The MCSE™ Migrating from NT 4 to Windows® 2000 Cram Sheet

This Cram Sheet contains the distilled, key facts about the Migrating from Microsoft Windows NT 4 to Microsoft Windows 2000 exam. Just before entering the test room, review this information, paying special attention to those areas where you feel you need the most review. You can transfer any of the facts from your memory onto a blank piece of paper before beginning the exam.

DEVELOPING THE MIGRATION STRATEGY

1. There are three migration paths:
   - *Domain upgrade (in-place migration)*—The system is upgraded, the network infrastructure does not change, and hardware does not change.
   - *Domain restructuring*—You can do interforest or intraforest restructuring:
     - *Interforest restructuring (between forests)*—Move and clone security principals into a pristine forest (using new equipment and a new infrastructure). Use tools such as ClonePrincipal and ADMT to *clone* objects.
     - *Intraforest restructuring (within a forest)*—Collapse a sprawling forest, and absorb resource and account domains into a single forest root. Use tools such as ADMT and MoveTree to *move* objects between domains.
   - *Domain upgrade and restructuring*—Perform a domain upgrade followed by a restructuring.

2. Order of migration for a domain upgrade:
   a. Upgrade account domains.
   b. Upgrade resource domains.
      1. Upgrade the domain PDC.
      2. Upgrade the domain BDCs and servers running DNS, WINS, and DHCP.

3. Upgrade the application and member servers.
4. Convert the domain to native mode after all domain controllers have been upgraded.

3. Order of migration for an interforest domain restructuring:
   a. Migrate account domains before resource domains to retain the **sIDHistory**.
      1. Create the Windows 2000 target domain (pristine forest).
      2. Use the ADMT Trust Migration Wizard or NETDOM to establish trusts between domains where the pristine forest is the trusting domain.
      3. Use the ADMT Group Migration Wizard or ClonePrincipal to migrate global groups.
      4. Use the ADMT User Migration Wizard to migrate user accounts.
      5. Decommission the source domain by demoting the domain controllers and moving the salvageable computers to the destination domain.
   b. Migrate resource domains.
      1. Use the ADMT Trust Migration Wizard to establish any needed trusts between domains.

2. Use the ADMT Service Account Migration Wizard to identify service accounts.

3. Use the ADMT Computer Migration Wizard to migrate workstations and member servers.

4. Use the ADMT Security Translation Wizard to migrate local profiles.

5. Use the ADMT Group Migration Wizard to migrate shared local groups.

6. Use the ADMT User Migration Wizard to migrate service accounts. These accounts were identified in Step 2.

7. Use the ADMT Security Translation Wizard to update service account user rights.

8. Migrate a domain controller from the resource domain.

9. Decommission source account domains by removing the last domain controller.

10. Decommission source resource domains by removing the last domain controller.

4. Order of migration for an intraforest domain restructuring:

   a. Migrate resource domains before account domains.

      1. Use the ADMT Service Account Migration Wizard to identify service accounts.

      2. Use the ADMT User Migration Wizard to migrate service accounts. These accounts were identified in Step 1.

      3. Use the ADMT Security Translation Wizard to update user rights and group memberships.

      4. Use the ADMT Group Migration Wizard to migrate domain local groups.

      5. Use the ADMT Computer Migration Wizard to migrate workstations and member servers.

      6. Migrate a domain controller from the resource domain.

      7. Decommission resource domains by removing the last domain controller.

   b. Migrate account domains.

      1. Use the ADMT Group Migration Wizard to migrate global groups.

      2. Use the ADMT Service Account Migration Wizard to identify service accounts.

      3. Use the ADMT User Migration Wizard to migrate users, service accounts, and roaming profiles.

      4. Use the ADMT Security Translation Wizard to upgrade user rights, group memberships and migrate local profiles.

      5. Migrate a domain controller from the account domain.

      6. Decommission account domains by removing the last domain controller.

5. DNS server facts:

   - There are three types of DNS zones: primary, secondary, and Active Directory Integrated.

   - Primary and secondary zones are not Active Directory Integrated.

   - Active Directory Integrated zones provide fault tolerance, secure transfers and updates, and DNS replication that's integrated with Active Directory replication.

   - Active Directory requires DNS that supports SRV records and dynamic updates. BIND 8.1.2 or greater supports these records.

   - The same DNS namespace must be used for all domains within an Active Directory tree.

   - Multiple DNS namespaces can be used for an Active Directory forest, assuming that there is a common global catalog, configuration, and forest root.

6. Trust facts:

   - Transitive trusts are two-way, dynamic, and automatically generated.

   - Explicit trusts are one-way and are manually created.

   - All trusts between Windows 2000 parent and child domains and tree root domains are transitive.

   - External, one-way, nontransitive trusts must be manually created between Windows 2000 domains and Windows NT 4 domains or between Windows 2000 domains that are in different forests.

   - Shortcut trusts can be created between two domains in the same forest and are one-way. These trusts send the authentication request directly to the target domain without having to traverse the forest root.

MCSE™
Migrating from NT 4 to Windows® 2000

Kurt Hudson
Doug Bassett
Deborah Haralson
Derek Melber

MCSE™ Migrating from NT 4 to Windows® 2000 Exam Cram

The Coriolis Group, LLC
14455 N. Hayden Road
Suite 220
Scottsdale, Arizona 85260

(480)483-0192
FAX (480)483-0193
www.coriolis.com

Library of Congress Cataloging-in-Publication Data
MCSE migrating from NT4 to Windows 2000 / by Kurt Hudson...[et al.].
    p. cm. -- (Exam cram)
    ISBN 1-57610-717-5
    1. Electronic data processing personnel--Certification. 2. Microsoft
software--Examinations--Study guides. 3. Microsoft Windows
(Computer file) I. Hudson, Kurt. II. Series.
QA76.3 .M3282 2001
005.4'4769--dc21   2001017334
                                CIP

President and CEO
Keith Weiskamp

Publisher
Steve Sayre

Acquisitions Editor
Shari Jo Hehr

Product Marketing Manager
Brett Woolley

Project Editor
Hilary Long

Technical Reviewer
Shawn McNutt

Production Coordinator
Todd Halvorsen

Cover Designer
Jesse Dunn

Layout Designer
April Nielsen

Printed in the United States of America
10 9 8 7 6 5 4 3 2 1

The Coriolis Group, LLC • 14455 North Hayden Road, Suite 220 • Scottsdale, Arizona 85260

ExamCram.com Connects You to the Ultimate Study Center!

Our goal has always been to provide you with the best study tools on the planet to help you achieve your certification in record time. Time is so valuable these days that none of us can afford to waste a second of it, especially when it comes to exam preparation.

Over the past few years, we've created an extensive line of *Exam Cram* and *Exam Prep* study guides, practice exams, and interactive training. To help you study even better, we have now created an e-learning and certification destination called **ExamCram.com**. (You can access the site at **www.examcram.com**.) Now, with every study product you purchase from us, you'll be connected to a large community of people like yourself who are actively studying for their certifications, developing their careers, seeking advice, and sharing their insights and stories.

I believe that the future is all about collaborative learning. Our **ExamCram.com** destination is our approach to creating a highly interactive, easily accessible collaborative environment, where you can take practice exams and discuss your experiences with others, sign up for features like "Questions of the Day," plan your certifications using our interactive planners, create your own personal study pages, and keep up with all of the latest study tips and techniques.

I hope that whatever study products you purchase from us—*Exam Cram* or *Exam Prep* study guides, *Personal Trainers*, *Personal Test Centers*, or one of our interactive Web courses—will make your studying fun and productive. Our commitment is to build the kind of learning tools that will allow you to study the way you want to, whenever you want to.

Visit ExamCram.com now to enhance your study program.

Help us continue to provide the very best certification study materials possible. Write us or email us at **learn@examcram.com** and let us know how our study products have helped you study. Tell us about new features that you'd like us to add. Send us a story about how we've helped you. We're listening!

Good luck with your certification exam and your career. Thank you for allowing us to help you achieve your goals.

Keith Weiskamp
President and CEO

Look for these other products from The Coriolis Group:

Migrating fron NT 4 to Windows 2000 Exam Cram Personal Test Center
CIP Author Team

MCSE Windows 2000 Network Design Exam Cram
by Kimberly Simmons, Jarret Buse, and Todd Halpin

MCSE Windows 2000 Security Design Exam Cram
by Phillip Schein

MCSE Exchange 2000 Design Exam Cram
by Michael Shannon

MCSE Exchange 2000 Administration Exam Cram
by David Watts and Will Willis

MCSE SQL 2000 Administration Exam Cram
by Kirk Hausman

To Laura Nelesen, a true love and inspiration.
—Kurt Hudson

ઓ

I dedicate this book to my grandmother, Helen Wells, for buying me my first computer, and to my grandfather, Lyle Wells, for not killing her.
—Doug Bassett

ઓ

This effort goes to my husband and my parents for their sacrifices, support, and advice in bringing me where I am today.
—Deborah Haralson

ઓ

I dedicate this book to Yvette and Alexa. They are ideal examples of patience and love.
—Derek Melber

ઓ

About the Authors

Kurt Hudson, president of HudLogic, Inc., has earned 30 different computer and networking certifications. He is certified as an MCSE in Windows 2000, NT 4 (MCSE+I), and NT 3.51, in addition to holding certifications from Cisco and CompTIA. Kurt is also a Microsoft Certified Trainer (MCT) and Certified Technical Trainer (CTT). Kurt completed a Master's in Business Management (MSM) from Troy State University in 1994. He began his technical career in the U.S. Air Force earning medals for systems efficiency, training excellence, and protecting national security. He has worked for Unisys, where he helped launch two Windows 95 support operations for Microsoft and Compaq, and Productivity Point International, where he trained hundreds of computer support engineers and system administrators. Today, he writes commercial technical publications, trains computer professionals in Windows 2000 (including migrations), and troubleshoots computer network problems. Kurt has also authored or co-authored over 30 different commercial computer networking books, some of which are in 12 languages.

Doug Bassett (MTS, MCSE and MCT) has been in the computer industry for over 20 years, starting with teaching computer science classes while still in high school. At college he taught programming and became the director of technical customer service for Business Computer Network. He was Instructor of the Year for Combat Systems Technical Schools Command where he taught advanced electronics and developed a 28-week Basic Electronics and Electricity course for the United States Navy. As a Gulf War Veteran, Doug has leveraged his unique insight and experience in everything from what was then called microcomputers to mainframes in a variety of opportunities ranging from computer assembler, end-user support professional, network administrator, network design engineer and now, senior technical instructor.

Doug is among the first 100 Windows 2000 MCSEs and has provided the latest in certification training to thousands of people worldwide. Doug has performed technical reviews and exam accuracy checks for five books, encompassing the entire spectrum of Windows 2000 support and certification.

When not knee-deep in winnowing out the mysteries of computers and protocol analysis, Doug can be found in his wood shop, trying to retain all of his typing appendages or with his family, trying to retain his sanity. You can email Doug at **Doug.Bassett@Knowledgenet.com.**

Deborah Haralson (MCSE, MCP+I) has been a computer geek since elementary school, learning BASIC programming on her father's Commodor VIC20. High school brought the technological bleeding edge, learning GWBASIC programming on an 8086 AT&T backplaned box with no hard disk drive. While going to school for engineering, she discovered that her true passion was IT, and began working on Windows, DOS, and Macintosh network clients, quickly graduating to network servers and WAN technologies. With over ten years of IT experience, she has worked for companies such as Honeywell, MicroAge, Moon Valley Software, and Mastering Computers. Along the way, she has become proficient in a wide array of hardware, software, and operating systems, along with both Windows and Novell networking technologies. Apart from an occasional stint as a PBX & ACD admin, DBA, trainer, webmaster, and application programmer, Deborah is currently working as an independent consultant with recent experience in IT management for large real estate companies.

Deborah has worked with Microsoft server products since the original NT 3.1 beta, and has <ahem> enjoyed the experience ever since then. While questing for the perfect ISP, Deborah can be reached at **deb.haralson@bigfoot.com.**

Derek Melber focuses on technical writing, instructing, professional speaking, and computer consultation. He has been able to work with Microsoft to help develop the Certification Skills and Assessment Program for Windows 2000. Derek has joined forces with IntenseSchool, which provide the most effective and powerful Windows 2000 MCSE and Cisco boot camps in the world. Although Derek focuses most of his efforts on Certification preparation for both Microsoft and CompTIA, he often finds himself consulting for companies to design and optimize their network infrastructure and Active Directory infrastructure. He has worked both as a network administrator for the University of Kansas and as a technology manager for a major commodities exchange company.

Derek currently has his Microsoft Certified Systems Engineer (MCSE) and CompTIA A+ certifications. Although a computer guy now, he has a Masters of Civil Engineering from the University of Kansas. Derek also runs his own business, Melber and Associates, which focuses on certification resources and technical education. Most recently, Derek launched a new Web presence, **www.braincore.net**, that provides access to Windows 2000 resources, as well as Exchange 2000, SQL 2000, and many other Windows tools. When he is not working on a computer, Derek is enjoying KU Jayhawk Basketball, "Rock Chalk Jayhawk!" You can catch up with Derek at **derek@melber.net.**

Acknowledgments

Hilary Long, you may have worked harder than all of us—thank you! It was truly a pleasure to work with you. Thanks to Derek, Deb, and Doug for their extensive work on this project. I'm sure you are glad it is finally finished. Shawn McNutt, thanks for keeping the bases covered and doing all that extra work. We truly appreciate it. Catherine Oliver, you had your work cut out for you and you certainly went above and beyond – thank you! Shari Jo, thanks for convincing me to do it.

—*Kurt Hudson*

I would like to acknowledge the efforts of Hilary Long for her patience in dealing with the myriad intricacies of juggling three authors' creative efforts. I would also like to acknowledge Shawn McNutt for keeping our facts, facts. I thank Catherine Oliver for not hunting me down like a wild animal when I mangled sentence structure and grammar. I would also like to thank Mike Foster for his efforts in the restructuring section. Last, but certainly not least, I would like to thank my wife, Shirley, and my children for giving me the time, space, and support that made this all possible.

—*Doug Bassett*

I would like to thank my husband Jeff, and my kids Johnathan and Raymond, for allowing mommy the time to write this book. Most especially to Jeff for running both the house and interference while supporting this effort 100 percent. Thank you, precious husband. Thank you to Mom and Dad for encouraging and supporting me all my life. Dad, your ever-curious quest for engineering and science are an inspiration to me without which I wouldn't be who I am today. Again, thanks to Jeff also for answering those infantile newbie IT questions I had when I first started out (and the occasional not-so-newbie that comes out today). Thanks also to Roberta Miller, Glenn Trotter, Jackie Kelly, Liz Devereaux, Terry Payne, Robert Fill, Hank Carbeck and Jim Johnson for answering questions over the years. Thank you to Roth Eddings for teaching me that I had a lot to teach you, and being a good friend in the process.

Thanks go to so many other people who are integral to this book: Hilary Long for her patient suffering while handling multiple authors, and yet still having a gracious and honest sense of humor; Catherine Oliver, our copyeditor, and Shawn McNutt, our technical reviewer, for questioning everything without making it come across like a federal crime. I think we all learned things here for which I'm grateful. Thank you to Lee Anderson for pulling me into this project, and Pam Poland at AFKA for bringing us together.

And finally, humble gratitude goes to my Heavenly Father, without whose blessings I would not have received this opportunity, and without whose trials and support I could not have succeeded.
—*Deborah Haralson*

I would like to thank my wife and daughter, Yvette and Alexa. Special thanks to Sheri Jo for her faith in me. Thanks go out to Hilary Long, the project editor who made sure this book was ready for prime time. Thanks to Shawn McNutt for his technical knowledge and his ability to communicate so effectively. To Coriolis for creating such incredible books for the IT industry. To IntenseSchool for giving me the chance to help lead the way. Last and not least, to the one who allows me to stop, think, and ask the question, WWJD?
—*Derek Melber*

Contents at a Glance

Table of Contents

Introduction

Welcome to *MCSE Windows 2000 Migrating from NT 4 to Windows 2000 Exam Cram*! Whether this is your first or your fifteenth *Exam Cram* book, you'll find information here and in Chapter 1 that will help ensure your success as you pursue knowledge, experience, and certification. This book aims to help you get ready to take—and pass—the Microsoft certification Exam 70-222, titled "Migrating from Microsoft Windows NT 4.0 to Microsoft Windows 2000." This Introduction explains Microsoft's certification programs in general and talks about how the *Exam Cram* series can help you prepare for Microsoft's Windows 2000 certification exams.

Exam Cram books help you understand and appreciate the subjects and materials you need to pass Microsoft certification exams. *Exam Cram* books are aimed strictly at test preparation and review. They do not teach you everything you need to know about a topic. Instead, we (the authors) present and dissect the questions and problems we've found that you're likely to encounter on a test. We've worked to bring together as much information as possible about Microsoft certification exams.

Nevertheless, to completely prepare yourself for any Microsoft test, we recommend that you begin by taking the Self-Assessment included in this book immediately following this Introduction. This tool will help you evaluate your knowledge base against the requirements for an MCSE under both ideal and real circumstances.

Based on what you learn from that exercise, you might decide to begin your studies with some classroom training or some background reading. On the other hand, you might decide to pick up and read one of the many study guides available from Microsoft or third-party vendors on certain topics, including The Coriolis Group's *Exam Prep* series. We also recommend that you supplement your study program with visits to **ExamCram.com** to receive additional practice questions, get advice, and track the Windows 2000 MCSE program.

We also strongly recommend that you install, configure, and fool around with the software that you'll be tested on, because nothing beats hands-on experience and familiarity when it comes to understanding the questions you're likely to encounter on a certification test. Book learning is essential, but hands-on experience is the best teacher of all!

The Microsoft Certified Professional (MCP) Program

The MCP Program currently includes the following separate tracks, each of which boasts its own special acronym (as a certification candidate, you need to have a high tolerance for alphabet soup of all kinds):

➤ *MCP (Microsoft Certified Professional)*—This is the least prestigious of all the certification tracks from Microsoft. Passing one of the major Microsoft exams qualifies an individual for the MCP credential. Individuals can demonstrate proficiency with additional Microsoft products by passing additional certification exams.

➤ *MCP+SB (Microsoft Certified Professional + Site Building)*—This certification program is designed for individuals who are planning, building, managing, and maintaining Web sites. Individuals with the MCP+SB credential will have demonstrated the ability to develop Web sites that include multimedia and searchable content and Web sites that connect to and communicate with a back-end database. It requires one MCP exam, plus two of these three exams: "70-055: Designing and Implementing Web Sites with Microsoft FrontPage 98," "70-057: Designing and Implementing Commerce Solutions with Microsoft Site Server 3.0, Commerce Edition," and "70-152: Designing and Implementing Web Solutions with Microsoft Visual InterDev 6.0."

➤ *MCSE (Microsoft Certified Systems Engineer)*—Anyone who has a current MCSE is warranted to possess a high level of networking expertise with Microsoft operating systems and products. This credential is designed to prepare individuals to plan, implement, maintain, and support information systems, networks, and internetworks built around Microsoft Windows 2000 and its BackOffice Server 2000 family of products.

To obtain an MCSE, an individual must pass four core operating system exams, one optional core exam, and two elective exams. The operating system exams require individuals to prove their competence with desktop and server operating systems and networking/internetworking components.

For Windows NT 4 MCSEs, the Accelerated exam, "70-240: Microsoft Windows 2000 Accelerated Exam for MCPs Certified on Microsoft Windows NT 4.0," is an option. This free exam covers all of the material tested in the Core Four exams. The hitch in this plan is that you can take the test only once. If you fail, you must take all four core exams to recertify. The Core Four exams are: "70-210: Installing, Configuring and Administering Microsoft Windows 2000 Professional," "70-215: Installing, Configuring and Administering Microsoft Windows 2000 Server," "70-216: Implementing and Administering a Microsoft Windows 2000 Network Infrastructure," and "70-217: Implementing and Administering a Microsoft Windows 2000 Directory Services Infrastructure."

To fulfill the fifth core exam requirement, you can choose from three design exams: "70-219: Designing a Microsoft Windows 2000 Directory Services Infrastructure," "70-220: Designing Security for a Microsoft Windows 2000 Network," or "70-221: Designing a Microsoft Windows 2000 Network Infrastructure." You are also required to take two elective exams. An elective exam can fall in any number of subject or product areas, primarily BackOffice Server 2000 components. The two design exams that you don't select as your fifth core exam also qualify as electives. If you are on your way to becoming an MCSE and have already taken some exams, visit **www.microsoft.com/trainingandservices/** for information about how to complete your MCSE certification.

Individuals who wish to remain certified MCSEs after 12/31/2001 must "upgrade" their certifications on or before 12/31/2001. For more detailed information than is included here, visit **www.microsoft.com/trainingandservices/**.

New MCSE candidates must pass seven tests to meet the MCSE requirements. It's not uncommon for the entire process to take a year or so, and many individuals find that they must take a test more than once to pass. The primary goal of the *Exam Prep* and *Exam Cram* test preparation books is to make it possible, given proper study and preparation, to pass all Microsoft certification tests on the first try. Table 1 shows the required and elective exams for the Windows 2000 MCSE certification.

➤ *MCSD (Microsoft Certified Solution Developer)*—The MCSD credential reflects the skills required to create multitier, distributed, and COM-based solutions, in addition to desktop and Internet applications, using new technologies. To obtain an MCSD, an individual must demonstrate the ability to analyze and interpret user requirements; select and integrate products, platforms, tools, and technologies; design and implement code, and customize applications; and perform necessary software tests and quality assurance operations.

To become an MCSD, you must pass a total of four exams: three core exams and one elective exam. Each candidate must choose one of these three desktop application exams—"70-016: Designing and Implementing Desktop Applications with Microsoft Visual C++ 6.0," "70-156: Designing and Implementing Desktop Applications with Microsoft Visual FoxPro 6.0," or "70-176: Designing and Implementing Desktop Applications with Microsoft Visual Basic 6.0"—*plus* one of these three distributed application exams—

Table 1 MCSE Windows 2000 Requirements

Core

If you have not passed these 3 Windows NT 4 exams	
Exam 70-067	Implementing and Supporting Microsoft Windows NT Server 4.0
Exam 70-068	Implementing and Supporting Microsoft Windows NT Server 4.0 in the Enterprise
Exam 70-073	Microsoft Windows NT Workstation 4.0
then you must take these 4 exams	
Exam 70-210	Installing, Configuring and Administering Microsoft Windows 2000 Professional
Exam 70-215	Installing, Configuring and Administering Microsoft Windows 2000 Server
Exam 70-216	Implementing and Administering a Microsoft Windows 2000 Network Infrastructure
Exam 70-217	Implementing and Administering a Microsoft Windows 2000 Directory Services Infrastructure
If you have already passed exams 70-067, 70-068, and 70-073, you may take this exam	
Exam 70-240	Microsoft Windows 2000 Accelerated Exam for MCPs Certified on Microsoft Windows NT 4.0

5th Core Option

Choose 1 from this group	
Exam 70-219*	Designing a Microsoft Windows 2000 Directory Services Infrastructure
Exam 70-220*	Designing Security for a Microsoft Windows 2000 Network
Exam 70-221*	Designing a Microsoft Windows 2000 Network Infrastructure

Elective

Choose 2 from this group	
Exam 70-019	Designing and Implementing Data Warehouse with Microsoft SQL Server 7.0
Exam 70-219*	Designing a Microsoft Windows 2000 Directory Services Infrastructure
Exam 70-220*	Designing Security for a Microsoft Windows 2000 Network
Exam 70-221*	Designing a Microsoft Windows 2000 Network Infrastructure
Exam 70-222	Migrating from Microsoft Windows NT 4.0 to Microsoft Windows 2000
Exam 70-028	Administering Microsoft SQL Server 7.0
Exam 70-029	Designing and Implementing Databases on Microsoft SQL Server 7.0
Exam 70-080	Implementing and Supporting Microsoft Internet Explorer 5.0 by Using the Internet Explorer Administration Kit
Exam 70-081	Implementing and Supporting Microsoft Exchange Server 5.5
Exam 70-085	Implementing and Supporting Microsoft SNA Server 4.0
Exam 70-086	Implementing and Supporting Microsoft Systems Management Server 2.0
Exam 70-088	Implementing and Supporting Microsoft Proxy Server 2.0

This is not a complete listing—you can still be tested on some earlier versions of these products. However, we have included mainly the most recent versions so that you may test on these versions and thus be certified longer. We have not included any tests that are scheduled to be retired.

* The 5th Core Option exam does not double as an elective.

"70-015: Designing and Implementing Distributed Applications with Microsoft Visual C++ 6.0," "70-155: Designing and Implementing Distributed Applications with Microsoft Visual FoxPro 6.0," or "70-175: Designing and Implementing Distributed Applications with Microsoft Visual Basic 6.0." The third core exam is "70-100: Analyzing Requirements and Defining Solution Architectures." Elective exams cover specific Microsoft applications and languages, including Visual Basic, C++, the Microsoft Foundation Classes, Access, SQL Server, Excel, and more.

➤ *MCDBA (Microsoft Certified Database Administrator)*—The MCDBA credential reflects the skills required to implement and administer Microsoft SQL Server databases. To obtain an MCDBA, an individual must demonstrate the ability to derive physical database designs, develop logical data models, create physical databases, create data services by using Transact-SQL, manage and maintain databases, configure and manage security, monitor and optimize databases, and install and configure Microsoft SQL Server.

To become an MCDBA, you must pass a total of three core exams and one elective exam. The required core exams are "70-028: Administering Microsoft SQL Server 7.0," "70-029: Designing and Implementing Databases with Microsoft SQL Server 7.0," and "70-215: Installing, Configuring and Administering Microsoft Windows 2000 Server."

The elective exams that you can choose from cover specific uses of SQL Server and include "70-015: Designing and Implementing Distributed Applications with Microsoft Visual C++ 6.0," "70-019: Designing and Implementing Data Warehouses with Microsoft SQL Server 7.0," "70-155: Designing and Implementing Distributed Applications with Microsoft Visual FoxPro 6.0," "70-175: Designing and Implementing Distributed Applications with Microsoft Visual Basic 6.0," and two exams that relate to Windows 2000: "70-216: Implementing and Administering a Microsoft Windows 2000 Network Infrastructure," and "70-087: Implementing and Supporting Microsoft Internet Information Server 4.0."

If you have taken the three core Windows NT 4 exams on your path to becoming an MCSE, you qualify for the Accelerated exam (it replaces the Network Infrastructure exam requirement). The Accelerated exam covers the objectives of all four of the Windows 2000 core exams. In addition to taking the Accelerated exam, you must take only the two SQL exams—Administering and Database Design.

➤ *MCT (Microsoft Certified Trainer)*—Microsoft Certified Trainers are deemed able to deliver elements of the official Microsoft curriculum, based on technical knowledge and instructional ability. Thus, it is necessary for an individual seeking MCT credentials (which are granted on a course-by-course basis) to pass the related certification exam for a course and complete the official Microsoft training in the subject area, and to demonstrate an ability to teach.

This teaching skill criterion may be satisfied by proving that one has already attained training certification from Novell, Banyan, Lotus, the Santa Cruz Operation, or Cisco, or by taking a Microsoft-sanctioned workshop on instruction. Microsoft makes it clear that MCTs are important cogs in the Microsoft training channels. Instructors must be MCTs before Microsoft will allow them to teach in any of its official training channels, including Microsoft's affiliated Certified Technical Education Centers (CTECs) and its online training partner network. As of January 1, 2001, MCT candidates must also possess a current MCSE.

Microsoft has announced that the MCP+I and MCSE+I credentials will not be continued when the MCSE exams for Windows 2000 are in full swing because the skill set for the Internet portion of the program has been included in the new MCSE program. Therefore, details on these tracks are not provided here; go to **www.microsoft.com/trainingandservices/** if you need more information.

Once a Microsoft product becomes obsolete, MCPs typically have to recertify on current versions. (If individuals do not recertify, their certifications become invalid.) Because technology keeps changing and new products continually supplant old ones, this should come as no surprise. This explains why Microsoft has announced that MCSEs have 12 months past the scheduled retirement date for the Windows NT 4 exams to recertify on Windows 2000 topics. (Note that this means taking at least two exams, if not more.)

The best place to keep tabs on the MCP program and its related certifications is on the Web. The URL for the MCP program is **www.microsoft.com/ trainingandservices/**. But Microsoft's Web site changes often, so if this URL doesn't work, try using the Search tool on Microsoft's site with either "MCP" or the quoted phrase "Microsoft Certified Professional" as a search string. This will help you find the latest and most accurate information about Microsoft's certification programs.

Taking a Certification Exam

Once you've prepared for your exam, you need to register with a testing center. Each computer-based MCP exam costs $100, and if you don't pass, you may retest for an additional $100 for each additional try. In the United States and Canada, tests are administered by Prometric and by Virtual University Enterprises (VUE). Here's how you can contact them:

➤ *Prometric*—You can sign up for a test through the company's Web site at **www.prometric.com**. Or, you can register by phone at 800-755-3926 (within the United States or Canada). For those outside the United States or Canada, visit Prometric's Web site for registration information.

➤ *Virtual University Enterprises*—You can sign up for a test or get the phone numbers for local testing centers through the Web page at **www.vue.com/ms/**.

To sign up for a test, you must possess a valid credit card, or contact either company for mailing instructions to send them a check (in the U.S.). Only when payment is verified, or a check has cleared, can you actually register for a test.

To schedule an exam, call the number or visit either of the Web pages at least one day in advance. To cancel or reschedule an exam, you must call before 7 P.M. pacific standard time the day before the scheduled test time (or you may be charged, even if you don't appear to take the test). When you want to schedule a test, have the following information ready:

➤ Your name, organization, and mailing address.

➤ Your Microsoft Test ID. (Inside the United States, this means your Social Security number; citizens of other nations should call ahead to find out what type of identification number is required to register for a test.)

➤ The name and number of the exam you wish to take.

➤ A method of payment. (As we've already mentioned, a credit card is the most convenient method, but alternate means can be arranged in advance, if necessary.)

Once you sign up for a test, you'll be informed as to when and where the test is scheduled. Try to arrive at least 15 minutes early. You must supply two forms of identification—one of which must be a photo ID—to be admitted into the testing room.

All exams are completely closed-book. In fact, you will not be permitted to take anything with you into the testing area, but you will be furnished with a blank sheet of paper and a pen or, in some cases, an erasable plastic sheet and an erasable pen. We suggest that you immediately write down on that sheet of paper all the information you've memorized for the test. In *Exam Cram* books, this information appears on a tear-out sheet inside the front cover of each book. You will have some time to compose yourself, record this information, and take a sample orientation exam before you begin the real thing. We suggest you take the orientation test before taking your first exam, but because they're all more or less identical in layout, behavior, and controls, you probably won't need to do this more than once.

When you complete a Microsoft certification exam, the software will tell you whether you've passed or failed. If you need to retake an exam, you'll have to schedule a new test with Prometric or VUE and pay another $100.

 The first time you fail a test, you can retake the test the next day. However, if you fail a second time, you must wait 14 days before retaking that test. The 14-day waiting period remains in effect for all retakes after the second failure.

Tracking MCP Status

As soon as you pass any Microsoft exam (except Networking Essentials), you'll attain Microsoft Certified Professional (MCP) status. Microsoft also generates transcripts that indicate which exams you have passed. You can view a copy of your transcript at any time by going to the MCP secured site and selecting Transcript Tool. This tool will allow you to print a copy of your current transcript and confirm your certification status.

Once you pass the necessary set of exams, you'll be certified. Official certification normally takes anywhere from six to eight weeks, so don't expect to get your credentials overnight. When the package for a qualified certification arrives, it includes a Welcome Kit that contains a number of elements (see Microsoft's Web site for other benefits of specific certifications):

➤ A certificate suitable for framing, along with a wallet card and lapel pin.

➤ A license to use the MCP logo, thereby allowing you to use the logo in advertisements, promotions, and documents, and on letterhead, business cards, and so on. Along with the license comes an MCP logo sheet, which includes camera-ready artwork. (Note: Before using any of the artwork, individuals must sign and return a licensing agreement that indicates they'll abide by its terms and conditions.)

➤ A subscription to *Microsoft Certified Professional Magazine*, which provides ongoing data about testing and certification activities, requirements, and changes to the program.

Many people believe that the benefits of MCP certification go well beyond the perks that Microsoft provides to newly anointed members of this elite group. We're starting to see more job listings that request or require applicants to have an MCP, MCSE, and so on, and many individuals who complete the program can qualify for increases in pay and/or responsibility. As an official recognition of hard work and broad knowledge, one of the MCP credentials is a badge of honor in many IT organizations.

How to Prepare for an Exam

Preparing for any Windows 2000 Server-related test (including "Migrating from Microsoft Windows NT 4.0 to Microsoft Windows 2000") requires that you obtain and study materials designed to provide comprehensive information about the product and its capabilities that will appear on the specific exam for which you are preparing. The following list of materials will help you study and prepare:

➤ The Windows 2000 Server product CD includes comprehensive online documentation and related materials; it should be a primary resource when you are preparing for the test.

➤ The exam preparation materials, practice tests, and self-assessment exams on the Microsoft Training & Services page at **www.microsoft.com/trainingandservices/default.asp?PageID=mcp**. The Testing Innovations link offers samples of the new question types found on the Windows 2000 MCSE exams. Find the materials, download them, and use them!

➤ The exam preparation advice, practice tests, questions of the day, and discussion groups on the **ExamCram.com** e-learning and certification destination Web site (**www.examcram.com**).

In addition, you'll probably find any or all of the following materials useful in your quest for Migration expertise:

➤ *Microsoft training kits*—Microsoft Press offers a training kit that specifically targets Exam 71-222. For more information, visit: **http://mspress.microsoft.com/findabook/list/series_ak.htm**. This training kit contains information that you will find useful in preparing for the test.

➤ *Microsoft TechNet CD*—This monthly CD-based publication delivers numerous electronic titles that include coverage of Directory Services Design and related topics on the Technical Information (TechNet) CD. Its offerings include product facts, technical notes, tools and utilities, and information on how to access the Seminars Online training materials for Directory Services Design. A subscription to TechNet costs $299 per year, but it is well worth the price. Visit **www.microsoft.com/technet/** and check out the information under the "TechNet Subscription" menu entry for more details.

➤ *Study guides*—Several publishers—including The Coriolis Group—offer Windows 2000 titles. The Coriolis Group series includes the following:

➤ *The Exam Cram series*—These books give you information about the material you need to know to pass the tests.

➤ *The Exam Prep series*—These books provide a greater level of detail than the *Exam Cram* books and are designed to teach you everything you need to know from an exam perspective. Each book comes with a CD that contains interactive practice exams in a variety of testing formats.

Together, the two series make a perfect pair.

➤ *Multimedia*—These Coriolis Group materials are designed to support learners of all types—whether you learn best by reading or doing:

➤ *The Exam Cram Personal Trainer*—Offers a unique, personalized self-paced training course based on the exam.

➤ *The Exam Cram Personal Test Center*—Features multiple test options that simulate the actual exam, including Fixed-Length, Random, Review, and Test All. Explanations of correct and incorrect answers reinforce concepts learned.

➤ *Classroom training*—CTECs, online partners, and third-party training companies (like Wave Technologies, Learning Tree, Data-Tech, and others) all offer classroom training on Windows 2000. These companies aim to help you prepare to pass Exam 70-222. Although such training runs upwards of $350 per day in class, most of the individuals lucky enough to partake find it to be quite worthwhile.

➤ *Other publications*—There's no shortage of materials available about Migration. The resource sections at the end of each chapter should give you an idea of where we think you should look for further discussion.

By far, this set of required and recommended materials represents a nonpareil collection of sources and resources for Migration and related topics. We anticipate that you'll find that this book belongs in this company.

About This Book

Each topical *Exam Cram* chapter follows a regular structure, along with graphical cues about important or useful information. Here's the structure of a typical chapter:

➤ *Opening hotlists*—Each chapter begins with a list of the terms, tools, and techniques that you must learn and understand before you can be fully conversant with that chapter's subject matter. We follow the hotlists with one or two introductory paragraphs to set the stage for the rest of the chapter.

➤ *Topical coverage*—After the opening hotlists, each chapter covers a series of topics related to the chapter's subject title. Throughout this section, we highlight topics or concepts likely to appear on a test using a special Exam Alert layout, like this:

This is what an Exam Alert looks like. Normally, an Exam Alert stresses concepts, terms, software, or activities that are likely to relate to one or more certification test questions. For that reason, we think any information found offset in Exam Alert format is worthy of unusual attentiveness on your part. Indeed, most of the information that appears on The Cram Sheet appears as Exam Alerts within the text.

Pay close attention to material flagged as an Exam Alert; although all the information in this book pertains to what you need to know to pass the exam, we flag certain items that are really important. You'll find what appears in the meat of each chapter to be worth knowing, too, when preparing for the test. Because this book's material is very condensed, we recommend that you use this book along with other resources to achieve the maximum benefit.

In addition to the Exam Alerts, we have provided tips that will help you build a better foundation for Migration knowledge. Although the information may not be on the exam, it is certainly related and will help you become a better test-taker.

This is how tips are formatted. Keep your eyes open for these, and you'll become a Migration guru in no time!

➤ *Practice questions*—Although we talk about test questions and topics throughout the book, a section at the end of each chapter presents a series of mock test questions and explanations of both correct and incorrect answers.

➤ *Details and resources*—Every chapter ends with a section titled "Need to Know More?" This section provides direct pointers to Microsoft and third-party resources offering more details on the chapter's subject. In addition, this section tries to rank or at least rate the quality and thoroughness of the topic's coverage by each resource. If you find a resource you like in this collection, use it, but don't feel compelled to use all the resources. On the other hand, we recommend only resources we use on a regular basis, so none of our recommendations will be a waste of your time or money (but purchasing them all at once probably represents an expense that many network administrators and would-be MCPs and MCSEs might find hard to justify).

The bulk of the book follows this chapter structure slavishly, but there are a few other elements that we'd like to point out. Chapter 11 includes a sample test that provides a good review of the material presented throughout the book to ensure you're ready for the exam. Chapter 12 is an answer key to the sample test that appears in Chapter 11. In addition, you'll find a handy glossary and an index.

Finally, the tear-out Cram Sheet attached next to the inside front cover of this *Exam Cram* book represents a condensed and compiled collection of facts and tips that we think you should memorize before taking the test. Because you can dump this information out of your head onto a piece of paper before taking the exam, you can master this information by brute force—you need to remember it only long enough to write it down when you walk into the test room. You might even want to look at it in the car or in the lobby of the testing center just before you walk in to take the test.

How to Use This Book

We've structured the topics in this book to build on one another. Therefore, some topics in later chapters make more sense after you've read earlier chapters. That's why we suggest you read this book from front to back for your initial test preparation. If you need to brush up on a topic or you have to bone up for a second try, use the index or table of contents to go straight to the topics and questions that you need to study. Beyond helping you prepare for the test, we think you'll find this book useful as a tightly focused reference to some of the most important aspects of Migration.

Given all the book's elements and its specialized focus, we've tried to create a tool that will help you prepare for—and pass—Microsoft Exam 70-222. Please share your feedback on the book with us, especially if you have ideas about how we can improve it for future test-takers. We'll carefully consider everything you say, and we'll respond to all suggestions.

Send your questions or comments to us at **learn@examcram.com**. Please remember to include the title of the book in your message; otherwise, we'll be forced to guess which book you're writing about. And we don't like to guess—we want to *know*! Also, be sure to check out the Web pages at **www.examcram.com**, where you'll find information updates, commentary, and certification information.

Thanks, and enjoy the book!

Self-Assessment

The reason we included a Self-Assessment in this *Exam Cram* book is to help you evaluate your readiness to tackle MCSE certification. It should also help you understand what you need to know to master the topic of this book—namely, Exam 70-222, "Migrating from Microsoft Windows NT 4.0 to Microsoft Windows 2000." But before you tackle this Self-Assessment, let's talk about concerns you may face when pursuing an MCSE for Windows 2000, and what an ideal MCSE candidate might look like.

MCSEs in the Real World

In the next section, we describe an ideal MCSE candidate, knowing full well that only a few real candidates will meet this ideal. In fact, our description of that ideal candidate might seem downright scary, especially with the changes that have been made to the program to support Windows 2000. But take heart: Although the requirements to obtain an MCSE may seem formidable, they are by no means impossible to meet. However, be keenly aware that it does take time, involves some expense, and requires real effort to get through the process.

Increasing numbers of people are attaining Microsoft certifications, so the goal is within reach. You can get all the real-world motivation you need from knowing that many others have gone before, so you will be able to follow in their footsteps. If you're willing to tackle the process seriously and do what it takes to obtain the necessary experience and knowledge, you can take—and pass—all the certification tests involved in obtaining an MCSE. In fact, we've designed *Exam Preps*, the companion *Exam Crams*, *Exam Cram Personal Trainers*, and *Exam Cram Personal Test Centers* to make it as easy on you as possible to prepare for these exams. We've also greatly expanded our Web site, **www.examcram.com**, to provide a host of resources to help you prepare for the complexities of Windows 2000.

Besides MCSE, other Microsoft certifications include:

➤ MCSD, which is aimed at software developers and requires one specific exam, two more exams on client and distributed topics, plus a fourth elective exam drawn from a different, but limited, pool of options.

➤ Other Microsoft certifications, whose requirements range from one test (MCP) to several tests (MCP+SB, MCDBA).

The Ideal Windows 2000 MCSE Candidate

Just to give you some idea of what an ideal MCSE candidate is like, here are some relevant statistics about the background and experience such an individual might have. Don't worry if you don't meet these qualifications, or don't come that close—this is a far from ideal world, and where you fall short is simply where you'll have more work to do.

➤ Academic or professional training in network theory, concepts, and operations. This includes everything from networking media and transmission techniques through network operating systems, services, and applications.

➤ Three-plus years of professional networking experience, including experience with Ethernet, token ring, modems, and other networking media. This must include installation, configuration, upgrade, and troubleshooting experience.

Note: The Windows 2000 MCSE program is much more rigorous than the previous NT MCSE program; therefore, you'll really need some hands-on experience. Some of the exams require you to solve real-world case studies and network design issues, so the more hands-on experience you have, the better.

➤ Two-plus years in a networked environment that includes hands-on experience with Windows 2000 Server, Windows 2000 Professional, Windows NT Server, Windows NT Workstation, and Windows 95 or Windows 98. A solid understanding of each system's architecture, installation, configuration, maintenance, and troubleshooting is also essential.

➤ Knowledge of the various methods for installing Windows 2000, including manual and unattended installations.

➤ A thorough understanding of key networking protocols, addressing, and name resolution, including TCP/IP, IPX/SPX, and NetBEUI.

➤ A thorough understanding of NetBIOS naming, browsing, and file and print services.

➤ Familiarity with key Windows 2000-based TCP/IP-based services, including HTTP (Web servers), DHCP, WINS, DNS, plus familiarity with one or more of the following: Internet Information Server (IIS), Index Server, and Proxy Server.

➤ An understanding of how to implement security for key network data in a Windows 2000 environment.

➤ Working knowledge of NetWare 3.x and 4.x, including IPX/SPX frame formats, NetWare file, print, and directory services, and both Novell and Microsoft client software. Working knowledge of Microsoft's Client Service For NetWare (CSNW), Gateway Service For NetWare (GSNW), the NetWare Migration Tool (NWCONV), and the NetWare Client For Windows (NT, 95, and 98) is essential.

➤ A good working understanding of Active Directory. The more you work with Windows 2000, the more you'll realize that this new operating system is quite different than Windows NT. New technologies like Active Directory have really changed the way that Windows is configured and used. We recommend that you find out as much as you can about Active Directory and acquire as much experience using this technology as possible. The time you take learning about Active Directory will be time very well spent!

Fundamentally, this boils down to a bachelor's degree in computer science, plus three years' experience working in a position involving network design, installation, configuration, and maintenance. We believe that well under half of all certification candidates meet these requirements, and that, in fact, most meet less than half of these requirements—at least, when they begin the certification process. But because all the people who already have been certified have survived this ordeal, you can survive it too—especially if you heed what our Self-Assessment can tell you about what you already know and what you need to learn.

Put Yourself to the Test

The following series of questions and observations is designed to help you figure out how much work you must do to pursue Microsoft certification and what kinds of resources you may consult on your quest. Be absolutely honest in your answers, or you'll end up wasting money on exams you're not yet ready to take. There are no right or wrong answers, only steps along the path to certification. Only you can decide where you really belong in the broad spectrum of aspiring candidates.

Two things should be clear from the outset, however:

➤ Even a modest background in computer science will be helpful.

➤ Hands-on experience with Microsoft products and technologies is an essential ingredient to certification success.

Educational Background

1. Have you ever taken any computer-related classes? [Yes or No]

   If Yes, proceed to question 2; if No, proceed to question 4.

2. Have you taken any classes on computer operating systems? [Yes or No]

   If Yes, you will probably be able to handle Microsoft's architecture and system component discussions. If you're rusty, brush up on basic operating system concepts, especially virtual memory, multitasking regimes, user mode versus kernel mode operation, and general computer security topics.

   If No, consider some basic reading in this area. We strongly recommend a good general operating systems book, such as *Operating System Concepts, 5th Edition*, by Abraham Silberschatz and Peter Baer Galvin (John Wiley & Sons, 1998, ISBN 0-471-36414-2). If this title doesn't appeal to you, check out reviews for other, similar titles at your favorite online bookstore.

3. Have you taken any networking concepts or technologies classes? [Yes or No]

   If Yes, you will probably be able to handle Microsoft's networking terminology, concepts, and technologies (brace yourself for frequent departures from normal usage). If you're rusty, brush up on basic networking concepts and terminology, especially networking media, transmission types, the OSI Reference Model, and networking technologies such as Ethernet, token ring, FDDI, and WAN links.

   If No, you might want to read one or two books in this topic area. The two best books that we know of are *Computer Networks, 3rd Edition*, by Andrew S. Tanenbaum (Prentice-Hall, 1996, ISBN 0-13-349945-6) and *Computer Networks and Internets, 2nd Edition*, by Douglas E. Comer and Ralph E. Droms (Prentice-Hall, 1999, ISBN 0-130-83617-6).

   Skip to the next section, "Hands-on Experience."

4. Have you done any reading on operating systems or networks? [Yes or No]

   If Yes, review the requirements stated in the first paragraphs after questions 2 and 3. If you meet those requirements, move on to the next section. If No, consult the recommended reading for both topics. A strong background will help you prepare for the Microsoft exams better than just about anything else.

Hands-on Experience

The most important key to success on all of the Microsoft tests is hands-on experience, especially with Windows 2000 Server and Professional, plus the many add-on services and BackOffice components around which so many of the Microsoft certification exams revolve. If we leave you with only one realization after taking this Self-Assessment, it should be that there's no substitute for time spent installing, configuring, and using the various Microsoft products upon which you'll be tested repeatedly and in depth.

5. Have you installed, configured, and worked with:

➤ Windows 2000 Server? [Yes or No]

If Yes, make sure you understand basic concepts as covered in Exam 70-215. You should also study the TCP/IP interfaces, utilities, and services for Exam 70-216, plus implementing security features for Exam 70-220.

 You can download objectives, practice exams, and other data about Microsoft exams from the Training and Certification page at **www.microsoft.com/trainingandservices/default.asp?PageID =mcp**. Use the "Exams" link to obtain specific exam information.

If you haven't worked with Windows 2000 Server, you must obtain one or two machines and a copy of Windows 2000 Server. Then, learn the operating system and whatever other software components on which you'll also be tested.

In fact, we recommend that you obtain two computers, each with a network interface, and set up a two-node network on which to practice. With decent Windows 2000-capable computers selling for about $500 to $600 apiece these days, this shouldn't be too much of a financial hardship. You may have to scrounge to come up with the necessary software, but if you scour the Microsoft Web site you can usually find low-cost options to obtain evaluation copies of most of the software that you'll need.

➤ Windows 2000 Professional? [Yes or No]

If Yes, make sure you understand the concepts covered in Exam 70-210.

If No, you will want to obtain a copy of Windows 2000 Professional and learn how to install, configure, and maintain it. You can use *MCSE Windows 2000 Professional Exam Cram* to guide your activities and studies, or work straight from Microsoft's test objectives if you prefer.

For any and all of these Microsoft exams, the Resource Kits for the topics involved are a good study resource. You can purchase softcover Resource Kits from Microsoft Press (search for them at **http:// mspress.microsoft.com/**), but they also appear on the TechNet CDs (**www.microsoft.com/technet**). Along with *Exam Crams* and *Exam Preps*, we believe that Resource Kits are among the best tools you can use to prepare for Microsoft exams.

6. For any specific Microsoft product that is not itself an operating system (for example, SQL Server), have you installed, configured, used, and upgraded this software? [Yes or No]

If the answer is Yes, skip to the next section. If it's No, you must get some experience. Read on for suggestions on how to do this.

Experience is a must with any Microsoft product exam, be it something as simple as FrontPage 2000 or as challenging as SQL Server 7.0. For trial copies of other software, search Microsoft's Web site using the name of the product as your search term. Also, search for bundles like "BackOffice" or "Small Business Server."

If you have the funds, or your employer will pay your way, consider taking a class at a Certified Training and Education Center (CTEC) or at an Authorized Academic Training Partner (AATP). In addition to classroom exposure to the topic of your choice, you get a copy of the software that is the focus of your course, along with a trial version of whatever operating system it needs, with the training materials for that class.

Before you even think about taking any Microsoft exam, make sure you've spent enough time with the related software to understand how it may be installed and configured, how to maintain such an installation, and how to troubleshoot that software when things go wrong. This will help you in the exam, and in real life!

Testing Your Exam-Readiness

Whether you attend a formal class on a specific topic to get ready for an exam or use written materials to study on your own, some preparation for the Microsoft certification exams is essential. At $100 a try, pass or fail, you want to do everything you can to pass on your first try. That's where studying comes in.

We have included a practice exam in this book, so if you don't score that well on the test, you can study more and then tackle the test again. We also have exams that you can take online through the **ExamCram.com** Web site at **www.examcram.com**. If you still don't hit a score of at least 80 percent after these tests, you'll want to investigate the other practice test resources we mention in this section.

For any given subject, consider taking a class if you've tackled self-study materials, taken the test, and failed anyway. The opportunity to interact with an instructor and fellow students can make all the difference in the world, if you can afford that privilege. For information about Microsoft classes, visit the Training and Certification page at **www.microsoft.com/education/partners/ctec.asp** for Microsoft Certified Education Centers or **www.microsoft.com/aatp/default.htm** for Microsoft Authorized Training Providers.

If you can't afford to take a class, visit the Training and Certification page anyway, because it also includes pointers to free practice exams and to Microsoft Certified Professional Approved Study Guides and other self-study tools. And even if you can't afford to spend much at all, you should still invest in some low-cost practice exams from commercial vendors.

7. Have you taken a practice exam on your chosen test subject? [Yes or No]

    If Yes, and you scored 70 percent or better, you're probably ready to tackle the real thing. If your score isn't above that threshold, keep at it until you break that barrier.

    If No, obtain all the free and low-budget practice tests you can find and get to work. Keep at it until you can break the passing threshold comfortably.

When it comes to assessing your test readiness, there is no better way than to take a good-quality practice exam and pass with a score of 80 percent or better. When we're preparing ourselves, we shoot for 85-plus percent, just to leave room for the "weirdness factor" that sometimes shows up on Microsoft exams.

Assessing Readiness for Exam 70-222

In addition to the general exam-readiness information in the previous section, there are several things you can do to prepare for the "Migrating from Microsoft Windows NT 4.0 to Microsoft Windows 2000" exam. As you're getting ready for Exam 70-222, visit the Exam Cram Windows 2000 Resource Center at **www.examcram.com/studyresource/w2kresource/**. Another valuable resource is the Exam Cram Insider newsletter. Sign up at **www.examcram.com** or send a blank email message to **subscribe-ec@mars.coriolis.com**. We also suggest that you join an active MCSE mailing list. One of the better ones is managed by Sunbelt Software. Sign up at **www.sunbelt-software.com** (look for the Subscribe button).

You can also cruise the Web looking for "braindumps" (recollections of test topics and experiences recorded by others) to help you anticipate topics you're likely to encounter on the test. The MCSE mailing list is a good place to ask where the useful braindumps are.

 You can't be sure that a braindump's author can provide correct answers. Thus, use the questions to guide your studies, but don't rely on the answers in a braindump to lead you to the truth. Double-check everything you find in any braindump.

Microsoft exam mavens also recommend checking the Microsoft Knowledge Base (available on its own CD as part of the TechNet collection, or on the Microsoft Web site at **http://support.microsoft.com/support/**) for "meaningful technical support issues" that relate to your exam's topics. Although we're not sure exactly what the quoted phrase means, we have also noticed some overlap between technical support questions on particular products and troubleshooting questions on the exams for those products.

Onward, through the Fog!

Once you've assessed your readiness, undertaken the right background studies, obtained the hands-on experience that will help you understand the products and technologies at work, and reviewed the many sources of information to help you prepare for a test, you'll be ready to take a round of practice tests. When your scores come back positive enough to get you through the exam, you're ready to go after the real thing. If you follow our assessment regime, you'll not only know what you need to study, but when you're ready to make a test date at Prometric or VUE. Good luck!

Microsoft
Certification Exams

Terms you'll need to understand:

✓ Case study
✓ Multiple-choice question formats
✓ Build-list-and-reorder question format
✓ Create-a-tree question format
✓ Drag-and-connect question format
✓ Select-and-place question format
✓ Fixed-length tests
✓ Short-form tests
✓ Simulations
✓ Adaptive tests

Techniques you'll need to master:

✓ Assessing your exam-readiness
✓ Answering Microsoft's varying question types
✓ Altering your test strategy depending on the exam format
✓ Practicing (to make perfect)
✓ Making the best use of the testing software
✓ Budgeting your time
✓ Guessing (as a last resort)

Exam taking is not something that most people anticipate eagerly, no matter how well prepared they may be. In most cases, familiarity helps offset test anxiety. In plain English, this means you probably won't be as nervous when you take your fourth or fifth Microsoft certification exam as you'll be when you take your first one.

Whether it's your first exam or your tenth, understanding the details of taking the new exams (how much time to spend on questions, the environment you'll be in, and so on) and the new exam software will help you concentrate on the material rather than on the setting. Likewise, mastering a few basic exam-taking skills should help you recognize—and perhaps even outfox—some of the tricks and snares you're bound to find in some exam questions.

This chapter, besides explaining the exam environment and software, describes some proven exam-taking strategies that you should be able to use to your advantage.

Assessing Exam-Readiness

We strongly recommend that you read through and take the Self-Assessment included with this book (it appears just before this chapter, in fact). This will help you compare your knowledge base to the requirements for obtaining an MCSE, and it will also help you identify parts of your background or experience that may be in need of improvement, enhancement, or further learning. If you get the right set of basics under your belt, obtaining Microsoft certification will be that much easier.

Once you've gone through the Self-Assessment, you can remedy those topical areas where your background or experience may not measure up to an ideal certification candidate. But you can also tackle subject matter for individual tests at the same time, so you can continue making progress while you're catching up in some areas.

Once you've worked through an *Exam Cram*, have read the supplementary materials, and have taken the practice test, you'll have a pretty clear idea of when you should be ready to take the real exam. Although we strongly recommend that you keep practicing until your scores top the 75 percent mark, 80 percent would be a good goal to give yourself some margin for error in a real exam situation (where stress will play more of a role than when you practice). Once you hit that point, you should be ready to go. But if you get through the practice exam in this book without attaining that score, you should keep taking practice tests and studying the materials until you get there. You'll find more pointers on how to study and prepare in the Self-Assessment. But now, on to the exam itself!

The Exam Situation

When you arrive at the testing center where you scheduled your exam, you'll need to sign in with an exam coordinator. He or she will ask you to show two forms of identification, one of which must be a photo ID. After you've signed in and your time slot arrives, you'll be asked to deposit any books, bags, or items you brought with you. Then, you'll be escorted into a closed room.

All exams are completely closed book. In fact, you will not be permitted to take anything with you into the testing area, but you will be furnished with a blank sheet of paper and a pen or, in some cases, an erasable plastic sheet and an erasable pen. Before the exam, you should memorize as much of the important material as you can, so you can write that information on the blank sheet as soon as you are seated in front of the computer. You can refer to this piece of paper anytime you like during the test, but you'll have to surrender the sheet when you leave the room. You will have some time to compose yourself and to record this information before you begin the exam.

Typically, the room will be furnished with anywhere from one to half a dozen computers, and each workstation will be separated from the others by dividers designed to keep you from seeing what's happening on someone else's computer. Most test rooms feature a wall with a large picture window. This permits the exam coordinator to monitor the room, to prevent exam-takers from talking to one another, and to observe anything out of the ordinary that might go on. The exam coordinator will have preloaded the appropriate Microsoft certification exam—for this book, that's Exam 70-222—and you'll be permitted to start as soon as you're seated in front of the computer.

All Microsoft certification exams allow a certain maximum amount of time in which to complete your work (this time is indicated on the exam by an on-screen counter/clock, so you can check the time remaining whenever you like). All Microsoft certification exams are computer generated. In addition to multiple choice, you'll encounter select and place (drag and drop), create a tree (categorization and prioritization), drag and connect, and build list and reorder (list prioritization) on most exams. Although this may sound quite simple, the questions are constructed not only to check your mastery of basic facts and figures about migration, but they also require you to evaluate one or more sets of circumstances or requirements. Often, you'll be asked to select more than one answer to a question. Likewise, you might be asked to select the best or most effective solution to a problem from a range of choices, all of which technically are correct. Taking the exam is quite an adventure, and it involves critical thinking. This book shows you what to expect and how to deal with the potential problems, puzzles, and predicaments.

In the next section, you'll learn more about how Microsoft test questions look and how they must be answered.

Exam Layout and Design: New Case Study Format

The format of Microsoft's Windows 2000 exams is different from that of its previous exams. For the design exams (70-219, 70-220, 70-221), each exam consists entirely of a series of case studies, and the questions can be of six types. For the Core Four exams (70-210, 70-215, 70-216, 70-217), the same six types of questions can appear, but you are not likely to encounter complex multiquestion case studies. When it comes to the Migration exam (70-222), you will presented with both multiquestion case studies and typical single-question formats.

Note: Keep in mind that Microsoft has stated that it can change the exam format at any time, so be prepared for any format.

Each case study or "testlet" presents a detailed problem that you must read and analyze. Figure 1.1 shows an example of what a case study looks like. You must select the different tabs in the case study to view the entire case.

Following each case study is a set of questions related to the case study; these questions can be one of six types (which are discussed next). Careful attention to details provided in the case study is the key to success. Be prepared to toggle frequently between the case study and the questions as you work. Some of the case studies also include diagrams, which are called *exhibits*, that you'll need to examine closely to understand how to answer the questions.

Once you complete a case study, you can review all the questions and your answers. However, once you move on to the next case study, you may not be able to return to the previous case study and make any changes.

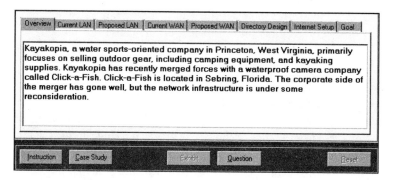

Figure 1.1 This is how case studies appear.

The six types of question formats are:

➤ Multiple choice, single answer

➤ Multiple choice, multiple answers

➤ Build list and reorder (list prioritization)

➤ Create a tree

➤ Drag and connect

➤ Select and place (drag and drop)

Multiple-Choice Question Format

Some exam questions require you to select a single answer, whereas others ask you to select multiple correct answers. The following multiple-choice question requires you to select a single correct answer. Following the question is a brief summary of each potential answer and why it is either right or wrong.

Question 1

> What is the recommended sequence for moving objects in a domain restructuring?
>
> ○ a. Users, computers, member servers, domain controllers
>
> ○ b. Computers, users, member servers, domain controllers
>
> ○ c. Domain controllers, member servers, users, computers
>
> ○ d. Member servers, domain controllers, computers, users

Answer a is correct. Microsoft recommends moving objects in the following order: users, computers, member servers, and domain controllers. This sequence allows you to take immediate advantage of the key features available only in Windows 2000, such as delegation of authority and the application of group policies.

This sample question format corresponds closely to the Microsoft certification exam format—the only difference on the exam is that questions are not followed by answer keys. To select an answer, you would position the cursor over the radio button next to the answer. Then, click the mouse button to select the answer.

Let's examine a question where one or more answers are possible. This type of question provides checkboxes rather than radio buttons for marking all appropriate selections.

Question 2

> Where are group policies stored? [Check all correct answers]
>
> ❑ a. Group policy template
>
> ❑ b. Group policy OU
>
> ❑ c. Group policy object
>
> ❑ d. Ntconfig.pol

Answers a and c are correct. Group policies are stored in the SYSVOL folder in the group policy template and in Active Directory in a group policy object. Answer b is incorrect as there is no defined group policy OU. Answer d is incorrect as ntconfig.pol is where NT system policies are stored, not group policies.

For this particular question, two answers are required. Microsoft sometimes gives partial credit for partially correct answers. For Question 2, you have to check the boxes next to items a and c to obtain credit for a correct answer. Notice that picking the right answers also means knowing why the other answers are wrong!

Build-List-and-Reorder Question Format

Questions in the build-list-and-reorder format present two lists of items—one on the left and one on the right. To answer the question, you must move items from the list on the right to the list on the left. The final list must then be reordered into a specific order.

These questions can best be characterized as "From the following list of choices, pick the choices that answer the question. Arrange the list in a certain order." To give you practice with this type of question, some questions of this type are included in this study guide. Here's an example of how they appear in this book; for a sample of how they appear on the test, see Figure 1.2.

Question 3

From the following list of famous people, pick those that have been elected President of the United States. Arrange the list in the order that they served.

Thomas Jefferson

Ben Franklin

Abe Lincoln

George Washington

Andrew Jackson

Paul Revere

The correct answer is:

George Washington
Thomas Jefferson
Andrew Jackson
Abe Lincoln

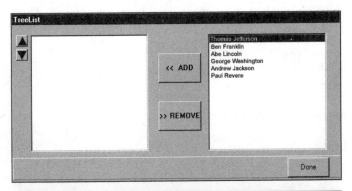

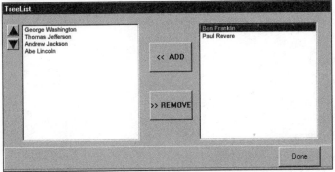

Figure 1.2   This is how build-list-and-reorder questions appear.

On an actual exam, the entire list of famous people would initially appear in the list on the right. You would move the four correct answers to the list on the left, and then reorder the list on the left. Notice that the answer to the question did not include all items from the initial list. However, this may not always be the case.

To move an item from the right list to the left list, first select the item by clicking on it, and then click on the Add button (left arrow). Once you move an item from one list to the other, you can move the item back by first selecting the item and then clicking on the appropriate button (either the Add button or the Remove button). Once items have been moved to the left list, you can reorder an item by selecting the item and clicking on the up or down button.

Create-a-Tree Question Format

Questions in the create-a-tree format also present two lists—one on the left side of the screen and one on the right side of the screen. The list on the right consists of individual items, and the list on the left consists of nodes in a tree. To answer the question, you must move items from the list on the right to the appropriate node in the tree.

These questions can best be characterized as simply a matching exercise. Items from the list on the right are placed under the appropriate category in the list on the left. Here's an example of how they appear in this book; for a sample of how they appear on the test, see Figure 1.3.

Question 4

The calendar year is divided into four seasons:

    Winter

    Spring

    Summer

    Fall

Identify the season when each of the following holidays occurs:

    Christmas

    Fourth of July

    Labor Day

    Flag Day

    Memorial Day

    Washington's Birthday

    Thanksgiving

    Easter

The correct answer is:

> Winter
>> Christmas
>>
>> Washington's Birthday
>
> Spring
>> Flag Day
>>
>> Memorial Day
>>
>> Easter
>
> Summer
>> Fourth of July
>>
>> Labor Day
>
> Fall
>> Thanksgiving

In this case, all the items in the list were used. However, this may not always be the case.

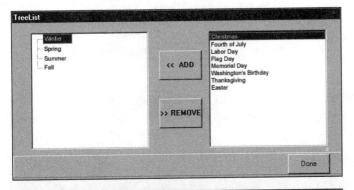

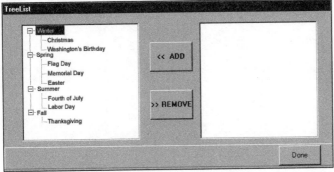

Figure 1.3   This is how create-a-tree questions appear.

To move an item from the right list to its appropriate location in the tree, you must first select the appropriate tree node by clicking on it. Then, you select the item to be moved and click on the Add button. If one or more items have been added to a tree node, the node will be displayed with a "+" icon to the left of the node name. You can click on this icon to expand the node and view the item(s) that have been added. If any item has been added to the wrong tree node, you can remove it by selecting it and clicking on the Remove button.

Drag-and-Connect Question Format

Questions in the drag-and-connect format present a group of objects and a list of "connections." To answer the question, you must move the appropriate connections between the objects.

This type of question is best described using graphics. Here's an example.

Question 5

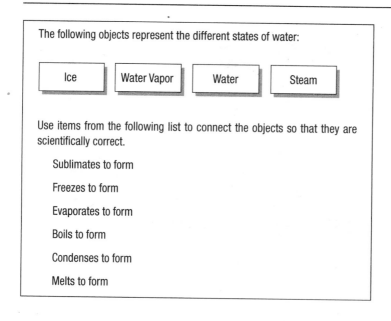

The correct answer is:

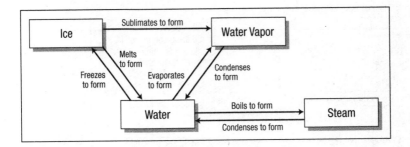

For this type of question, it's not necessary to use every object, and each connection can be used multiple times.

Select-and-Place Question Format

Questions in the select-and-place (drag-and-drop) format present a diagram with blank boxes, and a list of labels that need to be dragged to correctly fill in the blank boxes. To answer the question, you must move the labels to their appropriate positions on the diagram.

This type of question is best described using graphics. Here's an example.

Question 6

Place the items in their proper order, by number, on the following flowchart. Some items may be used more than once, and some items may not be used at all.

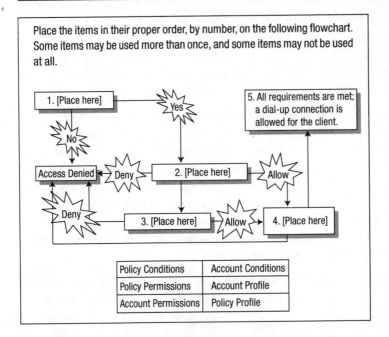

The correct answer is:

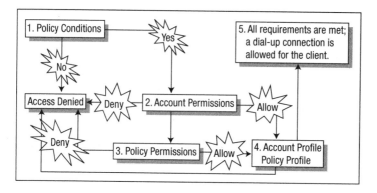

Microsoft's Testing Formats

Currently, Microsoft uses four different testing formats:

➤ Case study

➤ Fixed length

➤ Adaptive

➤ Short form

As we mentioned earlier, the case study approach is used with Microsoft's design exams and a portion of the Migration exam. These exams consist of one or more case studies that you must analyze to answer the related questions. Such exams include one or more case studies (tabbed topic areas), each of which is followed by 4 to 15 questions. The question types for design exams, the Core Four Windows 2000 exams, and the Migration exam are multiple choice, build list and reorder, create a tree, drag and connect, and select and place.

Other Microsoft exams employ advanced testing capabilities that might not be immediately apparent. Although the questions that appear are primarily multiple choice, the logic that drives them is more complex than older Microsoft tests, which use a fixed sequence of questions, called a *fixed-length test*. Some questions employ a sophisticated user interface, which Microsoft calls a *simulation*, to test your knowledge of the software and systems under consideration in a more or less "live" environment that behaves just like the original. The Testing Innovations link at **www.microsoft.com/trainingandservices/default.asp?PageID=mcp** includes a downloadable practice simulation.

For some exams, Microsoft has turned to a well-known technique, called *adaptive testing*, to establish a test-taker's level of knowledge and product competence.

Adaptive exams look the same as fixed-length exams, but they discover the level of difficulty at which an individual test-taker can correctly answer questions. Test-takers with differing levels of knowledge or ability therefore see different sets of questions; individuals with high levels of knowledge or ability are presented with a smaller set of more difficult questions, whereas individuals with lower levels of knowledge are presented with a larger set of easier questions. Two individuals may answer the same percentage of questions correctly, but the test-taker with a higher knowledge or ability level will score higher because his or her questions are worth more.

Also, the lower-level test-taker will probably answer more questions than his or her more-knowledgeable colleague. This explains why adaptive tests use ranges of values to define the number of questions and the amount of time it takes to complete the test.

Adaptive tests work by evaluating the test-taker's most recent answer. A correct answer leads to a more difficult question (and the test software's estimate of the test-taker's knowledge and ability level is raised). An incorrect answer leads to a less difficult question (and the test software's estimate of the test-taker's knowledge and ability level is lowered). This process continues until the test targets the test-taker's true ability level. The exam ends when the test-taker's level of accuracy meets a statistically acceptable value (in other words, when his or her performance demonstrates an acceptable level of knowledge and ability), or when the maximum number of items has been presented (in which case, the test-taker is almost certain to fail).

Microsoft also introduced a short-form test for its most popular tests. This test delivers 25 to 30 questions to its takers, giving them exactly 60 minutes to complete the exam. This type of exam is similar to a fixed-length test, in that it allows readers to jump ahead or return to earlier questions, and to cycle through the questions until the test is done. Microsoft does not use adaptive logic in this test, but claims that statistical analysis of the question pool is such that the 25 to 30 questions delivered during a short-form exam conclusively measure a test-taker's knowledge of the subject matter in much the same way as an adaptive test. You can think of the short-form test as a kind of "greatest hits exam" (that is, the most important questions are covered) version of an adaptive exam on the same topic.

Note: Some of the Microsoft exams can contain a combination of adaptive and fixed-length questions.

Microsoft tests can come in any one of these forms. Whatever you encounter, you must take the test in whichever form it appears; you can't choose one form over another. If anything, it pays more to prepare thoroughly for an adaptive exam than for a fixed-length or a short-form exam: The penalties for answering incorrectly are built into the test itself on an adaptive exam, whereas the layout remains the same for a fixed-length or short-form test, no matter how many questions you answer incorrectly.

The biggest difference between an adaptive test and a fixed-length or short-form test is that on a fixed-length or short-form test, you can revisit questions after you've read them over one or more times. On an adaptive test, you must answer the question when it's presented and will have no opportunities to revisit that question thereafter.

Strategies for Different Testing Formats

Before you choose a test-taking strategy, you must know if your test is case study based, fixed length, short form, adaptive, or some combination of these. When you begin your exam, you'll know right away if the test is based on case studies. The interface will consist of a tabbed window that allows you to easily navigate through the sections of the case.

If you are taking a test that is not based on case studies, the software will tell you that the test is adaptive, if in fact the version you're taking is an adaptive test. If your introductory materials fail to mention this, you're probably taking a fixed-length test (50 to 70 questions). If the total number of questions involved is 25 to 30, you're taking a short-form test. Some tests announce themselves by indicating that they will start with a set of adaptive questions, followed by fixed-length questions.

You'll be able to tell for sure if you are taking an adaptive, fixed-length, or short-form test by the first question. If it includes a checkbox that lets you mark the question for later review, you're taking a fixed-length or short-form test. If the total number of questions is 25 to 30, it's a short-form test; if more than 30, it's a fixed-length test. Adaptive test questions can be visited (and answered) only once, and they include no such checkbox.

The Case Study Exam Strategy

Most test-takers find that the case study type of test used for the design exams (70-219, 70-220, and 70-221) and Migration exam (70-222) is the most difficult to master. When it comes to taking a case study test, your best bet is to approach each case study as a standalone test. The biggest challenge you'll encounter is that you'll feel that you won't have enough time to get through all of the cases that are presented.

Each case provides a lot of material that you'll need to read and comprehend before you can effectively answer the questions that follow. The trick in a case study is to read the information in the ALL tab first. While reading the ALL tab of information, be sure to jot down any diagrams of the network that are objective based. After reading the information, you are ready to tackle the questions.

When studying a case, carefully read the tabbed information. It is best to read the ALL tab, which is a compilation of all other tabs, but in one location. This ALL tab does not have any buttons to push to see more information. It is important to answer each and every question. You will be able to toggle back and forth between case, exhibit, and all questions within a case testlet. You will be able to return to any portion of the exam. This will include reviewing the case studies or the questions associated with them. You may want to take notes while reading useful information so you can refer to them when you tackle the test questions. When taking notes, be sure to optimize your time. Many run out of time diagramming the perfect picture of the case.

The Fixed-Length and Short-Form Exam Strategy

A well-known principle when taking fixed-length or short-form exams is to first read over the entire exam from start to finish while answering only those questions you feel absolutely sure of. On subsequent passes, you can dive into more complex questions more deeply, knowing how many such questions you have left.

Fortunately, the Microsoft exam software for fixed-length and short-form tests makes the multiple-visit approach easy to implement. At the top-left corner of each question is a checkbox that permits you to mark that question for a later visit.

Note: Marking questions makes review easier, but you can return to any question by clicking the Forward or Back button repeatedly.

As you read each question, if you answer only those you're sure of and mark for review those that you're not sure of, you can keep working through a decreasing list of questions as you answer the trickier ones in order.

There's at least one potential benefit to reading the exam over completely before answering the trickier questions: Sometimes, information supplied in later questions sheds more light on earlier questions. At other times, information you read in later questions might jog your memory about Migration facts, figures, or behavior that helps you answer earlier questions. Either way, you'll come out ahead if you defer those questions about which you're not absolutely sure.

Here are some question-handling strategies that apply to fixed-length and short-form tests. Use them if you have the chance:

➤ When returning to a question after your initial read-through, read every word again—otherwise, your mind can fall quickly into a rut. Sometimes, revisiting a question after turning your attention elsewhere lets you see something you missed, but the strong tendency is to see what you've seen before. Try to avoid that tendency at all costs.

➤ If you return to a question more than twice, try to articulate to yourself what you don't understand about the question, why answers don't appear to make sense, or what appears to be missing. If you chew on the subject awhile, your subconscious might provide the details you lack, or you might notice a "trick" that points to the right answer.

As you work your way through the exam, another counter that Microsoft provides will come in handy—the number of questions completed and questions outstanding. For fixed-length and short-form tests, it's wise to budget your time by making sure that you've completed one-quarter of the questions one-quarter of the way through the exam period, and three-quarters of the questions three-quarters of the way through.

If you're not finished when only five minutes remain, use that time to guess your way through any remaining questions. Remember, guessing is potentially more valuable than not answering, because blank answers are always wrong, but a guess may turn out to be right. If you don't have a clue about any of the remaining questions, pick answers at random, or choose all a's, b's, and so on. The important thing is to submit an exam for scoring that has an answer for every question.

 At the very end of your exam period, you're better off guessing than leaving questions unanswered.

The Adaptive Exam Strategy

If there's one principle that applies to taking an adaptive test, it could be summed up as "Get it right the first time." You cannot elect to skip a question and move on to the next one when taking an adaptive test, because the testing software uses your answer to the current question to select whatever question it plans to present next. Nor can you return to a question once you've moved on, because the software gives you only one chance to answer the question. You can, however, take notes, because sometimes information supplied in earlier questions will shed more light on later questions.

Also, when you answer a question correctly, you are presented with a more diffi-cult question next, to help the software gauge your level of skill and ability. When you answer a question incorrectly, you are presented with a less difficult question, and the software lowers its current estimate of your skill and ability. This contin-ues until the program settles into a reasonably accurate estimate of what you know and can do, and takes you on average through somewhere between 15 and 30 questions as you complete the test.

The good news is that if you know your stuff, you'll probably finish most adaptive tests in 30 minutes or so. The bad news is that you must really, really know your stuff to do your best on an adaptive test. That's because some questions are so convoluted, complex, or hard to follow that you're bound to miss one or two, at a minimum, even if you do know your stuff. So the more you know, the better you'll do on an adaptive test, even accounting for the occasionally weird or un-fathomable questions that appear on these exams.

 Because you can't always tell in advance if a test is fixed length, short form, or adaptive, you will be best served by preparing for the exam as if it were adaptive. That way, you should be prepared to pass no matter what kind of test you take. But if you do take a fixed-length or short-form test, remember the tips from the preceding section. They should help you improve on what you could do on an adaptive test.

If you encounter a question on an adaptive test that you can't answer, you must guess an answer immediately. Because of how the software works, you may suffer for your guess on the next question if you guess right, because you'll get a more difficult question next!

Question-Handling Strategies

For those questions that take only a single answer, usually two or three of the answers will be obviously incorrect, and two of the answers will be plausible—of course, only one can be correct. Unless the answer leaps out at you (if it does, reread the question to look for a trick; sometimes those are the ones you're most likely to get wrong), begin the process of answering by eliminating those answers that are most obviously wrong.

Almost always, at least one answer out of the possible choices for a question can be eliminated immediately because it matches one of these conditions:

➤ The answer does not apply to the situation.

➤ The answer describes a nonexistent issue, an invalid option, or an imaginary state.

After you eliminate all answers that are obviously wrong, you can apply your retained knowledge to eliminate further answers. Look for items that sound correct but refer to actions, commands, or features that are not present or not available in the situation that the question describes.

If you're still faced with a blind guess among two or more potentially correct answers, reread the question. Try to picture how each of the possible remaining answers would alter the situation. Be especially sensitive to terminology; sometimes the choice of words ("remove" instead of "disable") can make the difference between a right answer and a wrong one.

Only when you've exhausted your ability to eliminate answers, but remain unclear about which of the remaining possibilities is correct, should you guess at an answer. An unanswered question offers you no points, but guessing gives you at least some chance of getting a question right; just don't be too hasty when making a blind guess.

Note: If you're taking a fixed-length or a short-form test, you can wait until the last round of reviewing marked questions (just as you're about to run out of time, or out of unanswered questions) before you start making guesses. You will have the same option within each case study testlet (but once you leave a testlet, you may not be allowed to return to it). If you're taking an adaptive test, you'll have to guess to move on to the next question if you can't figure out an answer some other way. Either way, guessing should be your technique of last resort!

Numerous questions assume that the default behavior of a particular utility is in effect. If you know the defaults and understand what they mean, this knowledge will help you cut through many Gordian knots.

Mastering the Inner Game

In the final analysis, knowledge breeds confidence, and confidence breeds success. If you study the materials in this book carefully and review all the practice questions at the end of each chapter, you should become aware of those areas where additional learning and study are required.

After you've worked your way through the book, take the practice exam in the back of the book. Taking this test will provide a reality check and help you identify areas to study further. Make sure you follow up and review materials related to the questions you miss on the practice exam before scheduling a real exam. Only when you've covered that ground and feel comfortable with the whole scope of the practice exam should you set an exam appointment. Only if you score 80 percent or better should you proceed to the real thing (otherwise, obtain some additional practice tests so you can keep trying until you hit this magic number).

> If you take a practice exam and don't score at least 80 to 85 percent correct, you'll want to practice further. Microsoft provides links to practice exam providers and also offers self-assessment exams at **www.microsoft.com/trainingandservices/**. You should also check out **ExamCram.com** for downloadable practice questions.

Armed with the information in this book and with the determination to augment your knowledge, you should be able to pass the certification exam. However, you need to work at it, or you'll spend the exam fee more than once before you finally pass. If you prepare seriously, you should do well. We are confident that you can do it!

The next section covers other sources you can use to prepare for the Microsoft certification exams.

Additional Resources

A good source of information about Microsoft certification exams comes from Microsoft itself. Because its products and technologies—and the exams that go with them—change frequently, the best place to go for exam-related information is online.

If you haven't already visited the Microsoft Certified Professional site, do so right now. The MCP home page resides at **www.microsoft.com/trainingandservices** (see Figure 1.4).

Note: This page might not be there by the time you read this, or may be replaced by something new and different, because things change regularly on the Microsoft site. Should this happen, please read the sidebar titled "Coping with Change on the Web."

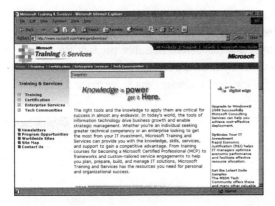

Figure 1.4   The Microsoft Certified Professional home page.

Coping with Change on the Web

Sooner or later, all the information we've shared with you about the Microsoft Certified Professional pages and the other Web-based resources mentioned throughout the rest of this book will go stale or be replaced by newer information. In some cases, the URLs you find here might lead you to their replacements; in other cases, the URLs will go nowhere, leaving you with the dreaded "404 File not found" error message. When that happens, don't give up.

There's always a way to find what you want on the Web if you're willing to invest some time and energy. Most large or complex Web sites—and Microsoft's qualifies on both counts—offer a search engine. On all of Microsoft's Web pages, a Search button appears along the top edge of the page. As long as you can get to Microsoft's site (it should stay at **www.microsoft.com** for a long time), use this tool to help you find what you need.

The more focused you can make a search request, the more likely the results will include information you can use. For example, you can search for the string

```
"training and certification"
```

to produce a lot of data about the subject in general, but if you're looking for the preparation guide for Exam 70-222, "Migrating from NT 4 to Windows 2000," you'll be more likely to get there quickly if you use a search string similar to the following:

```
"Exam 70-222" AND "preparation guide"
```

Likewise, if you want to find the Training and Certification downloads, try a search string such as this:

```
"training and certification" AND "download page"
```

Finally, feel free to use general search tools—such as **www.search.com**, **www.altavista.com**, and **www.excite.com**—to look for related information. Although Microsoft offers great information about its certification exams online, there are plenty of third-party sources of information and assistance that need not follow Microsoft's party line. Therefore, if you can't find something where the book says it lives, intensify your search.

Active Directory vs. NT 4 Directory Service Structure

Terms you'll need to understand:

- ✓ Directory service
- ✓ Active Directory
- ✓ Primary domain controller (PDC)
- ✓ Backup domain controller (BDC)
- ✓ Single domain model
- ✓ Single-master domain model
- ✓ Multimaster domain model
- ✓ Complete trust domain model
- ✓ Forest
- ✓ Tree
- ✓ Domain
- ✓ Organizational unit (OU)
- ✓ Site
- ✓ DNS (Domain Name Service)
- ✓ WINS (Windows Internet Naming Service)

Techniques you'll need to master:

- ✓ Identifying and contrasting the logon processes of NT and Active Directory
- ✓ Identifying the roles of the primary and backup domain controllers in a variety of domain models
- ✓ Identifying the role of the Active Directory domain controller
- ✓ Identifying the Flexible Single Master Operations (FSMO) server roles in a forest
- ✓ Identifying the Flexible Single Master Operations server roles in a domain
- ✓ Identifying the purpose and placement of a tree in an Active Directory forest
- ✓ Identifying the purpose and placement of a site in an Active Directory forest
- ✓ Identifying the purpose and placement of a domain in an Active Directory tree
- ✓ Identifying the purpose and placement of an organizational unit in an Active Directory domain
- ✓ Identifying the purpose of DNS in Active Directory

The largest learning curve that confronts the MCSE2K wanna-be is the completely alien vocabulary and undiscovered pitfalls of Windows 2000. The purpose of this chapter is to demystify Active Directory and compare it to NT's way of doing things. If you consider yourself a master of NT and Active Directory, we recommend that you peruse the section titles for areas you might want to review. Microsoft is extremely interested in ensuring that migration specialists are conversant with the old ways and the new ways of ensuring successful access to network resources. This level of concern is easily evident in the depth of testing that probes material mastery. Skip this chapter at your own peril.

Purpose of a Directory Service

The purpose of a directory service is simple—you use a directory service to locate something. Once you have that something located, you can then gather information about it and use it for your desired purpose.

An example of a directory is the phone book. It contains white pages listing residential phone numbers and yellow pages listing business services. The purpose of a phone book is to locate people or services. If we apply this analogy to Windows 2000, we can say that Active Directory is a listing of user accounts that correspond to the residential phone entries. Active Directory also holds a listing of services that are offered on a network. This is like looking in the yellow pages for the nearest dry cleaners or pizza delivery outlet. The services advertised in Active Directory can include anything from a file server, a printer, or even the nearest domain controller. Obviously, we don't call these listings phone numbers. Microsoft calls pretty much everything in Active Directory an *object*.

Active Directory—The Nickel Tour

Objects in Active Directory are like records in a database. Let's say you have a record that lists a person's first name and last name. That record could be called a *user record*. In Active Directory, this information would be contained in a *user object*. There are user objects, server objects, printer objects, and file-share objects; the list goes on and on. If Active Directory doesn't have the object you want, you can always make more objects. Each of these objects has a variety of attributes. These attributes would correspond to the database record's field for the first name or the last name in a user record.

Active Directory is a place to store all of the objects and attributes in an enterprise environment. We use Active Directory to locate these various objects—either by name or by one of the many attributes the objects contain. Active Directory is pretty much the foundation of a Windows 2000 network.

NT—SAM I Am

Windows NT's directory service is called the Security Accounts Manager database (SAM). This database's purpose is the same as that of Active Directory: The SAM is used to find something and to get information about what you found. One of the major differences is that the SAM contains only the white pages of our phone book. The NT SAM has only user accounts, groups, and machine accounts. It doesn't offer nearly the wealth of information that even the most bare-bones Active Directory implementation does.

Basic Structure and Terminology

It is difficult, if not impossible, to understand the nature of a forest without being familiar with the nature of a tree. In Active Directory's case, you have to know about the forest, the tree, the organizational unit, and the site. To successfully pass the exam on migration from NT SAM to Windows 2000 Active Directory, you must master each of the elements contained in *both* NT and Windows 2000. If you are completely familiar with how NT and 2000 interoperate and you want to get into the meat of migration, you can skip to Chapter 3, which discusses group policy. Be warned, however, that the exam assumes an extremely thorough understanding of the way NT does things and of what a transformation professional must do to ensure similar and enhanced performance.

NT—There Can Be Only One!

If you are entirely familiar with how NT distributes and acts on the Security Accounts Manager database, you might want to skip ahead and read the sections prefaced with the title Active Directory. But if you want a refresher or are new to NT, this section is solid gold. Without understanding how NT works in comparison to Active Directory, you won't get as much out of the sections on Active Directory.

The undisputed king and tyrant in the NT world is the primary domain controller (PDC). This beast will not tolerate anyone usurping its role in the network. If a PDC comes back after a well-deserved reboot and finds an impostor claiming the throne, it will throw a fit, shut down its services, and sulk. This is by design. The PDC in an NT domain is the only server that has the keys to the kingdom. The PDC holds the only Read/Write copy of the Security Accounts Manager database. If any changes need to be made—such as adding a user or changing a password—the PDC is the one you must deal with. Sulking is NT's way of preventing two PDCs from fighting it out for ultimate supremacy. The PDC doesn't have to do its job entirely alone. Any administrators worth their salt will add fault tolerance and load balancing by installing backup domain controllers (BDCs). The BDC holds a Read-Only copy of the SAM.

Any time someone, hopefully an administrator, changes the Security Accounts Manager database, the PDC replicates the new information to the BDC(s) throughout the network. If the PDC happens to be down, no changes can occur and administration of the user accounts is impossible. This creates a single point of failure.

> ➤ PDC—This machine holds the only Read/Write copy of SAM.
>
> ➤ BDC—These machines have a Read-Only copy of SAM.

Active Directory—A Domain Controller Is a Domain Controller

Active Directory uses a multimaster replication model. This means that *every* Windows 2000 domain controller has a Read/Write copy of Active Directory. When an administrator needs to add a user account, or update one of the several attributes associated with the account, he or she can contact *any* domain controller. After the changes are made, this domain controller notifies other domain controllers, and they come get the latest information. This scheme ensures a certain level of fault tolerance and network load balancing. Active-Directory-aware clients—such as Windows 2000 Professional or Windows 95/98/NT running the Active Directory client—can contact a domain controller close to them to perform routine account maintenance, such as changing passwords. Gone are the days of rushing to the PDC every 45 days because the password is expiring.

Understanding the multiple-master aspect of Active Directory is critical to managing migration properly. In the old days, password changes would sometimes have to traverse WAN links to find the PDC. This led to the proliferation of multiple domains so the user accounts could have a PDC located nearby. The PDC mindset is one hurdle that you must overcome when shifting to Windows 2000.

NT Domain Validation

NT domain controllers have many jobs, but their main purpose is to validate users. Users must be validated by a domain controller before they are allowed access to network resources. You need to fully comprehend how each of the important points works. That way you can support users throughout the 2000 transformation and, what's more important, laugh at those feared case-study questions.

Note: In the following procedures, the steps in boldface type are the primary concerns when you're moving from NT domains to Active Directory. It's not necessary to memorize them for the exam, but you should be familiar with them.

In Windows NT, when a user does the three-finger salute by pressing Ctrl+Alt+Del, the following events are triggered:

1. The computer presents the user with a dialog box that asks for a username, a password, and a domain.

2. This information is presented to the Local Security Authority (LSA) for validation.

3. The LSA checks whether the user is attempting to validate against the local machine's SAM or whether domain validation is being requested.

4. The machine tries to **locate a domain controller** to which it can send the username and password for domain validation.

5. The logon username and password are passed to the domain controller that was found.

6. The domain controller **locates the username in the SAM** and verifies the password.

7. The domain controller **returns the user account's security identifier (SID),** which uniquely identifies that account in the network.

8. The domain controller returns **group membership tokens that list the SIDs of any groups** that contain the user account.

9. The domain controller returns the **path of any user logon scripts** that were associated with the user account.

10. The domain controller returns the **path to the user's roaming profile,** if one is assigned.

11. The computer then goes to the validating domain controller's **NETLOGON share to look for any system policies** associated with the machine SID, the user account SID, or group SIDs that have the user account as a member.

12. All **policies are applied,** the user profile is downloaded, and any user logon scripts are executed.

13. The user then gets access to the desktop.

Active Directory Domain Validation

In Windows 2000, when a user does the three-finger salute by pressing Ctrl+Alt+Del, the following events are triggered:

1. The computer presents the user with a dialog box that asks for a username and a password. The domain is displayed only if the user requests it or if the previous logon attempt failed.

2. This information is presented to the Local Security Authority (LSA) for validation.

3. The LSA checks whether the user is attempting to validate against the local machine's SAM or whether domain validation is being requested.

4. The machine tries to **locate a domain controller** for domain validation.

5. Windows 2000 creates a Kerberos authentication request containing the username and a random number. This random number is embedded twice in the request message: once in clear text and once encrypted using the user's typed-in password. This message is passed to the domain controller that was found. Notice that the password itself never hits the wire. L0PHTCRACK can't break a password that never leaves the computer. This process ensures that only a real domain controller from your real domain can respond to the authentication request because any responses are also encrypted. The famous man-in-the-middle attacks, in which the evil computer criminal impersonates your domain controller and steals information from your user credentials or off of your machine, are no longer as likely.

6. The domain controller **locates the username in Active Directory** and decrypts the encrypted number with the password stored in Active Directory. If the clear text and decrypted numbers match, the user is authenticated. If they don't match, the attempt fails.

7. The domain controller **returns the user account's security identifier (SID),** which uniquely identifies that account in the network.

8. The domain controller and the global catalog server return **group membership tokens that list the SIDs of any groups** that contain the user account.

9. The domain controller returns the **path of any user logon scripts** that were explicitly associated with the user account. This is primarily for backward compatibility.

10. The domain controller returns the **path to the user's roaming profile,** if one is assigned.

11. The domain controller provides the machine with the user portion of the assigned group policies associated with that user account. The computer portion of the group policy was already activated when the computer booted.

12. **All policies are applied**, the user profile is downloaded, and any user logon scripts are executed.

13. The user then gets access to the desktop.

Windows Active Directory adds security, stability, load balancing, and flexibility to an already impressive array of tools provided to the network administrator. With this power comes responsibility. One of the few opportunities you have to fundamentally change the way you do business arises when you are moving from one network enterprise infrastructure to another. Proper understanding of the interrelationships and contrasts between NT and 2000 will make it a lot easier to solve those case-study problems. Typically you are presented with a set of challenges, and you will leverage your understanding of the inner workings of Active Directory and NT to ensure that all of your bases are covered. We will now examine and contrast each of the critical points in the validation process. You must know the difference because that is the key that unlocks this exam.

NT—Locating a Domain Controller

You have only four methods for locating either the PDC or a BDC, and these methods are always used in the order in which they're listed here. Realize that once you locate a domain controller, you stop and don't use any of the other methods. This makes it easier to troubleshoot a validation problem.

1. *Check the NetBIOS name cache*—If you contacted a domain controller in the past 10 minutes or if it broadcast a service advertisement in the past two minutes, the special entry that identifies the machine as a domain controller will be stored in the cache. You can also preload the cache with #PRE entries in the LMHOSTS file.

2. *Query the WINS server*—Query a Windows Internet Naming Service (WINS) server for a list of all domain controllers that are registered for your domain. The PDC is identified with the sixteenth character of 1bh. BDCs identify each other by 1Ch entries that specify the domain as a special group. The WINS server returns a list of up to 25 BDCs to the host, and the host sends requests to a select few domain controllers. The first one that responds will take over the validation process. This can be an issue if your BDCs aren't roughly matched in speed.

I have personal experience in which a newer, faster machine was installed in a satellite office, and this machine was validating nearly all 15,000 users in the corporate home office through the WAN link. This BDC was designed to be a file server and, as a side job, to provide local validation to the remote office. But the BDC was so busy validating everyone in the company that it was a very sluggish file server, and the department that paid for the server was less than pleased. We ended up having to reinstall the operating system on the server as just a file server and then add a second, older box for local validation.

3. *Broadcasts*—Shouting down the wire locates only a PDC or BDC that happens to be on your local subnet. You can configure your routers to forward these types of broadcasts, but that typically uses up bandwidth and eliminates one of the larger reasons (logical segmentation of traffic) to have subnets.

4. *Use the LMHOSTS file*—Use this archaic text file, which should contain a **#DOM:mydomain** entry (where **mydomain** is the NT domain name), to identify a domain controller. LMHOSTS files are static files that are typically stored in the %systemroot%\system32\drivers\etc directory.

The LMHOSTS files have two main problems: They are checked only after a broadcast has been attempted, and they are static. Changes made in them have to be manually propagated throughout the company.

For more information on the LMHOSTS file and formatting, look at the LMHOSTS.SAM file on any Windows NT or Windows 2000 system. To access the LMHOSTS.SAM, click on Start, click on Run, and then type "notepad %systemroot%\system32\drivers\etc\lmhosts.sam" and click on OK. This will open the LMHOSTS.SAM file in notepad.

Active Directory—Locating a Domain Controller

In a pure Windows 2000 environment, Active Directory gives you a single option. You will query DNS looking for a service locator (SRV) record advertising Kerberos authentication services. If one can't be located, you will log on with cached credentials.

Note that NetBIOS domain resolution services are not used with a Windows 2000 client talking to a Windows 2000 domain. Legacy clients such as 95, 98, and NT use the older method as described for NT.

NT—Locating a Username in the SAM

NT domain controllers load the entire SAM into their memory. This domain SAM differs in fundamental structure from the local SAM. That is why you are forced to reinstall NT when you move from a server to a domain controller or vice versa. Each domain controller takes the passed username and finds it in the loaded SAM. The password that was sent over the wire is also compared. If there is a proper match, the user is authenticated. Remember, there is an approximate 40,000-user limit to the SAM. Also remember that this is why remote administration is such a pain. When you open the User Manager For Domains tool, the entire SAM is transferred over to your machine. On a 56K link, that will take awhile.

Active Directory—Locating a Username

The Local Security Authority on the domain controller queries Active Directory for the user object that contains the requested username and password. If a user principal name (UPN) is used, the global catalog is queried to locate the appropriate username, and the authentication is passed to a domain controller associated with the appropriate domain.

The password contained in Active Directory is used as the decryption key on the random number embedded in the logon request. This decrypted number is then compared to the clear text version. If the two match, the user is authenticated. If they don't match, the logon fails.

NT and Active Directory—The User Account's Security Identifier

The resource permissions assigned are not assigned by a username. Instead they are assigned to a security identifier (SID). Even if you rename the account, or if you move the account (possible only in Active Directory), the SID remains the same.

The SID has a format of S-1-5-21-domain's SID-relativeID. An example would be S-1-5-21-1763464350-544365479-500. The 500 suffix is a special relative identifier (RID) for the administrator account. In this example, this is the administrator account for domain 1763464350-544365479. The domain portion is important because it tells a resource which domain the user comes from; then the resource has to go to that domain to verify the credentials. The SID plays a critical role in migrating user accounts from NT to 2000. If you don't retain the SID, the user account loses resource access. Retaining resource access is one of the major goals of the administrator migrating or restructuring an old NT domain.

NT—Group Membership Tokens

NT user accounts can be members of two types of groups: local and global. The approved method of using groups is to place user accounts into global groups and then place global groups into the local groups. Each of these group types is assigned a SID. The SIDs are presented to users as part of their membership tokens. These membership tokens are transmitted to a resource machine when a user requests access. The resource machine then goes through all of the access control entries (ACEs) to find a SID match that provides the requested level of access. Remember that SID-granted permissions are cumulative, so permissions can be pieced together from several group memberships and from the SID of the user account itself. Because NT groups can't be nested any further than global groups into local groups, the access control list (ACL) can get rather large.

Active Directory—Group Membership Tokens

In Windows 2000, user accounts can be members of three Active Directory groups: domain local, global, and universal. Universal groups appear only when the domain is running in native mode. The approved method of using groups is to place the user account into the global group. You then place the global group into the domain local group, and you assign permissions to the domain local group.

Local Groups

Local groups (used in NT) still exist in Windows 2000, but they are really limited in scope. You can use them only to assign access to resources local to the machine, and they can only contain user accounts local to the same machine. Local groups are not shared or even entered into Active Directory. You typically use local groups in a workgroup environment only. They operate strictly within the boundary of the local SAM, and their use can really add to the administrative burden. Local groups can be found on all Windows 2000 Professional, standalone, and member servers. Local groups do *not* exist on domain controllers.

Domain Local Groups

Domain local groups can be used to assign access to resources located within a single domain with user accounts or groups from several domains. These groups are typically used to hold global groups, and then resource access is assigned once to the domain local group.

Global Groups

Global groups can be used to assign access to resources located in any domain in the enterprise, but these groups can contain only user accounts and global groups from the local domain. In a native 2000 domain, you can nest global groups. This setup provides the advantage of keeping the ACL (access control list) short. The downside is that the administrator needs to document the nesting, or it rapidly evolves into a nightmare.

Universal Groups

Universal groups are new to Windows 2000. They can be used to assign resource access in any domain, and they can contain user accounts and global groups from any domain. They are truly universal. Many administrators new to 2000 try to use universal groups almost exclusively. This practice should be discouraged because the membership of universal groups is stored and replicated to all global catalog servers in the entire enterprise. When you have multiple global groups that need to be assigned identical resource permissions, you should place the global groups in the universal groups, and then add the universal group to the domain local group. This practice keeps the ACL nice and short and ensures that you need to query only the global catalog server, not the various domain controllers, when you need to verify access credentials.

Membership in universal groups can have a significant side effect. Universal group membership is stored only in the global catalog server. No user can authenticate with a native-mode domain if a global catalog server isn't available. This is true because the user account can belong to a universal group that has been assigned a Deny Access security setting. Without this restriction, a hacker would need only to stop the global catalog server to bypass any universal group's Deny Access restriction. That could be simply accomplished by one of the many Denial Of Service attacks, such as simple port flooding, that seem to be cropping up with dismaying regularity.

Group SIDs

Each group type has a SID assigned to it. These SIDs are returned to the client, and the client uses the group SIDs to collect sufficient permissions to perform their tasks. All the administrator has to do to grant or deny access permission to a resource is to add or remove the user account from the appropriate group. This setup eliminates the need to change the ACL on the resource. The downside is that these group membership tokens are generated only when the user logs on. Many administrators have torn their hair out trying to figure out why user accounts that were just dropped into groups still don't have the requested, and assigned, access. The fix is to have the users log off; when they log back on, their memberships are updated.

The challenge during a migration or restructure is to ensure that the group and user SIDs are maintained, at least until the resource's ACL list can be updated. The whole idea is to minimize the downtime anyone experiences, and the mark of a perfect transformation is that no one notices the change. The additional features and benefits will become apparent to users as time passes and features roll out. But initially, it should go so smoothly that users have nothing, or at least nothing out of the ordinary, to complain about.

NT—User Logon Scripts

Logon scripts are the hook the administrator has to the user's machine. Administrators can use logon scripts to map drives, update virus tables, inventory machines, and distribute updates. The default path for the scripts is %systemroot%\system32\repl\import\scripts. The **import** portion of the path is automatically shared out as the NETLOGON share. The odd path is due to the archaic and unreliable method of script replication using the LAN Manager Replication Service.

In NT, you configure one machine, normally the PDC, to replicate logon scripts to all domain controllers. You place the scripts to be replicated in the %systemroot%\system32\repl\export\scripts folder. This folder is sent to all domain controllers, including the PDC to the import path just described. The problem is that this process is a one-way, full-copy replication. Any changes have to be made on the PDC, and administrators have to wait until replication occurs. Users can be assigned personal scripts, normally by using the **%username%** environment variable. This process rapidly becomes a massive administrative burden, so we typically settle with a logon script that tries to be all things to all people.

Active Directory—User Logon Scripts

Administrators who have well-crafted DOS batch files that they are emotionally attached to are in luck. Windows 2000 supports full compatibility with the old batch-file logon scripts. You can still set old logon scripts as an attribute of the user object. But Windows 2000 goes beyond the old method by storing script pointers directly in Active Directory.

In Windows 2000, you are not limited to batch files but can now use VBScript, JScript, or the Windows Script Host. The scripts are normally assigned using group policies, and the scripts have startup, logon, logoff, and shutdown opportunities for execution. Startup and shutdown scripts are assigned to machines and are executed before the WINLOGON dialog box is presented. Logon and logoff scripts are assigned to users. Logon scripts are executed before the users get their desktops; logoff scripts are executed before the WINLOGON dialog box reappears.

NT—Roaming User Profiles

Roaming user profiles contain desktop and machine settings that are specific to a user account. These profiles can contain documents that are stored on the desktop, Internet shortcuts, color schemes, and other items. The contents of the profile are downloaded when the user logs in and uploaded when the user logs off. This process can greatly increase the time it takes for users to get their desktops or shut down their computers. Administrators can use roaming user profiles to control the corporate appearance and can reduce trouble calls by making profiles mandatory. This means that any changes that users make on their desktops will be discarded when the users log off. You set up this system by renaming the ntuser.dat file to ntuser.man. You have to be cautious, though, because this will cause any file that is saved on the desktop to be discarded when the user logs off.

The administrator sets the Universal Naming Convention (UNC) path to the profile by using the Active Directory Users and Computers MMC snap-in. The usual format is \\server5\profiles\%username% where **server5** is the server name, **profiles** is the share name and the **%username%** is an environmental variable. This format makes the user's machine go to this path and create the underlying file structure, which includes the desktop, the Start menu, and so on. The username is normally granted full control permissions to this path. If this profile is to be used by several people, you should assign access permission to the appropriate local group. Shared profiles are normally configured as mandatory to prevent one user's changes from affecting everyone who uses the machine. Otherwise, the last person to log off gets his or her settings saved and everyone else's settings are lost.

While users are logged in, the local copy of their profiles normally reside in the %systemroot%\profiles\%username% directory. This directory is what is modified when a user changes his or her setting, and this directory is what is uploaded to the server when the user logs off. This path is important because it changes in Windows 2000.

Active Directory—Roaming User Profiles

Roaming user profiles in Windows 2000 are quite similar, in some aspects, to profiles in NT. The file names ntuser.dat and ntuser.man are the same. In fact, the same profile can be used with NT and Windows 2000. Any Windows-2000-specific Registry entries are simply ignored. Remember, this compatibility exists only with NT 4. Windows NT 3.51 machines and earlier are not compatible with Windows 2000 profiles.

Slow connections of 500Kbps or less will cause the user to log on with the locally cached profile. This makes it critical to log on to a laptop at least once to get a local copy of the user's profile created on the local drive.

The path to the profile is still added as an attribute of the user account and still follows the same UNC naming convention. The difference is where Microsoft decided to address the problem of slow logins due to massive transfer of files. You have three options. First, you don't use roaming profiles, and you force everyone to have different desktops if they log in on different machines. Second, you have users warned via a group policy when their profiles exceed a certain limit. Last, and probably best, you can use folder redirection to split out the parts of the user's environment that are stored separately from the normal mass of colors, pointers, and background graphics.

Folder Redirection

Folder redirection can split off the My Documents folder, Start Menu folder, Desktop folder, and other large folders. When the user logs on, these are not downloaded from the profile path. Instead, these folders can exist on any number of servers or shares, and that includes Distributed File System (DFS) shares. Folder redirection is set in a group policy that can be defined at multiple levels in the enterprise. Folder redirection allows the centralization of classes of files without the baggage of massive uploads and downloads when a user logs on or off.

Note: An important warning about mandatory profiles and the My Documents folder: The My Documents folder is included when you use a mandatory user profile with the standard settings. That means that any files that are stored in the My Documents folder are automatically and irretrievably deleted when the user logs off. This can cause severe distress to the normal user—and lots of hate mail directed at the uninformed administrator. When you use mandatory user profiles, folder redirection of the My Documents folder is essential.

NT System Policies and Windows 2000 Group Policies

System and group policies are the single most complex topic you are going to find in Windows 2000. It is vital that you understand the similarities and differences. We have decided to devote an entire chapter to System and group policies. This helps to ensure you will have "one stop shopping" in your quest to understand all the aspects of this critical management tool. You need to make sure that you understand where they fit in the logon process, but for an in-depth discussion, please refer to Chapter 3.

Logical Structure of NT Domains

Before you can decide what type of Active Directory you want to create, you need to understand what you currently have. Present domain structure might have a significant impact on your migration strategy because connectivity and access need to be maintained throughout the migration process. This section will explore how NT domains conduct business. Later in the chapter, we will explore the logical structure of Active Directory and will then examine some of the strategies advanced administrators can use to fit the domain structure to the administrative functions that are required in their particular enterprise.

You must understand Windows NT 4 domain models.

Single Domain Model

The single domain model is the easiest model to understand and implement. User accounts and resources are centrally controlled in one domain. All access to all shares, printers, and files are set in a single domain SAM database. There is only one primary domain controller and any number of backup domain controllers to provide redundancy. Figure 2.1 illustrates the single domain structure.

The single domain model is designed for centralized administration of both user accounts and resources. There is a single security boundary so that an administrator of the domain is an administrator of all user accounts and resources throughout the company. Single seat administration and simple design are the advantages of this structure. The disadvantages are that the single domain model doesn't scale well. An administrator is limited to approximately 40,000 user accounts. This is a design limitation of the SAM database. The single domain model can also have communications problems because some operations that the users may perform require direct contact with the primary domain controller. An example of this type of operations would be a simple password change. Any user that changes a password has to have their request handled by the only machine in the enterprise that has a Read/Write copy of the SAM database. If the PDC is on the far side of a WAN length, this operation may time out. If the domain has a password expiration policy and the users can't change their passwords, they will be locked out. In a distributed environment with limited WAN bandwidth, this model's limitations would make the single domain model unusable.

Administrators also need to pay particular attention to the political and financial realities of business. Many business units will expend large amounts of capital to acquire expensive resources like color printers. These units may not want to share, or may desire freedom from any outside administration. Administrators may find

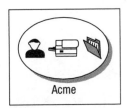

Figure 2.1   Single domain model.

they are required to provide administrative access to individuals who need to only manage single assets, but inherit massive permission due to the lack of granularity in NT permissions. The luckless admin may also find that units have great resistance to any form of central control over resource access. The "one domain fits all" solution may not be optimal, or even possible, in a politically-charged or geographically dispersed environment.

Single-Master Domain Model

The single-master domain model is specifically designed to address the concerns of department or business units in regard to administration and access to resources. The single-master domain model is comprised of a single user domain and multiple resource domains. The top domain is the user domain. This user domain is where all user accounts in the enterprise are located. To facilitate localized control of resource access and administration, the single-master domain model will have one or more resource domains. These resource domains are designed to hold all file and print shares. An illustration of a typical single master domain model is found in Figure 2.2.

The resource domains are separate domains that are controlled by a separate set of domain administrators. These resource domains will have their own PDC and BDCs and will trust the user account domain.

An advantage of the single-master domain model is that departments and business units can control administrative access to their resources. They can also have autonomous administrators who configure the security and admin functions, and this provides the control that may be politically or organizationally necessary. Remember that all of the user accounts are still contained in the master domain, so the WAN and scalability limitations of the single-domain model still apply.

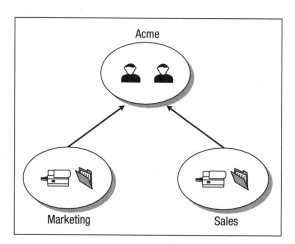

Figure 2.2 Single-master domain model showing trust relationships.

Trusting and trusted are methods of identifying whose SIDs are located in which ACL. The trusted domain contains the user accounts and these SIDs are used in the access control lists of the trusting domain's resources. An easy way to remember who is trusted and who is trusting is: Ed is a user and he is in the trustED domain. The trusting domain has the "tings" to share. A single-headed arrow, pointing from the trusting domain to the trusted domain, usually represents the trust relationships. If you see a double-headed arrow, it simply illustrates two, one-way trusts where the domains are both trusted and trusting.

Multimaster Domain Model

The multimaster domain model is designed to provide distributed resource administration but steps beyond a single master model in WAN access and scalability. The multimaster domain model is a variation of the single master domain model in that the resource and user domains are separate entities. The difference lies in the number of user domains. In the single master model, all user accounts are in a single domain and there may be several resource domains. In the multimaster domain model, there are still several possible resource domains, but we also add additional user account domains. Figure 2.3 illustrates a typical multimaster domain configuration.

The existence of two user domains that have a bi-directional trust relationship is an important difference between single and multimaster domains. The multiple-user domains provide separation of administrative authority but, more importantly, allows for infinite scalability as you simply add additional user domains to accommodate additional user accounts. An interesting feature of the multimaster

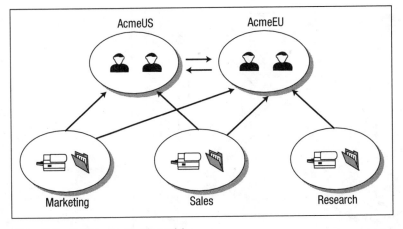

Figure 2.3   Multimaster domain model.

domain model is that you can use this design to overcome the problems associated with slow WAN links. If you have two locations that are separated by limited bandwidth, you can create separate domains on each side of the link. Users will validate against PDCs and BDCs from their local domain and will be able to perform functions like password modification on their local PDC. Multimaster domains can be more complex to manage, but you can have some level of centralized control through judicious assignment of administrative authority.

Complete Trust Domain Model

The complete trust domain model is also known as the chaos model. This model is designed for when there is a complete lack of central IT control. Each domain is comprised of a combination of user accounts and resource assets. An example of the complete trust domain model is illustrated in Figure 2.4.

Each domain in the model is both trusted and trusting. The number of trust relationships that must be maintained is the biggest disadvantage to the complete trust model. Each additional domain that is added only adds to the complexity. The advantages of the complete trust domain model are the absolute autonomy that is enjoyed by each and every domain. User accounts can be assigned access to any resource but no domain is under the administrative control of any other domain. WAN links are not a problem, except in the realm of pass-through authentication. Every user account that is from a trusted domain has to be authenticated to a domain controller from that domain. Since there is no centralized SAM database, the authentication request must be forwarded to a

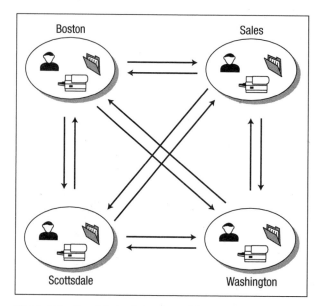

Figure 2.4 Complete trust domain model.

PDC or BDC from the user's domain. This can cause an increase in WAN traffic and add to the complexity of the administrative need to ensure domain resolution via WINS or LMHOSTS files is possible. The complete trust model operates best in environments where there is no centralized authority and resource access between geographically dispersed domains is relatively rare.

Logical Structure of Active Directory

When you are moving from a well-known NT directory structure to the relatively new Active Directory, one of the most important points to understand is the level of hierarchical management that is available. The Active Directory structure consists of forests, trees, domains, organizational units, and sites. Before developing a migration or restructuring plan, the enterprise engineers should divide the destination environment into its component pieces. An advanced administrator needs to be fully conversant with each element in order to properly plan the logical and timely transformation from the old to the new. In this section, we will explore the logical structure of Active Directory to help ensure that your migration occurs at an appropriate level. If you roll out multiple forests when you only need organizational units, you are adding huge levels of administration. One of the goals of a migration is to streamline and restructure the administration of the network, not to heighten its complexity.

 You must understand Active Directory structure.

The Forest—There Should Be Only One

The forest is the overriding body that describes and controls every other aspect of Active Directory. Inside the forest you can have any number of trees, domains, organizational units, and sites. The inside can be as ordered or as chaotic as you desire. The forest creates the first level of organization and provides the overall administrative structure.

Unless you have compelling reasons to the contrary, you should have only one forest for your entire organization. The advantages are many. You have a common directory schema, a common global catalog, and a common configuration. These features help to reduce the levels of cumbersome administration and the number of hoops you have to jump through to perform the tasks that make up an administrator's day.

> Even though there should be only one forest in a good single company Active Directory design, be prepared for situations involving multiple forests. You will get practice with this later.

The first domain that is upgraded or created from scratch forms the *forest root domain*. This domain can have a name that represents the organization as a whole. An example of a forest root domain would be **acme.com**. Any domains that you want to add to the forest have to be able to access the forest root domain during promotion. The domains that join can have a contiguous namespace, thereby forming a child domain off of the forest root. Figure 2.5 shows the child domain of **marketing.acme.com** added to the forest root of **acme.com**.

You can also create domains that maintain a completely separate identification, thereby creating a new tree in an existing forest. Separate trees help maintain separate name recognition to differing business units, but ensures that the many advantages of a single forest are maintained. One way to identify separate trees is the non-contiguous naming convention. Figure 2.6 illustrates how we can add **acme.com** and **scooters.org** to the same forest, but maintain separate trees.

Naming the Forest Root

Understanding the components of the forest root makes it easier for you to plan its creation. Realize that when you are rolling this out, you must make several design decisions that are then written in stone.

One of the first design decisions in implementing the forest root is the domain name. This is very important because after the domain is named, you cannot rename it without reinstalling the *entire forest*. Microsoft recommends one of two approaches to naming the root: Either select a name that represents the entire company; or select a "generic" name, such as "corporate" or "root."

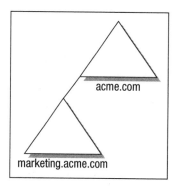

Figure 2.5 **Acme.com** parent and child domains.

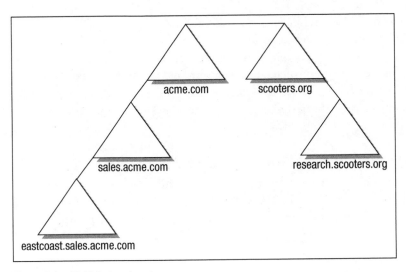

Figure 2.6 Multiple-tree forest.

The first approach might seem like a good idea, but the downside is that if your company is acquired or renamed, you will be stuck with a root name that makes no sense or, in the worst case, is a reminder of times past. This can be particularly burdensome in the event of a hostile takeover in which the new owners want to divest themselves of any shred of the old identity.

The second approach—using something generic like "corporate" or "root" or "home" or "blank" as the forest root—gives you unprecedented levels of flexibility. Figure 2.7 illustrates a typical approach to a generic forest root.

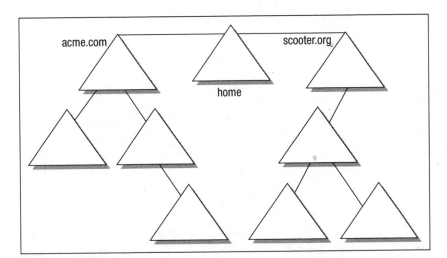

Figure 2.7 Generic forest root.

Because the name isn't linked to any portion of the company, any future reorganizations, acquisitions, and company spin-offs will have no effect. You can add and remove tree structures at will. This approach also helps secure the structure because hackers and users will not be aware of the hidden structure of the unknown root. Because this name will most likely not follow the Internet standard naming conventions, it will be next to impossible for external forces to penetrate security and do any form of damage.

The Flexible Single Master Operations Servers

The forest root contains both of the forest-level Flexible Single Master Operations (FSMO) servers. These are the schema master and the domain naming master. Only one server, per role, in the entire forest can maintain these roles at any one time.

 You can manage the Domain Naming Master via the Active Directory Domains and Trusts snap-in or the NTDSUTIL command line utility. You can manage the Schema Master role via the Schema snap-in or NTDSUTIL. The Schema stap-in must be registered before it can be added to an MMC console. To register the Schema snap-in, go to the Run dialog box or a command line and enter the following command: **regsvr32 %systemroot%/system32 schmmgmt.dll**.

The Schema Master

The schema master is responsible for maintaining and extending the schema. One of the important aspects of a forest is that its objects share a common schema. The schema master defines and controls the types of objects that are available in the directory structure. These objects are defined in object classes that make up the fundamental structure of Active Directory.

The schema master is also responsible for maintaining the attributes that are assigned to the various objects available in Active Directory. Some of the attributes are Must Contain, and others are May Contain. An example of a Must-Contain attribute is the logon name in the user object. Every user must have a logon name when his or her user account is created in Active Directory. An example of a May-Contain attribute is an email address that is part of the user object. The good news is that potential attributes that aren't filled out will not occupy any space in the Active Directory database.

Certain directory-aware applications, such as Exchange 2000, modify the schema. These applications add object classes and attributes. These forms of schema modification can have some severe consequences if they are not well thought out. One of the challenges of schema extensions is that after an object or attribute class is created, it can never be deleted. You can disable the object or attribute, but once it is in Active Directory, it is there to stay.

With the permanence of schema extensions in mind, we must carefully consider securing the directory against malicious and/or accidental damage. The best defense against irreparable damage is the well-worn policy of frequent backups. Before any modification to the schema, you must back up the system state of your network environment. You should perform a complete backup of your schema master. If your extension should fail, you will need to do an authoritative restore. This forces all of the other domain controllers to accept the restored settings as the latest and greatest structure, and they will modify their internal directory settings to comply.

Microsoft has also placed some stringent requirements on who and what can extend the schema. There is a special group called Schema Admins; administrators belonging to this group have the unique ability to place the schema into a Read/Write state. They can then use scripts or the Active Directory Service Interfaces (ADSI) to change the structure manually.

If you are installing an Active-Directory-aware application, such as Exchange 2000, the installation will occur in two stages. The first is the extension of the schema. This requires the rights and privileges of a schema administrator. The second part of the installation involves the file copying and directory population of the new objects. This part doesn't require schema modification and can be performed by anyone who has the appropriate Create Child permissions at the correct layer in the hierarchy. By default, the only user account that is a member of the Schema Admins group is the default administrator account that was created in the forest root domain as part of the installation of the first domain controller.

Because schema extension is such a rare event, it is advisable to remove the default administrator account from the Schema Admins group and create a special user account that is just for schema modification. The schema is common throughout the entire forest, so any changes should be approved by a cross section of decision makers throughout the company. This should be a difficult process and should occur rarely. If you are thinking of extending the schema, first consider examining the alternatives. Once the deed is done, there are few ways to undo the damage.

Remember, the schema master contains the overall structure of the Active Directory. The schema master doesn't, however, contain a list of all the created objects that populate your enterprise. The objects are all listed in the global catalog server's database. But even the global catalog doesn't contain a complete set of all the attributes of all of the objects. Realize that if there is a business reason to extend the schema, but the changes can't be reflected throughout the enterprise, the administrator will need to create a separate forest. This decision is not to be taken lightly because the many advantages of a forest—with its full transitive trust relationships and common global catalog—are lost. You are also unable to join an existing domain or tree to a different forest. You will be stuck creating the old-style explicit one-way trusts, and then you are pretty much back to the NT style of administration.

The Domain Naming Master

The domain naming master is responsible for tracking domain names that are assigned throughout the forest. The role of a naming master comes into play only when a domain is added to or deleted from the forest. This server must be up and operational any time a new domain is created, even if it is just a child domain added to an existing parent.

Because schema extensions and domain additions are rare operations that generate minimal traffic, Microsoft recommends that the schema master and the domain naming master be placed on the same domain controller in the forest root. Microsoft also recommends that the forest root contain at least two domain controllers for fault tolerance. Never forget that if the forest root goes away, the entire forest goes along with it. (You did print extra copies of your résumé?)

Domain Level FSMO Roles

There are three FSMO roles that are specific to each Active Directory domain. These roles are the PDC Emulator, RID Master, and Infrastructure Master. You can manage these FSMO roles via the Active Directory Users and Computers MMC snap-in or the NTDSUTIL command line utility.

The PDC Emulator provides backwards compatibility with Windows NT 4 domains. When in mixed mode (see "Domain Modes" later in this chapter) the PDC Emulator is responsible for propagating account database changes to any existing NT 4 BDCs on its domain. The PDC Emulator is also responsible for password changes in mixed- or native- mode domains. For example, if a user attempts to logon to the domain, but provides an incorrect password, the PDC Emulator is checked before denying the user the ability to logon. The reason is that the user's password may have recently changed and the PDC Emulator is primarily responsible for handling password changes.

The RID Master is responsible for giving out relative identifiers (RIDs) to domain controllers. RIDs are unique numbers for a domain that allow a domain controller to assign unique SIDs to newly created objects.

The Infrastructure Master is responsible for updating user and group memberships in a multidomain environment. This FSMO role makes it possible to grant users and groups from other domains rights, permissions, and membership in groups on your local domain. When you have a multidomain environment, you should never place the Infrastructure Master on a Domain Controller configured as a global catalog.

 Any domain controller can be configured to be a global catalog. However, by default the only Global Catalog Server (GCS) is the forest root domain controller. You can configure additional GCS through the Active Directory Site and Services MMC snap-in. By default, all FSMO roles for the forest and the forest root domain are assigned to the first domain controller installed (a.k.a. the forest root domain controller).

Joining Multiple Forests

Microsoft recommends that the overall structure of the enterprise should be a single forest. If you have established your Active Directory forest and then your company merges with another company (with its own forest), or another company needs access to your company's resources, you will need to join the forests together.

Joining forests is actually a process that runs home to the old NT way of doing things. You will need to set up a manually configured trust relationship. This goes back into the old trusted and trusting scheme. Again, easiest way to remember this is to think of "Ed" as a user account. Ed, the user, lives in the trustED domain. Resources are always in the trusting domain.

When you create explicit trust relationships, you don't have the advantages that are inherent in a Windows 2000 forest. The trusts are not transitive. If domain A trusts domain B, and domain B trusts domain C, domain A does not automatically trust domain C. Windows is not limited to trusting just Microsoft domains. Windows 2000 is compatible with the MIT version 5 of Kerberos realms. As companies standardize on a Kerberos format, you will see additional opportunities to merge network operating system directories.

It really boils down to this: To gain all of the advantages of Windows 2000, you need to be in the same forest. If you want complete autonomy, including no enterprise administrators, or a different global catalog, or a different schema, you will need to create a new forest and set up old-style trust relationships. Just don't forget where Ed lives.

Trees—Just Don't Add Too Many Branches

A tree is a set of Windows 2000 domains that share a common schema and configuration and a contiguous namespace. This means that the child domains will build their names based on the parent's name. Trees ensure a logical flow up through the parents until authentication requests reach the tree root. Once the tree root is located, the requests can move laterally through the forest root and down a neighboring tree.

There is really only one advantage of inhabiting a single tree versus multiple trees in a forest. If you inhabit a single tree, it's really easy to find out where you exist in the corporate food chain. I know that if my domain is **greenwaypkwy .scottsdale.az.westernus.production.foo.com,** I am down the line from **scottsdale,** who is down the line from **az,** who is under **westernus,** who reports to **production,** which is a wholly owned subsidiary of **foo,** which, hopefully, is a commercially successful business venture. Figure 2.8 shows how messy this can become.

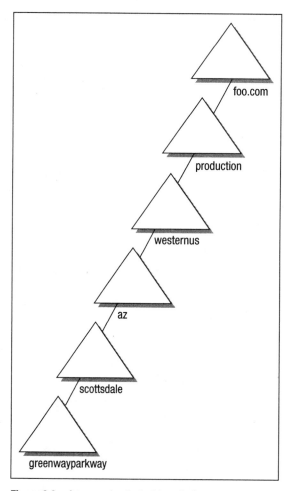

Figure 2.8 An example of a bad tree design.

This illustrates one important rule of tree creation. Whenever possible, do not, do not, *do not* create your Active Directory structure by looking at a company's organization chart. If you follow the chart, you will get domain names that are impossible to remember and near-impossible to administrate. The cold, hard fact is that Active Directory is designed for one thing: administrative ease. Never fall into the trap of creating "vanity" Active Directory domains. Most users will never see the structure, and added levels of complexity will make your design inefficient and burdensome.

It can give you a warm feeling to know that Microsoft has put so much thought into the care and feeding of us administrators. Before you get all weepy, though, realize this: It is the administrators who provide access to resources. It is also administrators who recommend network operating systems. Most end users don't really care what is running on their machines as long as they can do their jobs. Our job is to help them do theirs. Proper Active Directory design takes administrative tasks into consideration. The mess we just mentioned shows you how *not* to do it. You can, but you shouldn't create a leviathan domain structure that makes a nice big chart, but gives administrators nice, big headaches.

But what if political realities rear their pointy heads and take us out of our blissful administrative nerdvana? Because all domains in a forest share a transitive trust relationship, users from any domain can have access to any resources in the enterprise where they were granted permissions. These trust relationships ensure that administrators in any domain can assign access to any user or global group from any domain. Gone are the days when administrators from domain A had to find an administrator in domain AAA to set up a trust relationship just so Bob in accounting could get a file from server 23 in the Scottsdale office.

All this trust and cooperation might lead you to think that security must be lacking. But this isn't the case.

Domains—Fortresses or Sieves?

The core unit of the logical structure of Active Directory is the domain. The domain is probably the most familiar feature for administrators moving from Windows NT to Windows 2000. A domain has users and computers. It even has trust relationships. But many of the new features of Windows 2000 go far beyond what experienced NT administrators are used to. This section highlights some of the important features—important in the real world and very important on the exam.

Domains Are Security Boundaries

Windows 2000 provides many layers of administration and security. We also see an unprecedented level of interoperability through delegation and inheritance.

An advanced administrator must thoroughly understand the various implications of security to prevent locking administration staff out or, worse yet, letting the wrong people in.

The domain is an entity all its own. The Enterprise Admins group is automatically added to the Domain Admins group whenever a domain is created. This occurs whether the domain is installed as a child or a tree to an existing forest. The Domain Admins group is added to the built-in Administrators domain local group. The Administrators group has the most rights and privileges of all groups in Active Directory. The Domain Admins and Enterprise Admins groups inherit these powers due to their automatic placement in every domain's Administrators group.

Password Policy—It Is Domain Specific

Another area where the domain reigns supreme is in certain areas of group policy. Password, account, Kerberos, and Public Key Trust List policies can be truly controlled only at the domain level. You can create a policy at the OU level, but Active Directory will ignore it.

If a case study discusses how a department wants a different password length than other departments, that department will need a separate domain. Pay particular attention if a department asks for a longer password history or for changes in the account lockout settings. To facilitate any of these changes, you will need to set them in a different domain.

Domains Are Units of Replication

Active Directory can contain millions of objects, and each of these objects can contain any number of attributes. Some of the attributes, such as a username, are important to the entire enterprise. Other attributes, such as parking space, have meaning only within a local area. Active Directory is designed to be scalable, and part of that is controlling how much information has to be shared with the furthest reaches of a network.

In a pure Windows 2000 domain, all domain controllers are masters of replication, or more correctly, replication masters. They all have a Read/Write copy of Active Directory. Any changes that are performed on one of the domain controllers are sent to all other domain controllers. The gotcha is that *all* properties and *all* attributes of every domain object is sent to all domain controllers. It is intelligent replication in that only changes are replicated, but every domain controller receives the complete set regardless.

If you want a smaller subset of all of the attributes, you have a couple of options. One option is to create a new domain where you will only replicate your complete set of attributes that is specific to your domain. You will rely on a global catalog server to provide information on all of the other objects in the enterprise. Another, much worse option is to install a separate forest. Because the global catalog is common throughout the forest, the only way to get away from having a complete copy of everything is to split off into a new forest. If you do this, you lose all of the benefits of a transitive trust relationship, a common schema, and a common configuration. The biggest price to pay is the fact that global policies are not inherited past the boundary of a domain. Policies can be assigned to a site, but each client will then have to wander around in the directory forest and locate a domain controller from the domain that is hosting the policy. This really adds to logon time and increases network traffic. Such is the price of freedom. Unless you really need this level of isolation, stick with a single domain or, at most, a new domain. Try to leave multiple forests to the lumberjacks.

Domain Modes

Domains have two modes of operation: mixed mode and native mode. The names sound a bit odd, but the overriding point is that they have nothing to do with the client. You can have a mixture of Windows 95, 98, NT, and 2000 clients and non-domain controllers, and it doesn't affect the domain mode one iota.

The only thing that mandates your domain mode is the type of domain controllers that are operating in the domain. If you have any NT backup domain controllers, you must be running in mixed mode. Notice we said "backup domain controllers." If you have any Windows 2000 servers operating as a domain controller, one of them has to be the primary domain controller. Windows 2000 will not join as a domain controller unless it is an upgrade of a PDC or unless another Windows 2000 server is already the PDC. Once the PDC is upgraded, you can add any number of Windows 2000 or NT domain controllers. In a mixed-mode network, the BDCs think they are in NT domain, and the Windows 2000 domain controllers know better. If we upgrade or replace all of the NT BDCs with Windows 2000,we are still in a mixed-mode environment until we explicitly order a conversion.

The only way to convert to a native-mode environment is to have only Windows 2000 domain controllers and then go into the Active Directory Domains and Trusts Microsoft Management Console (MMC), right-click on the domain name, and upgrade.

Changing from mixed to native mode is a one-way process. You cannot go back. After the conversion, you cannot add any NT 4 BDCs. From then on, you can use only Windows 2000 domain controllers. You can, however, still support Windows NT and Windows 9x clients when in native mode.

Remember, clients and non-domain controllers don't care what domain mode you are in. You can still have a mixture of Windows 95, 98, NT, and even Windows for Workgroups clients, and they will still operate—fat, dumb, and happy. They are completely oblivious to the change. You can shatter their illusion by installing the Active Directory client. This makes a couple of changes. The older, or legacy, clients can now change their passwords on any domain controller instead of running to the PDC. These clients can also participate in domain-based DFS (Distributed File System), and they can perform searches against Active Directory for resources. They still can't take advantage of group policies, and they will fall under the old logon scripts and the tyranny of NETLOGON.

The Cost of Creating a New Domain

Creating a new domain is not a trivial decision. You have to determine where in the forest it is to be located. You have to identify the domain namespace and ensure that DNS knows about you and will support your endeavor. You also need to concern yourself with fault tolerance and administration. You will need at least two domain controllers, and you will need to designate someone, or better yet a group of someones, to create and manage your new domain. Do yourself a rather large favor; try really, really hard to stick to a single domain. If you find that impossible, keep each domain as flat as possible. The headache and heartache of a layered tree or multiple trees or multiple forests do little to reduce the total cost of ownership. You are going to find on the exam, as in real life, that the main tendency is to gravitate to a single-domain solution. But how do you manage all the users and resources and maintain departmental independence? Simple; you roll out the organizational units.

Organizational Units

Organizational units (OUs) are the way to go for delegating administrative authority. OUs relieve the wise administrator of the burden of having to manage each and every aspect of a domain. You can use organizational units to divide your domain into administrative-level pieces. Some call this system the hierarchy of the oppressors and the oppressed.

The Oppressors—OU Level Administration

If it has an administrative segment, it should probably be an OU. The lowest level of an organizational unit hierarchy will probably be the help desk. These staunch individuals have to deal with the day-to-day operations of MAC, or *move, add, change*. Help-desk staffers are on the front lines and need to have limited administrative authority. Although these professionals are good at what they do, what they do doesn't require the keys to the domain. In other words, they are performing some administrative duties, but don't need to be full-blown administrators. You can use the Delegate Administration wizard to delegate a subset of your awesome power to these hardworking professionals.

When you are designing your Active Directory system, you want to orient it toward the business goals and the administration that make these goals possible. The best part about Active Directory is that its structure is completely transparent to the users. Set OUs at levels of administration. If you find a common administrative task that encompasses many individuals, groups, or computers, you should think really hard about adding an OU.

The Oppressed—Control through Security Groups

End users, including the CEO, should not be delegated special administrative abilities. Hopefully, you couldn't find the company's organization chart when you designed your forest. You need to keep that chart lost when you design the OU structure. The "oppressed," or end users, should be grouped by global security groups. This lumps them into a nice manageable section where the administrator or, better yet, the delegated OU administrator can provide them with the necessary management and control. *Never* create "vanity" OUs. If the director of sales wants an OU called WAYCOOLSALESGUYS, tell them you will get right on it and try to keep a straight face until they wander off. No one will ever know because users have no idea how the OU structure is organized. Unless they have been attending night classes in the intricacies of X.500, they will probably never know. The point was made previously: The purpose of Active Directory is *administrative convenience*. It is there to make your job easier (so that you'll recommend more easy-to-manage Microsoft products).

The Power of Well-Developed OUs

OUs are an administrator's dream, especially if the administrator is fairly high in the IT food chain. It is through OUs that group policies can really flex their muscles. Remember, group policies flow from the site to the domain and throughout our administratively-oriented OU structure. OUs are also used to distribute software applications to the user's logon or to individual computers. OUs can be used to selectively implement "desktop lockdowns" where the opportunity for computer customization can be greatly limited or loosened. You can even use OUs to hide users, computers, groups, printers, and even shares from the rest of the enterprise. In order to search Active Directory for an object, you must have Read permission to the OU.

OUs Create Flexibility to Design

One of the most powerful advantages of the organizational unit is its ability to react to the never-ending threat of the reorganization. As companies grow, or collapse for that matter, things change. Users need to move from one department to another, the administrative authority over a server or share changes, or departments pop into existence or die on the vine. If we designed our directory structure based on the company organizational chart, I hope we can find those installation disks. If we did the smart thing, and set it all up with OUs, we simply right-click on the object that needs to be relocated (for the fourth time) and select Move. Microsoft, as of this writing, is promising a drag-and-drop solution to OU reorganization. Either way, this absolutely rocks as far as moving within a domain.

OUs are the mainstay of a mature, stable, and scalable Active Directory design. OUs exist to serve mankind, and I don't mean with a cookbook.

Sites Provide the Power to Localize Traffic

Forests, trees, domains, and OUs are all parts of the logical structure of Active Directory. As we know, sometimes logic has nothing to do with the real world. The way we force our utopian Active Directory into the cold, cruel world is through the proper design and maintenance of sites.

Sites are designed to deal with one basic reality: WAN connections stink, and some stink more than others. In a perfect environment, we would be in a single LAN with a 10Gbps connection right to the desktop. Well, that isn't quite the case, although some rather fascinating technologies are coming out of the labs recently, and 10Gbps may soon become a cost-effective reality. The fact is that LAN connectivity, under most normal circumstances, is adequate to replicate directory changes between all domain controllers that are on the same local network. Users will probably suffer only limited logon delay and can access local shares with minimal lag. Your mileage may vary, especially if your CIO is addicted to networked first-person shooters. In this environment of ample bandwidth, a single site is probably sufficient. Everyone can replicate with everyone, and users can validate with the first domain controller that responds to the request.

But remember, WANs exist. Some WANs have fairly decent connectivity, and others barely have any. Microsoft has designed a way to control bandwidth utilization and logon traffic by designating one or more IP subnets as a site.

A site is nothing more than a collection of IP subnets that have been designated by some administrator as high-speed and well-connected. By default, all subnets fall into a single site that is named, somewhat appropriately, First-Site-Name. Remember, the administrator is responsible for deciding what is good available bandwidth and what is less than good.

Site Membership

Sites can contain several IP subnets. However, and this is a *big* however, an IP subnet can belong to only a single site. Administrators will need to get together with the network people and carefully examine available bandwidth. Available bandwidth is the critical measurement because 100Mbps with only 15Kbps available is worse than 10Mbps with 100Kbps available. You need to identify usage trends, not just an average or a localized snapshot.

Creating a site is simple; all you have to do is to go to the Active Directory Sites and Services MMC snap-in and select Sites. Right-click and fill out the magic wizard. Notice that the network and subnet portion of the IP address should match your actual assigned address, but the subnet mask is only used to identify what part of the provided address is to be used to identify the network, as opposed to the host portion of the address.

The Possibly Negative Results of Site Creation

Sites are extremely powerful and let advanced administrators take control of their networks. When you properly configure sites, you localize logon and searching traffic. You provide priority services for Active Directory replication. You also steer the users to local resources, including files, catalog servers, and domain controllers. If you get it wrong, people will be going across WAN links when the resources they want are right next to them.

When a domain controller is installed, it compares its IP address with all of the sites that are listed in Active Directory. Remember that sites are a forest thing, not a domain thing. If a domain controller can't find a site that fits, the DC drops into the site cleverly called Default-First-Site-Name. If the DC can find a site, it drops itself in there and sits, smug in knowing its work is finished.

Herein lies the problem. If you install a domain controller in your deployment offices in Orlando, you have to give it an IP address that makes sense to your local subnet. The domain controller sniffs around and registers in the Orlando-FL site. You then box this shiny new server up and ship it to Tokyo. When the local Tokyo administrator fires the server up, it doesn't care that its IP address has changed. It has registered and now considers itself above such things. The server's Kerberos SRV record has been updated in DNS to reflect the new IP address, but we have a problem waiting to happen.

Bill comes in on Monday morning and fires up his laptop in the local Orlando office. After forever, he finally gets his machine up and running. You notice that a lot of your clients are complaining. Not only that, but your WAN utilization is going through the roof. After much wailing and gnashing of teeth, someone fires up a command prompt, types **SET**, and presses Enter. Lo and behold, over half of your users have the **%validatingserver%** variable showing as Tokyo7. Doh!

When users log in, they contact a DNS server to locate a list of domain controllers. The domain controllers are sorted and returned by site name. The clients then attempt to ping UDP port 389 to every DC that happens to be in their site. The first DC that answers wins and authenticates the client. How does the computer know what site it is in? When the machine boots, it gets its site information from the domain controller that authenticates the computer from Active Directory. How does the computer know which domain controller to contact for machine validation? The last site the client was assigned to is stored in the registry under HKLM\System\CurrentControlSet\Services\Netlogon\Parameters\ DynamicSiteName. The client uses that site for the initial DNS query. The only way to fix this DC placement problem is to have your sites fully configured before you install additional domain controllers. You should also try to install the DCs in their local subnets. In the case of a configuration and deployment facility, as with Tokyo7, you will need to *manually* move the domain controller from the original site to the correct site. Otherwise, ticked-off users and high WAN bills result.

 Remember, Windows 2000 Professional and Windows 2000 Server, all flavors, are fully conversant with automatic site placement. The important fact that Microsoft wants you to know, and what it tests you on, is that domain controllers do not change their assigned site membership, except during the initial installation. Failure to remember this could cost you a few points, and a few points could cost you the exam.

The Positive Side of Site Creation

Now that you are a bit gun-shy about sites, here is the good news. If you have configured the sites and the domain controllers properly, all the rest is automatic. When a client gets an IP address, either manually assigned or via DHCP, that client is placed into the appropriate site. The DNS server responds to all queries with a sorted list of services, based on site information. That means that when a client wants to find a global catalog server, DNS will steer that client to the nearest server hosting the global catalog. When we are looking for a domain-based DFS share, Active Directory will point us to a local share, not the one in Guam. When we are looking to change our domain password, the DC in the closet over there will hook us up. We won't have to run to the PDC.

Site membership works for only those clients that understand how to query Active Directory. Windows 95/98/NT will need to have the Active Directory client installed to find local domain controllers, global catalog servers, and DFS root servers and links. Without this client, they can go anywhere and ask anyone.

Another important point about sites is that there is no such thing as preferred domain controllers in Active Directory. If your entire network is well-connected, the only way to segment your clients based on subnets is to create sites.

Sites Aid in Directory Replication

The advantages of Active Directory don't stop at validation. This multimaster replication model can certainly become chaotic if there isn't some mechanism to control communications between machines. In a simplistic design, we could let everyone replicate with everyone, but this would create an unnecessary level of duplicated traffic on our wires. Microsoft has borrowed a page from routers and implemented a spanning-tree algorithm; Microsoft has also snagged technology from Exchange Server to use the Knowledge Consistency Checker to control it all.

The Knowledge Consistency Checker (KCC) is designed to view the entire topology. First it looks at the local site. The KCC tries to create a topology that ensures that each domain controller is no further than two hops away from every other domain controller in the site. When we are talking hops, we aren't talking about routers. We are saying that each domain controller in a site will tolerate only information that has gone through two other domain controllers. This is similar to the children's game where everyone sits in a circle. One of the kids whispers a phrase in their neighbor's ear. That neighbor whispers what they heard to the next person in the circle. Over time, the message gets so garbled that it completely changes. To prevent this the KCC only tolerates replicated information that has been whispered through a maximum of two domain controllers. If the KCC determines that there are more than two hops between any two DCs, the KCC will create a direct replication path with the offending domain controller. If we add additional domain controllers to the mix, the KCC will review the topology and may direct domain controllers to directly replicate with any newbies.

This intrasite replication uses remote procedure calls (RPCs) over the TCP/IP routed protocol. The traffic is uncompressed, and the replication can occur at any time. Domain controllers replicate only with domain controllers from their domain. Remember, domains are a replication boundary. If we want to share information between domains, we rely on global catalog servers. These global catalog servers reside as an additional service on designated domain controllers. Global catalog servers rely on infrastructure master FSMO servers to update any changes in a domain's internal structure that is of interest to the rest of the forest.

Because replication can occur at any time in a site, we may find ourselves sitting around twiddling our thumbs waiting for the latest change to show up at our local DC. You can use the utility REPLMON to view replication status on a DC-by-DC basis. If you want to force replication between servers, you can do this in the Active Directory Sites and Services MMC. All you need to do is to move into the tree of the server to which you want the replication to flow. Remember, all connectors are inbound. Right-click on the connector, and select the Replicate Now command. This will send the RPC, and the data should shortly follow. If you want to do this from the command line, you can get the Replication Administrator utility, **Repadmin**, from the Windows 2000 resource kit. Then type **repadmin /syncall <DSA> <NC>** where DSA is the fully qualified domain name of the server you want to send your changes to, and NC is the naming context you want to replicate. An example of this command is:

```
repadmin /syncall dc23.sales.acme.com "DC=sales,DC=acme,DC=com"
```

This will force the domain controller to replicate the sales child domain information to a server named DC23 in the **sales.acme.com** domain.

Replication between Sites

Sites really shine in controlling replication traffic between domain controllers and global catalog servers. In a single site, DCs can talk to anyone at any time. Between sites, communications are tightly controlled by the KCC (Knowledge Consistency Checker).

Domain controllers that belong to the same domain always communicate via RPCs over IP. You may want to note that for the exam. Global catalog servers that are from different domains have the option of using SMTP (Simple Mail Transfer Protocol). These servers basically send email to each other. You always have the option to use RPCs, but SMTP is only for domain controllers in different domains that are in different sites.

Another difference between intrasite and intersite replication is that intrasite replication is push/pull. I can tell you I have changes, and you come and get them, or you can ask me if I have changes, and I will send them to you. Intersite (between site) replication is always pull. I come to you and ask if you have changes. If you have changes, you then send them to me. This polling is controlled by two factors: schedule and interval.

The schedule specifies when the site link between the sites is available for replication. The polling interval is how often a domain controller is allowed to "run across the WAN" to check for changes. You have to match both the schedule and the interval to talk across the wire. Administrators typically set the schedule for lower utilization time, depending on the desired and tolerable levels of Active Directory latency. The greater the interval and the narrower the schedule, the more "drift", or loss of directory synchronization, will occur. Eventually you may find that it takes too long for information entered in one site to travel throughout your network.

Sites make it possible to control the amount of traffic that goes across our WAN links. We can control logon, search, file access, and replication traffic. The wise administrator will take available bandwidth and directory latency into account when planning the proper implementation of this powerful feature.

Integration with DNS

The Domain Name System (DNS) is the single most important service that exists in Windows 2000. Without DNS, users can't log on, domain controllers can't find each other, and pretty much nothing works. As an administrator, you must understand how this critical service supports hostname and service resolution and how Microsoft's Active Directory works with DNS to ensure that information is up-to-date and complete.

The whole purpose of DNS is to resolve hostnames like **server5.sales.northernus.acme.com** to an IP address like 10.5.23.1. This is known as a *forward lookup*. A *reverse lookup* takes a known IP address, like 10.5.23.1, and finds the hostname, which in this case would be **server5.sales.notthernus.acme.com**.

 A thorough understanding of DNS is expected on almost every Windows 2000 exam and this one is no exception. Be sure to review these DNS topics before you take the exam.

DNS Zone Types

Three zone types are supported with the Microsoft version of DNS. Each type has its role in the stability and overall structure of our internal and external namespaces. You must know how each type differs from the others and how to properly utilize this standard service during the transformation to Windows 2000.

The Standard Primary Zone

The standard primary zone provides PDC-like functionality in DNS. The server that is designated as holding the primary zone has a Read/Write copy of the zone file. Any changes that need to be made to the file have to be performed on the server that holds the primary zone.

There is normally only one server that holds the primary zone file. This file is replicated to all other secondary servers by using a full or incremental zone transfer. The incremental zone transfer sends only the changes to the secondary DNS server. A full zone transfer occurs when the secondary server doesn't support incremental transfers or when the number of changes exceeds the tracked storage cache on the server that received the transfer request.

The Standard Secondary Zone

The standard secondary zone is like the BDC of the DNS world. A server with a secondary zone file has a Read-Only copy. This server will resolve names contained in the file until the file expires. If the server cannot be refreshed, it will no longer support the zone.

Secondary servers can act as masters to other secondary servers. In this case, the secondary server is also a master server. There can be any number of secondary servers and masters, but there is only one primary server. Secondary servers can be configured to reduce overall replication load on the primary server; secondary servers can also assist in staging information and creating bridgeheads of replication between server branches with poor connectivity.

The Active Directory Integrated Zone

When you set the zone as Active Directory Integrated, you lose all the concerns of a single master DNS server. Active Directory Integrated zones exist only on Windows 2000 domain controllers that are also configured as DNS servers. You gain a lot in stability and functionality. Active Directory Integrated is the preferred implementation of DNS as far as Microsoft and the exam are concerned.

Any DNS server that is also a domain controller can update the zone file. You also gain the advantage that you no longer have two replications to manage: one for DNS and the other for Active Directory. The DNS zone is automatically and incrementally transferred right along with Active Directory.

You also gain the advantage of security. When you allow for Dynamic DNS, anyone can update the zone file on the standard primary server. An evil hacker person could simply send an update to your Web server address and steal all of your traffic. The only way to prevent this is to change the zone to Integrated and then select the Secure Update Only option. In Secure Update mode, the DNS records are protected by an ACL. Only authorized people and machines are allowed to modify the records. Individual computers that are identified by their machine SIDs are allowed to update their records. DHCP servers can also be given permission to update client records.

DNS—SRV Records

Service locator (SRV) resource records are designed to help find a TCP/IP-based service with a single DNS query. These SRV records are automatically registered when the domain and the domain controllers are created. These records provide information about sites and services that are available throughout your enterprise.

Lightweight Directory Access Protocol (LDAP) is used to query for services over TCP port 389. The DNS server then searches the zone to locate the requested SRV record(s). The server returns all records that match the query. In the case of domain validation, the client pings all domain controllers that are in its site. The first one that responds will be selected for validation services.

DNS—Compatibility Issues

DNS is an Internet standard that is advertised and controlled by the Internet Engineering Task Force (IETF). Microsoft's version of DNS tries to follow the rules as outlined. If you decide to go with an Active Directory Integrated DNS zone, you can still provide services to non-Microsoft clients and servers.

If you have a Unix DNS server that needs to act as a secondary server, you can point it to an Active Directory Integrated DNS server as the Unix server's master. The Microsoft DNS server will provide full replication services to the Unix box. Because the Unix box is acting as a secondary server, it will receive a Read-Only copy of the zone file and will not try to update the Microsoft Active Directory (AD) DNS server. AD DNS servers can act as primaries and masters. If you have a zone that is hosted by a non-Windows 2000 DNS server acting as a primary server, you can have Windows 2000 perform the roles of a secondary server and a master server to other secondary servers as desired.

To support Windows 2000, your DNS server must support certain specific features of later versions of DNS. If the service supports incremental zone transfers and dynamic updates, so much the better. The later versions of BIND integrate nicely. If the existing DNS servers don't support SRV records, you might need to split your namespace into a separate external and internal namespace or maybe into a subzone where your Active Directory needs are maintained by Windows 2000 DNS.

If you create a forward lookup zone and then add a domain controller, you need to ensure that the SRV records are created. A common mistake is to set up the zone but not to configure it for dynamic updates. If that is the case, the domain controller will not be able to create the required records, and the clients and other servers won't be able to locate the needed resources. If you have created a zone and you changed the zone to handle dynamic updates, simply stop and then restart the NETLOGON service on the domain controller, and it will automatically register the required records.

WINS—Throw the Old Dog a Bone

WINS, with its NetBIOS names, is not necessary in a completely Windows 2000 network. Everything is resolved by DNS. WINS is primarily supported for older clients such as NT and Windows 9x. To its credit, Microsoft has added some nice features to make the old veteran operate in its remaining years with added style and comfort.

WINS now supports persistent connections. Older WINS servers would always have to re-establish connections whenever they wanted to replicate with their partners. This can lead to a lag in responsiveness because we have to wait for the servers to resolve the target IP address, authenticate, and then send the replication request. A persistent connection means that all of that goes away. WINS servers running on a Windows 2000 platform maintain communications channels. This helps ensure speedy resolution and faster response times for the clients.

WINS used to be a two-man show. You were assigned a primary and a secondary WINS server, and those were the only ones you were allowed to use. With Windows 2000, each client can be assigned up to 12 WINS servers. You will still have a primary and a secondary, but if you are unable to contact them, you will move down your list. When a server finally responds, it will become your primary WINS server. So it not only gives you more options, but it also auto-adjusts for success.

Clients aren't the only ones who benefit. Administrators will love the new and improved editing features. You can now manually tombstone records to prevent a replication from replacing a record that has been marked for deletion. You can also delete both dynamic and static records. You can sort, filter, and even select multiple records. Last but not least, Windows 2000 will export your WINS database as a comma-separated variable (CSV) text file. This lets you import the information into spreadsheets and databases. It makes configuring an IP address exception list on your routers a snap.

Microsoft has put a lot of time, effort, and money into providing better services to WINS clients. Microsoft has improved stability, database consistency, and overall administrative functionality. It is *almost* a shame to see it go away, but I will still take Dynamic DNS (DDNS) any day.

Active Directory is a service that is head and shoulders above the old NT SAM days. With the multimaster replication model, you improve fault tolerance. By embracing Internet standards such as LDAP and DNS, Microsoft has truly moved from a painfully proprietary shop to a true team player. Due to the internal restructuring of Active Directory, we now have the scalability numbered in the millions of objects, unlike the NT 40,000-user limit.

Active Directory does require some TLC. It also requires careful planning and a thorough understanding of the web of dependencies that are created due to the massive utilization of this service. Microsoft knows that if you understand where you are coming from and understand where you are trying to go, you will have a greater chance of success. It looks good and you look good. This is a true win/win situation.

Practice Questions

Question 1

> Remaining in mixed mode after upgrading all domain controllers provides greater administrative flexibility and increased functionality.
>
> O a. True
>
> O b. False

Answer b (False) is correct. Native mode brings group nesting, universal groups, and full functionality to all portions of Active Directory. As soon as all domain controllers are upgraded to Windows 2000, upgrade to native mode.

Question 2

> When the last domain controller has been upgraded to Windows 2000, what mode are you now running in?
>
> O a. Native mode
>
> O b. Mixed mode

Answer b is correct. You are still in mixed mode. Conversion to native mode is not automatic. You will need to go into the Active Directory Domains and Trusts MMC snap-in and manually make the one-way transition to native mode.

Question 3

> Which of the following statements is true when a domain is operating in mixed mode?
>
> O a. Windows 2000 domain controllers use the Security Accounts Database until the domain is upgraded because NT 4 BDCs can't administrate Active Directory.
>
> O b. All Active Directive security groups are available in native and mixed mode.
>
> O c. After all BDCs are upgraded to 2000, you have greatly increased scalability options.
>
> O d. Group policies are available to all client computers in mixed mode.

Answer c is correct. After all of the BDCs are upgraded to 2000, you can go beyond the 40,000-user limit established by the SAM. Answer a is incorrect because Windows 2000 domain controllers always use Active Directory. Answer b is incorrect because universal groups are not available in mixed mode. Answer c is incorrect because group policies are available only to Windows 2000 clients, even when the older clients are running the Active Directory client.

Question 4

> Which are valid reasons for an organization to use multiple forests in Windows 2000? [Check all correct answers]
>
> ❏ a. To restrict resource access provided by transitive trusts
>
> ❏ b. To allow domains that are geographically separated to have independent administration
>
> ❏ c. To prevent custom schema extensions from affecting a domain
>
> ❏ d. The organization is too large for a single forest

Answers a and c are correct. Transitive trust relationships are created by default in a Windows 2000 forest. To eliminate these relationships, you would need to be in a different forest. The forest contains a shared schema. Any extensions will affect every domain in the forest. To prevent schema extensions from reaching a domain, you would need to be in a different forest. Answer b is incorrect because locations can have independent administration because the domain is a security boundary. Answer d is incorrect because organizations might become too large for a domain, but you can segment the full replication of all attributes by creating additional domains. It is highly unlikely that a company could outgrow a forest.

Question 5

> What FSMO roles does the first domain controller assume in a newly created forest? [Check all correct answers]
>
> ❏ a. Infrastructure master
>
> ❏ b. Global catalog server
>
> ❏ c. Domain naming master
>
> ❏ d. PDC Emulator
>
> ❏ e. Schema master
>
> ❏ f. RID master

Answers a, c, d, e, and f are correct. Answer b is incorrect because the first domain controller in a new forest is a global catalog server, but a global catalog server isn't an FSMO role. Global catalog servers can exist on any number of domain controllers so the single part of Flexible Single doesn't work.

Question 6

> Why can users move between NT and Windows 2000 machines, yet use the same roaming user profiles?
>
> ○ a. The registry settings held in systemroot\%username%\ are translated without intervention.
>
> ○ b. The profiles actually do change. In fact, new settings specific to Windows 2000 are added to the user profiles every time users log into Active Directory. These changes are removed when users log on to an NT machine.
>
> ○ c. The users' SIDs don't change when users log on via different operating systems, and any non-applicable settings are ignored by the client operating systems.
>
> ○ d. The local profiles held on each machine are automatically modified to include only the settings for the machine, not for the users.

Answer c is correct. SIDS don't change, so users still have ACL-determined access to their defined profiles, and any settings that aren't relevant are retained, but are ignored. Answer a is incorrect because that is not an appropriate path to a user profile. Answer b is incorrect because profiles don't change. Answer d is incorrect because local profiles are simply copies of the latest roaming profile and they include settings for user accounts.

Question 7

How can you control bandwidth consumption when you migrate to Windows 2000?

○ a. After the first domain controller has been upgraded, you create sites, subnets, and links as defined by Active Directory. This ensures that site topology will control replication.

○ b. Replication is not a problem because all synchronization between newly created Windows 2000 domains is sent in compressed format. You merely configure schedules.

○ c. Domain controllers automatically assign themselves to the proper sites as they are moved around on the network. This causes each client to log on to the nearest domain controller that is in its site. You simply create site records in DNS to ensure the correct site mappings.

○ d. Configure SMTP as the preferred replication method between domain controllers in the same domain, but in different sites. This format is smaller than sending RPCs over IP and will compress to conserve bandwidth.

Answer a is correct. You must manually create sites, assign subnets, and create site links. As you add additional domain controllers, you will be able to configure replication timing based on site topology. Answer b is incorrect because replication within a site is not compressed. Answer c is incorrect because domain controllers do not update their site membership as they are moved between subnets. You don't manually create any form of site record. Site membership is tracked as a property of the SRV records that are automatically maintained by each domain controller. Answer d is incorrect because domain controllers in the same domain can only use RPCs over IP for Active Directory replication. SMTP is used only between domain controllers from different domains, replicating to different sites.

Question 8

We upgraded the PDC and all the NT BDCs to Windows 2000. When we converted to native mode, clients were no longer able to validate. What could cause this problem?

- ○ a. NT, 95, and 98 computers can't validate against Active Directory.
- ○ b. Validating Domain Controller can't locate a global catalog server.
- ○ c. Every site must contain at least one domain controller.
- ○ d. WINS doesn't have the correct SRV records registered to locate domain controllers.

Answer b is correct. If you are in a native-mode domain, you must be able to contact a global catalog server to enumerate all of your universal group memberships. This prevents users who would be explicitly denied access based on universal-group-assigned SIDs from bypassing security. Answer a is incorrect because NT, 95, and 98 machines can validate against an Active Directory domain. Answer c is incorrect because it is recommended that each site has at least one domain controller. But if I can't find a DC in my site, I will go to any domain controller in my domain, regardless of location. Answer d is incorrect because WINS doesn't store SRV records.

Question 9

Which services are required for Windows 2000 native-mode network authentication? [Check all correct answers]

- ❏ a. DHCP
- ❏ b. DNS
- ❏ c. Global catalog
- ❏ d. Active Directory
- ❏ e. WINS
- ❏ f. RIS

Answers b, c, and d are correct. Answer a is incorrect because you can have statically assigned addresses. Answer e is incorrect because you can use LMHOST files or broadcasts for legacy systems, and DNS is used for Windows 2000 clients. Answer f is incorrect because Remote Installation Server (RIS) is used to automatically deploy operating systems, not to validate users.

Question 10

> Which of the following Active Directory objects should be used to delegate administrative authority whenever practical?
>
> ○ a. Forest
>
> ○ b. Tree
>
> ○ c. Site
>
> ○ d. Domain
>
> ○ e. Organizational unit
>
> ○ f. Local group
>
> ○ g. Machine SID

Answer e is correct. You delegate administrative authority at the OU level whenever possible.

Question 11

> What are the methods Windows 2000 Professional uses to locate a domain controller to validate in a native mode domain? Select from the following list and place them in the proper order. Not all items have to be used.
>
> LMHOSTS
>
> DNS
>
> WINS
>
> DHCP
>
> NetBIOS broadcast
>
> NAT
>
> NetBIOS name cache

The correct answer is DNS. This is the only method used to validate when a Windows 2000 client is validating in a pure Windows 2000 domain. An NT client, on the other hand, will use, in order: NetBIOS name cache, WINS, NetBIOS broadcast, and LMHOSTS.

Need to Know More?

 Boswell, William. *Inside Windows 2000 Server*. Indianapolis: New Riders, 1999. ISBN 1562059297. This is THE bible as far as Windows 2000 is concerned. This will give you tons of information about the step-by-step internals of the operating system. Every section is near solid gold.

 Microsoft Corporation. *MCSE Training Kit Windows 2000 Active Directory Services*. Redmond, Washington: Microsoft Press, 2000. ISBN 0735609993. Chapter 2 goes into particular detail about the logical structure of Active Directory and the overall concepts you must master when migrating to this new directory service. Chapter 4 provides great information on planning and implementing Active Directory.

 Microsoft Corporation. *The Microsoft Windows 2000 Server Resource Kit*. Redmond, Washington: Microsoft Press, 2000. ISBN 1572318058. The encyclopedia of everything for 2000 Server. The volume devoted entirely to deployment will be of particular interest to migration professionals. It has an outstanding poster of a fictitious migration and deployment that covers nearly every situation a true professional will face in the real world and the exam.

 Gulbrandsen, A. and Vixie, P. RFC 2782, "A DNS RR for Specifying the Location of Services (DNS SRV)." Internet Engineering Taskforce. This is the Internet standard document that sets the rules for SRV DNS records.

 Reynolds, J. and Postel, J. RFC 1700, "Assigned Numbers." Internet Engineering Taskforce. This document sets the stage for number assignment for private IP addresses, port numbers and anything that has to have a unique service ID on the Internet.

 Pummill, T. and Manning, B. RFC 1878, "Variable Length Subnet Table for IPv4." Internet Engineering Taskforce. This really demystifies IP addressing. Extremely informative when setting up sites and subnets. Truly, a must-have document.

Group Policy

Terms you'll need to understand:

✓ SYSVOL share

✓ Group policy object (GPO)

✓ Group policy template (GPT)

✓ Group policy container (GPC)

✓ Group policy link

✓ Group policy inheritance

✓ Policy loopback

✓ Inheritance blocking

✓ No Override setting

✓ Assigned software

✓ Published software

Techniques you'll need to master:

✓ Understanding group policy inheritance order

✓ Explaining settings that can be created by group policies

✓ Blocking inheritance

✓ Overriding inheritance blocking

✓ Identifying domain controller group policy differences

✓ Understanding difference between NT system policies and Windows 2000 group policies

✓ Leveraging the difference between published and assigned software

✓ Controlling policy linking

✓ Identifying advantages and disadvantages to assigning a policy to a site

✓ Selecting which policies are effective only when set at the domain level

✓ Filtering group policies

Group policies in Active Directory are custom-made for all those control freaks who land jobs as domain administrators. Group policies are also wonderful if you want an opportunity for single-seat administration. You can use group policies to control just about every aspect of the user's computing experience. You still have the old powers, such as removing regedit from the list of available toys, but the level of granularity extends much further.

Group policies apply only to Windows 2000 systems. Windows 95, 98, and NT still use the old system policies, even if they are running the Active Directory client. Part of the transformation strategy is to support older, legacy operating systems.

Group polices do not rely on a single file that is stored in the NETLOGON share. Instead, pointers to group policies are stored directly in Active Directory or on the local machine. The local policies are stored in the %systemroot%\system32\GroupPolicy folder. These policies affect just the local machine and anyone who logs on to this machine. These local policies, when there is a conflict, are subordinate to policies stored throughout the site, the domain, and the various OU structures where the machine resides. The only exception to this rule concerns domain controllers. A domain controller's local policy overrides *all other* inherited policies. This is an important point if you are trying to change the rights and permissions assigned to domain controllers.

General Group Policy Settings

Some policy settings are unique to Windows 2000. They are fairly simple in concept and are described in the following list:

➤ *Disk quota policies*—These policies ensure that the administrator can control the amount of space that each user consumes in an overall policy. This feature works only on NTFS drives and is a volume-by-volume setting. This feature can also be set individually on each drive that is exposed to the network.

➤ *Folder redirection policies*—Earlier in Chapter 2, we explored the implications of mandatory user profiles and the requirement to redirect the My Documents folder. You can use folder redirection to standardize items such as Start menus and desktops. You can also personalize the redirection by using environmental variables such as **%username%**. Many administrators set up a folder structure that follows the home directory\profile\folder redirection format, which looks something like this:

\\servername\sharename\%username%\%username%

The double **%username%** lets you configure the top layer as a profile location and the second layer as the location for the user's home and folder redirection.

➤ *Encrypting File System (EFS) recovery policies*—EFS is designed to provide strong security for laptops and for particularly sensitive information. EFS is not designed to be used for shared files because the encryption and decryption usually involve an individual's assigned private and public keys. EFS files are also subject to increases in processor activity because all encrypted files have to be decrypted prior to use. EFS can also lock out administrators because the only accounts that can decrypt a file are, by default, the account that originally encrypted it and the designated recovery agent. By default, the only key recovery agent is the administrator account that was created when the new domain was first implemented. Before you allow widespread encryption, you should select and implement recovery agents at the appropriate levels of your domain.

➤ *Registry configuration*—You can use group policies to configure your favorite registry hacks and then send them out to your entire organization. This makes it easy to fine-tune individual settings for computers and users. Because the changes aren't permanent, corrections are as easy as removing the offending policy.

Group Policy Locations

Active Directory group policies are located in one of two places. Most group policies are stored in a group policy template (GPT) in the SYSVOL share. The SYSVOL share is replicated to each domain controller in your domain. This share usually maps to the winnt\sysvol\sysvol folder. This winnt folder doesn't have to be the same winnt as %systemroot%. The SYSVOL location is selected during Active Directory installation.

The second location for group policies is the actual Active Directory. These policies are stored as a group policy object (GPO) in a group policy container (GPC) that is associated with the appropriate site, domain, or OU container. Group policies are normally created domain by domain, but they can be assigned, or linked, to any domain in the entire forest.

With group policies, unlike NT system policies, changes that are made to the local Registry are not tattooed (they aren't permanent). Any changes to the computer configuration are still applied to the HKEY_Local_Machine Registry hive. Changes to the user settings are applied to HKEY_Current_User. But these changes are applied to the copy of the Registry stored in memory. These changes are not permanent. If you are unable to contact a domain controller, all restrictions are lifted. This system keeps administrators from permanently locking themselves out of a machine.

Some administrators are concerned because it seems that all a user would have to do to bypass security would be to disconnect the network cable. This is partially true except for the fact that the security administrators can set local policies on the local machine. These policies are always in operation, regardless of the link to the network. One point to remember is that local policies, when conflicting with any other level of group policy, are overwritten so you might want to use local policies just as a fail-safe or for baseline protection.

Another difference between NT system policies and Active Directory group policies is update frequency. NT system policies are Read-Only when the user logs in. Group policies are put into effect as soon as the computer boots. They are also refreshed approximately every 90 minutes until the user logs off. This ensures that new restrictions will take effect without having to wait for the user to log off and then back on. Certain portions of the group policy (software distribution, for example) are not refreshed on the local computer until the user logs off.

GPO Replication and Implementation

Group policies are stored on all domain controllers for a particular domain. These policies need to be replicated any time a new policy is created or an existing policy is modified. It is vital to understand when and how policies are created and promulgated throughout your enterprise environment.

 Microsoft wants to call everything an "object." Group policies are no exception. Any time you see "GPO," it means group policy object, but you can just think "group policy."

Group Policy Creation

For a group policy to be replicated, you have to create it. This is accomplished in Active Directory Users And Computers for most policies, but you can also create site-level policies in Active Directory Sites And Services. Whether you create a group policy for a site, domain or OU, the process is the same. You simply right-click on the object where you want to configure the group policy and then select Properties. In the Properties dialog box, you then select the Group Policy tab. Figure 3.1 shows what this dialog box looks like.

The New button creates a new policy, and the Add button links an existing policy from any domain in the forest to this object. After you click on the New button, Windows 2000 creates a new policy titled New Group Policy Object. You then select Edit to make any configuration changes in the blank policy. Figure 3.2 displays a new policy, ready for you to modify.

The individual configuration items listed in the group policy aren't important for the Migration exam. It is important to know that there are two sections labeled

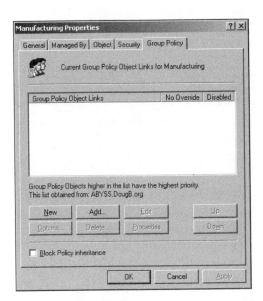

Figure 3.1   The Group Policy tab of the Properties dialog box.

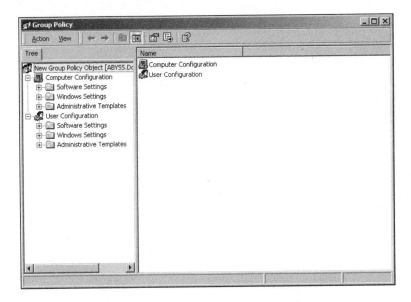

Figure 3.2   A new group policy object, ready to be configured.

Computer Configuration and User Configuration because these are critical to policy inheritance. The relationship of these sections to policy execution is discussed in further detail in the section titled "GPO Inheritance, Blocking, and No Override" later in this chapter.

Applying Policies to Groups

The assignment scope of a group policy can be restricted to certain groups. This powerful feature allows you to fine-tune policy targeting. It's simply a matter of selecting the policy you want to assign, selecting properties, and selecting the Security tab. Figure 3.3 displays the Security tab of the Properties dialog box for our new group policy.

Only users or groups that have Read and Apply policy permissions will be affected by an assigned policy. Advanced administrators can use this security feature to plan test rollouts of new policies or to limit the number of users who fall under a particularly restrictive or liberal policy. Assigning Read access to the Authenticated Users group means that any user who authenticates in the domain can be assigned to the policy.

Group Policy Replication

The folder that contains the group policy files is called a group policy template (GPT). These files are stored on each domain controller's SYSVOL share, which normally maps to %systemroot%\sysvol\sysvol. These folders are populated and

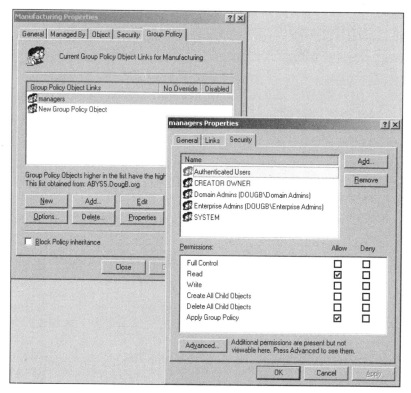

Figure 3.3　The Security tab of the Properties dialog box for a new group policy.

maintained by the File Replication Service (FRS) and is multimastered. Any changes that are made on any machine are automatically sent to all other domain controllers in the domain.

The set of group policies that is stored in Active Directory is the group policy container (GPC). Because the GPC is part of Active Directory, the various GPCs are replicated to all domain controllers through the normal Active Directory replication process.

An important point to remember is that when you are running the Group Policy Microsoft Management Console (MMC), it is always focused on the primary domain controller (PDC) operations master. This focus ensures that all changes to a group policy occur at a single location.

If the PDC operations master is unavailable, you receive an error message and you are given the option of selecting a different domain controller. You need to ensure that another administrator isn't modifying the same policy but on a different domain controller. If there is a duplication of effort, the last policy saved will have the latest time-date stamp and will be the one that overwrites all other copies on all of the other domain controllers.

Select another domain controller only when you are certain that no one else is editing the policy and you are certain that the replication of all GPCs and GPTs has been completed successfully. Otherwise, you might inadvertently edit an old copy of the group policy.

Group Policy Linking

After a policy has been created, it can be linked anywhere in your organization. You typically create policies in a central location and then link to them from other sites, domains, or organizational units. This linking provides flexibility and reusability.

You need to be cautious when linking to policies in other domains. All users and computers that have the policy assigned to them will need to contact a domain controller from the source domain. This can cause a performance slowdown across slow WAN links. You also need to plan carefully when using policies assigned to sites because users will need to access domain controllers from a remote domain. Figure 3.4 shows how group policies are replicated and linked throughout a typical enterprise.

You can link a single policy to multiple containers, such as OUs and domains. You can also link multiple policies to a single container. Many administrators create single-purpose policies—such as folder redirection and software distribution—and selectively link them to the appropriate containers in Active Directory. This makes

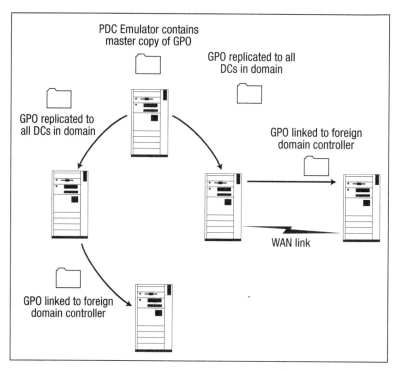

Figure 3.4 Group policy linking.

it easy to add and remove individual policy settings without having to hunt for the individual setting in a morass of policies. Just make sure you thoroughly document what each policy does, and make sure that all administrators responsible for policies have access to this documentation.

GPO Inheritance, Blocking, and No Override

One of the goals of group policies is single-seat administration, and inheritance brings this dream closer to reality. An experienced administrator will carefully plan policy placement to maximize administrative control but minimize administrative function. Most of the group-policy questions you will see on the Microsoft exams deal with placing the policies in the appropriate location to get the desired results.

GPO Inheritance Flow

Group policies are *additive*. Policies that are set above me in the parent/child hierarchy are normally in effect. But being additive also means that the last policy setting to be set persists and overwrites any conflicting settings applied earlier in the inheritance process. If I remove the Run command high in the hierarchy and then grant the Run command lower down in the food chain, the result will be that the user gets the Run command. You will retain higher settings only when they don't conflict with lower policies.

It is critical that you understand the order of inheritance as far as group policies are concerned. Figure 3.5 illustrates the multiple layers that compose the final policy that is applied to the end user.

NT System Policies

Windows 2000 machines are designed to be backwardly compatible with any old system policies you may be implementing. Any settings that aren't understood, or simply don't apply, are ignored. This brings forth the real danger that you might have configured an ntconfig.pol file for your older machines, and your shiny new Windows 2000 Professional machines might be experiencing some problems. One of the more interesting effects of an NT system policy is that it still tattoos

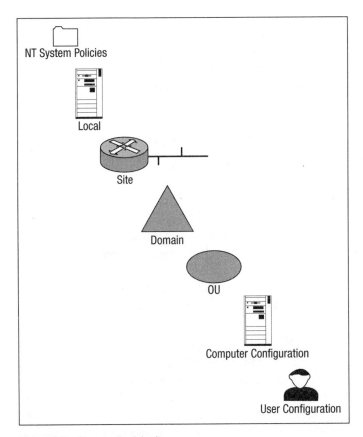

Figure 3.5   Group policy inheritance.

the local Registry, making those undesired changes permanent. We recommend that you are really careful when you replicate old NT system policies to Windows 2000 domain controllers.

Local Group Policies

Once we get past the old NT system policies, we are hit with any local policies that are configured on the local machines. These policies are normally fairly limited because all other policies overwrite any of their settings. The exception to this rule occurs with domain controllers. On domain controllers, local policies are applied last and overwrite any other configured policies. You can use local policies to prevent clever users from disconnecting their machines from the network and thereby eliminating any security that was imposed by the various Active Directory policies.

Site Group Policies

Site policies are applied to every computer assigned to the site. The major issue with site policies is where the machines have to go to obtain the policy. Sites are the physical structure of Active Directory and are based purely on subnets. This means that machines from several domains can be in the same site. If a particular policy is not stored on a domain controller that happens to be in the same site as the user, that user's machine crosses potentially slower WAN links to locate a domain controller from a domain that hosts the site-level policy. This can result in slower logons and increased traffic over bandwidth-constrained connections.

Site policies should be limited to policies that are locally hosted on domain controllers that are physically present in the actual site. These policies are typically limited to settings having to deal with the physical location. Research and development sites, for example, may require more stringent security settings than would normally be required. To ensure that any visitor, particularly those with laptops, are subject to the restrictions, you'll need to assign the policy to the site. To download the policy, these client machines will need to contact a domain controller from the domain where the policy is stored. Place one of those domain controllers locally to ensure the download occurs in a reasonable amount of time.

Domain Group Policies

Domain group policies are where the majority of generic policy settings should reside. The two default policies are stored in the domain container and in the domain controller container. These policies are stored on each domain controller in the domain so that if a user can validate, he can download the policy. Certain policy settings—namely, security settings—can be effectively set only at the domain level. An examination of domain security policies and security analysis will shortly follow.

OU Group Policies

Organizational units are wonderful for granular control. You can place computers and users in OUs based on location, job role, or any number of logical or administrative subdivisions. Each of these OUs can have a separate group policy that dictates software installation, user rights and privileges, or desktop settings. Don't forget that machines and users can reside in different OUs and have the policies of each OU applied separately.

Computer vs. User Group Policy Settings

Each group policy has two sections. One is specific to the computer, and the other is specific to the users. Settings are fairly specific to the particular the sections; for example, a computer setting is a startup script, and a user setting is a logon script. Because these two settings are unrelated, both policy settings are applied. Figure 3.6 illustrates a typical group policy and shows the Computer Configuration and User Configuration sections.

Certain computer and user policy settings are duplicated. When this occurs, the computer policy is applied first and is then overwritten by the user policy setting. Realize that user policy settings are applied only when a user logs in. If you have a server that is just sitting there, displaying a logon screen, no user policy is applied because no user is present. Once someone logs on, the user policy wins all conflicts with the computer policy.

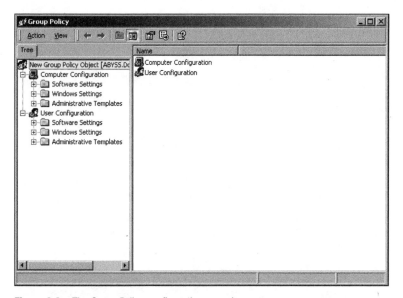

Figure 3.6   The Group Policy configuration console.

The Loopback Processing Mode

The loopback processing mode enables you to overcome the user's group policy, preventing undesired levels of access to restricted machines. According to the loopback help files, loopback is typically applied to "closely managed environments such as kiosks, laboratories, classrooms, and reception areas." Because the more restrictive computer configuration settings can be re-applied on top of more liberal user configuration settings, the loopback feature can help prevent someone from using a stolen, high-level user account to gain unauthorized access to network resources. Figure 3.7 shows how to enable loopback in a group policy.

Loopback should be set on the OU that contains the machine account, not the computer account. You also need to be cautious about setting the loopback too high in the inheritance hierarchy. If you limit access to administrative tools at the domain level, user configurations that loosen this policy will be ignored.

Blocking Inheritance

Besides enabling loopback, you might want to modify which policies are inherited and which are ignored. Blocking inheritance does this with a click of the mouse. Figure 3.8 shows the dialog box you need to configure to remove group policy inheritance from your OU.

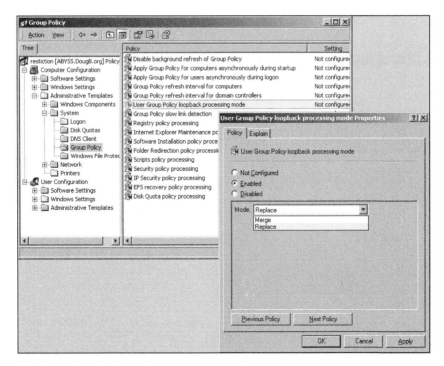

Figure 3.7   Enabling the loopback processing mode.

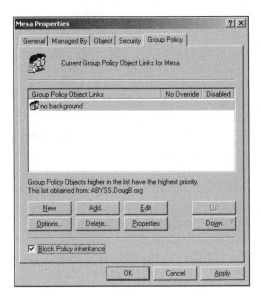

Figure 3.8 Blocking inheritance.

You need to exercise a degree of caution because when you block policy inheritance, you block *all* policy inheritance. This means that the carefully crafted domain policy will also be ignored in favor of the settings created at the blocked point. You also need to realize that an OU that has blocked inheritance still provides inheritance for any OUs that reside underneath it. Imprudent and arbitrary use of inheritance blocking can lead to unexpected policies being implemented for users and groups. In extreme cases, administrators have severely complicated their administrative burden by scattering inheritance blocking throughout the enterprise. This will cause innumerable headaches as the administrator tries to locate the settings' sources because Microsoft does not provide tools that identify policy sources.

Preventing Inheritance Blocking (Using No Override)

To prevent capricious policy blocking, Microsoft has included the No Override setting for group policies. When No Override is selected for a group policy, child OUs are not allowed to block inheritance of that particular policy. No Override should be used only with the mission-critical policies that must never be overridden. These policies can include preventing chains of OUs from executing any but designated applications.

Inheritance blocking and No Override settings should be limited in use, and wise administrators always follow the "Rule of the Three D's": document, document, and document. Documenting any nonstandard configuration change is an excellent habit to form, particularly during the early portion of an administrator's career. You might need to look up obscure but vital settings, and you can do this only if you've got excellent and exhaustive documentation. Do yourself a favor; grab all those cocktail napkins you've been using to document your migration and at least put them in a binder.

Domain Security

One of the first arenas an advanced administrator will control with group policies is domain security. With a single stop, the administrator can control password length, control Kerberos authentication, and limit access to destructive applications such as REGEDT32. Certain portions of domain security can be set only at the domain level. Other configuration settings can vary based on policy placement throughout the OU structure of the domain.

 Some of the exam questions will be directly related to settings that can reside only at the domain level. You must memorize the settings that are ignored at the OU level and are in effect only at the domain level.

Security That Can Be Set Only at the Domain Container

Certain policies will work only when set at the domain level. These three policies are:

➤ Password policy

➤ Account lockout policy

➤ Kerberos policy

These policies can be set at the OU level, but they will be ignored during group policy processing.

The password policy comprises settings associated with password length, complexity, and change frequency. Figure 3.9 shows the various settings you can configure.

Account lockout policy settings determine what happens when a user fails authentication, normally by entering an incorrect password or failing smart card authentication. Figure 3.10 gives you an idea of the many settings that are available.

Kerberos policies control the security authentication settings allowed for domain and interdomain security. Figure 3.11 shows some of the many options available.

 If you are faced with a case study that requires differences between password, lockout, or Kerberos policies, you will be required to create separate domains.

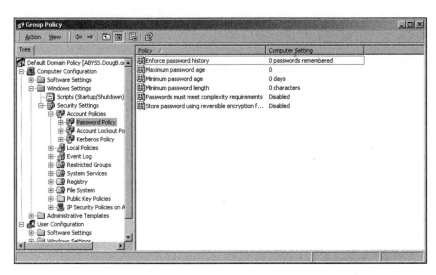

Figure 3.9   Password Policy settings.

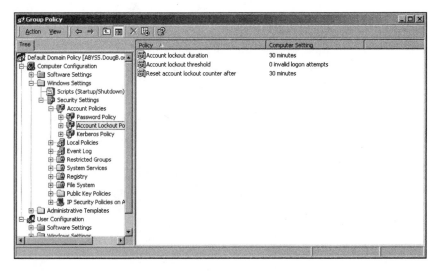

Figure 3.10   Account Lockout Policy settings.

Security Configured at the OU Level

OU group policy assignment combines the best of Windows 2000 to give you the most control in your organization. Group policies are typically used at the OU level for software assignment, desktop standardization, and system stability.

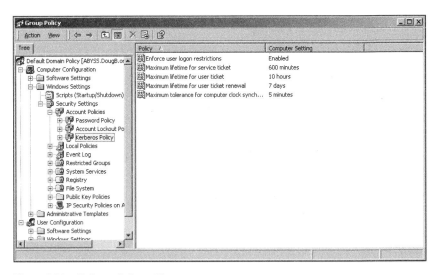

Figure 3.11   Kerberos Policy settings.

User Management

The user configuration settings in a group policy have, with the exception of domain controllers, the highest priority of all applied policies. The GPO assigned to the OU that holds the user's account is applied last. Any settings that are configured—either through inheritance to the user or through the entire hierarchy of the computer account—are overridden by the user account's assigned policy.

Users and the Containers Used to Manage Them

The user configuration settings of a group policy are arranged in three categories:

➤ *Software Settings*—These settings are for assigning and publishing software. This is an aggregate function. Software assignment is particularly useful for having certain utilities and applications follow support staff members around, regardless of which machine they log on to.

➤ *Windows Settings*—These include Internet Explorer policies and settings, logon and logoff scripts, user security settings, remote installation service policies, and folder redirection. Logon and logoff scripts are assigned using group policies at various areas in the enterprise structure. The scripts can be created using DOS batch files, but JScript, VBScript, and the Windows Script host are also supported. As with all group policies, create scripts as high as possible in the hierarchy of your organization. Group policies follow the standard rules of inheritance. Scripts set up at the site level flow through the various domain machines in that site. Scripts at the domain and site levels flow down to the OU. Troubleshooting logon scripts can become difficult if you add too many layers.

➤ *Administrative Templates*—This section is where the meat of the administrative power in group policies resides. Using administrative templates, you can restrict access to applications, desktop settings, and network and system configuration options. This is the section that most closely relates to NT system policies.

Figure 3.12 shows the various sections that are available to you in the user configuration portion of group policies.

 Specific settings aren't likely to be covered in the Migration exam. A general knowledge of available settings, with identified exceptions, should be sufficient.

Computer Control

Computer settings are configured when a machine boots up and connects to the network. Several powerful options are available to you. Because computer configuration is completely separate from user configuration, the settings you select will be immediately implemented.

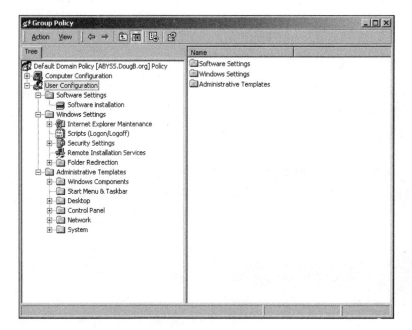

Figure 3.12 User Configuration sections of a group policy.

Computers and the Containers Used to Manage Them

A group policy's computer configuration enables you to fine-tune settings affecting your computing environment based on computer location and purpose. You must be generally familiar with the various options available to determine if migration settings can be controlled via a group policy or will require a manual visit to the selected.

 The computer configuration portion of a group policy has three sections. As with the user configuration portion, you don't need to memorize each and every configuration option; just be aware of the general categories.

The computer configuration settings of a group policy are arranged in three categories:

➤ *Software Settings*—This section has the settings for assigning software to a machine. You cannot publish software to a computer because the computer is incapable of using the Control Panel to add or remove applications. Instead, software is immediately installed when the machine boots.

➤ *Windows Settings*—Windows gives you the ability to configure machine-oriented configuration settings for the startup and shutdown scripts as well as for any security settings. Remember that the security settings for passwords are effective only when set at the domain level. For information on domain-only settings, review the section entitled "Security That Can Be Set Only at the Domain Container," earlier in this chapter.

➤ *Administrative Templates*—These templates are similar to the configuration options found in the old NT system policies, with additional options specific to the computer. This section doesn't offer as many configuration settings, such as the Start menu customization, as the user configuration section offers.

Figure 3.13 shows the computer configuration dialog box.

Domain Controllers and Computer Control

Domain controllers are an exception to the normal policy execution procedure. Local policies that are placed on domain controllers have the highest priority, regardless of site, domain, or OU group policy assignments. Administrators must be cautious in setting local policies because they are always available on the machine, even when network connectivity is lost.

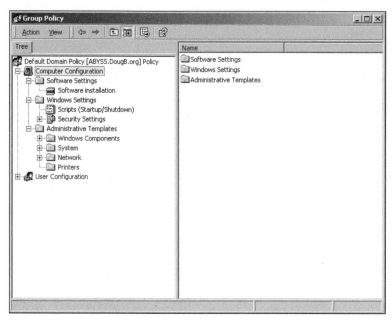

Figure 3.13 Computer Configuration sections of a group policy.

Disabling the Computer or User Configuration of a Group Policy

The numerous settings that are available in the group policy can take awhile for the computer to process. Many administrators will create policies for a single purpose. To avoid having to parse through all of the settings that are not configured, you can simply disable the unused portion of the group policy.

To disable the computer configuration or user configuration sections, do the following:

1. Open the Properties dialog box of the Active Directory container that holds the group policy, and select the Group Policy tab.

2. Select the group policy that you want to configure, and then click on the Properties button. Select the Advanced tab of this Properties dialog box, and select what you want to disable. Figure 3.14 shows this dialog box.

Software Distribution

You can use group policies to centrally manage software distribution in your organization. You can assign and publish software for groups of users and computers. This facility is in no way designed to replace Microsoft Systems Management Server (SMS). SMS has much greater control over software distribution and

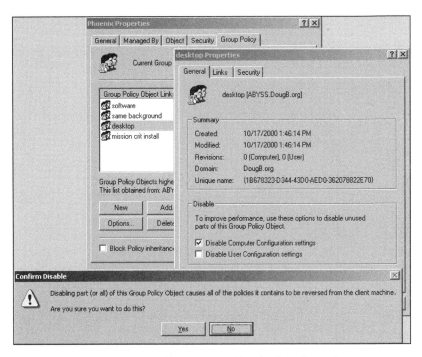

Figure 3.14   Disabling Computer Configuration or User Configuration settings.

metering. Group policies are merely a convenient method for administrators to add applications to groups of computers or to a selected set of users.

Assigning Software

When software is *assigned to a computer,* the software package is installed when the machine boots. All users who log onto the machine will have the application available for their use. When software is *assigned to a user,* the software already appears to be installed. The Start menu and any desktop shortcuts are already present, and any file extension assignments are already made in the classes library. When a user clicks on an icon or activates a file with the assigned extension, the software is automatically installed. This can be rather disconcerting to users as they watch dialog boxes flying by. Many users have been known to hit the power switch, fearing that a virus is being installed on their machines. It's usually a good idea to let users know when you are rolling out a package. You must also remember that software distribution can cause a significant delay in logging on, and you might want to warn users.

The advantage of software assignment is that the applications are resilient. If a user happens to delete DLL files or other critical components, the group policy will automatically reinstall the missing components. Another advantage of software assignment is that the applications are installed only when they are used. If you are a roving administrator, all of your applications will appear to be loaded and available when you log onto any machine, but you will install only the applications that you actually need. This system saves hard drive space and helps with controlling licenses because users will be able to install only the software that has been assigned to them or to groups to which they belong. You have to be careful who has access to applications because, without using third-party software metering applications, there is no way to determine how many people have had the applications installed.

Assigned applications can also be modified automatically with a Microsoft Transform (MST) file. These applications are deployed the same way as the original application. Assigned applications can be used to add features, such as adding multiple-language support to word processing applications. You can also update applications by upgrading to the next version or applying a service pack. These upgrades can be made mandatory or optional. This capability ensures that the feature set desired by the local user can be maintained, or that the version supported by the IT department can be controlled.

Publishing Software

The other method of application deployment is *application publishing*. Applications can be published to users, but not to machines. Application publishing causes the applications to appear in the Add/Remove Programs portion of a computer's Control Panel. Administrators can assign categories to ease application selection. Published applications can also be installed using document invocation. Active Directory contains a list of assigned extensions assigned to the applications. When a user attempts to open an application with an unassigned extension, the computer queries Active Directory to see if there are any published applications associated with the unknown extension. When an application is found, it is automatically installed.

Note: Published applications are not resilient. If a user decides to help out the administrator by deleting some of those pesky DLL files, the application will crash.

GPOs vs. System Policies

In Windows NT, you can use system policies to lock down end-user computers. You can set policies and restrictions to add to the system's overall security and stability. Microsoft has discovered the power of policies and has made them the centerpiece of Active Directory. In this section, we will discuss the operation and limitation of NT system policies and explain how to bring system policies into the new world of group policies in a 2000 environment.

NT group policies are stored in a file that has to be named ntconfig.pol. Group policies for Windows 95 and 98 clients are stored in the config.pol file. These files are normally stored in the NETLOGON share of every domain controller, and this share normally maps to the %systemroot%\system32\repl\import directory. These policies are replicated by the LAN Manager Replication Service. Windows NT computers pull their system policies from the validating domain controller. Windows 95 and 98 clients normally go to the PDC to pull down their policies. This behavior, which can slow down your network and overwhelm your PDC, can be corrected by enabling the Load Balancing policy setting. Once that is set, Windows 95 and 98 machines will get their policies from the validating domain controller.

You typically configure system policies by using the System Policy Editor (poledit.exe). The system policy is nothing more than a collection of Registry keys and values. These individual keys and values are edited when you change the selections with the System Policy Editor. Specific changes can be assigned to all users, all computers, specific computers, specific groups, or individual user accounts. The downside is that all these different settings are contained in a single file. This makes it more difficult to manage. Also, there is no way to apply settings to a group of computers.

When a user logs onto the network, his or her machine goes to the server's NETLOGON share (see the exceptions mentioned earlier) and opens the ntconfig.pol file. The machine then checks to see if any of the settings apply. If it finds a policy for the computer account, that policy is applied, and the All Computers setting is ignored. If there is a policy setting for that particular user's account, both the group policy and the All Users setting are ignored. This scheme makes it difficult to have domain policies that are enhanced by group membership and further defined by user settings.

NT System Policies Are Permanent Registry Changes

A major limitation of Windows NT system policies is the fact that the Registry changes are made through the process of tattooing; that is, the Registry changes that are mandated make permanent changes to the local machine's Registry. Many administrators have implemented an insufficiently tested policy only to find that certain mistakes required a personal visit to several hundred, or several thousand, machines.

It is also possible, using the custom policy script language, to create custom settings for the system policy. Remember, system policies are nothing more than a series of Registry settings, and the scripting language reflects that fact. Many administrators have flexed their creative muscles and, much to their dismay, have had to reinstall the operating system when the system policy decided to lock them out permanently.

Translating System Policies to Group Policies

During the exam, most of your policy translation will be accomplished by the administrator manually creating the group policy based on the old system policy. Microsoft tends to be more concerned about policy placement than about policy translation. However, the Windows 2000 Server Resource Kit provides several tools that you may want to pay attention to. Microsoft has been testing knowledge of some of the add-on tools in its other exams, and the Migration exam is no different. We recommend becoming familiar with the names and functions of the tools described here.

Be ready for questions concerning the following GPO utilities on the exam.

Gpolmig.exe

Gpolmig.exe is the only utility specifically designed to migrate NT system policies to Windows 2000 group policies. Windows 2000 will use NT system policies when they are located on the NETLOGON share of the validating domain controller. These policies are dangerous because they change the local Registry permanently. You can't migrate NT system policies directly to Windows 2000, but you can extract the various settings embedded in the ntconfig.pol file. Gpolmig.exe opens the desired file and creates a policy that has the relevant settings.

This utility can convert only the settings that apply to Windows 2000. Also, this is a one-way procedure. Gpolmig.exe does *not* convert Windows 2000 group policies to NT system policies. It is important to remember that Windows NT, even with the Active Directory client software installed, cannot use group policies. Windows NT uses system policies, and Windows 2000 uses system and group policies, with group polices being the preferred, and tested, method of administration.

Gpotool.exe

This command-line tool gives you the ability to ensure that group policies that are linked in Active Directory are still intact. You can also use Gpotool.exe to identify replication status and failure points. This is a great utility if you find that policies are taking an inordinate amount of time to execute or are failing completely. This utility also has the unique ability to set preferred domain controllers for policy downloads.

Gpresult.exe

This is Microsoft's primary utility for diagnosing and troubleshooting group policy configuration errors. It is unfortunate that it has so many limitations. Gpresult.exe is a command-line utility that must be run locally on each machine. This utility gives you a text list of all the configurations that have occurred as a result of assigned group policies. The major limitation is that Gpresult.exe does not reveal any details of an applied security policy, nor does it identify where the individual settings were implemented. This illustrates the need for careful placement of group policies and judicious use of inheritance blocking because it can be difficult to identify exactly where the configuration error occurred. Gpresult.exe displays the last time a policy was applied and which domain controller applied the policy for both the computer and the user configuration. This information, combined with the replication information gleaned from Gpotool.exe, can ease administrative frustration when you're troubleshooting replication errors.

Practice Questions

Question 1

> You are concerned about placing the newly configured group policy in the correct location. Place the following list in the correct order of inheritance for a system that is not a domain controller.
>
> OU
>
> Domain
>
> Site
>
> Local policy
>
> NT system policy
>
> User configuration
>
> Computer configuration

The correct order is:

> NT System Policy
> Local policy
> Site
> Domain
> OU
> Computer configuration
> User configuration

The old NT system policies are applied first, followed by local, site, domain, and any OUs. Finally, any conflicting configuration that is applied to the computer will be overwritten by user configuration settings.

Question 2

> What can you use to ensure that all sales machines have the client tracking software installed, regardless of the logged-on user?
>
> ○ a. Software publishing to computer OU
>
> ○ b. Software assignment to computer OU
>
> ○ c. Software publishing to user OU
>
> ○ d. Software assignment to user OU

Answer b is correct. Assigning software to the OU that contains the computer account will install the application when the computer starts. Answer a is incorrect because you cannot publish software to a computer. Answers c and d are incorrect because publishing and assigning software to users doesn't install software and is user-specific.

Question 3

> You have applied your group policy to ensure that users in the Accounting OU must change their passwords every month. Jasmine, who resides in the Accounts-Rec OU, which is underneath the Accounting OU, hasn't had to change her password in the last year. How can you repair this serious security breach?
>
>
>
> ○ a. Remove the inheritance block at the Accounts-Rec OU.
>
> ○ b. Configure the Accounting password policy as No Override.
>
> ○ c. Change the domain group policy.
>
> ○ d. Place Jasmine in the Accountants group, and ensure that the Accountants group has Read and Apply policy permissions to the Accounting OU's group policies.

Answer c is correct. Password policies are set only at the domain level. Any password policies set at any OU level are simply ignored. The remaining answers are valid troubleshooting steps that you would use to ensure that policies are being implemented. But, because of what is being configured, this situation is the exception to normal practice. Answer a is incorrect because you cannot block password restrictions. Answer b is incorrect because the OU policy, even with the No Override setting, cannot configure password policies. Answer d is incorrect because the Accounting OU's group policy is unable to configure password settings.

Question 4

> What can you configure on a kiosk machine to prevent someone from logging in with a stolen user account and overwriting the Computer Configuration restrictions?
>
> ○ a. Loopback processing mode
>
> ○ b. Shortcut
>
> ○ c. No Override setting
>
> ○ d. Inheritance blocking

Answer a is correct. When you enable the loopback processing mode, you can merge, reapply, or overwrite any settings that were changed when the User Configuration portion of the applied group policy was implemented. Answer b is incorrect because shortcuts refer to trust relationships in a forest as opposed to group policy processing. Answer c is incorrect because the No Override setting prevents inherited policies from being blocked but does not modify the order of inheritance. Answer d is incorrect because blocking inheritance will block only the settings that are set higher in the policy hierarchy. Blocking inheritance will not change the processing order of the actual policy.

Question 5

> What can you use to implement a change to the Registry of a targeted machine? [Check all correct answers]
>
> ❑ a. Ntconfig.pol
>
> ❑ b. Site-level GPO
>
> ❑ c. Logon script
>
> ❑ d. Startup script
>
> ❑ e. Regpol.exe

Answers a, b, c, and d are correct. Answer a is correct because Windows 2000 uses old Windows NT system policies to permanently tattoo Registry changes. Answer b is correct because any level of GPO, site included, can add Registry changes. Answers c and d are correct because batch files, VBScript, and JScript can all modify the Registry and can run during user logon or machine startup. Answer e is incorrect because there is no such utility.

Question 6

> Where are group policies stored? Select all that apply.
>
> ❑ a. Group policy template
>
> ❑ b. Group policy OU
>
> ❑ c. Group policy object
>
> ❑ d. Ntconfig.pol

Answers a and c are correct. Group policies are stored in the SYSVOL share in the group policy template and in Active Directory in a group policy object. Answer b is incorrect as there is no defined group policy OU. Answer d is incorrect as ntconfig.pol is where NT system policies are stored, not group policies.

Question 7

> What can be done to improve group policy processing performance? [Check all correct answers]
>
> ❑ a. Create a separate policy for each configuration entry.
>
> ❑ b. Specify loopback processing.
>
> ❑ c. Place a domain controller from the domain that hosts the group policies in the local site.
>
> ❑ d. Disable User Configuration processing for policies that are strictly for computer configuration.

Answers c and d are correct. Placing a hosting domain controller in the local site will improve group policy processing by eliminating the requirement for the request to travel across the slower WAN link. Disabling unused portions of the group policy will speed processing as the computer can skip reading unconfigured sections.

Need to Know More?

 Boswell, William. *Inside Windows 2000 Server.* Indianapolis: New Riders Publishing, 1999. ISBN 1562059297. Chapter 15, "Managing the User Operating Environment," goes into quantum detail on the ins and outs of group policy. The discussion of modifying the local Registry by using the registry.pol file in the USER folder of the GPT is particularly good.

 Microsoft Corporation. Microsoft Official Curriculum course 1560, "Updating Support Skills from Microsoft Windows NT to Microsoft Windows 2000." Module 8, "Using Group Policy to Manage Desktop Environments," goes into great detail on configuring and securing workstations by using group policies. Module 9, "Using Group Policy to Manage Software," has an awesome discussion on creating software packages and using group policies to assign and publish them.

 Microsoft Corporation. *The Microsoft Windows 2000 Server Resource Kit.* Redmond, Washington: Microsoft Press, 2000. ISBN 1572318058. Chapter 22, Part 4, "Desktop Configuration Management," has an excellent in-depth discussion of nearly all aspects of group policies. The section titled "Active Directory and Group Policy" is of particular interest because it explains how the GPT and the GPC interrelate.

 Microsoft Corporation. "Defining User Interface Standards," which is a reprint from *The Microsoft Windows 2000 Server Resource Kit.* Redmond, Washington: Microsoft Press, 2000. ISBN 1572318058. Chapter 23 "Defining Client Administration and Configuration Standards" provides wonderful administrative tips on evaluating user environments with regard to user experience and configuring the interface to assist users as opposed to making them fit into the IT department's idea of nerdvana. This can be located at: **www.microsoft.com/TechNet/win2000/dguide/chapt-23.asp**.

 Microsoft Corporation. "TechNet Article Q231287 Loopback Processing of Group Policy." Redmond, Washington, 2000. This article goes into detail on the loopback option of group policies and discusses the configuration choices you have to fine-tune your resultant policies. This article can be located at: **http://support.microsoft.com/support/kb/articles/Q231/2/87.asp**.

Planning Migration

Terms you'll need to understand:

✓ Domain upgrade
✓ Domain restructuring
✓ Mixed-mode domain
✓ Native-mode domain
✓ Mixed environment
✓ Active Directory
✓ DNS (Domain Name Service)
✓ WINS (Windows Internet Naming Service)
✓ LMRepl (LAN Manager Replication Service)
✓ FRS (File Replication Service)
✓ Account domain
✓ Resource domain
✓ Master domain

Techniques you'll need to master:

✓ Knowing domain migration types
✓ Determining the best method of domain migration based upon the network environment
✓ Establishing the appropriate order for migrating systems within a single domain
✓ Establishing the appropriate order for migrating multiple domains
✓ Determining the impacts upon resource access in a multidomain migration

Considering all of the new features of Windows 2000, migrating your enterprise from Windows NT 4 can appear to be a matter of some concern to both management and systems engineers alike.

Microsoft, in recognizing the schism between a multiple-master domain model and an Active Directory domain, has provided a very powerful, modular approach to migrating NT 4 domains to Windows 2000. One particularly outstanding feature of this migration model is that each migration plan can be utilized individually for smaller single and multiple domains, while still enabling a "phase two" approach for larger enterprises.

In this chapter, we will discuss the process of evaluating the current environment in order to determine the best migration strategy, and we'll discuss how the different migration strategies can be applied appropriately to the evaluated network.

Migration Methods

There are basically three methods for upgrading or migrating your Windows NT 3.51 or 4 domains to Windows 2000:

➤ *A domain upgrade*—The literal process of upgrading the existing domain controllers and member servers to Windows 2000.

➤ *A domain restructuring*—The exact opposite of a domain upgrade, a restructuring basically involves replacing the current hardware with native Windows 2000 controllers, and restructuring enterprise environments appropriate to new Windows 2000 features.

➤ *A domain upgrade and reconfiguration*—Being a mixture between the two prior migration types, a domain upgrade and reconfiguration basically consists of upgrading the system to Windows 2000, and then restructuring multi-domain environments to take advantage of the enterprise-enabled features of Windows 2000.

The word "domain" is listed in each of these migration types because the Microsoft exam primarily addresses servers within existing domain models. Although workstations might be members of a domain, they are covered only in the context of server connectivity and resource access. This is also a great reminder of what the Windows 2000 upgrade path is: Windows NT 3.51 and 4 servers can be upgraded because they can be configured as domain controllers.

Domain Upgrade

A domain migration can also be considered as a domain upgrade because a migration is basically an operating system upgrade.

 Be careful of wording here. The exam usually refers to an upgrade as the actual process of upgrading a server. The process of upgrading or restructuring a domain will often be termed a migration. The key is to ask yourself if the domain structure is changing. If not, they are referring to a domain upgrade. On the other hand, if the word upgrade does appear, you can be sure that they are referring to at least to an upgrade and at most, an upgrade and restructuring.

Domain upgrades provide the following advantages:

➤ Users and groups are retained.

➤ The existing domain structure is retained.

➤ Access control lists (ACLs) do not change.

➤ Most system settings and preferences remain intact.

➤ Compatible applications and programs remain unaffected.

➤ Domain upgrades are ideal for incremental migrations and smaller domain infrastructures.

➤ It is relatively easy to fall back to Windows NT if complications arise.

➤ Domain upgrades are fully backward-compatible with other Windows NT domain controllers.

➤ Client configuration is unnecessary.

Because users, groups, system settings, and preferences are retained, the domain name remains the same also. As a result, it is not necessary to "walk the floor" to reconfigure all workstations and client computers to authenticate them against a new or different domain.

It's important to remember that after you've upgraded the first Windows NT 4 primary domain controller (PDC) to a Windows 2000 domain controller (DC), you don't have to immediately upgrade all NT backup domain controllers (BDCs) within the same domain. This is true because the Windows 2000 DC is fully backward-compatible via a service called the *PDC Emulator*. Among other things, the PDC Emulator deals with time synchronization and with group policy object editing, and it broadcasts the Windows 2000 DC as a Windows NT domain controller. Unless significant DNS or WINS changes occur network clients can access the Windows 2000 system without additional configuration, and other

Windows NT computers will view the Windows 2000 computer as they did before the upgrade. This situation is especially ideal for networks containing too many BDCs and member servers to upgrade in a single setting.

 Despite the advances of Active Directory, services like the PDC Emulator are still exclusive to a single server. Controllers with services like this are called FSMO servers (Flexible Single Master Operations).

Another advantage of a domain upgrade is an easy fallback if complications arise. The Windows NT domain structure allows for a single primary domain controller and any number of backup domain controllers. In Windows NT, a PDC's most important roles are that of providing logon and authentication to users and of maintaining the Security Accounts Manager (SAM) database. If the PDC in a domain goes down, a BDC will promote itself to a PDC in order to provide those mission-critical services. That same method of promoting a BDC can be manually triggered for scheduled PDC upgrades and system maintenance. The same is true for the operating system upgrade to Windows 2000. The key is to designate a Windows NT BDC and remove it from the network during the actual installation of Windows 2000. If it becomes necessary to fall back to the old domain, simply remove the Windows 2000 system from the network, bring the BDC online, and promote it to a PDC.

 For the exam, remember that creating a BDC fallback is a necessary task during the upgrade process prior to the actual upgrade. To create a BDC fallback, synchronize your NT 4 domain, then remove the BDC from the network.

A domain upgrade is essentially the only migration process necessary in a single-domain environment. A domain upgrade should also be considered as a first step in the overall migration for networks following a master or multimaster domain model. In these multidomain environments, you will need to consider the effects on resource access further along in the planning process.

Keep in mind that, during any domain migration, the production environment is affected. This can also be a contributing factor in determining the type of domain migration that should occur and the upgrade schedule of domain servers.

As mentioned earlier, a Windows 2000 migration is based primarily upon domains. Windows NT 3.51 and 4 servers can be upgraded because they can be configured as domain controllers. Domain controllers contain copies of the SAM database, whose conversion during upgrade is a huge feature of Windows 2000.

Windows NT 3.51 and 4 Workstation, as well as Windows 9x, can be upgraded into Windows 2000 Professional, but workstation upgrades are not covered in Exam 70-222.

 Various workstations running different operating systems (including Windows 2000) will be shown in the network layout of questions on the exam. Do not be fooled—client OS configuration does not come into play. This information is presented merely to guide you toward choosing the appropriate upgrade order during the exam. Account and resource domains should be upgraded prior to standard child domains in order to better take advantage of the features of Active Directory.

Domain Restructuring

A domain restructuring is basically an advanced migration process, ideal for complex and mixed network environments. A domain restructuring involves the purchasing of new server hardware, configuring that hardware as a separate Windows 2000 test lab forest, creating test user groups and computers, and then basically changing the lab forest into a production environment by migrating pilot users and computers over to the new system. Once the pilot groups are safely and happily migrated, the remainder of users, groups, and computers can be migrated appropriately.

Advantages of a domain restructuring include the following:

➤ Minimal impact on the production environment

➤ Incremental migration and fallback

➤ More time for testing applications and interoperability

➤ Lower administrator training

➤ Greater scalability

➤ Ideal opportunity to reorganize and consolidate resource and account domains

Because a domain restructuring first begins with a test lab, the impact upon a production environment is virtually nonexistent. Furthermore, if a failure should occur with a pilot user group, the fallback strategy would be to allow the users to log on to the original production NT domain rather than to the new Windows 2000 domain.

A significant advantage of a domain restructuring lies in the fact that all resource access, applications, and interoperability can be thoroughly tested before affecting any users or computers outside the test realm. This is ideal for mixed environments (where other operating systems, such as Windows 9x, Windows 3.x, NT 3.1, NT 3.51, and Unix, reside) and complex environments (such as client/server and other enterprise applications).

Another important advantage of having a test lab for a domain restructuring is the impact upon administrative and resource training. Using a test lab enables people to become more familiar with and qualified to administer the Windows 2000 domain with little or no risk of interfering with mission-critical systems. Downtime can be reduced due to the experience gained during the test and pilot portions of the restructuring.

Most multidomain environments were created to solve two complications with Windows NT: geography and limitations on the SAM database size. The geography problem stems from the need to have a remote administrator control resources specific to that remote location. Windows 2000 makes this easier.

Quite often, because a remote business unit dealt primarily with specific non-shared resources, system administrators would need to create a Windows NT resource domain containing files and services specific to that business unit, and would then need to configure trusts between the resource and parent domains to allow access to resources outside the remote domain. Reasons for this often revolved around the need for local administration of the resource domain. Windows 2000 has a new feature that allows you to delegate resource and object administration; this feature has tremendous advantages in both domain structure and server administration.

Any multidomain structure created around the size limitation of the Windows NT 4 SAM (Security Accounts Manager) database is no longer necessary with Windows 2000 Active Directory. As a result, account domains originally created to deal with the SAM limitations can be reorganized into a single domain, allowing centralized user and group administration and providing greater control over resource access and user permissions.

Consolidating a multidomain or master domain model into a single domain can reduce administrative overhead. Allowing remote administrators to control only specific resources can reduce downtime because these administrators are not involved in server and system-related maintenance and administration.

Before you decide upon a domain restructuring, consider the following:

➤ A domain restructuring takes longer than a domain upgrade.

➤ Because the test lab will eventually become a production environment, the equipment cost might become unreasonable. If, however, the existing equipment is incapable of supporting Windows 2000, the equipment cost of a domain restructuring might be the same as for a domain upgrade.

➤ Even though the cost of reconfiguring users, shares, permissions, and trusts can be spread out over time, the resources necessary might become prohibitive.

Note: A domain reconfiguration should be considered only when the corporate goals for the migration (that is, Active Directory functionality, increased security, Windows 2000-specific applications, reduced administration) do not concern time, money, or initial administrative configuration. The most compelling reason for a reconfiguration is the minimal impact upon the production environment.

Domain Upgrade and Restructuring

In many ways, a domain migration combined with a "phase two" reconfiguration might be the best of both worlds. Beginning with a single-domain migration, you can take any number of steps: migrate another domain into the existing domain; migrate another domain into the existing forest; or migrate another domain into its own forest and then join it to the first forest.

Advantages of a domain upgrade and restructuring include the following:

➤ The greatest visible returns are made available with a domain upgrade.

➤ Multiple mixed-mode domains can be migrated and consolidated into a single domain structure relatively quickly, while giving you time to go back and finish the migration into a native-mode domain.

➤ Although a combined upgrade and restructuring might take longer than would a domain upgrade or a domain restructuring by itself, the extra time can be well used by administrative personnel to both train and troubleshoot Windows 2000 issues specific to the environment.

➤ The combined upgrade and restructuring involves little or no initial equipment cost.

➤ This method provides incremental migration and fallback.

➤ This method provides more testing time for applications and interoperability.

➤ This method reduces the level of administrator training needed.

➤ This method provides greater scalability.

➤ The combined upgrade and restructuring involves little or no inital equipment cost providing current hardware meets minimum system requirements for Windows 2000.

The combined domain upgrade and restructuring method is specifically tuned for those multiple-domain environments in which a single cut-over is either too risky or physically impossible. After you create the initial Windows 2000 forest during the first domain upgrade, it becomes easy to troubleshoot any issues that arise while you're planning and implementing a subsequent domain upgrade and restructuring. This two-prong approach can save time, money, and resources while creating a "happy medium" for issues such as security, redundancy, and fallback.

Pay careful attention to wording during the exam. If even one piece of new equipment is brought into the picture, or if the domain structure changes at all, what would have been an upgrade has now become an upgrade/restructuring. In situations where a new system is brought into the computer, it is configured as a forest root domain controller.

Evaluating the Network

To better determine the appropriate domain migration method, you need to take a look at the current network and domain structure. Several lesser factors can make or break what would otherwise be a clean migration plan. These factors range from protocol services all the way out to legacy DNS namespaces, and back again to applications residing on and serviced by domain controllers.

The Existing Structure

Several network infrastructure questions need to be answered before you commit to a domain migration plan. Table 4.1 addresses these questions.

Additionally, you will need to document and thoroughly understand the trusts that exist between domains.

Trusts

A quick overview of trusts will be essential to understanding how the operating system upgrade process will treat existing Windows NT trusts and how trusts are established in a Windows 2000 forest. Resource access as a result of these trusts is also very important because it could affect the projected milestones and deadlines for pieces of the migration process.

Table 4.1	Network infrastructure Q&A.
Question	**Answer**
Is this a single domain?	If yes, then a domain upgrade is appropriate.
Resource or account domain?	If yes, then an upgrade might be most appropriate, followed by a restructuring into a single domain.
Single master domain?	If yes, then upgrading and restructuring into the same domain is appropriate only after resource and account domains have been converted to Windows 2000.
Child domain?	If yes, then investigate the purpose of this domain. If it exists due to geography, bandwidth, and provides little or no resource access, then an upgrade followed by a restructuring into an existing forest will be most appropriate. If the child domain's existence is based upon Windows NT SAM database limitations, then a migration into a new forest will be most appropriate.
Multimaster domain?	If yes, then consider the three previous questions for each master domain, and subsequently restructure each one into the same forest.

Be sure to study the following different types of trusts and their limitations.

Windows 2000 one-way trusts exist:

➤ Between Windows 2000 domains in separate forests

➤ Between Windows 2000 and Windows NT domains

➤ Between Windows 2000 and Kerberos v5 realms

Windows 2000 two-way trusts:

➤ Are also known as Kerberos trusts

➤ Exist between all Windows 2000 domains in a Windows 2000 forest

Windows 2000 transitive trusts:

➤ Are dynamic and are automatically updated by the system when a new Windows 2000 domain joins the forest

➤ Exist between all domains in a Windows 2000 forest

➤ Do not cross between forests

Windows 2000 nontransitive trusts:

➤ Are not dynamic and are exclusive to the two domains involved

➤ Are all trusts to Windows NT domains

➤ Are the only possible way to create trusts between the following:

  ➤ Windows 2000 domains and Windows NT domains

  ➤ Windows 2000 domains in forest 1 and Windows 2000 domains in forest 2

  ➤ Windows 2000 domains and Kerberos v5 realms

Windows 2000 explicit trusts:

➤ Are manually created by an administrative authority

➤ Can be external, enabling authentication to domains outside the forest

➤ Can be shortcut trusts, which are special performance enhancers that remove time-consuming associative trust layers from the authentication process

During the initial Windows 2000 upgrade process, all prior trusts (to Windows NT domains) will be converted into Windows 2000 transitive one-way trusts.

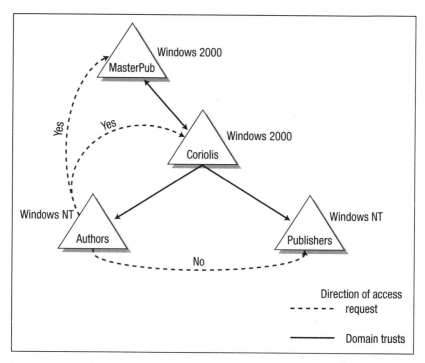

Figure 4.1 The resource access capabilities in a mixed Windows NT and Windows 2000 forest.

Subsequent child domains that upgrade, migrate, and restructure into the existing forest will be created with two-way transitive Kerberos trusts to the parent domain. Figure 4.1 illustrates resource access between domains based upon domain resources requested. By-and-large, the rule of thumb here between mixed Windows 2000 and Windows NT domains is that both upstream and downstream resource requests will be successful; however, mixed up-and-downstream requests will fail, thus requiring that an additional manual trust be established in order to maintain resource access across affected domains.

Here's one more thing to keep in mind regarding trusts. As shown in Figure 4.1 let's say that the domain **coriolis** is migrated to Windows 2000, while the child domains **authors** and **publishers** remain in Windows NT. By default, transitive one-way trusts are created during migration from the original trusts (those that existed before the Windows 2000 upgrade). A user residing in the **authors** domain will be able to access resources located in the **coriolis** domain (with appropriate authority, of course) and in other domains to which **coriolis** is a child. The beauty of transitive trusts is that they are dynamic. That same user residing in the **authors** domain will not be able to access resources located in the **publishers** domain because both trusts are one-way by default. If such a situation exists within a network, you will need to create an additional explicit trust between the

Windows 2000 domain and the Windows NT domain. The same concept applies for any resource that will need to be accessed downstream from a Windows 2000 domain, provided that the target domain is a Windows NT domain.

Existing Services

Before implementing a domain configuration, you will need to consider the services and applications running on each of the domain controllers and servers that are slated for upgrade to Windows 2000.

DNS

DNS (Domain Name Service or Domain Name System) is an integral part of the functionality of Active Directory. In short, DNS is a naming resolution service that resolves fully qualified domain names (FQDNs) to TCP/IP addresses. DNS is what enables a ping to **www.microsoft.com** to come back with **207.46.230.219**.

DNS basically consists of a database that is populated with this information in one of four ways: forward lookups, replication, manual updates, and WINS (Windows Internet Naming Service). When a user issues a request that requires name resolution (such as entering a Web page address or finding a particular computer on the network), a query is sent to the primary DNS server. This server is defined in the local computer's TCP/IP configuration or is provided by DHCP (Dynamic Host Configuration Protocol). The DNS server checks the database for the TCP/IP address that matches the requested name. If a match is not found, the DNS server will then check with a WINS server (when configured to do so) for a match. If a match is still not found, then the name remains unresolved, and the original event associated with the query fails.

Quite often, the DNS server will receive updated information via a replication process within a day or so, and if the requested name is valid, a subsequent query will succeed. This is common when users are accessing servers on the Internet or across a wide area network (WAN). When such an automatic update is not possible or is still incomplete, the DNS database must be updated manually. It is safe to say that for every DNS change on the Internet, someone somewhere must manually change a DNS database. This is also true for local resources, where DNS updates will never be retrieved from replication or a forward lookup query.

With Windows NT's DNS, it was something of a mystery why the Domain Name Service didn't follow the same structure as the domain itself. Windows 2000 DNS, coupled with Active Directory, allows us to create and maintain domains that live within the DNS infrastructure. Because DNS and Active Directory are so tightly coupled, any Windows 2000 computer joining the network is dynamically updated within DNS. Other Microsoft client systems can also be automatically updated when Windows 2000 Dynamic DNS (DDNS) is enabled. This feature can reduce the administration traditionally necessary to update and maintain domain servers and clients within DNS.

For this functionality and the WINS resolution functionality (described in more detail in the next section) to be supported, every domain controller must function as a DNS primary server if it contains an editable copy of the lookup zone. The DNS database is stored within Active Directory, so traditional DNS replication issues are addressed by Active Directory replication—which is far more comprehensive and fault tolerant than the Windows NT replication of the SAM database.

As Chapter 2 discussed, the Active Directory structure consists of forests, trees, domains, and organizational units. When you're planning a Windows 2000 migration, you need to research the current DNS infrastructure and compare it with the proposed Active Directory structure.

 Windows 2000 requires DNS that supports SRV records and dynamic update. UNIX DNS servers running BIND version 8.1.2 or above are compatible with Windows 2000. BIND 8.1.1 has a special problem with dynamic updates and it will fail if a system tries to dynamically update it. Therefore, you cannot use BIND 8.1.1 to support Windows 2000 clients. If you must use BIND and you have a BIND 8.1.1 server, you must upgrade the BIND server.

In environments where DNS is handled by a legacy system such as Unix, you will need to determine if the current version of BIND (Berkeley Internet Name Domain) is 8.1.2 or above or if it supports dynamic updates. If the existing Windows NT domain structure relies upon this type of legacy DNS system, if the BIND version is appropriate, *and* if the proposed Active Directory layout conforms to the business rules of the existing DNS layout, then there is no reason *not* to use the same DNS domain for the Active Directory forest root that was previously used as the Windows NT primary zone. Forward lookup queries and upstream replication will simply go to the legacy DNS servers, as they have in the past. If the BIND version is older than 8.1.2, or if the Active Directory layout differs from the DNS layout, it may be more feasible to create a delegated subdomain as the Active Directory forest root, as discussed in Chapter 5.

If the current DNS structure conforms with the proposed Active Directory layout, then DNS can be migrated during the process of upgrading to Windows 2000, and the structure can be maintained. If the current DNS structure differs from the proposed Active Directory layout, you'll need to consider a domain restructuring or a domain upgrade and restructuring. Table 4.2 describes domain naming conventions.

Table 4.2 **Domain naming conventions.**	
Domain root	A fully qualified domain name, such as **www.microsoft.com**.
Top-level domain	Usually a three-letter domain name, such as **.com**, **.net**, **.org**, and **.edu**.
Second-level domain	Usually a business name or a descriptive name, such as **microsoft**, **yahoo**, or **download**.
Subdomain	An additional name derived from the domain root. Often indicates a department or geographical location, such as **redmond**, **accounting**, or **bldga**.
Host	A computer name or hostname. Usually describes functionality (as in **RAS1**), a primary user (**Harry**), or an asset tag (**at356**).

WINS

In a traditional Windows network, computers are given NetBIOS names during installation in order to make resource access and sharing more user-friendly. This practice creates a new set of names that need resolution to TCP/IP addresses so that computers can understand and communicate with these systems. This NetBIOS name resolution can happen in one of two ways: using the local data file, or using WINS. The local data file (LMHOSTS) resides on the local hard drive and must be manually updated on every server and client on the network. In a network environment, distributing these updates to each computer can lead to accuracy issues and be very time-consuming. The solution to centralizing this lookup process came in the form of WINS. WINS, being centralized, eliminated the need to update multiple files in multiple locations. In addition, WINS is dynamic. Every time a network client starts up, it registers itself with WINS.

Another method by which DNS can update its database is through a WINS lookup query. This provides another method by which DNS can answer queries and allows administrators to avoid manually updating the database.

The beauty of Windows 2000 Active Directory naming is that traditional computer names appear and act no differently than they did before. Active Directory, however, treats these names as aliases. For example, Jodi's computer is named **shesells**, and it is a member of the **seashells** subdomain in the **seashore** domain. Jodi's full domain name is **shesells.seashells.seashore**. The Windows Network Neighborhood sees Jodi's computer as **shesells**; the UNC (Universal Naming Convention) code for the system is still **shesells**; and resources can be accessed in the same manner as they have been in the past.

The largest impact of this is that because DNS will resolve against the FQDN (fully qualified domain name) of the host computer, and the computer will be registered with DNS either on its own or through DDNS (Dynamic DNS), a WINS lookup is no longer necessary to resolve any local queries.

Replication

Generic data replication for Windows NT domains consists of a process that uses the *LAN Manager Replication Service* (*LMRepl*). LMRepl is often used to replicate login scripts from an NT PDC to any number of BDCs. LMRepl can also be used for file replication with member servers (see Figure 4.2). LMRepl requires that import and export replication links be established between servers. Microsoft determined that LMRepl was used primarily to replicate information to all domain controllers in the network. While designing Windows 2000, Microsoft opted to discontinue support for the LMRepl process. Instead, Microsoft created the more robust File Replication Service (FRS). FRS replicates all data located in a primary domain controller's SYSVOL (system volume) share with every other controller in the domain (see Figure 4.3). This eliminates complex replication links.

To maintain appropriate replication during a mixed-mode domain upgrade where Windows NT script hosts will exist, you will need to disassemble any current export/import LMRepl links dealing with the upgraded servers, centralize data to be replicated, and reestablish a replication link to the SYSVOL share on any single Windows 2000 domain controller (see Figure 4.4). Also, because LMRepl is push-only, a process will need to be created whereby Windows 2000 scripts

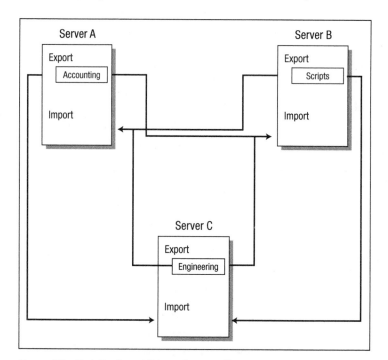

Figure 4.2   Each line to and from each server illustrates a separate administrative step in configuring LMRepl to replicate a single file on each server to all other servers.

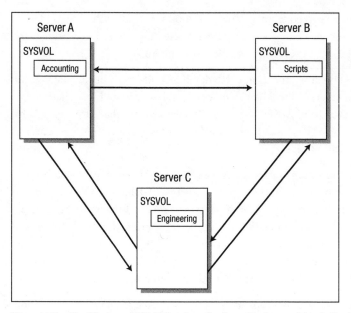

Figure 4.3   The Windows 2000 FRS automatically replicates anything in the SYSVOL share to all other domain controllers.

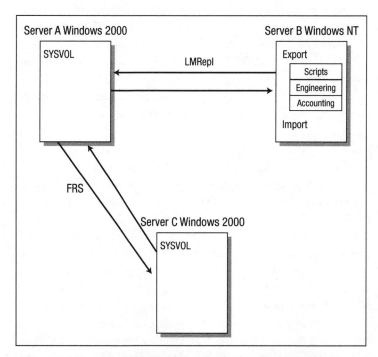

Figure 4.4   The method of maintaining replication in a mixed-mode domain.

and policies can be copied from a Windows 2000 DC to the Windows NT central replication server. This process is known as creating a replication bridge, and will be discussed in further detail in Chapters 5 and 6.

Just like Active Directory, the local DNS database updates replicated data within a given Active Directory site when changes occur. In addition, DNS changes in a zone are replicated to only the domain controllers within that same zone. This feature saves a lot of bandwidth because DNS changes specific to a zone will generally stay within that zone.

DNS database replication occurs as part of the Active Directory replication process. To conserve bandwidth, the Active Directory database can be compressed specifically for transport during the replication process. Intersite Active Directory replication can be scheduled for a specific span of time during off hours, and intervals can be configured to check for changes during the scheduled time span. During a multidomain upgrade, replication can best be maintained and optimized by creating a DNS zone for every Active Directory site.

WINS replication occurs as a separate process from Active Directory replication. Despite the new features available in DNS, Active Directory, and Dynamic DNS, WINS remains much the same as it was for Windows NT. Any given WINS database can replicate with multiple WINS servers by sending, receiving, or both sending and receiving requests for WINS updates. These capabilities are known as *push, pull,* and *push/pull partnering.* By default, WINS replication partners are configured for push/pull replication. If WINS is required for application or client functionality, it is a good idea to install or upgrade the appropriate WINS servers and to monitor network performance. You might need to configure a specific push or pull schema in order to appropriately replicate the WINS database.

Applications

Several applications run as services on a Windows NT server or domain controller. While you're planning a domain upgrade, you'll need to research the applications and services running on all servers. This is because applications such as tape backup, RAS (Remote Access Service), SQL Server, and most monitoring programs don't require an active session in order to be running in the background. Many applications access specific properties based on local service and local system account-specific to the Windows NT server. Many service and system accounts log in with the NULL password. Windows 2000 Active Directory does not support NULL password sessions. This lack of support can cause problems when an application attempts to authenticate against or access resources within a Windows 2000 mixed domain. Because that member server will authenticate against a Windows 2000 domain controller, the login will fail. During the migration process, consider the following workarounds:

➤ Place the application server programs on a Windows NT backup domain controller. Due to backward replication between Windows 2000 and Windows NT, the BDC will have a local SAM database to query against and will allow the application server to perform its tasks.

➤ Force the application server to contact a Windows NT backup domain controller for authentication.

➤ Loosen Active Directory permissions to give everyone Read permissions for any objects within the Active Directory database.

➤ Loosen Active Directory permissions during the upgrade process.

Any applications that rely upon a current Windows NT domain structure should also be investigated. One example is Microsoft Exchange Server. Environments where the domain structure has been built around specific applications need to be considered for potential impact during a domain upgrade.

 A good rule of thumb for applications residing on Windows NT servers is that anything that "comes with the package" of Windows NT or Windows 2000 will be upgraded automatically. These include Terminal Services, Internet Information Server, and Site Services. Certificate Server, however, will need to be re-installed after the upgrade.

As with all applications and hardware, it's a good idea to contact the manufacturer to determine Windows 2000 compatibility and to test the software and hardware.

Upgrade Sequence

During a single-domain upgrade, the primary domain controller should always be upgraded first. User and group information is automatically synchronized between Windows 2000 and Windows NT backup domain controllers, so you don't have to immediately upgrade the backup domain controllers unless critical applications are affected or required. It becomes far more important to upgrade any necessary application servers appropriate to their service continuity and ease of administration. A good rule of thumb after upgrading the PDC is this: He with the most security risks wins, with applications running a close second.

During a multiple-domain upgrade, Microsoft recommends that account domains be upgraded first. Why? Account domains, by definition, contain large numbers of users and groups, which are migrated automatically during the upgrade process. An account domain should be the easiest and quickest domain upgrade available and should have the greatest visible success rate. Advantages to an account-domain upgrade include the following:

➤ Hundreds or thousands of users can be upgraded; this feat impresses management.

➤ Most Active Directory features become immediately available.

➤ The 40MB SAM database restriction is removed.

➤ User and group administration can be delegated to responsible people with little or no administrative training.

 When upgrading child domains, always make sure a server acting as the forest root within the master domain has been upgraded first. Otherwise, the child DC won't have a forest to join, and realistically this becomes an upgrade/restructuring rather than just an upgrade.

With multiple account domains to choose from, the first to be migrated should be:

➤ A domain that is easily accessible to the migration team. A resource-domain upgrade potentially has the greatest immediate impact upon the end user. If complications arise, it is important to be able to service and troubleshoot a new Windows 2000 domain without having to schedule a plane flight.

➤ A domain that is smaller and therefore has a lesser potential impact upon the rest of the production system.

➤ A domain that will eventually be restructured at a later date, allowing the migration environment itself to stabilize. Administrative experience grows during this time, and this will be an advantage during the subsequent restructuring.

After all account domains have been upgraded, Microsoft recommends migrating resource domains. Why? Resource domains, by definition, contain computers and resources; the computer accounts and other system settings are automatically converted during the upgrade process. Be aware that a resource domain will be a slower migration—not necessarily because the access control lists have changed, but rather because resource domains tend to contain application servers, which might have unforeseen complications within a Windows 2000 environment. Again, make sure that all applications are known to run in Windows 2000 before you perform any domain migration.

With multiple resource domains to choose from, the first to be migrated should be:

➤ Any domain where software or hardware has been specifically designed or optimized for Windows 2000—for example, Exchange 2000, which requires Active Directory.

➤ Any domain containing large numbers of workstations. IntelliMirror features can be implemented immediately.

➤ A domain that will eventually be restructured at a later date.

Incremental Migration

Concepts and benefits of incrementally upgrading servers during a domain upgrade have been discussed throughout this chapter. It becomes necessary, however, to examine the process in further detail when you're creating a domain upgrade plan.

Advantages of incrementally performing a domain upgrade include the following:

➤ The network does not become 100 percent Windows 2000 overnight.

➤ Additional training and troubleshooting time is available between server upgrades.

➤ Windows 2000 can synchronize with Windows NT backup domain controllers.

➤ Fallback plans can be recycled for subsequent pieces of the incremental upgrade.

➤ The impact on users is minimized and distributed over a longer period of time.

As we will see in subsequent chapters, performing even a single Windows 2000 upgrade on an existing domain controller can be time-consuming, especially if multiple protocols, services, and applications are being hosted on the controller. It is a tremendous advantage to be able to pause, step back, appropriately test, and gauge the effectiveness of the ugprade. In addition, the training and experience gained during this time will be valuable during subsequent server upgrades.

Windows 2000 fully supports Windows NT domain controllers within a Windows 2000 domain. This is done through backward synchronization of the Active Directory database into the Windows NT flat SAM database format. Client systems will continue to successfully authenticate against a Windows NT backup domain controller. If this backward compatibility feature were not available, you would need to perform a domain upgrade on all domain controllers at the same time.

Creating a Windows NT backup domain controller during the PDC upgrade process will enable continuity if the upgrade encounters complications. During this time, the BDC could easily be brought back online and promoted to a PDC. Let's say that the PDC upgrade is performed successfully, and a BDC upgrade is performed a few days later. Should any subsequent upgrade attempt fail, the

Windows NT backup domain controller can be brought back online and installed with the applications and services appropriate to the upgraded server. Specific file and print data will have to be either re-created or restored from backup.

A Windows 2000 domain upgrade from a Windows NT domain should affect end-user authentication and resource access less than a domain restructuring would. Incrementally migrating the domain should lessen and distribute potential negative implications.

Practice Questions

Question 1

> Which of the following is an example of a domain restructuring plan?
>
> ○ a. The Windows NT primary domain controller is upgraded to Windows 2000. One by one, the NT backup domain controllers are also upgraded. Windows 95, Windows 98, and Windows NT workstations remain the same.
>
> ○ b. A Windows 2000 domain controller is created in a test lab. Applications and servers are installed, and user accounts are copied from Windows NT to Windows 2000. A pilot group of users is configured and migrated from the Windows NT domain to Windows 2000.
>
> ○ c. The Windows NT domain is upgraded to Windows 2000. Windows NT backup domain controllers still exist within the domain. Data is configured to be synchronized from Windows 2000 Active Directory to the Windows NT backup domain controller.
>
> ○ d. The Windows NT domain is upgraded to a Windows 2000 domain running in native mode. During the upgrade process for another domain, the option to join an existing tree is selected.

Answer b is correct. A domain restructuring begins in a lab environment in order to reduce the impact on users. Answer a is an example of an upgrade because no new equipment is present and the domain structure is not changing. Answer c is incorrect because no new equipment is present and the domain structure has not changed. Answer d is incorrect because no new equipment has been introduced, and the domain structure remains the same. The option to join an existing tree can be presented during any Active Directory installation.

Question 2

> A PDC Emulator is no longer required after a domain contains all Windows 2000 domain controllers and is converted to a native-mode domain.
>
> ○ a. True
>
> ○ b. False

Answer b (False) is correct. Even within a native-mode domain, the PDC Emulator performs time synchronization and group policy object editing.

Question 3

> You are the administrator in a network containing one master domain, two account domains, and two resource domains. Your management decides that the Active Directory features of Windows 2000 will be necessary in order to maintain growth within the company. What is the order of upgrading these domains?
>
> The master domain
>
> The account domain with the most users
>
> The account domain with the least users
>
> The resource domain with the most computers
>
> The resource domain with the least computers

The correct order is:

The account domain with the least users

The account domain with the most users

The resource domain with the least computers

The resource domain with the most computers

The master domain

The account domain with the least users should be upgraded first in order to take advantage of the most active directory features quickly while minimizing user impact. The account domain with the most users should be upgraded next because of the added active directory features. The resource domain with the least systems should be next in order, again, to take advantage of active directory management functionality, while having a lesser effect on the network than upgrading the resource domain with the most users, which is upgraded next. The master domain is always upgraded last, although this can cause some confusion because in order to avoid an upgrade/restructure, it will be necessary to create a forest root DC (upgrade a single DC within the master domain) in order to maintain synchronization and FSMO functionality appropriately.

Question 4

James is a member of the Windows NT 4 domain **art**, which is a child domain belonging to the Windows 2000 domain **finearts**. James needs to access a folder located on a server that is a member of the **dance** domain, which is also a Windows NT 4 child domain belonging to the Windows 2000 domain **finearts**. James hasn't been able to access that data since the **finearts** domain was migrated to Windows 2000. When you look at James's privileges for both servers, you find everything in order. What's the problem?

○ a. James needs an account within the **finearts** domain.

○ b. James needs an account within the **dance** domain.

○ c. The Windows 2000 trusts that were created during the upgrade are only one-way trusts.

○ d. The destination folder doesn't exist.

Answer c is correct. All previous trusts to Windows NT domains will be converted into transitive one-way trusts from the Windows 2000 domain to the Windows NT domains. Answer a is incorrect because James doesn't need to access data within the **finearts** domain. Answer b is incorrect because James was able to access the data prior to the upgrade; therefore, we assume that he either has an account within the **dance** domain, or he didn't need one to begin with. Answer d is incorrect because the question does not mention deleting files or folders; therefore, we must assume that the target folder still exists.

Question 5

Which of the following does not describe a Windows 2000 transitive trust?

○ a. A transitive trust never crosses forest boundaries.

○ b. All domain trusts within a Windows 2000 forest are transitive.

○ c. Transitive trusts can be manually created.

○ d. Transitive trusts are dynamic.

Answer c is correct. Transitive trusts are created automatically. Explicit trusts are created manually.

Question 6

The network infrastructure at the state university was created with several account and resource domains, which are all interconnected within the same building campus. The only reason for this setup is that Windows NT could not contain the number of users necessary within a single domain. While considering domain migration strategies, management decides that Active Directory features need to be implemented as soon as possible. Although it is important to minimize the impact on the production system, it is more important that Active Directory be installed. Which domain migration strategy should be considered?

○ a. Domain upgrade

○ b. Domain restructuring

○ c. Domain upgrade and restructuring

Answer c is correct. The SAM database limitation no longer exists in Windows 2000; therefore, you no longer have to maintain separate resource and account domains. This indicates that a domain restructuring is in order because consolidating these resource and account domains would be more efficient. Considering that it isn't necessary to bypass the production environment during the migration, an upgrade would be faster and easier to implement than a domain restructuring. Answer a is incorrect because the question indicates that the multidomain configuration is based upon the SAM limitation that no longer exists, thus requiring a restructuring. Answer b is incorrect because management indicated that production system impact is less important than getting the upgrade done quickly, which is a feature of an upgrade.

Question 7

> You are considering upgrading your Windows NT domain to Windows 2000. Your research indicates that Windows 2000 will require DNS to be available to every domain controller. This may cause problems because a Unix DNS server is already running on the network, and all Windows NT clients are resolving against the Unix DNS system. What are the Unix DNS requirements that will allow Windows 2000 to integrate with the Unix DNS? [Check all correct answers]
>
> ❏ a. The DNS infrastructure must conceptually match the proposed Active Directory infrastructure.
>
> ❏ b. There are no requirements; Windows 2000 will function.
>
> ❏ c. The DNS version of BIND must be 8.1.2 or above.
>
> ❏ d. The DNS version of BIND must support dynamic updates.

Answers a, c, and d are correct. The DNS infrastructure must match because an Active Directory site will resolve itself against DNS. If the applicable DNS zone is not located nearby, replication issues will arise. The BIND version must either be version 8.1.2+ or support dynamic updates in order for Active Directory to both register resources and perform dynamic DNS updates. Answer b is incorrect because Windows 2000 will not function without a DNS system that is available, and that supports SRV records and dynamic update.

Question 8

> You recently upgraded your primary domain controller from Windows NT to Windows 2000. You are working on upgrading your backup domain controllers when you notice that several clients are not receiving drive-letter mappings when they log on to the network. What's the problem?
>
> ○ a. FRS is not supported in Windows 2000.
>
> ○ b. The SYSVOL directory is empty.
>
> ○ c. Windows NT LMRepl hasn't been reconfigured to replicate logon scripts with the Windows 2000 domain controller.
>
> ○ d. The scripting host must be upgraded before the PDC upgrade.

Answer c is correct. LMRepl must be disconnected and then reconnected to replicate information to and from the Windows 2000 system. Answer a is incorrect because File Replication Service (FRS) is supported in Windows 2000. Answer b is incorrect because although the SYSVOL directory will contain login scripts, it cannot be empty because not all clients are having this particular problem. Answer d is incorrect because a scripting host can be any Windows NT system, and is not linked to upgrading the domain whatsoever.

Question 9

RAS is running on a Windows NT member server located in the **widgets** domain. Since the Windows NT primary domain controller was upgraded, users have been able to connect to connet, but unable to remotely access the network. What's the problem?

- O a. Windows 2000 does not support Windows NT RAS.
- O b. RAS is not running.
- O c. The RAS server must be configured to join the new Windows 2000 domain.
- O d. Windows 2000 will not accept the LocalSystem account credentials.

Answer d is correct. The LocalSystem account credentials used by Windows NT RAS are NULL and will not be accepted by Windows 2000 unless Active Directory security is relaxed. Answer a is incorrect because Windows 2000 not only supports RAS, but it also upgrades the service to RRAS. Answer b is incorrect because if RAS was not running, users would not be able to connect at all. Answer c is incorrect because this is an upgrade; therefore, the RAS server is already a member of the upgraded Windows 2000 domain.

Question 10

Which of the following can be upgraded to Microsoft Windows 2000 Server? [Check all correct answers]

- ❏ a. Windows NT 3.1 Advanced Server
- ❏ b. Windows NT 3.51 Server
- ❏ c. Windows 9x
- ❏ d. Windows NT 4 Server
- ❏ e. Windows NT 3.51 Workstation

Answers b and d are correct. Windows NT 3.51 Server and Windows NT 4 Server can both be upgraded to Windows 2000 Server.

Question 11

Friday night you upgrade your Windows NT domain controllers to Windows 2000 with no problems. DNS is installed appropriately, but you remove WINS from the Windows 2000 configuration because DNS can now handle WINS-like resolution. Monday morning, the network appears to be functioning normally, but you receive email from several users indicating that they cannot connect to the database server. What's the most likely problem?

○ a. The database server is down.

○ b. The users are not logged onto the network.

○ c. DNS was not configured appropriately during the Active Directory installation.

○ d. The database clients use NetBIOS names to connect to the database server.

Answer d is correct. NetBIOS names are resolved by WINS. Answer a is incorrect because the database server, in being part of the network, appears to be functioning normally. Answer b is incorrect because the users are able to send email; therefore, they are logged onto the network. Answer c is incorrect because DNS was upgraded and should function in the same manner (albeit better) than it did prior to the upgrade.

Need to Know More?

 Microsoft Corporation. *Deployment Planning Guide.* Redmond: Microsoft Press, 2000. Vol. 1 of *Microsoft Windows 2000 Server Resource Kit.* ISBN 1572318058. Although this publication is primarily tuned toward deploying Windows 2000 from scratch, it does provide several tips and tricks towards upgrade and migration.

 Microsoft Corporation. *MCSE Training Kit Microsoft Windows 2000 Server.* Redmond: Microsoft Press, 2000. ISBN 1572319038. Although migration is not covered specifically in the server exam, this book contains several sections on migrating and upgrading specific portions of Windows NT to Windows 2000.

 Willis, W., David Watts, and J. Peter Bruzzese. *MCSE Windows 2000 Directory Services Exam Cram.* Scottsdale: The Coriolis Group, 2000. ISBN 1576106888. An invaluable guide to the functionality of Active Directory, including replication processes.

 Microsoft Corporation. *Planning Migration from Windows NT to Windows 2000 White Paper.* Redmond: Microsoft Press, 2000. This guide is useful for covering a broad array of migration environments and processes. Probably the most complete reference from Microsoft on the migration topic.

 http://www.microsoft.com provides *Microsoft Windows 2000 Server Documentation.* Redmond: Microsoft Press, 2000. A thorough reference for overall Windows 2000 Server and domain features and functionality.

 http://www.microsoft.com/TechNet/win2000/upgrnt.asp provides *Upgrading a Windows NT Domain to Windows 2000 Active Directory.* Redmond: Microsoft Press, 2000. A great resource to use as a 20,000 foot guideline in upgrading, but lacks in specific details necessary. It does, however, provide several hyperlinks to more detailed information, some of which is listed here.

Preparing for Migration

Terms you'll need to understand:

✓ Performance Monitor

✓ Delegated DNS domain

✓ Forward lookup

✓ Reverse lookup

✓ DNS zone

✓ DHCP Scope

✓ Replication schema

Techniques you'll need to master:

✓ Documenting current DNS, WINS, and DHCP configurations

✓ Cleaning current DNS, WINS, and DHCP databases

✓ Using the Jetpack utility to compress WINS and DHCP databases

✓ Creating appropriate failsafe and backout plans

✓ Using Performance Monitor to check for memory, disk, and CPU bottlenecks

✓ Using Network Monitor to check for NetBIOS network activity

✓ Reconfiguring replication for a mixed domain

✓ Manually forcing replication and synchronization

Based upon the migration types and their benefits and drawbacks outlined in Chapter 4, hopefully you have a good idea of what structures and services will be required for the network types covered in the exam. This chapter covers the footwork required prior to a successful migration.

 During the exam, pay careful attention to context because quite often the term "migration" can refer to an upgrade, a restructuring, or a combined upgrade and restructuring. All upgrades are migrations, but not all migrations are upgrades. This chapter specifically addresses migrations that do not involve a restructuring.

Hardware Requirements

The first and foremost thing to do is to look at the Windows NT servers on the network and ask the question: Can the server that is to be upgraded be physically upgraded? Minimum hardware requirements for Windows 2000 Server are:

➤ Pentium 133

➤ 1GB hard-disk space

➤ 128MB RAM (256MB recommended)

➤ 3.5-inch floppy drive or a bootable CD

➤ VGA monitor

➤ Keyboard, mouse

➤ CD-ROM drive

➤ Network interface card

You can use the WINNT32 /**checkupgradeonly** command to find out if a system is capable of running Windows 2000. Also consider any additional system requirements for third-party applications and services. Additional means of doing this are described later in this chapter.

Windows 2000 uses hardware detection and PnP (plug-and-play) hardware similar to the way Windows 95 and Windows 98 do. Check the Microsoft Hardware Compatibility List (HCL) carefully to ensure that the current hardware used with Windows NT is compatible with Windows 2000. In most cases, the hardware will be compatible, but some non-PnP devices have been removed from the Windows 2000 HCL due to compliance issues.

After determining whether the hardware is compatible, you'll still need to perform several tasks before the Windows 2000 upgrade. One of the first tasks is to upgrade the system BIOS (basic input/output system) and enable plug and play within the BIOS options. Be careful here: Plug and play might have been disabled within the BIOS due to compatibility issues with Windows NT, so it may be wise to enable PnP just before the upgrade.

Document all IRQs and memory addresses for any non-PnP devices (or any other devices that you may be unsure of), and manually assign those devices within the BIOS itself. Most non-PnP devices require specific IRQs. Because Windows 2000 automatically detects hardware both during the upgrade and on the fly, it's important to reserve those memory addresses within the BIOS. This will prevent the Windows 2000 auto-detect feature from dynamically allocating a PnP device to an address that is currently being used by a non-PnP device on existing hardware addresses and rendering those non-PnP devices unusable.

Obtain Windows 2000 drivers for all printers, modems, shared resources, and other peripherals *before* the upgrade. Most devices will be auto-detected during the upgrade process, but you might need to manually upgrade the drivers. Better to have all drivers on-hand during the installation, rather than frantically searching the Web for elusive drivers. And while you're at it: Download and retrieve the same print drivers for all other clients, such as Windows 3.1, Windows 95, Windows 98, and Windows NT.

Check the relnotes.htm file provided on the Windows 2000 CD. This file contains valuable post-upgrade information regarding hardware and applications; this information might come in handy in eliminating potential problems.

Use Performance Monitor to make sure that there are no memory, disk, or CPU (central processing unit) bottlenecks occurring during high-usage periods. To do this, you'll need to open Performance Monitor from within Administrative Tools and add several counters, as indicated in Figure 5.1. To monitor CPU usage, select the Processor Object, along with the %Processor Time counter. Each of

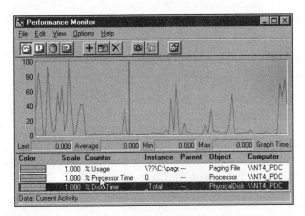

Figure 5.1   Using Performance Monitor to determine Windows 2000 hardware needs.

these counters should be monitored over a period of time spanning your highest production usage hours. It's easy to forget that when the CPU performs a task, it goes at it with gusto. Windows 2000 will run successfully on a Pentium 133 processor, but additional applications and services may require a more robust processor. If the majority of processor time is spiked or is consistently at 100 percent, you'll need to upgrade the CPU prior to the upgrade.

Several hardware-related items need to be added to a "just before upgrade" checklist:

1. At an appropriate off-hours time—let's say a day or so before the upgrade—run a tape backup, verify that the tape has written appropriately, and do a test restore to ensure that a tape backup will work if a mid-upgrade backout is necessary.

2. Designate a current BDC (backup domain controller) as the fallback system, as discussed in Chapter 4. If a BDC is unavailable, you should configure one specifically for this purpose. In a situation where a recovery becomes necessary, the BDC can be brought online to provide authentication and logon services while a tape restore is being performed on the affected server, resulting in less overall downtime.

3. Make sure that the BDC is synchronized and up-to-date when it is taken offline.

4. Disconnect any non-essential peripherals, such as a UPS (uninterruptible power supply) serial cable, and remove the system from any CPU or KVM (keyboard, video, mouse) switches. During the hardware detection phase of installation, the Windows 2000 installer may incorrectly allocate any of these devices, potentially resulting in lack of keyboard, mouse, or loss of power.

5. Run a disk defragmenter utility. This may seem like a mundane thing to do just before an upgrade, but it's very important to ensure that all disk drives are clean and as contiguous as possible, and that any bad blocks are flagged appropriately. Unlike other operating system installations, the Windows 2000 upgrade will blue-screen with an ambiguous (in other words, friendly, but useless) message when it encounters disk errors or I/O timeouts.

6. Immediately before the upgrade, run a tape backup again after the systems are locked down and the end users have gone home for the day.

Create a backup domain controller for fallback purposes. This is especially ideal if you have any domain controllers or member servers that do not meet the necessary hardware requirements. Just before the upgrade is performed, force any synchronization of authentication information by doing the following steps:

1. Open Server Manager, and highlight the primary domain controller.

2. From the menu bar, choose Computer|Synchronize Entire Domain. Depending upon the size of the domain, it may take awhile before the synchronization is complete.

Login scripts and replication items also need to be distributed before the upgrade. After synchronization, stop and restart the Directory Replicator service from within Control Panel|Services.

After verifying that synchronization is complete and any script replication is done, shut down and disconnect the designated fallback BDC. Appropriately planned upgrades should not need this fallback, but it's available if the primary domain controller fails during the upgrade and cannot be recovered.

Overall, the hardware analysis and upgrade process will be the most time-consuming and potentially expensive phases of the entire migration. It is absolutely essential to remember that unresolved hardware issues could be more expensive in resources and money after the migration.

Operating System

Although several questions on the exam will cover specific services such as DNS and WINS, other preparatory jobs involving the overall operating system will also be addressed in some detail. These jobs are discussed next.

Quite often, large companies will not regularly use their administrator logon to administer the servers. Instead, the administrator credentials are put into an envelope along with all other mission-critical usernames and passwords, and filed somewhere in case of emergency. If this is the case, break open the administrator password and make sure it's correct. Also, create an additional administrator-equivalent user, and test the capabilities to ensure that a proper authoritative login will be available.

Choose a Directory Services Restore Mode administrator password. You'll need this password if a failure occurs further along in the migration process when it might become necessary to restore directory services. You will be prompted for it during AD installation.

Make sure that you have both NT 4 and Windows 2000 tape drivers available. Also ensure that a Windows NT Server disk is on hand and that tape backup software (if you need something other than ntbackup.exe) is available for installation if a drastic failure occurs during the upgrade. Although the BDC can be utilized immediately in order to minimize user interruption, non-replicated services and applications that reside on a failed server might trigger the need to completely restore from tape and return to the Windows 2000 migration drawing board.

If the production environment can support additional downtime, run a Registry cleanup tool. It's best to do this after a tested tape backup, but not immediately before the upgrade-specific tape backup. The reason for this is that Registry scrubbers will occasionally mistakenly remove necessary Registry entries. While it is an advantage to clean the Registry, it is still a risk, so timing this necessary downtime should be after a successful tape backup so that any major glitches can be immediately fixed by a tape restore, and some time before the upgrade itself in order to allow time to troubleshoot any less-critical errors that may result. During the upgrade process, Windows 2000 will carefully analyze the Windows NT Registry and restructure it to handle new and upgraded services and Active Directory features that will be installed. Eliminating erroneous Registry entries will not only speed up this analysis but also prevent Windows 2000 from unnecessarily tracking and potentially getting hung up on erroneous or obsolete entries.

Consider installing Service Pack 4 or higher because it is compatible with NTFS 5. During the installation process, any NTFS 4 partitions will be converted to NTFS 5. If an upgrade fails after this conversion, yet before any significant OS files have been altered, Service Pack 4 might increase instant-recovery possibilities just because NT 4 with Service Pack 4 will be able to read NTFS 5. Balance this consideration with any other patches and service packs that have been applied for security, application compatibility, or stability purposes. Updating to Service Pack 4 could lead to disastrous results if security is compromised in the process.

 Applying Windows NT Service Pack 4 or later is typically recommended when you want to support Windows NT 4 systems in your Windows 2000 environment.

Take a look at the hard disk and partition structures. Determine where the Active Directory (AD) database and SYSVOL share should be. It's recommended that they each live in separate partitions from the system partition. Because the SYSVOL share contains login scripts and replication data, it's important to consider this placement very carefully—particularly in large enterprises where a lot of authentication and replication traffic might affect disk performance. Best performance would be obtained by placing the AD database and SYSVOL share in separate drives. If the current PDC doesn't have the disk structure to allow this placement in the short term, and a BDC does, then do the following: force replication; take the PDC offline; promote the BDC to a PDC; and then proceed with the upgrade. Before doing this, make sure that all of the services and applications running on the PDC are also running on the BDC, and vice versa. Instead of the previously mentioned BDC, the offline PDC will be our failsafe backup during the upgrade. While the PDC is offline, consider performing appropriate hardware and software upgrades. A similar concept applies across the board: Any domain controller or server that doesn't immediately meet hardware requirements can become the failsafe-backup domain controller during the initial upgrade, and can remain so for as long as it's necessary. While it's offline, after the initial upgrade is complete and the failsafe is no longer quite so critical, upgrade the hardware to your heart's delight.

When the BDC doesn't run the same services as the PDC, another failsafe option that is particularly appealing is to create a standby server (by restoring from tape) that has the same name, services, applications, and even machine name as the PDC. The biggest advantage here is that if the upgrade fails, you can bring back the Windows NT network just by connecting the system to the network and turning it on. It is absolutely necessary, however, to pay attention to what happens on the network immediately after the upgrade. As soon as the first user changes a password or access privileges, the failsafe backup (be it PDC or BDC) begins to become obsolete. A large network where changes happen constantly can render the failsafe obsolete in minutes, whereas within a smaller, more stable network, it may take several days for the failsafe to pass into obsolescence.

Immediately before the upgrade, uninstall any non-critical virus scanners and other utilities. Now is the time to uninstall any UPS software also. Even if the installed software is Windows-2000 compliant, uninstall it anyway. Also uninstall any third-party network services—sniffers, bandwidth monitors, and so on. Basically, if it falls under the "utility" framework, uninstall it because these robots will be attempting to do their jobs during the upgrade and might interfere with the appropriate component installations.

DNS

DNS (Domain Name System) is probably the single most important factor in a successful Windows 2000 upgrade. Therefore, the process of preparing for the advent or continuance of DNS within a given network is one of the more complex tasks during a migration.

Microsoft highly recommends an Active-Directory-integrated DNS just because of the dynamic update functionality. An additional huge advantage is security: Dynamic updates can occur only from domain-authenticated systems. However, it is possible to configure DNS just as it was configured within Windows NT. Just be sure to keep in mind that when DNS is integrated into Active Directory, DNS will be available only when AD is available. For the purpose of the exam, we will focus on Active-Directory-integrated DNS.

When you're planning Active Directory domains, keep in mind that every AD domain must also have a DNS zone against which to reference. Also, when you're running DNS under Active Directory, keep in mind that AD-integrated DNS must be on a domain controller. Plan the hardware and memory appropriately. If you intend to maintain WINS (Windows Internet Naming Service), then WINS Forwarding should be enabled. Know the WINS server IP address prior to the upgrade.

If DNS does not reside on the NT 4 domain controller, be prepared with a dedicated IP address. By and large, all Windows NT and Windows 2000 servers should have dedicated IP addresses; however, dedicated IP addresses will definitely be required for any DNS servers. Also, if a Windows 2000 DNS server (or another DNS server that supports dynamic update and SRV records) already exists on the network, document the address of that DNS server.

Note: Also keep in mind that DNS zone names can include the following characters: A-Z, a-z, 0-9, - (dash).

In environments where older, non-compatible DNS exists, you can create a completely separate namespace. However, this is ill-advised due to the administrative overhead in maintaining two completely separate DNS systems.

 It's possible to upgrade BIND on the existing DNS structure, but it might be politically difficult or near-to-impossible. The same political friction may occur on the subject of completely replacing legacy DNS servers. The preferred solution is to create a delegated subdomain under the existing DNS structure, forward to the legacy DNS as appropriate, and create the DNS zones and structures in a manner similar to the Active Directory domain structures.

Determine the DNS forwarding and reverse lookup servers and their TCP/IP addresses. For a system already running DNS in a single-domain environment, the forwarding server usually is an ISP. For larger environments already running DNS, this can be a Unix or Windows NT flavor of DNS. If legacy non-Windows DNS exists on the network and is not compatible with BIND 8.1.2, it is recommended that a delegated DNS domain be created specifically for Windows 2000 to live in, as illustrated in Figure 5.2. This way, Windows clients can thrive happily with the functionality of DDNS (Dynamic DNS), while you can cut down on the administrative overhead of maintaining separate DNS zones.

Because of the importance of DNS in a successful upgrade of Windows NT to Windows 2000, let's run through a few scenarios based upon Figure 5.2:

> ➤ *Scenario 1*—Let's say that this is the DNS structure in a large corporation called WidgetsRUs. The current DNS is Unix-based and not running BIND 8.1.2 or above. You have determined that it will be impossible to upgrade the BIND servers appropriately, so you'll need to obtain a delegated DNS

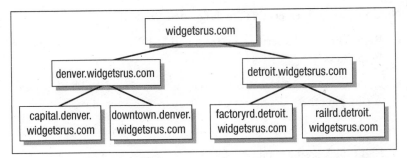

Figure 5.2 Example of a DNS domain structure. Each object under **widgetsrus.com** is a delegated subdomain.

domain in order to proceed with a Windows 2000 upgrade. A delegated domain name of **adminbldg.denver.widgetsrus.com** is added to the **denver. widgetsrus.com** domain specifically for this purpose. The forwarding and reverse lookup server for this domain should be **denver.widgetsrus.com**.

➤ *Scenario 2*—This is the DNS structure in the same corporation. The current DNS is NT-based, and you are responsible for upgrading the **factoryrd.detroit.widgetsrus.com** domain from Windows NT to Windows 2000. The forwarding and reverse lookup server for this domain should be **detroit.widgetsrus.com**—but make sure that you check the current DNS configuration to confirm this.

➤ *Scenario 3*—This is the DNS structure in the same corporation. The current DNS is both NT- and Unix-based. The first domain to be upgraded is **downtown.denver.widgetsrus.com**, which is currently running NT-based DNS with forward and reverse lookups pointing to **denver.widgetsrus.com**, which is Unix-based. Because the delegated domain name has already been created, simply check the forward and reverse lookups in the current NT DNS to ensure that they are correct, and upgrade as planned in Scenario 1. If any non-Windows clients will be looking toward Windows 2000 DNS for resolution, make a note to disable Unicode after DNS is installed.

In a Windows NT 4 DNS system, several major things need to happen prior to upgrade:

1. Document and note any static A records and make sure they are correct. To do this:

   a. Start the Domain Name Service Manager, and select the appropriate server, zone, and domain (as applicable).

   b. As shown in Figure 5.3, several records are listed. Ensure that the records associated with servers are correct. (The easiest way to ensure accuracy is to ping the IP addresses listed.) Document the associations.

2. Note any forward servers that are designated. To do this:

   a. Right-click on the server icon from within DNS Manager, and choose Properties.

   b. Click on the Forwarders tab and make a note of any IP addresses listed. Again, ping these IP addresses to ensure that they are alive.

3. Determine any WINS servers that are designated for WINS lookup. To do this:

   a. Right-click on the applicable DNS zone, and choose Properties.

   b. Click on the WINS lookup tab. Note any WINS-server IP addresses listed. Ensure that the addresses are valid by pinging them. Also ensure that the addresses are appropriately listed in Zone Info.

4. Change the NT domain name to match the DNS domain name before the migration. If they're different, you'll have to walk the floor to change the client configuration anyway. If a delegated subdomain is in order, the name of the delegated subdomain should be the name of the NT domain.

5. Last, but definitely not least: Clean up the current DNS database as much as possible. As shown in Figure 5.3, you'll notice that the hosts where and why now both have the same IP address. The correct address needs to be determined and corrected for the affected host. Any other similar errors for servers should be corrected by double-clicking on the record and correcting the IP address. We'll go into more details in the DHCP section of this chapter, but be aware here and now that any systems running static IP addresses should be checked and corrected. These should include any DHCP, WINS, and IIS servers as well as any lesser-known application servers.

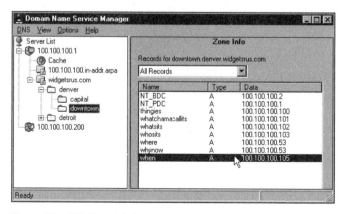

Figure 5.3   DNS Zone Info for the **downtown** subdomain located in the **denver** subdomain, which belongs to the **widgetsrus.com** zone.

Also be sure to check the reverse lookup zone. You can do this by selecting the zones labeled with **in-addr-arpa**. If there are multiple zones labeled as such, select the one that is preceded by the same backwards address as that of the server itself. For example: A server whose address is **10.20.30.40** would have a reverse lookup zone labeled **30.20.10.in-addr.arpa**.

As shown in Figure 5.4, several Pointer (PTR) records such as 100.100.100.1 appear to be duplicated. As in the previous processes, ping the addresses listed, and ping the names listed. If the name resolution brings back the appropriate pinged address, all is well. Delete any duplicate records that are not correctly resolved by this process. Be very thorough here, and take careful note of the static IP addresses listed both here and in the appropriate domain lookup zone. The bulk of the DNS database resides between these two screens, with each screen essentially mirroring each other. One screen has the standard Name-to-IP lookup, and the other has the reversed IP-to-Name lookup. Although it's not necessary to spend time with every single host record, it is essential to ensure that any static IP addresses listed in the domain Zone Info are also appropriately listed in the reverse Zone Info screen. While looking through both forward and reverse lookup zones, keep in mind that every record in the forward zone should have an equal and opposite record in the reverse lookup zone. For example, as you may notice in Figures 5.3 and 5.4, nearly all of the records listed in **downtown.denver. widgetsrus.com** are not represented within **100.100.100.in-addr.arpa**. Similarly, the record for **100.100.100.10** that is located in **100.100.100.in-addr.arpa** does not appear as sqlserv record in the **downtown.denver.widgetsrus.com** zone. In database terms, this particular DNS database needs to be normalized before the upgrade to Windows 2000. That is to say that all records need to be checked and corrected for consistency and accuracy across the board.

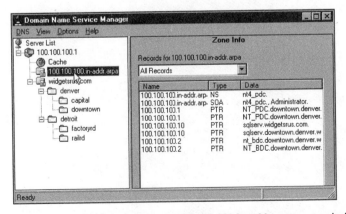

Figure 5.4   Zone information for the **100.100.100.in-addr.arpa** reverse lookup zone.
The reverse lookup zone will contain PTR records that enable reverse lookups.

DHCP

The largest part of preparing DNS, DHCP (Dynamic Host Configuration Protocol), and WINS (Windows Internet Naming Service) for Windows 2000 involves cleaning up the existing DNS, WINS, and DHCP databases and ensuring their accuracy.

The first thing to do when you're checking the accuracy of the DHCP database is to make sure that there are no address inconsistencies. You do this by checking scopes, exclusions, and reservations to make sure that they are all correct and that they match up to entries in any current Windows NT 4 DNS database.

To check Scope Properties, follow these steps:

1. Open DHCP Manager.

2. Double-click on a server. Each scope should be listed with a light bulb icon next to it. Inactive scopes will be gray, and active scopes will be indicated by an icon of a lit yellow light bulb.

3. Highlight an active scope. Then choose Scope|Properties.

   As shown in Figure 5.5, the Scope Properties dialog box will appear. In particular, check the list of exclusions shown on the right. If necessary, research what each exclusion is for.

Traditionally, there are two basic ways of implementing DHCP on a network. The first is to create scopes that contain exclusions for every static IP address necessary, and the second is to create scopes that utilize reservations for the same

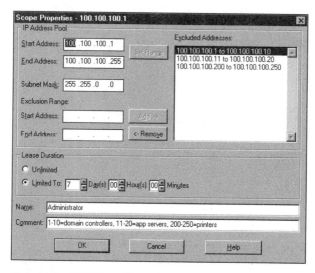

Figure 5.5 DHCP Scope Properties.

static IP addresses. Exclusions can be significantly easier to configure and maintain, but creating reservations is quite often more appropriate in environments where it's important to have a single source of documented IP address assignments. This automatic documentation is created because, unlike scope exclusions, reserved addresses are still leased and managed by DHCP. Figure 5.5 is an example of the first method of using exclusions. Note that the basic IP addressing schema has been documented under the Comment box at the bottom of the Scope Properties dialog box.

While attempting to configure DHCP to manage all IP addressing needs, keep in mind Windows NT DHCP may have been brought into a statically-addressed IP network with the potential for several non-Windows hosts and devices to obtain IP addresses from across the network. Therefore, it may be difficult to define a set DHCP schema, such as the one shown in the Comment box at the bottom of Figure 5.5. In environments where DHCP is configured to handle all IP addressing needs on the network, the current NT DHCP may have been configured with global options so that an array of IP addresses has been set aside for lease to specific types of servers, such as time servers and DNS servers. You can view any of these address arrays by choosing DHCP Options from the menu bar and selecting Global. Ensure that the address arrays are valid and useful. If they are not, delete them.

Be sure also to check any addresses listed in the Option Configuration window for each scope. These are the specific addresses that are served to the DHCP clients via the DHCP Scope, Global, and Defaults options.

If you're migrating from static clients, take note of any IP addresses that should be maintained as static addresses. Now is the perfect time to configure the ideal IP addressing scheme. For example, you can decide that all servers reside between 10.0.0.1 and 10.0.0.100, printers reside between 10.0.101 and 10.0.0.200, and so forth. Again, Figure 5.5 has accomplished this via exclusions.

If DHCP doesn't exist on the current network, make sure to map out all of the scopes, exclusions, and so on. Don't forget that it will be necessary to touch every client computer to fully implement DHCP. This means either walking the floor the night of the upgrade, or setting additional exclusions to handle current static clients while enabling the client cutover over a longer period of time.

Before the upgrade, you must accomplish two tasks. The first is to set a time when all address leases will expire. The second is to compress and optimize the DHCP database by running jetpack.exe.

Although setting a time for all address leases to expire is not absolutely essential for an upgrade, it is important when a network reorganization is in order. The easiest way to do this is to set the lease duration as appropriate for when the upgrade will occur, as shown in Figure 5.5. For example, let's say that the upgrade is scheduled to occur in seven days. Any system requesting a new lease will be up for renewal on the day of the upgrade. That's fine for today. Tomorrow, however, the seven-day setting means that new leases will expire the day after the upgrade. This is not the desired result. Tomorrow, set the lease duration to six days; the next day, set it to five days; and so on. What this will do is gradually get all of the clients in step with each other to expire on the same day.

The other job that should be done a day or two before the upgrade is to compress and optimize the DHCP database by running the Jetpack utility (jetpack.exe). The process for this is as follows:

1. Determine what the DHCP database name is. By default it is **dhcp.mdb**. The easiest way to do this is to check the \winnt\system32\dhcp directory for any file with an .mdb extension.

2. Stop the DHCP service. You can do this from within Control Panel|Services or by opening a command prompt and entering the **NET STOP DHCPSERVER** command.

3. Open a command prompt, and enter the **JETPACK DHCP.MDB** command. Replace **dhcp.mdb** with the appropriate database name.

4. Errors may occur if the service is not appropriately stopped, if the database is not named dhcp.mdb, or if a temp.mdb file already exists. The **temp.mdb** portion of the syntax can be named anything else as long as it ends with an .mdb extension.

5. Restart the DHCP service. You can do this from within Control Panel|Services or by entering **NET START DHCPSERVER** at the command prompt.

 Running Jetpack on the DHCP database will eliminate obsolete entries and compress the database so that it will be more stable and will run through the upgrade faster.

WINS

Determine what machines use NetBIOS (Network Basic Input/Output System) or NetBEUI (NetBIOS Extended User Interface) on clients and servers. This will help you figure out whether WINS can be eliminated in the short term, long term, or never. The best means of doing this is to use the NBTSTAT utility.

1. Open a command prompt and enter the following command: **NBTSTAT -r**.

2. Take note of the results. If the listed results are too numerous, rerun the command as follows: **NBTSTAT -r>NOTES.TXT** (where **notes.txt** can be replaced by any valid path and file name).

3. Enter the following command: **NBTSTAT -s**.

4. Take note of the results. Again, if the list is too long, run **NBTSTAT -s>NOTES.TXT**.

Upon looking through the results of the **NBTSTAT -r** command, you'll notice that there are two lines indicating names resolved by the name server. If this number is above 0, WINS is still not only alive but also being utilized on the network. The **NBTSTAT -s** command will list active and inactive NetBIOS connections. Basically, anything that's listed as Connected would merit some concern with regard to removing WINS from the network.

Microsoft would prefer to see WINS quietly and happily made an extinct animal. However, because interoperability and support are still necessary, the rest of this section will focus upon current WINS preparations with the intent of maintaining a post-migration WINS environment.

Take careful note of situations in which NetBEUI might be in place for security purposes, such as when communications to an outside-the-firewall system are exclusively NetBEUI. If this is the case, it doesn't necessarily mean that WINS must exist on this network solely for this one application. What it does mean, however, is that DNS can handle the name resolution if the machines in question are Windows 2000 clients or servers, or if they will be appropriately accommodated within DHCP and Dynamic DNS.

Make sure that all WINS records for all domain controllers match the corresponding DNS records. To do this, you must view the current database from within WINS Manager. (Choose Mappings|Show Database from the menu.) As you can see in Figure 5.6, there is no way to easily search for items in the Show Database window from within WINS Manager. This is where having a TCP/IP naming scheme may come in handy. Be cautious, however, because incorrectly mapped addresses might fall outside the schema. Correct any inappropriate addresses or hostnames by double-clicking the incorrect record and updating the appropriate information.

Because WINS is a dynamically updated database, get rid of obsolete records by using the scavenging option within WINS Manager. From the WINS Manager menu, choose Mappings|Initiate Scavenging. A dialog box will appear indicating that the task has been queued for execution.

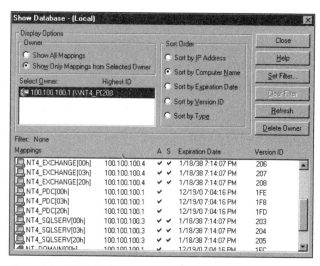

Figure 5.6 WINS database mappings.

Although this is outside the WINS scope, it is a good idea to check the local LMHOSTS and HOSTS files to ensure that all controllers and statically assigned systems are correct. These files are located by default in the \winnt\system32\drivers\etc folder.

As with DHCP, you should run jetpack.exe on the WINS database a day or two before the upgrade. The process for this is as follows:

1. Determine what the WINS database name is. By default it is **wins.mdb**. The easiest way to do this is to check the \winnt\system32\wins directory for any file with an .mdb extension.

2. Stop the Windows Internet Naming Service. You can do this within Control Panel|Services or by entering **NET STOP WINS** at the command prompt.

3. Open a command prompt and enter the **JETPACK WINS.MDB TEMP.MDB** command. (Replace **wins.mdb** with the appropriate database if applicable.)

   Errors may occur as outlined previously, in the section on DHCP.

4. Restart the Windows Internet Naming Service. You can do this within Control Panel|Services or by entering the command **NET START WINS** at the command prompt.

Running jetpack.exe on the WINS database will result in increased performance and a faster upgrade.

Replication

By this stage in the game, you should already have a good idea of what Active Directory will look like, as well as what sites and site links will be established after the Windows 2000 upgrade, as outlined in Chapter 2 on Active Directory. Keep in mind that a good guideline is to establish site link boundaries everywhere a remote subnet exists. Site links themselves can be generally considered as WAN links—anything that particularly requires a gateway on both ends, such as a router can and should be considered a site link. Another great guideline for site link placement is to place a site link anywhere bandwidth can be an issue.

If you haven't already, consider planning a global catalog server for sites whose site/WAN links are unstable or unreliable, or whose configurations are planned intermittence. Specific global catalog servers are not installed by default, might be bandwidth intensive for large multidomain enterprises, and aren't necessary for a single domain.

Active Directory replication occurs based upon two concepts: intersite replication and intrasite replication. Intersite replication occurs every 3 hours for 15 minutes. Update notification between servers does not occur. Replication packages are compressed in order to decrease bandwidth utilization. Intersite replication packages can even be automatically compiled into an email message for delivery via SMTP. This, in particular, is ideal for sites whose site links are unstable or specifically designed to be intermittent, such as dialup links. Remember that, for these unstable sites, you might do well to consider creating a site link bridge in order to funnel replication traffic through a single server. Intrasite replication, on the other hand, occurs once every five minutes after a change occurs, or when replication is requested by a domain controller. Replication is requested after changes to a given server prompt it to notify its replication partners of changes. Ideally, the definition of a site does not include any WAN links and consists of what we would normally term a LAN or MAN (Metropolitan Area Network) running at 10/100 Mbps speeds. This is why intrasite replication is not compressed.

Intrasite replication maintains a full replica of the AD database. Considering the sheer size capabilities of a given Active Directory database, it would be impractical to have the entire database replicated every night within a given domain or site, let alone across WAN boundaries. This is why only object properties—and not the objects themselves—are replicated. In addition to this, global catalog properties are replicated across multiple domains—specifically to other global catalog servers. This is why it may be wise to create a GC server at sites where the site link is unstable or unreliable. It is these compression-type features of AD replication that ultimately reduce interdomain authentication traffic significantly over Windows NT interdomain bandwidth usage.

Keep in mind another factor for integrating DNS into Active Directory: DNS replication will occur during standard Active Directory replication. This can be a good thing because it lessens the administrative overhead for dealing with replication, unlike Windows NT DNS and WINS replication. Active Directory-integrated DNS replication can be of concern also, however, because of the added considerations of Active Directory replication during the planning stages of any upgrade or migration.

If you choose not to take advantage of DDNS and AD-integrated DNS, standard DNS replication will be upgraded with the same configuration that any existing systems have—with primary, secondary, and caching-only servers. Again, this can decrease the necessary planning involved with Active Directory replication, but still maintain the same administrative overhead that goes into any current DNS replication scheme.

Only two basic replication-related tasks need to be performed before the upgrade itself: analyze current bandwidth utilization, and document the current replication schema. For the most part, these jobs need not be done immediately before the upgrade, and do not involve much preparation work on the NT servers themselves.

Spend some time analyzing the current bandwidth utilization both within the site and between sites across WAN links. Based upon current bandwidth utilization across different periods of time, determine if the default intrasite replication schedule of 15 minutes should change and which time ranges would be most appropriate.

Windows 2000 domain controllers will automatically replicate among themselves any login scripts and other data located in the Sysvol directory. This is great if the network is in native mode, however, it is unlikely that a migration will instantly produce a native-mode domain. As a result, we need to consider how data will be replicated amongst remaining NT servers, and how that same data will replicate between Windows 2000 servers and the remaining NT servers. After the first domain controller upgrade, and while the domain is still in mixed mode, you'll need to re-configure replication in two ways: the first being to re-configure replication (if necessary) between the NT servers, and the second being to configure a single replication bridge between an NT server and a Windows 2000 domain controller. Because both of these events will occur after the upgrade, they will be addressed in Chapter 6. In the meantime, it becomes necessary to thoroughly understand and document the current replication schema across the network.

In order to properly understand how we should document the replication schema, it is a good idea to consider how the network will look after the upgrade. The example in Figure 5.7 shows a basic network with five Windows NT servers, all performing replication amongst themselves. The plan is to upgrade each server according to its number on the network, starting with NT Server 1, and finishing with NT Server 5. While planning replication, start with the server that will be performing replication between the NT network and the Windows 2000 network. This is called the replication bridge. This NT export server should be among the last to be migrated to Windows 2000. Otherwise, you would have to constantly reconfigure the replication bridge every time the NT server was upgraded. Let's say that in phase 1 of the migration, NT Server 2 was designated as the replication bridge, phase 2 might become a problem, because once NT Server 2 is upgraded according to plan, the replication bridge would need to be reconfigured for a different server. In our example, it is far better to designate NT Server 5 as the replication bridge. You might also need to move the current replication functionality to a different server. In Figure 5.7, keep in mind that once NT Server 2 is upgraded, NT Server 3 will need to be reconfigured to no longer replicate with NT Server 2 because the replication to that server will automatically be handled as a member of the Windows 2000 network. Also keep in mind that, because any NT member server can be configured for replication, each server that owns a given replicated directory can also be an export server. Understanding and documenting the current NT replication schema becomes critical at this point because of the additional replication links that need to be dismantled and reconfigured after every server upgrade. If you take this opportunity to tidy up the current replication schema on the NT network, also ensure that the new replication schema is slated for inclusion on the designated fallback BDC in case it ceases to be a fallback and is brought back online post-migration as a standard NT BDC.

The first step in documenting the current replication schema is to determine where the LMRepl export servers are. Check replication on a given server by checking the properties of a server within Server Manager and clicking on the Replication button. Take note of any items listed under Export Directories. Anything listed under Export Directories makes this server an export server. Again, it is recommended that all export server functionality be centralized in a single server to avoid constantly reconfiguring the export functionality every time a server is upgraded to Windows 2000. Also document any items listed on the right pane under Import Directories. This documentation will give you a clearer picture of what other export servers are on the network. After the upgrade, and when an export server is designated, a replication bridge will be established to handle replication to Windows 2000, and NT replication links will be reconfigured or rebuilt as appropriate for all other import servers on the network. Import servers, in turn, should be rebuilt to pull the replication data from export servers.

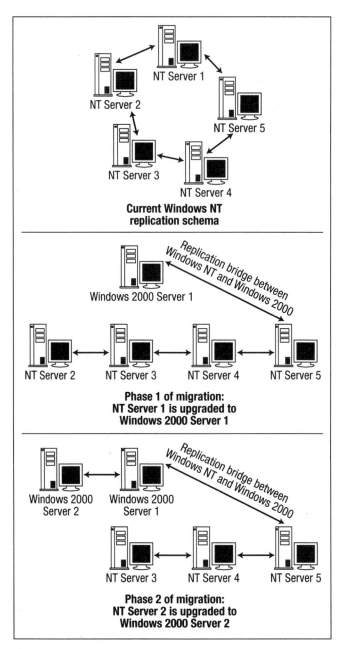

Figure 5.7 Windows NT replication schema as the servers become upgraded to Windows 2000 in mixed mode.

Practice Questions

Question 1

> While preparing to upgrade your Windows NT domain controllers, you need to determine which systems can be upgraded to Windows 2000 Server. Which of the following apply? [Check all correct answers]
>
> ❑ a. Pentium 133, Windows NT 3.5, 2GB HDD, 80MB RAM, bootable CD, Super VGA monitor, keyboard, mouse, network interface card
>
> ❑ b. Pentium 266, Windows NT 3.51, 1GB HDD, 64MB RAM, floppy drive, Super VGA monitor, keyboard, mouse, network interface card
>
> ❑ c. Pentium 300, Windows NT 3.51, 1 GB HDD, 128MB RAM, floppy drive, CD-ROM, Super VGA monitor, keyboard, mouse, network interface card
>
> ❑ d. Pentium 166, Windows NT 4, 40GB HDD, 256MB RAM, floppy drive, CD-ROM, Super VGA monitor, keyboard, mouse, network interface card

Answers c and d are correct. Minimum system requirements are a Pentium 133, with a 1GB HDD, 128MB RAM, 3.5 floppy drive or bootable CD, VGA monitor, keyboard, mouse, CD-ROM, and network interface card. Answer a is incorrect because of the RAM requirements and because there is no direct upgrade path from Windows NT 3.5 to Windows 2000. Answer b is incorrect because the memory is insufficient and there is no CD-ROM listed.

Question 2

> You have been given the task of upgrading the Windows NT domain control-lers to Windows 2000 in order to take advantage of Active Directory func-tions and features. You need to determine the most efficient placements of the Sysvol directory and the Active Directory database. Which of the follow-ing scenarios would produce the best performance based upon the stated location of the Sysvol and AD database?
>
> ○ a. The server has a single disk drive. Create three partitions. Place the system files on the first partition, the Sysvol directory on the second partition, and the Active Directory database on the third partition.
>
> ○ b. The server has a single disk drive. Create two partitions. Place the system files on the first partition, and the Sysvol directory and Active Directory database on the second partition.
>
> ○ c. The server has a single disk drive. Create two partitions. Place the system files on the first partition, and place the Sysvol directory on the second partition. Purchase a new disk drive, install it, create the appropriate partitions, and place the Active Directory database on the new drive.
>
> ○ d. The server has a single disk drive. Create two partitions. Place the system files on the first partition. Purchase a new disk drive, install it, create the appropriate partitions, and place the Active Directory database and the Sysvol directory on separate partitions of the new drive.

Answer d is correct. Placing the Active Directory database and the Sysvol direc-tory on separate partitions of the new drive optimizes performance by separating these functions from the system partition. Answers a, b, and c are incorrect be-cause placing either of these components on the same drive as the system parti-tion will result in slower disk I/O—particularly if you have a large network with a lot of replication traffic.

Question 3

> You are the network engineer for a large company with offices in Phoenix, Detroit, and Denver. While the entire company runs on Windows NT Workstation, each client still relies upon a DNS server that runs using BIND 4.0.2. Which of the following are appropriate options when you're considering a Windows 2000 upgrade? [Check all correct answers]
>
> ❑ a. Upgrade to BIND 8.1.2.
>
> ❑ b. Create a new DNS domain.
>
> ❑ c. Create a new DNS subdomain within the existing structure.
>
> ❑ d. DNS is not necessary.

Answers a and c are correct. Answer a is correct because upgrading to BIND 8.1.2 will provide the dynamic update and SRV records that are required for Active Directory to function. Creating a new DNS subdomain, as indicated in answer c, will allow for the functionality of Windows 2000 without requiring the additional resources that would be required to maintain a completely separate DNS namespace. Answer b is incorrect because creating a new DNS domain will result in the additional resources of maintaining two separate DNS systems. Answer d is incorrect because a working DNS system running BIND 8.1.2 or above must be available to the Windows 2000 network in order to function.

Question 4

> You are responsible for planning the Windows 2000 migration for a large company called WidgetsRUs. The current DNS is Unix-based and is running BIND 4.0.2. You have determined that it will be impossible to upgrade the BIND servers appropriately, so you'll need to obtain a delegated DNS domain in order to proceed with the Windows 2000 upgrade. What is the best possible DNS subdomain name?
>
> ○ a. **widgetsrus.com**
>
> ○ b. **detroit.widgetsrus.com**
>
> ○ c. **detroit_factoryrd.widgetsrus.com**
>
> ○ d. **denver@widgetsrus.com**

Answer b is correct. Answer a is incorrect because **widgetsrus.com** is not a subdomain. Answers d and c are incorrect because they both contain invalid characters.

Question 5

You are preparing to upgrade your DHCP server to Windows 2000. What must be done? [Check all correct answers]

- ❑ a. Stop the service, run jetpack.exe, and restart the service.
- ❑ b. Every day before the upgrade, change the lease duration to expire on the day of the upgrade.
- ❑ c. Scavenge the database.
- ❑ d. Stop the service.

Answers a and b are correct. Running the Jetpack utility will compress and optimize the database. Resetting the lease duration will graciously expire all TCP/IP leases on the day of the upgrade. Answer c is incorrect because scavenging the database is a WINS function. Answer d is incorrect because simply stopping the service does nothing to prepare for the upgrade.

Question 6

Before proceeding with a Windows 2000 upgrade, you need to create a failsafe plan in the event of a failure during the upgrade process. Which of the following do not apply?

- ○ a. Create a backup domain controller and take it offline during the upgrade. Bring it online if a failure occurs.
- ○ b. Create a duplicate primary domain controller by restoring from tape backup, and take it offline. Bring it online if a failure occurs.
- ○ c. Create a tape backup. Reinstall Windows NT 4 and restore from tape backup if a failure occurs.
- ○ d. Configure replication to copy the system files to a member server before the upgrade. Upgrade the server to a domain controller if a failure occurs.

Answer d is correct. System files cannot be reliably replicated, and member servers cannot be upgraded to a domain controller. Answer a is incorrect because a BDC can be brought back online and promoted to a PDC in the event that a Windows 2000 backout becomes necessary. Answer b is incorrect because a duplicate server can be brought online to provide the functionality of the failed server. Answer c is incorrect because a tape restore is a reliable method of recovering from failure.

Question 7

> You have configured Performance Monitor to check %Disk Time under the Physical Disk Object. Performance Monitor shows that the hard drive is operating at 80 percent. You also notice that pagefile usage is below 30 percent. What should be done to improve the system performance before the upgrade?
>
> ○ a. Upgrade RAM.
>
> ○ b. Upgrade the hard drive.
>
> ○ c. Upgrade the CPU.
>
> ○ d. Increase network bandwidth.

Answer b is correct. The pagefile utilization in this situation is not indicating excessive usage of memory; therefore, the hard disk usage is completely attributable to insufficient disk space. Answer a is incorrect because the pagefile usage would be higher if there weren't enough RAM on the system. Answer c is incorrect because CPU utilization doesn't impact the performance of RAM, hard drive, or network bandwidth. Answer d is incorrect because bandwidth does not affect the performance of RAM, hard drive, or CPU.

Question 8

> You are considering whether or not to remove the WINS server from your network during the Windows 2000 upgrade. Using the **NBTSTAT -s** command on each domain controller indicates that all servers are listening with the exception of the data server that serves the Internet server located outside the firewall. Is it safe to decommission the WINS server?
>
> ○ a. Yes; because the Internet server communicates with the data server, name resolution can occur through DNS.
>
> ○ b. No; you haven't checked for activity from any of the clients.
>
> ○ c. Yes; any NetBIOS communications from the clients should be going to the servers, whose resolution will be handled by DNS.
>
> ○ d. No; all the clients are Windows NT or Windows 2000 clients.

Answer b is correct. It is important to remember that WINS primarily serves clients, not necessarily servers.

Question 9

> Site links should be planned based upon what criteria? [Check all correct answers]
>
> ❏ a. Anywhere a remote subnet exists
>
> ❏ b. Anywhere network speeds are low
>
> ❏ c. Anywhere network connectivity is intermittent
>
> ❏ d. Anywhere between Active Directory domains

Answers a, b, and c are correct. Multiple Active Directory domains can exist within a subnet and therefore should not be considered as criteria for determining site links.

Question 10

> You work for a midsize engineering firm that has two offices, located in Denver and Phoenix. The corporate offices, located in Phoenix, contain several domains and domain controllers. The Denver office, however, contains only one domain with several domain controllers. The WAN link between the two offices resides on a 256K frame relay service. What planning can be done in order to minimize replication traffic after Windows 2000 is installed?
>
> ○ a. Plan on compressing the data.
>
> ○ b. Create a site link bridge.
>
> ○ c. Turn off the update-notify feature between the sites.
>
> ○ d. Upgrade from a 256K link to a 640K link.

Answer b is correct. Answers a and d are incorrect because if 256K is appropriate under Windows NT, it should be even more so under Windows 2000 due to the added *default* replication features data compression and the fact that bandwidth isn't utilized to perform update notifications. Answer b is correct because creating a site link bridge will limit traffic between each site to a single point of contact. This will eliminate the possibility of having multiple domain controllers replicating with the remote domain at the same time. Answer c is incorrect because update-notify does not occur between sites.

Need to Know More?

 Boswell, William. *Inside Windows 2000 Server.* Indianapolis: New Riders, 2000. ISBN 1562059297. Arguably the most outstanding operating system book ever written. There is no doubt that upgrading DNS can be the largest glitch in a successful migration. Boswell thoroughly and appropriately emphasizes the role of DNS both during and after migration.

 Microsoft Corporation. *MCSE Training Kit Microsoft Windows 2000 Server.* Redmond, Washington: Microsoft Press, 2000. ISBN 1572319038. The chapter on Active Directory contains information on replication, site links, and how they function.

 Microsoft Corporation. *Windows 2000 Server Resource Kit.* Redmond, Washington: Microsoft Press, 2000. ISBN 1572318058. Contains valuable information on Windows 2000 replication and establishing replication bridges.

 Minasi, Mark, Christa Anderson, and Elizabeth Creegan. *Mastering Windows NT Server 4,* 7th ed. San Francisco: Sybex Network Press, 1997. ISBN 0782126936. Ideal for the basics on Windows NT DNS, DHCP, and WINS configuration.

 Nielsen, Morton Strunge. *Windows 2000 Server Architecture and Planning.* Scottsdale, Arizona: The Coriolis Group, 1999. ISBN 1576104362. Chapters 17, 18, and 19 contain valuable information on migrating from Windows NT to Windows 2000.

 Willis, Will, David V. Watts, and J. Peter Bruzzese. *MCSE Windows 2000 Directory Services Exam Cram.* Scottsdale, Arizona: The Coriolis Group, 2000. ISBN 1576106888. Chapter 3 covers DNS planning in more detail.

 Planning Migration from Windows NT to Windows 2000 White Paper. Redmond, Washington: Microsoft Corporation, 2000. A great source for practical applications of an upgrade process. You can find it at **www.microsoft.com/TechNet/win2000/win2ksrv/technote/migntw2k.asp.**

Migrating to Windows 2000

Terms you'll need to understand:

✓ CD-ROM installation

✓ Network installation

✓ Automatic installation

✓ Replication bridge

✓ DCpromo.exe

✓ Active Directory Installation Wizard

Techniques you'll need to master:

✓ Using three methods to install Windows 2000

✓ Installing DNS

✓ Upgrading domain controllers within a domain in the proper order

✓ Upgrading domains in the proper order

By this time, you should have thoroughly planned your upgrade. This includes establishing the order of upgrades, checking compatibility on both hardware and resident software, and also checking for healthy DNS, WINS, and DHCP seervices on the domain controllers slated for upgrade. This chapter is about the actual upgrade process, including those tasks that need to be done after the upgrade. It is important to keep in mind that migrating any domain, environment, or enterprise is usually not a one-step process. Although we discuss the upgrade only once, the process may need to be repeated several times, depending on the environment. Likewise, several post-upgrade tasks may be performed just once or twice, or they may be performed several times in between upgrade processes.

Upgrading Domain Controllers

There are three methods of launching a Windows 2000 upgrade process: CD-ROM installation, network installation, and automatic installation with Setup Manager.

Perhaps the easiest and most straightforward method, a CD-ROM installation is highly recommended for those first few domain controller upgrades in order to reduce the risk of network connectivity problems during the installation. The easiest method of beginning the CD upgrade is to enable the boot-from-CD feature in the BIOS of the server that is to be upgraded, and then simply reboot the system and follow the prompts. If the system can't be booted from CD, or doesn't have a BIOS that supports booting from CD, then you can start the upgrade by running Setup.exe from the CD.

A network-based upgrade is another option for upgrading Windows NT domain controllers. Consider this option only if you plan to upgrade a plethora of servers and domain controllers. A network upgrade might save you the hassle of keeping track of a CD, but there are two primary reasons not to plan a network upgrade. The first reason is that the network I/O (input/output) will result in a slower upgrade process than would occur if the process were run from the CD. The second reason is simply that network-based upgrades are generally used for mass workstation rollouts. The efforts involved in creating a network-based upgrade are not justified by the time savings of installing just a few servers over the network. As with the older Windows NT installation process, when you install Windows 2000, you need to create a network share, copy the I386 directory from the installation CD to that share, and run Winnt32.exe from within Windows NT. The only hitch: You must create a network client boot disk from within Windows NT in order to boot to the network and subsequently access the distribution share that contains the I386 directory.

Setup Manager is also an option for upgrading to Windows 2000, but it's somewhat more impractical than a network-based upgrade. The reason for this is that

Setup Manager was designed to script unattended installations for large numbers of workstations. What's more, it is designed less for upgrades and more for installations. Therefore, I won't go into Setup Manager details here.

As shown in Figure 6.1, after Winnt32.exe is run from within Windows NT, the Installation Wizard will appear. If you're upgrading, you'll need to select the Upgrade To Windows 2000 option. For restructuring or for fresh installations, select Install A New Copy Of Windows 2000. Remember that Windows NT 3.51 and 4 can be upgraded to Windows 2000, but Windows 9x and Windows 3.x cannot.

After the main upgrade process is complete, the system will automatically detect that the upgraded server is a domain controller and will therefore run Dcpromo.exe. This utility, also known as the Active Directory Installation Wizard, installs and configures Active Directory, and prompts for DNS installation. You don't need to run the wizard in order to have a functioning Windows 2000 system. Therefore, you can cancel the application at any time. However, keep in mind these few things:

➤ The server will not function as a domain controller until Active Directory installation is completed. DNS will function as it did before the upgrade, but because the system cannot authenticate users, DNS becomes useless.

➤ During the Active Directory installation process, if you feel like a mistake has been made, you can cancel the installation. You can then begin it again by running Dcpromo.exe from the Start menu's Run line or by restarting the system.

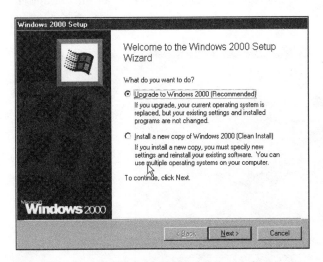

Figure 6.1   The initial Windows 2000 installation window.

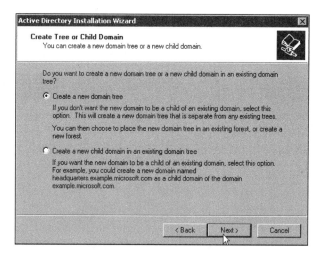

Figure 6.2　Determining what type of domain to create.

As shown in Figure 6.2, the Active Directory Installation Wizard prompts you to create a new domain tree or to create a new child domain in an existing domain tree. Basically, when you're upgrading any master domain or an isolated single domain, you should choose to create a new domain tree. Child domains are the Windows 2000 equivalent of resource, account, and other subdomains within a Windows NT master or multimaster domain model.

As shown in Figure 6.3, the Active Directory Installation Wizard then prompts you to create a new forest of domain trees or to place this new domain tree into an existing forest. It's easy to become confused here, so remember this: A forest

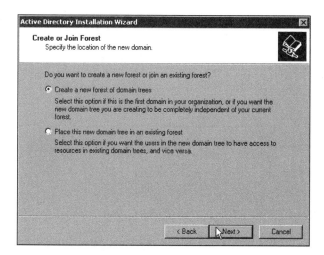

Figure 6.3　Determining whether to create or join a forest.

consists of several domains that trust each other. The NT equivalent of a forest would be a set of master, child, resource, or account domains where several trusts have been established between all of the domains. Therefore, for any domain that belongs to one of these multidomain models and is not a master domain, you should choose to place the new domain tree into an existing forest. Otherwise, for the master domain or any standalone domains, you should create a new forest of domain trees.

To better understand what options you should choose for specific servers, examine Table 6.1.

When you are prompted to enter a full DNS name for a new domain, make it the same name as the old domain, if possible. If the current network DNS is running an older version of BIND, this is where you enter the delegated subdomain name as discussed in Chapter 5.

After you choose the appropriate domain and forest options, the Active Directory Installation Wizard prompts you for the Active Directory database and log locations. Remember that the system will perform better if the database, logs, and SYSVOL share are all located on a drive separate from the drive containing the system partition.

Table 6.1   Wizard options to choose for various servers.

When Upgrading:	Choose	Then:	And Move on to:
The PDC in an isolated domain	Create A New Domain Tree	Create A New Forest	Enter a FQDN (fully qualified domain name) for DNS.
The first PDC in a master domain	Create A New Domain Tree		Enter a FQDN for DNS.
The first PDC in the first master domain that is a member of a master domain model	Create A New Domain Tree	Create A New Forest	Enter a FQDN for DNS.
The first PDC in a secondary master domain	Create A New Domain Tree	Join An Existing Forest	Provide administrative credentials for the forest root domain.
The first PDC in any resource, account, or child domains	Create A Child Domain In An Existing Domain Tree		Provide administrative credentials to the parent domain.
A BDC anywhere	Create A Replica Of An Existing Domain		Provide administrative credentials to the domain.

Take special note here: The SYSVOL share, in particular, must reside on an NTFS 5 partition. Existing NTFS 4 volumes will be converted to NTFS 5 during the Windows 2000 upgrade. If FAT partitions are maintained after the upgrade, be aware that the Active Directory Installation Wizard will fail.

The SYSVOL share must be installed on an NTFS-formatted partition. If one does not exist, it's a good idea to run the Convert.exe program either within Windows NT or after the upgrade and before the Active Directory installation, and convert a FAT or FAT32 partition to NTFS.

After you define the locations of the Active Directory database, log files, and SYSVOL share, the Active Directory Installation Wizard searches the network for the DNS server that was entered earlier. If the wizard does not find the named DNS server, it will prompt you to install DNS.

As shown in Figure 6.4, the Active Directory Installation Wizard also prompts you to loosen permissions in order to make Active Directory compatible with pre-Windows 2000 servers. This is for applications such as RAS that generally don't reside on a domain controller, yet still need to access the database in order to verify access permissions for dial-in users. If this is the case, or if any other applications will need to access user account information anonymously or through a system account, you can loosen permissions by choosing the Permissions Compatible With Pre-Windows 2000 Servers option. Keep in mind, however, that this option also allows for a potential security breach. If security is paramount within the organization, be sure to select the Permissions Compatible Only With Windows 2000 Servers option, and upgrade the RAS (Remote Access Service) or other application server ahead of schedule.

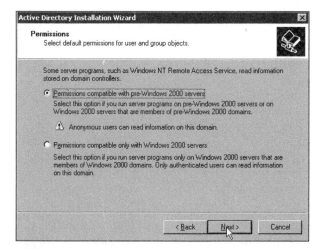

Figure 6.4   Changing permissions in order to accommodate applications that refer to account security information.

A mysterious post-upgrade failure for Windows NT RAS is probably due to the permissions not being set as compatible with pre-Windows 2000 servers.

After you choose a Permissions option, the Active Directory Installation Wizard installs Active Directory. This may take some time, depending on whether or not DNS will be installed. As Figure 6.5 shows, one or more services will be disabled during the installation. As with upgrading, you should install Active Directory in an off-hours time when users will not be attempting to use the system.

Installing DNS

You can install DNS in one of two ways: either add the service, or let the Active Directory Installation Wizard do it for you.

To add the service, you open the Control Panel, choose Add/Remove Programs, and then choose Add/Remove Windows Components. From here, you can install lots of stuff, such as Certificate Services, IIS (Internet Information Server), RIS (Remote Installation Server), and Terminal Services. Under the Windows Components Wizard, select Networking Services and click on the Details button. This is where you select options to install DNS, DHCP (Dynamic Host Configuration Protocol), and WINS (Windows Internet Naming Service).

After you've added the protocol via the Control Panel, you still need to configure DNS. Unlike the DNS installation and configuration process for Windows NT, DNS configuration for Windows 2000 is now integrated into a DNS

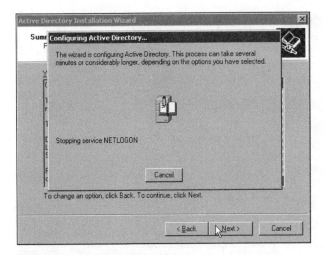

Figure 6.5 Active Directory installation.

Configuration Wizard that does it all for you. Start this wizard by selecting Configure This Server from the Action menu within DNS manager. The wizard prompts you for a domain name and asks if you want to create forward and reverse lookup zones. Keep in mind that, if DNS already exists, existing zones will not be overwritten.

Another means of configuring DNS is by manually creating the DNS domain and its appropriate forward and reverse lookup zones. Forward Lookup Zone and Reverse Lookup Zone folders are created by default when DNS is installed. Create a forward lookup zone by clicking on the Forward Lookup Zone folder and choosing New Zone from the Action menu. In the next window, which contains options for what kind of zone to install, select Standard Primary. Create a reverse lookup zone by clicking on the Reverse Lookup Zone folder and choosing New Zone from the Action menu. Enter the network ID when prompted, and the new file should be filled in as the IP address .in-addr.arpa.dns.

The Active Directory Installation Wizard attempts to contact the server that hosts the DNS zone listed earlier in the installation. If no DNS is detected, the wizard installs it for you. The DNS Configuration Wizard will follow, and it will guide you through the creation of forward and reverse lookup zones.

If the referenced DNS server is not on the current Windows 2000 machine, the Active Directory Installation Wizard tries to find it on the network. If the wizard does not find the DNS server, you will receive the message shown in Figure 6.6. If the wizard does find the server, the wizard then checks it for the dynamic update and SRV record functionality required for Active Directory DNS. If these things are present, the Active Directory installation will move forward to the permissions dialog as shown in Figure 6.4. If dynamic update and SRV record

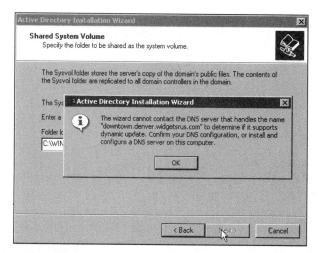

Figure 6.6   Active Directory notification that the DNS server is unavailable.

functionality are not present, a dialog box will appear, notifying you that dynamic update is not supported on the named server, and prompting you to install DNS on the local machine.

Upgrading DNS

The Windows 2000 upgrade automatically upgrades any installed, clean, and functional Windows NT DNS before running the Active Directory Installation Wizard. Actually, the upgrade application also upgrades any installed, dirty, and broken Windows NT DNS system before running the Active Directory Installation Wizard. The key here is that during Active Directory installation, if the Active Directory Installation Wizard cannot detect the server that is hosting the named DNS, the prompt shown in Figure 6.6 will appear. If DNS already exists on the network or on the current system, the Active Directory Installation Wizard will not prompt for installation, but rather will display the dialog box shown in Figure 6.5 and proceed to configure Active Directory. Therefore, it might be a good idea to pause or cancel the Active Directory installation process and check on the healthiness of the DNS server.

If you are positive that DNS is running, yet the Active Directory Installation Wizard isn't talking to the DNS server, the first thing to do is to monitor DNS via the server properties within DNS manager. As shown in Figure 6.7, you can select A Simple Query Against This DNS Server to have the DNS server test its own name resolution functionality, and determine if it will work appropriately. A

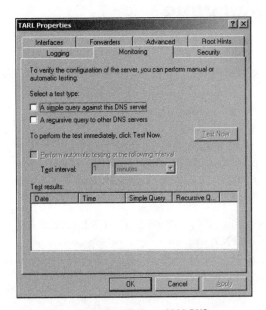

Figure 6.7 Monitoring Windows 2000 DNS.

successful test will show positive results in the test results window. If the test is successful, and the Active Directory Installation Wizard still does not detect the DNS server, try pinging the indicated domain name and checking Event Viewer for any DNS problems. You can also attempt to run the DNS Configuration Wizard by choosing Configure This Server from the Action menu. This will completely reconfigure DNS for you, but it will not overwrite the current zone files. What you can do instead is point the wizard at the zone files that already exist. This will basically serve the purpose of re-initializing DNS for you.

It is also possible to create new zones and point them to the older files. However, the redundancy and file sharing issue requires that you delete the original zones while preventing their underlying zone files from being deleted also, so that they can survive to be the basis for new zones. Considering the risk factors associated with this particular plan, it's recommended that you exhaust all other measures before proceeding down this road.

 Although the Active Directory Installation Wizard behaves just like any other application in that you can pause the progress and press Alt+Tab to check on DNS, it's a good idea to cancel the Active Directory Installation Wizard while troubleshooting DNS. The Active Directory Installation Wizard can be restarted at any time by running Dcpromo.exe from the Start menu, Run command.

Installing DHCP and WINS

The Windows 2000 upgrade will automatically upgrade DHCP and WINS. Both DHCP installation and WINS installation have improved significantly over Windows NT DHCP and WINS configuration. Both protocols can be installed easily by running the Add/Remove Programs applet from within the Control Panel and selecting the Add/Remove Windows Components button. Select Networking Services, and click on the Details button. The details will list available network-flavored services that can be installed. Among these are DNS, DHCP, and WINS. Select DHCP, click on OK, and then click on install. The installation will request the Windows 2000 CD. After that, the installation is quick and seamless and doesn't even require a reboot of the server.

After each of these protocols is installed, they will need to be configured. Configuration is very similar to Windows NT, with entry into the appropriate management program via Start|Programs|Administrative Tools|WINS Manager or DHCP Manager.

As far as the exam is concerned, DHCP configuration will need to be correct for not only the IP address but also items such as the default gateway address, the DNS server address, and WINS server addressing.

Handling Replication

As discussed briefly in Chapters 4 and 5, replication in a mixed-mode environment can be tricky. At this stage, you should have as much replication as possible centralized within the Windows NT network, and you should have planned to upgrade that centralized export server after every other server on the network.

After doing the upgrade, you need to configure a replication bridge in order to handle the replication between the Windows 2000 system and the Windows NT systems. Just like building a bridge between two cities, we have an NT city and a Windows 2000 city. First we need to anchor the sides of the bridge by designating a Windows NT replication server and a Windows 2000 domain controller. Then we make sure that the roads on the NT side of the bridge are open to designated locations (servers) within the NT city. Next, we open traffic going to the NT city, and then open traffic going to the Windows 2000 city. It is not necessary to make sure that the roads on the Windows 2000 side are open to designated locations because the Windows 2000 city is a much more advanced city that automatically conveys traffic where it needs to go. The steps are as follows:

1. Anchor each side of the bridge to a designated Windows NT replication server and a Windows 2000 domain controller. In order to avoid rebuilding the bridge after every server upgrade, the Windows NT replication server should be one of the last to be upgraded. Figure 5.7 in Chapter 5 will help you gain a better idea of this concept.

2. Make sure that the roads on the NT side are open. Using the known list of import and export servers on the network, re-configure all Windows NT import servers to expect data from the appropriate designated central replication server. We configure these roads going from the NT side of the bridge by checking the properties of each import server within Server Manager and clicking on the Replication button. Remove any entries from the import window, and then add the appropriate entries back into the import window so that they point to the NT replication server.

3. Allow traffic to go to the NT city. Create a batch file on the Windows 2000 domain controller that will be the Windows 2000 replication server. The batch file will copy the contents of the SYSVOL share into the import directory of the NT replication server. A similar batch file called 1-bridge.cmd

can be found in the Windows 2000 Resource Kit. The batch file should basically look like this:

```
XCOPY \\WIN2K\SYSVOL \\NTREPL\EXPORT /S /D
```

where **WIN2K** represents the Windows 2000 replication server, and **NTREPL** represents the NT replication server. **/S** will copy subdirectories, and **/D** will copy updated files. Within the batch file, another similar line should be implemented that brings any Windows NT data into the Windows 2000 system appropriately. The export directory must be shared with appropriate permissions such that the Windows 2000 replication server can access and write to that directory. Configure the Windows 2000 Task Scheduler to run this batch file as often as necessary.

4. Open traffic to go to the Windows 2000 city. Configure the NT replication server to ship all the data located in the export directory out to the other NT import servers on the network. Again, do this via Server Properties within Server Manager. Steps 1 and 4 will handle the NT side of the replication bridge.

5. The Windows 2000 replication of the SYSVOL volume will occur automatically, thus handling the Windows 2000 replication bridge.

Lbridge.cmd is a Windows 2000 Resource Kit script that can be used to synchronize Windows 2000 and Windows NT 4 replication. This file defaults to using Xcopy, but can also employ the services of Robocopy.

Establishing Sites

After upgrading multiple domains, you need to establish Active Directory sites and site links between subnets. From within Active Directory Sites And Services, you'll notice that a default first site has been created automatically. Windows 2000 domain controllers will be added to the default site as they are upgraded into the domain.

It's highly recommended that any domain controllers residing on a separate subnet be added to a separate site within Active Directory Sites And Services. The exception to this guideline would normally be a situation in which a subnet has been created in the same physical location to isolate and reduce traffic and to increase security.

Create a site within Active Directory Sites And Services by choosing Create A New Site from the Action menu. After you create the new site, you'll need to configure additional subnet information; however, keep in mind that this information will not be covered in the exam.

Practice Questions

Case Study

Company

Ipwitch, Inc., is a manufacturer of popular holiday and celebratory costumes. Although security is not the company's main concern, it is an important factor in day-to-day operations. Management's main concern at Ipwitch involves maintaining the production schedule, which is 24 hours a day, 7 days a week.

Background

To take advantage of the additional stability and security features available with Active Directory, and to best maintain the production schedule, Ipwitch has decided that the network needs to be running Windows 2000. The company has determined that an upgrade will have the least impact on the production environment. The company has also determined that the Windows 2000 domain name will be **ipwitch.net**.

Ipwitch, Inc., consists of three major departments: administration, engineering, and manufacturing. The administration group consists of 100 computers running Windows 95 and Windows 2000 Professional. The engineering group consists of 50 computers running Windows 3.1 and Windows 2000 Professional. The manufacturing group consists of 500 computers running Windows NT Workstation 4 SP3.

Existing Domain Configuration

Ipwitch has three domains: **admin, mfg,** and **engineering.** Both the **engineering** and **mfg**domains trust the **admin** domain. The **admin** and **engineering** domains both reside on the same subnet network. The **mfg** domain is connected to the other two domains via a 56Kbps WAN link.

Existing Network Infrastructure

The **admin** domain contains a Windows NT 4 PDC; a Windows NT 4 BDC running DNS, WINS, and DHCP; an Exchange 5.5 server running on Windows 3.51; and a member server running a proprietary human-resources application.

The **engineering** domain contains a Windows NT 3.51 PDC running DHCP, and a member server running several server-based CAD (computer-aided design) applications.

The **mfg** domain is running with a Windows NT 4 PDC, an NT 4 BDC running DHCP, an Exchange server, and a member server running a proprietary manufacturing application that runs all of the robots on the assembly line.

Your Assignment

Upgrade the network—starting with the **admin** domain and finishing with the **mfg** domain—in such a manner as to produce as little downtime for members of the **mfg** domain as possible.

The following five questions are based upon this case study.

Question 1

List the steps that need to occur to upgrade the PDC located in the **admin** domain. [Check all correct answers]

❏ a. Run Setup32.exe from the Windows 2000 installation CD.

❏ b. Run Winnt32.exe from the Windows 2000 installation CD.

❏ c. Promote the human-resources member server to a BDC and take it offline.

❏ d. Take the PDC offline, and promote the BDC to a PDC.

❏ e. Install DNS on the PDC.

❏ f. Name the DNS server **ipwitch.net**.

❏ g. Loosen permissions to be compatible with non-Windows 2000 servers.

❏ h. Take the BDC offline.

Answers b, e, f, g, and h are correct. Answer b is correct because Winnt32.exe will begin the upgrade process whenever a boot CD-ROM drive is unavailable. Answer e is correct because you'll need to install DNS on the PDC. Not only is the DNS server offline, but Windows NT 4 DNS does not support dynamic update or SRV records, and the Active Directory Installation Wizard will reject it as an appropriate DNS server. Answer f is correct because **ipwitch.net** is the designated name of the new domain. Answer g is correct because the domain will be running in mixed mode with other Windows NT servers. Answer h is correct because you'll need to take the BDC offline. Because DNS is installed on this system, DNS should be removed when it's safe to bring the BDC back online. Because the BDC also handles DHCP and WINS, this system should be the next to be upgraded. Answer a is incorrect because Setup32.exe will not install Windows 2000. Answer c is incorrect because you cannot promote a member server to a domain controller without reinstalling it. This would violate the requirement of reducing downtime as much as possible. Answer d is incorrect.

Although taking a PDC offline and promoting a BDC is a viable backout solution (especially because upgrading DNS, WINS, and DHCP might be more reasonable), taking a BDC offline is the preferred method for providing a fallback in the event of an upgrade failure.

Question 2

> List the correct order for the following steps for upgrading the network.
>
> Upgrade the PDC in the **admin** domain.
>
> Upgrade the PDC in the **mfg** domain.
>
> Upgrade the PDC in the **engineering** domain.
>
> Upgrade the BDC in the **admin** domain as a replica of the **admin** domain.
>
> Define the PDC in the **admin** domain as the forest root.
>
> Configure the PDC in the **mfg** domain to join an existing forest.
>
> Configure the PDC in the **engineering** domain to join an existing forest.
>
> Upgrade the BDC in the **mfg** domain as a replica of the **mfg** domain.
>
> Switch the domains to native mode.

The correct order is:

Upgrade the PDC in the **admin** domain.

Define the PDC in the **admin** domain as the forest root.

Upgrade the BDC in the **admin** domain as a replica of the **admin** domain.

Upgrade the PDC in the **engineering** domain.

Configure the PDC in the **engineering** domain to join an existing forest.

Upgrade the PDC in the **mfg** domain.

Configure the PDC in the **mfg** domain to join an existing forest.

Upgrade the BDC in the **mfg** domain as a replica of the **mfg** domain.

Switch the domains to native mode.

The first thing to do is to upgrade the PDC in what would be considered the master domain, which is **admin** (a), and define it as the forest root (e). Then, because the BDC in the **admin** domain is running DHCP and WINS, and because it serves systems on the entire network, the BDC should be upgraded next (d). Because it is a BDC, it should be configured as a replica of an existing domain—the **admin** domain (d). Next, upgrade the PDC in the **engineering** domain (c), and join it to the existing forest under the **admin** domain (g). Then upgrade the **mfg** domain (b), and configure it to join an existing forest (f). Finally, upgrade the BDC in the **mfg** domain as a replica of the **mfg** domain (h), and because all of the domain controllers have been upgraded, switch to native mode in each domain (i).

Question 3

After upgrading the PDC and BDC computers located in the **admin** domain, James, a member of the **admin** domain, is unable to use resources located in the **mfg** domain. You ping the fully qualified domain name of the PDC in the **mfg** domain and determine that the server is unreachable. What should be done to solve this problem?

○ a. Create a replication bridge.

○ b. Reconfigure DHCP with the new DNS address.

○ c. Add a new record in WINS for the PDC in the **mfg** domain.

○ d. Modify the LMHOSTS file located on James's computer with the IP address of the PDC in the **mfg** domain.

Answer b is correct. The DNS server changed from the **admin** BDC to the **admin** PDC; therefore, DHCP needs to be configured to serve the appropriate DNS server address. Answer a is incorrect because creating a replication bridge will not change the authentication or accessibility of any servers. Answers c and d are incorrect because name resolution would come into play if only pinging the IP address of the PDC were successful and pinging the name of the PDC were unsuccessful.

Question 4

After upgrading the PDC in the **admin** domain, you find it necessary to change the logon script on the Windows 2000 PDC to add more drive mappings. You create a site link bridge on the **admin** PDC to copy the contents of the SYSVOL share to the **admin** Exchange computer, and set it up to run every two hours. You notice that when users log in, sometimes they don't receive the appropriate drive mappings. What do you need to do to finish creating the site link bridge? [Check all correct answers]

- ❑ a. Configure the Exchange server with appropriate permissions on the export directory.
- ❑ b. Configure the Exchange server to replicate to the BDC.
- ❑ c. Configure the BDC import directory to receive data from the Exchange server.
- ❑ d. Configure the BDC import directory with appropriate permissions.

Answers a, b, c, and d are correct. Because the problem happens only occasionally, it's safe to assume that the affected users are logging onto the domain via the BDC. You then know that the BDC is not receiving the logon scripts appropriately. To finish creating the site link bridge, you need to check all of the replication components associated with the Windows NT side of the bridge. This includes checking permissions on both the Exchange server and the BDC, and configuring the export and import replication on the Exchange server and the BDC, respectively.

Question 5

Before upgrading the **admin** domain, you configured the DNS located on the BDC with the same DNS configuration that you planned for the Windows 2000 DNS. What's the best way to use the current DNS in the upgraded domain?

- ○ a. Run jetpack.exe on the DNS database.
- ○ b. Manually copy the database into the new DNS database structure.
- ○ c. Run dnsexp.exe on the NT 4 DNS to export the database, and run Dnsexp.exe on the Windows 2000 DNS database to bring the data in.
- ○ d. Copy the DNS database files to the PDC. During the Windows 2000 DNS installation, select the database files for the appropriate forward and reverse lookup zones.

Answer d is correct. During DNS installation and specifically during the DNS Configuration Wizard, DNS allows for another DNS zone file to be used instead of creating a new one. Answer a is incorrect because jetpack.exe is a DHCP and WINS utility. Answer b is incorrect because copying the databases will not cause DNS to recognize them. Answer c is incorrect because there is no dnsexp.exe utility.

Question 6

After upgrading the PDC and BDC computers located in the **admin** domain, James, a member of the **admin** domain, is unable to use resources located in the **mfg** domain. You ping the IP address of the PDC in the **mfg** domain and determine that the server is unreachable. Upon further examination, you determine that none of the systems in the ADMIN domain are able to reach resources in the **mfg** domain, yet systems in the MFG domain are functioning appropriately. What should be done to solve this problem?

- ○ a. Configure DHCP with the default gateway address.
- ○ b. Reconfigure DHCP with the new DNS address.
- ○ c. Add a new record in WINS for the PDC in the **mfg** domain.
- ○ d. Modify the LMHOSTS file located on James's computer with the IP address of the PDC in the **mfg** domain.

Answer a is correct. Because no resources located in the **mfg** domain are available, an incorrect default gateway is the best answer. Answer b is incorrect because DHCP is not being used when pinging an IP address. Answers c and d are incorrect because name resolution would come into play only if pinging the IP address of the PDC were successful and pinging the name of the PDC were unsuccessful.

Need to Know More?

 Boswell, William. *Inside Windows 2000 Server*. Indianapolis: New Riders Press, 2000. ISBN 1562059297. Boswell has spent incredible amounts of lab and field time determining exactly how all functions of Windows 2000 work. He provides incredible information on Active Directory Sites And Services replication.

 Microsoft Corporation. *MCSE Training Kit Microsoft Windows 2000 Server*. Redmond, WA: Microsoft Press, 2000. ISBN 1572319038. Chapter 2, on installing and configuring Windows 2000 Server, contains valuable information on the installation process.

 Willis, W., David Watts, and J. Peter Bruzzese. *MCSE Windows 2000 Directory Services Exam Cram*. Scottsdale, AZ: The Coriolis Group, 2000. ISBN 1576106888. Contains valuable information on Active Directory installation and post-upgrade functionality.

 www.microsoft.com/technet/win2000/win2ksrv/technote/ migntw2k.asp—"Planning Migration from Windows NT to Windows 2000." This white paper is a great source for practical applications of an upgrade process.

 www.microsoft.com/windows2000/upgrade/pathwinnt4351serv.asp— "How to Upgrade from Windows NT Server 3.51 or 4.0." This document provides an awesome central guide for the entire upgrade process, soup-to-nuts. The document contains several links to more detailed information on the upgrade process.

 www.microsoft.com/windows2000/upgrade/path/winnt4ent.asp— "How to Upgrade from Windows NT Server 4.0, Enterprise Edition." This is similar to the previous document, but provides additional information for larger, multidomain enterprises.

Planning the Restructuring

Terms you'll need to understand:

✓ Domain restructuring
✓ Site
✓ Forest
✓ Transitive trust
✓ Nontransitive trust
✓ Explicit trust
✓ Shortcut trust

✓ Tree
✓ Domain
✓ Organizational unit (OU)
✓ Interforest restructuring
✓ Intraforest restructuring
✓ Cloning

Techniques you'll need to master:

✓ Describing and recognizing the differences between the various components of the physical and logical structures of Active Directory

✓ Describing the effect on trust relationships when you're migrating source domains to target domains

✓ Describing and understanding the differences between the four common NT 4 domain models and the effect of migrating each of these to a Windows 2000 environment

✓ Understanding the different requirements for moving security principals and for cloning security principals

✓ Understanding the difference between interforest and intraforest restructuring

✓ Understanding the implications, including the effects on SIDs and resource access, when you move or clone security principals

Earlier chapters have discussed domain upgrades. This chapter discusses domain restructuring, which is usually done when the existing model is out-of-date or no longer supports the needs of the business. Restructuring can include migrating users, groups, and resources from a Windows NT 4 domain to a Windows 2000 domain, or from a Windows 2000 domain in one forest to a Windows 2000 domain in another forest.

You need to be familiar with two types of domain restructuring: interforest restructuring and intraforest restructuring. An interforest restructuring involves copying (cloning) security principals to a target domain that is in a different forest than the source domain. An intraforest restructuring requires that you move security principals between two domains in the same forest. Security principals include Active Directory objects like user accounts, groups, and machine accounts. Cloning and moving security principals do share some similarities, but each method also raises its own issues that need to be addressed for a successful migration. Before we get into the details of each of these restructuring scenarios, it's probably a good idea to review some of the fundamentals of both the Windows 2000 and the NT 4 domain environments so that we have a baseline to build from when we get into the more advanced topics. Therefore, we'll begin with an overview of the domain structure for each of these operating systems.

The Windows 2000 Active Directory is divided into two distinct and separate structures: the physical structure and the logical structure. Each of these serves a different purpose, and this section will help you understand each structure's roles and components. A complete understanding of these two structures will help you to decide on the appropriate restructuring path based on the specific needs of your organization.

Purpose of the Physical Structure

The purpose of the Active Directory physical structure is to control replication traffic and the authentication process through the use of sites, subnets, and site links. A *site* is defined as one or more "well-connected" IP subnets; that is to say, the subnets in a site have a fast and reliable connection between them. "Fast" and "reliable" are fairly ambiguous and are defined by an administrator based on the available bandwidth. Each organization has different types and speeds of connections, so Microsoft has left the definition of a high-speed connection up to you, to base on your own environment. One thing that sites do have in common is that they generally correspond with specific geographical areas because a local LAN connection is usually much faster than a WAN connection between geographically dispersed locations.

When you install Active Directory, Windows creates an initial default site called "Default-First-Site-Name." If you don't manually configure additional sites, all subsequent domain controllers created in the forest will be placed in this site by default. Sites are created by associating IP subnets to a particular site name. Machines will automatically join their assigned sites when they boot by querying Active Directory when they first boot up. The exception to this is domain controllers. Domain controllers will place themselves in the site associated to their subnet only upon initial installation. From that point on, administrators will need to manually move domain controllers. This is so you can assign domain controller to sites without regard to IP subnet. Microsoft designed this system so that administrators could control two types of bandwidth-intensive traffic: authentication and replication.

Every site has at least one subnet associated with it. The IP address of the site-aware client from which a user logs on also determines what site the client is a member of, based on the subnets associated with a specific site. Site-aware clients include members of the Windows 2000 operating system family, plus NT 4, Windows 98, and Windows 95 clients with the DS (Directory Services) client software installed. During the logon process, a client queries DNS for a list of domain controllers. For site-aware clients, DNS returns a list based on the site that the client is in. At the top of the list will be the domain controllers that are members of the same site as the site-aware client. The client will always try to authenticate with a domain controller located in its own site first. This has a major impact on cross-domain authentication traffic because the only time a site-aware client will contact a home-domain controller in another site is when a domain controller in its own site does not respond to the authentication request.

One of the biggest disadvantages of Windows NT 4 domains is that it is difficult to schedule when directory replication will occur across a slow WAN connection. This means that you cannot schedule replication to occur during periods of low WAN usage to avoid using the link during business hours when traffic is the highest. In Windows 2000, in what's called *multimaster replication,* the replication of the Active Directory database occurs between all domain controllers within a domain. This is where sites come in handy. You can create a site for every geographical location that is separated by a slow connection, and you can then configure when directory replication occurs across each link. You do this by setting a replication schedule and an interval on the site link. The schedule identifies the time the link is available and the interval is the polling times that the domain controllers will use to contact the controllers across the link. Remember, site links only affect replication traffic. Resource access can occur anytime. You can use sites to limit resource access when combined with the Distributed File System (DFS), but for the most part sites are primarily used to prevent the link from being used for directory replication during times of peak usage.

Purpose of the Logical Structure

The purpose of the Active Directory logical structure is to allow the simplification of both the design of the network architecture and the administration of the network. The Active Directory logical structure is significantly more scalable than the Windows NT 4 directory service structure. With Windows 2000, there is no longer a 40,000-user account limit, and Active Directory can theoretically contain millions of objects. The logical structure of Active Directory consists of four primary components:

➤ Forests

➤ Trees

➤ Domains

➤ Organizational units (OUs)

In Windows NT 4, domains were used to define specific administrative boundaries. This is still applicable in Windows 2000, but now you can also replace the resource domains in Windows NT 4 with organizational units (OUs) in an Active Directory environment. You then have the benefit of delegating administrative authority over the resources located in an OU to one or more users. This granularity helps simplify administration by reducing the number of domains and trust relationships that existed between these domains in the old NT 4 environment.

Forests

The first component of the logical structure is a forest. A *forest* is defined as one or more trees that share a common global catalog, schema, and configuration. When you create the first Windows 2000 domain, it becomes the *forest root domain*. Certain built-in groups created by the operating system exist only in the forest root domain. These groups include:

➤ Enterprise Admins

➤ Schema Admins

Every domain has a built-in Administrators group, but the forest root domain has these two additional default groups in addition to the Domain Admins group. These special forest-level groups have even more privileges than the Domain Admins group. The Enterprise Admins group initially contains only one member, which is the administrator account on the first domain controller in the forest. This root domain administrator has forest-wide administrative rights and is capable of creating sites and authorizing services. The Schema Admins group also contains only one default member, which is that same administrator account.

This is the only account that, by default, can change the schema. Because Enterprise Admins and Schema Admins are groups like any other, the enterprise administrator can place additional users into either of these groups.

Note: It is critical that you have a well-thought-out forest root domain because after it's implemented, it cannot be renamed. To rename the forest root domain, you have to re-create your entire forest structure.

All of the trees in a forest share several common components:

➤ A schema

➤ A global catalog

➤ Transitive trusts

 For the exam, remember that to perform a migration between forests, the user account performing the migration has to be a member of the Enterprise Admins group in both the source and destination forest.

The Schema

The schema can be thought of as the Active Directory database template because it defines the types of object classes and object attributes that can be created in the directory. The schema is also *extensible,* which means that an administrator with the appropriate permissions can add object classes or attributes to the schema in order to meet the unique requirements of an organization. To modify the schema, you must first enable Schema Modification in the Active Directory Schema MMC snap-in, and you must be a member of the Schema Admins group, which is found only in the forest root domain. A default schema is created when you promote the first domain controller in the forest. The default schema contains those objects and attributes that Microsoft has determined to be the most widely used in most organizations.

The Global Catalog

A global catalog (GC) server is a specialized role held by a domain controller. The GC contains a list of all of the objects in the entire forest but maintains only a partial list of each object's attributes. A domain controller that is not a global catalog server contains a list of only the objects within its own domain, plus all of the attributes of those objects.

The first domain controller installed in a forest is automatically configured as a global catalog server. Other global catalog servers must be
created manually; you do this by configuring a domain controller as a
GC server in the Active Directory Sites and Services MMC snap-in.

Trusts

A *domain trust* is a relationship, established between two domains, that enables
users in one domain to be authenticated by a domain controller in the other
domain. The authentication requests follow a trust path. A *trust path* is the series
of trust relationships that authentication requests must follow between domains.
Before a user can access a resource in another domain, Windows 2000 security
must determine whether the *trusting* domain (the domain containing the resource that the user is trying to access) has a trust relationship with the *trusted*
domain (the user's logon domain). To determine this, the Windows 2000 security system computes the trust path between a domain controller in the trusting
domain and a domain controller in the trusted domain. Windows 2000 provides
several types of trusts:

➤ Two-way transitive trusts

➤ Nontransitive, explicit trusts

➤ External trusts

➤ Shortcut trusts

Two-Way Transitive Trusts

Active Directory automatically establishes two-way transitive trusts between a
parent domain and a child domain when a new child domain is added to the
forest. Active Directory also establishes two-way transitive trusts between all tree
root domains located in the same forest. A two-way transitive trust is a combination of a two-way trust and a transitive trust. In a *two-way trust*, each domain
allows users to access resources in the other domain. A *transitive trust* means that
I will trust you and anyone you trust. This makes it easy to manage access as you
have the ability to assign resource access to anyone in your forest without having
to create and maintain a complex trusted and trusting relationship.

Figure 7.1 shows two trees: **yoohoo.com** and **boohoo.com**. The three domains in
the same tree—**yoohoo.com**, **old.yoohoo.com**, and **new.yoohoo.com**—show how
two-way transitive trusts work between domains in the same tree. The child domains **old.yoohoo.com** and **new.yoohoo.com** have two-way transitive trusts established with their parent domain, **yoohoo.com**; these trusts were established by
default when the child domains were created. If a user in **old.yoohoo.com** wants

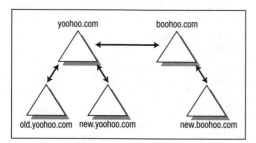

Figure 7.1   Two-way transitive trusts.

to access a resource, such as a server, in **new.yoohoo.com**, the user first accesses **yoohoo.com** through the transitive trust between **old.yoohoo.com** and **yoohoo.com**, and then accesses **new.yoohoo.com** through the transitive trust between **yoohoo.com** and **new.yoohoo.com**. This means that a user with the appropriate permissions in one domain in a forest has access to resources in all other domains in the forest.

The two-way transitive trust between **yoohoo.com** and **boohoo.com** would be established by default when **boohoo.com** was joined as a separate tree in the existing **yoohoo.com** forest. As with the interdomain resource access discussed earlier, a user with the appropriate permissions in any domain in this forest would have access to resources in all other trees in the forest.

Note: Transitive trusts are the default trusts in Windows 2000 domains. In Windows NT 4, only explicit (one-way) trusts were used. For a two-way trust to exist, an administrator had to create two explicit one-way trusts, one in each direction, between the two NT 4 domains. For a Windows 2000 domain and an NT 4 domain to have a trust relationship, you must manually create an explicit trust relationship between the two domains.

Nontransitive Trusts

A *nontransitive trust*, which is an *explicit trust*, is bounded by the two domains in the trust relationship and does not flow to any other domains in the forest. In most cases, you must manually (explicitly) create nontransitive trusts. Explicit trusts are one-way trusts that give a user access to resources in only the trusting domain. When you're creating an explicit trust, one domain becomes the trusting domain, and the other becomes the trusted domain. The trusted domain is the domain that contains the users to whom you want to grant access to the resources. One way to remember this is to think that Ed is a user in the trustED domain and the trusTING domain has the TINGS you want to share. The trusting domain is the domain that contains the resources you want to grant access to. There are two kinds of nontransitive trusts: external trusts and shortcut trusts.

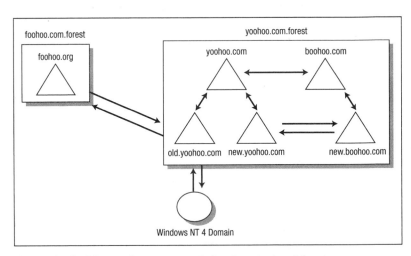

Figure 7.2 Explicit trusts between separate forests and external domains.

External trusts allow user authentication to a domain outside a forest. Figure 7.2 shows an example of external explicit trusts created between a Windows 2000 forest and both an external Windows 2000 domain (**foohoo.org**) and a Windows NT 4 domain.

Shortcut Trusts

Shortcut trusts shorten the trust path between two Windows 2000 domains in a complex forest. A shortcut trust allows direct access to resources in one of the two corresponding domains, as opposed to traversing the entire domain tree between **new.yoohoo.com** and **new.boohoo.com** as shown in Figure 7.1. A shortcut trust is a special kind of Windows-2000-only explicit (one-way) trust and therefore must be created in both directions to allow access to and from both domains. Shortcut trusts, due to their explicit nature, are not transitive. Figure 7.3 shows an example of two shortcut trusts that have been manually created to allow direct resource access between the **new.yoohoo.com** domain and the **new.boohoo.com** domain. You create and manage nontransitive trusts by using the Active Directory Domains and Trusts MMC snap-in.

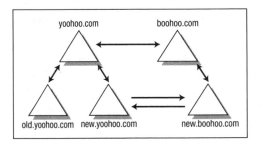

Figure 7.3 Shortcut trusts.

Trees

A *tree* consists of one or more domains arranged, in a hierarchical structure, that all share a contiguous DNS namespace. The parent and child **yoohoo.com** domains in Figure 7.1 are an example of a single tree in a forest with more than one tree. All new domains added to the existing tree will share the namespace of the parent domain, which in this case is **yoohoo.com**. Therefore, the fully qualified domain name of the "old" domain is **old.yoohoo.com**.

If your Active Directory design requires support for a single contiguous namespace, then a single tree should suffice. Having more than one tree would result in a non-contiguous DNS namespace, such as the one shown in Figure 7.1. This figure shows two trees, **yoohoo.com** and **boohoo.com**, in the same forest, with each tree having its own domain namespace. The addition of separate trees in a forest allows an organization to incorporate multiple DNS namespaces into a single forest.

Domains

Domains act as security boundaries and replication boundaries in Windows 2000. A *domain* is a logical grouping of resources that share the same security or administrative needs. Each Windows 2000 domain can be a member of only one forest. By default, all domain controllers in the same domain replicate Active Directory object information to every other domain controller in the same domain every five minutes. This default interval is configurable with a Registry change.

Organizational Units

OUs are similar to the NT 4 concept of domains, but OUs offer a lot more flexibility. You can create multiple OUs in order to logically organize Active Directory objects—such as users, groups, and computers—into a structure that will simplify management. One common use for OUs is to allow existing Windows NT 4 domains to be collapsed into a single Windows 2000 Active Directory domain. In this scenario, you move or clone the objects from an existing NT 4 resource domain into a Windows 2000 Active Directory OU. This shift reduces the number of domains from the old environment and has the added benefit of allowing the administrator to delegate authority of the OU to the previous domain administrator or to another user. This way the previous domain administrator still has full administrative control over the same objects but not over any other objects outside that OU. OUs are designed to minimize and replace Windows NT 4 account and resource domains.

NT 4 Domain Structure

This section discusses the Windows NT 4 domain models and suggests planning solutions for their migration to Active Directory. Four basic NT 4 domain models are used by the majority of organizations. These models include:

➤ Single domain model

➤ Single-master domain model

➤ Multiple-master domain model

➤ Complete trust model

The Single Domain Model

This is the simplest domain architecture possible in a Windows NT 4 topology. In this model, you have one primary domain controller (PDC), which holds the master copy of the Security Accounts Manager (SAM) database. In addition, there is usually one or more backup domain controllers (BDCs). All user accounts, computer accounts, and resource definitions (such as shares and printers) are represented by unique security identifiers (SIDs) within the SAM database on the PDC. These accounts are granted rights based on access control entries (ACEs) in the access control lists (ACLs) that exist for each resource that is being shared or restricted. By definition, there is only one Read/Write copy of the SAM database that can be modified at any given time, and the database is always stored on the computer that is functioning as the PDC.

Note: Almost all domains will also contain BDCs (backup domain controllers), which contain a Read-Only copy of the SAM database. BDCs receive all changes from the PDC in a way that's similar to a zone transfer in DNS.

When you're migrating a single domain, the result is almost always another single domain in Active Directory. However, many of the new features of Active Directory, such as the OU hierarchy and the delegation of administrative rights, can be used to better arrange and administer this single domain.

Organizing users and resources into an Active Directory hierarchical OU namespace gives you a much clearer representation of the actual business structure reflected in the domain. The new delegation features also allow an administrator to assign users or groups very granular administrative rights, such as allowing the ability to reset passwords in only a single OU, or allowing only the ability to create computer accounts in the domain. Figure 7.4 shows the result of restructuring a single domain.

Migrating a single domain is usually done through a domain upgrade, which was discussed in an earlier chapter. In a domain upgrade, the domain's PDC will be the first domain controller upgraded to Windows 2000, followed by all BDCs. Your domain's existing NetBIOS name will remain for backward compatibility, and a DNS name will be assigned to your new Windows 2000 domain.

Upgrading the PDC in a Windows NT 4 domain to Windows 2000 will automatically upgrade the PDC to a Windows 2000 member server and then promote this member server to a domain controller (using the Active Directory Installation Wizard, dcpromo.exe). When the promotion is completed, all user accounts will reside in the Users container, and all computer accounts will reside in the Computers container, by default.

 The Users container and the Computers container are not OUs and therefore cannot have group policies applied to them. You might want to plan for migrating these objects to an OU that you have created in advance for their use.

The Single-Master Domain Model

The single-master domain model in NT was a logical choice for organizations that required decentralized resource administration or the ability to logically organize resources. This model normally consists of one account domain,

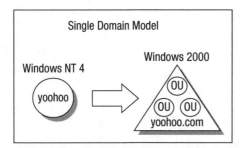

Figure 7.4 Restructuring a single NT domain into an Active Directory domain with organizational units.

containing all of the user accounts and global groups, along with additional resource domains, containing all of the resources. The single-master domain containing the user accounts is trusted by all of the resource domains. You might find this model used in a larger organization that creates a single account domain for all company employees, and creates individual resource domains for each department or geographical location. The resources, such as files and printers, can then be located within each departmental resource domain and administered in either a centralized or a decentralized manner.

An NT single-master domain is typically migrated in a top-to-bottom manner. The master domain is the first domain to be migrated, and the resource domains are migrated later. Depending on whether the company has a centralized or decentralized administrative model, you may find that your entire organization can be restructured into one domain. If you are using a centralized administrative model, you can use the existing organizational structure to mirror the proposed target domain structure. Figure 7.5 shows two possible restructuring scenarios.

This model also allows you to move resources gradually from resource domains to the new target domain. This can be a very effective approach if an organization wants to migrate from several domains to a single domain and wants to convert

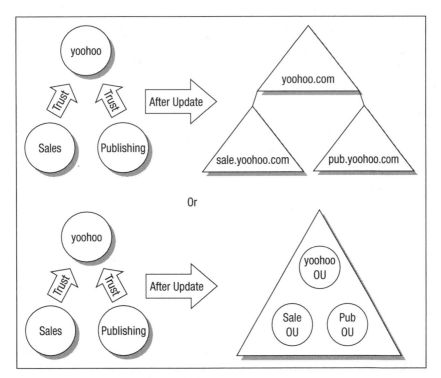

Figure 7.5 Two scenarios for restructuring an NT singlemaster domain.

the resource domains into OUs in the new target domain. This approach also allows administrators to maintain centralized control while allowing a finer granularity of administrative delegation.

Another approach is to use the flexibility of domain trees by assigning the resource domains to their own tree(s) and moving the user accounts to a domain where they can be administered separately; this could even be into their own designated tree. This scheme can result in a more decentralized administrative structure that allows individual users and groups to be managed independently of the resources they access.

This model can also work well for an organization that is often involved in mergers and acquisitions because it allows the company to buy and sell business units while treating them as separate companies. These business units can then have complete independence in areas where they might differ, such as their accounting and hiring decisions, but there is still an overall framework for running the enterprise network. For these companies, a domain tree with multiple domains might just be the best solution.

The Multiple-Master Domain Model

In the multiple-master domain model, the network has more than one account domain. The multiple-master domain model requires the creation and administration of more trusts because each resource domain should be configured to trust all account domains. In addition, all account domains should be configured to trust each other; you do this by creating two one-way trusts, one in each direction. A multiple-master domain model might be necessary for any number of reasons. For example, the business might need to have a direct correlation between its actual business structure and the domain model. Remember that business structure refers to the processes and informational systems administrative flow, not the company's organization chart. Always design your structure based on resource and account administration. In this way, different business units can manage their own respective account domains and resource domains. This system can also be used when an organization needs to split up the network because of political, economic, or IT-infrastructure issues (such as domain replication) arising in geographically separated areas.

For migrating a multimaster domain model, an organization can choose from two migration approaches. The first approach is to build a single tree. This requires that the business units agree on one root domain and on who will own that root domain (preferably the IT department). The individual business units can then be implemented as child domains on the next lower level of the tree, and they can again implement their resource domains on a lower level, using their own security policies.

The root domain is a good place to offer global resources, such as a corporate Web server or a public folders database, that should be available for all users. This setup provides central resource and IT management while allowing the business units to retain their independence by implementing their own structures and security policies in their child domains.

 If you are moving a multiple-master domain model to Windows 2000, the OU approach to converting resource domains gives you the highest level of flexibility. This is something to keep in mind if the exam talks about frequent reorganizations or acquisitions.

The second approach, which is even more decentralized, is to build one tree for each NT master domain and its associated resource domains. Each of these separate trees will still be in a single forest. The forest concept allows these trees to retain a common schema, a common global catalog, and the default two-way transitive Kerberos trust relationships so that users can still access resources from anywhere. This setup can also eliminate the need to administer cross-domain trusts because each domain requires only one default two-way transitive trust to its parent domain. Figure 7.6 shows a possible restructuring scenario.

Using the forest approach, business units can implement their own trees by using their own structures and security policies. The only thing the business units' trees have in common is the connection to the other trees in the forest. No administrative work is necessary for this. All administration happens on the tree level. This very flexible model is particularly appropriate for companies that buy and sell business units and want to treat them independently.

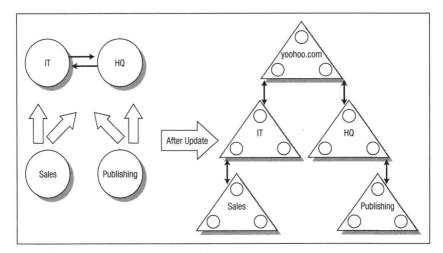

Figure 7.6   Restructuring an NT multiple-master domain.

Using separate domain trees when restructuring a multiple-master domain model should normally be used when there is a business reason to retain the existing domain name space. Look for name retention when evaluating case studies revolving around multiple-master domain restructuring.

The Complete Trust Model

Some organizations are so decentralized that they cannot agree on a common centralized administrative framework (such as a central IT department) that can manage common resources or establish a common root in a tree. In the past, this has led to companies using the complete trust model, and they had to assume the corresponding burden of maintaining all of the manual trust relationships required for resource access between the domains.

With Windows 2000 Server and Active Directory, it is still possible to retain this independence. The organization can choose either to introduce some centralization and build one tree, or to fully retain the decentralized structure and build a forest with several trees (the former domains). In both cases, this results in a less complex structure, in which the trust relationships will be much easier to manage and more scalable.

Note: Structures without centralized control normally result in multiple trees in a single forest.

If you want the advantages of Active Directory, but have no desire to share the structure, global catalog, or schema, you would need to create multiple forests. This is typically used when creating resource access for external companies. They don't what your schema and you don't want theirs. This allows complete decentralization and independent control. The down side is that you have none of the advantages, such as a centralized global catalog, available in a single forest structure. The results of restructuring a complete trust model are very similar to those of restructuring a multiple-master domain model, so refer to Figure 7.6 again to see possible outcomes.

To summarize, all domain models can be easily migrated to Active Directory. Depending on your organization's administrative structure, the flexibility of Active Directory allows you to reflect a centralized or a decentralized business structure even more than you could with Windows NT 4. On the other hand, a migration offers the opportunity to change the structure of your domain environment to better meet your current business needs.

Opportunities for Improvement

The Active Directory design allows the simple migration of both centralized and decentralized Windows NT 4 domain models. The concept and design of the typical single, master, or multiple-master domain model can be easily migrated to an Active Directory tree or forest.

The combination of the improved administrative features of Active Directory and the enhanced security model allows customers to reduce the number of domains in the enterprise. The primary reason organizations choose a master domain model is to allow local staff to administer local resource domains without granting these users unlimited administrative rights to user accounts in the master domain. This setup is useful for both the central Information Technology (IT) departments and local users. Central IT staff members do not have to travel to remote locations or perform administrative operations over slow WAN links, and local users receive support more quickly from local support staff. Local support personnel often tend to have a better understanding of the daily requirements and special needs of their local users.

The origin of many multiple-master domain implementations can be found in the limitations of Windows NT 3.1 domain controllers. In the first release, Windows NT could not hold more than approximately 10,000 objects in the database, which was insufficient for larger companies. Therefore, customers had to create additional account or master domains and establish trust relationships between these domains to provide resource access. With NT 4, the SAM database limit was estimated to be in the area of 40,000 user accounts, but this was generally considered to be an unachievable number in production environments. The scalability inherent in Active Directory ensures its ability to store all objects in one domain.

The source domain structure can be reestablished within a target domain using an OU hierarchy. A company can use the migration to Active Directory as a means of reducing the number of domains and can thus simplify and consolidate both its network administration and its network structure. The company can then reorganize the domain structure to bring it into alignment with the actual IT administration requirements. Besides simplifying administration, this has the added benefits of lowering the TCO (total cost of ownership) and bringing a considerably faster ROI (return on investment) from the migration to Windows 2000.

Examining the Implications of Restructuring Domains

After you have determined why and when you need to restructure domains, you need to examine the implications of such a restructure. The following section describes some of the most important considerations for a restructuring plan:

➤ Migrating security principals

➤ Moving users and global groups

➤ Moving computers

➤ Moving member servers

➤ Establishing trusts

➤ Cloning security principals

Migrating Security Principals

What makes a domain restructuring possible in Windows 2000 is the ability to move security principals and domain controllers between domains. This ability raises several issues, including how security principals are identified by the system and how access to resources is controlled and maintained. These issues could affect your preferred approach to domain restructure.

Effect on SIDs

The domain-specific nature of SIDs has the following consequence: When you move or copy (also known as cloning) a security principal (such as a user or a group) between domains, the security principal must be issued a new SID for the account in the new domain. Realize that moving deletes the source security principal. If you want to keep the old security principal, clone it instead.

In both the Windows NT 4 and Windows 2000 security models, access to resources is affected by the way the operating system looks at the user's access token and compares the primary SID of the user—as well as the SIDs of any groups the user is a member of—to the ACEs on the resource ACLs. Because the SIDs contained in the ACL have information that can cause access to be granted or denied to the SID of any security principal, changing the SID has far-reaching implications for authentication and resource access. The implications of changing the SID are illustrated in the example discussed in the following section.

Effect on Global Group Membership

A global group can contain members from only its own domain. Therefore, moving a global group to a new domain would cause that group's user accounts to be denied access to the resources in any resource domains because the moved global group would no longer have the same primary SID as the source global group. If sufficient trust relationships exist between the new domain and the resource domains, you can fix this situation in a number of ways, including the following two:

➤ *Adding the new SID to the resource ACLs*—You can maintain access to resources by adding the new SID for the migrated user or group account to the ACLs on all the resources to which the account formerly had access. This fix would be time-consuming and complicated for many reasons, including the following:

➤ Many domain restructuring operations are carried out incrementally over-time. There is no guarantee that during this time, access to new or additional resources will not be granted for the original global group. This means that resource repermissioning would have to continue for the duration of the restructuring, and beyond.

➤ If an affected user changed job functions and no longer needed to be a member of a restructured global group, it would be much easier to remove that user from the global group than to change the ACLs of all of the resources referring to that user. For this reason, Microsoft has always recommended that you set up ACLs using groups rather than individuals, because users and their specific job functions can change over time.

➤ *Moving the global group*—Because security principals can be moved in Windows 2000, the global group can be moved to the new domain. However, the ACLs referring to the group also refer to the original group SID, so the resources would have to be repermissioned to refer to the new SID.

Effect on ACLs Directly Referring to the User

Let's say that in our scenario, the affected user account is also granted direct access to some resources on a member server, which means that the user account SID also appears on ACLs on that server. It is perfectly legitimate to add users to ACLs on resources, but moving the user account would require repermissioning resources on that server. This would require adding the migrated user account's new SID to the ACLs on the original and/or migrated resources, depending on the resource access you wanted to maintain and on which phase of the server migration plan you were in.

The sIDHistory Attribute

In many instances, the issues regarding moving or cloning security principals between domains can be eliminated due to a new Windows 2000 feature called **sIDHistory**. This is a schema object attribute of Active Directory security principals that is used to store the former SIDs of moved objects, such as users and security groups.

When a user is moved or cloned using the Windows 2000 migration tools provided by Microsoft, the **sIDHistory** attribute of the object in Active Directory could be updated with the former SID. When the migrated user logs on to the system, the system retrieves the entries in the user's **sIDHistory** attribute and adds them to the user's access token.

Groups can also be moved, so the system also retrieves the **sIDHistory** attributes of all the migrated groups to which the user belongs and adds these to the user access token as well. The **sIDHistory** entries in the token appear to the system like normal group memberships during authorization checks and therefore allow the appropriate access, even on previous operating systems that know nothing about Windows 2000 or Active Directory.

 For the exam, you must understand the issues with SIDs and the purpose of **sIDHISTORY**.

Moving Users and Global Groups

A global group can contain members from only its own domain. Therefore, when a user moves between domains, any global groups of which the user is a member must also be moved. This must occur to maintain access to resources protected by ACLs that refer to global groups. A corollary of this rule is that if a global group is moved, its members must also be moved.

In this situation, Windows 2000 uses the concept of a closed set. A *closed set* is a collection of users and global groups for which the following conditions are true:

➤ For each user being moved, all corresponding global groups of the set are also being moved.

➤ For each group being moved, all of the users who are members of the group are also being moved.

If the source domain is a native-mode domain, global groups can also contain other global groups. This means that all of the members of each nested group, and all of the global groups that have members in that nested group, must also be moved.

Using closed sets to move global groups that are already populated can have particularly restrictive results. You might have to depopulate and repopulate large global groups, and this can be very time-consuming. In some cases, the smallest closed set that can be moved is the entire source domain.

Fortunately there are several other ways to solve this problem. These include:

➤ Creating a "parallel" group in the target domain

➤ Reconsidering your migration strategy

➤ Leveraging the power of universal groups

Creating a "Parallel" Group in the Target Domain

Moving a global group requires creating parallel global groups in the target domain for each group to be moved, finding all resources in the enterprise containing ACLs referring to the original group, and repermissioning them to include a reference to the parallel target domain group. This method is likely to be a large undertaking in the following instances:

➤ Resources in any trusting domain can refer to the group.

➤ Domain local groups from native-mode source domains can be used on any computer in the domain.

Reconsidering Your Migration Strategy

A certain amount of flexibility is in the migration process, and you might be able to avoid having to face some of the more complex issues, depending on the path you choose. The point here is that cloning (copying) security principals, unlike moving security principals, does not require the use of closed sets. Cloning does require that you copy accounts between two forests, so your choice here would be to perform an interforest restructuring directly from an existing NT 4 domain or from a separate Windows 2000 forest.

Leveraging the Power of Universal Groups

This method requires that both the source and target domains are running in native mode. Once this requirement is met, you can change the group type from a global group to a universal group, migrate the group, and then change the group type back to a global group. When using this method, be aware that the universal group membership is stored on all global catalog servers, and changes to this group's membership can have a direct impact on the amount of replication traffic.

Moving users will have an impact in several more areas, and therefore these should also be included in your migration plan. Some of these areas include:

➤ Moving profiles and **sIDHistory** attributes

➤ Copying profiles

➤ Sharing profiles

Moving Profiles and **sIDHistory** Attributes

When formulating your domain restructuring plan, you must be aware that migrated users receive new SIDs, and this can affect their profile use. Users logging on to a computer after migration could lose access to their logon profiles because their primary SIDs will have changed, while their old profiles might still be stored under their old primary SIDs. This can occur in any of the following circumstances:

➤ A user has been cloned from a Windows NT 4 domain.

➤ A user has been cloned from a Windows 2000 domain.

➤ A user has been cloned from a Windows 2000 domain but is logging on at a Windows NT 4 workstation.

If users lose access to their logon profiles, you have two options for making a profile available to a migrated user: copying profiles or sharing profiles. The preferred method is to copy the profiles.

Copying Profiles

The first option is to copy the original profile from its current location—under the key named after the user's original SID—to a key named after the user's new SID. Each account is associated with its own separate copy of the profile. Updates to one are not reflected in the other.

The advantage of using this method is that the behavior of Windows 2000 is more predictable. Because data is not shared between the profiles, there is no chance of one profile allowing access to another account's data in the same or another domain or forest.

One disadvantage of using this method is that it consumes extra disk space because two profiles are stored. Another disadvantage of this method is that it creates unpredictable fallback results in resource access. This highlights the need for thoroughly testing the impact of installing applications that use group policies so that you are prepared for any contingency.

Copying profiles is the preferred method of migrating profiles. The advantage is isolation where one user's updates will not affect another. The disadvantages are in the extra consumption of disk space and that fallback results may be unpredictable.

Sharing Profiles

This option makes the same profile available to both the user's original account and the new account. This option allows one copy of the profile to be accessed and updated by both accounts. This method has a couple of advantages:

➤ Updates to the profile while a user is logged on to one account, such as changes to the My Documents folder, are accessible when the user subsequently logs on to another account.

➤ Disk space is minimized because only one copy of the profile is stored.

The disadvantage of using this method is that there are unknown variables that could alter the predictability of its use. For example, if you create a new Windows 2000 group policy that refers to an account profile, you will need to test the impact of falling back to a source account for which the group policy is different or has not been used.

 Sharing a profile ensures synchronization between accounts without consuming additional disk space. The disadvantage is that Windows 2000 variables could affect the performance of the older account.

Moving Computers

Shared local groups residing on Windows NT 4 domain controllers, along with other domain local groups, exist only within the domain in which they are created. Therefore, moving such a group can leave unresolvable references to the group in the source domain ACLs.

In this instance, you have a closed set of computers and shared or domain local groups if the following conditions are true:

➤ For each computer being moved, you also move all shared or domain local groups referred to in ACLs on that computer's resources.

➤ For each group being moved, you also move all computers in the domain containing ACLs referring to that group.

Moving Member Servers

The implications of moving domain controllers—including the need to ensure that shared local groups and domain local groups are maintained—have been described earlier in this book. However, those implications are different from the ones involved in moving a member server or a client computer.

In our previous example, a user has access to some resources on a member server through ACLs referring to a computer's local group and referring to the user's domain account directly. If the member server is moved to a domain that has trust relationships with the new account domain for the migrated user account, the **sIDHistory** attribute will ensure that the new account can access resources with ACLs referring to the user account directly. ACLs referring to the computer's local group will also continue to function because the group exists in the account database of the local computer. This means that the group is unaffected by the move, so its SID would not need to be changed.

Establishing Trusts

During domain upgrades, it is assumed that sufficient trust relationships exist from the target domain to any relevant resource domains so that access to resources is maintained. However, such trusts must first be established in any domain restructuring scenario. Netdom is a tool used to carry out tasks such as enumerating domain trusts and establishing new trusts. This tool is also useful for creating computer accounts and updating the domain membership of a client or server.

Moving vs. Cloning Security Principals

Moving or cloning security principals raises many additional concerns that need to be addressed early on in the planning process. Moving security principals creates a new identical account in a destination domain and removes the account from the source domain. The move operation does not allow a return to the old account status if there are problems with the migration.

To ensure that you can recover from problems during the pilot project or production migration, it is recommended that you migrate users incrementally to a Windows 2000 domain while maintaining the old accounts in the source domain. This is possible through *cloning*, which is creating a duplicate user or group by using either the Active Directory Migration Tool (ADMT) or the ClonePrincipal command-line utility. This utility consists of a set of Microsoft Visual Basic (VB) scripts that perform tasks such as cloning users and global groups. The specific use of these and other migration tools will be discussed in Chapter 8.

Creating a Restructuring Strategy

The restructuring strategy you choose will be based on several factors, including your existing environment and the business goals that drive the decision to migrate to Windows 2000. Figure 7.7 provides a sample migration flow chart that you can use to make the necessary decisions based on your organization's goals for the migration.

When you create your restructuring strategy, keep in mind several planning steps that every organization should be aware of. You may find that your organization requires additional steps based on the needs of your existing network environment. At a minimum, you'll need to do the following:

1. Identify your pre-restructuring tasks.

2. Determine the order of restructuring within your domain.

3. Identify your post-restructuring tasks.

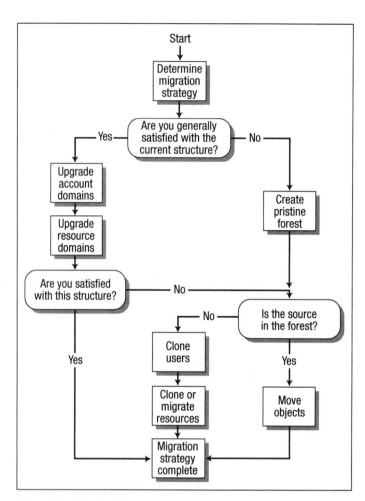

Figure 7.7 Migration flow chart.

Identifying Your Pre-restructuring Tasks

Documenting your pre-restructuring tasks will ensure that you have a thoroughly planned restructuring strategy. This plan should address several areas, including the following:

➤ Examining your existing environment

➤ Choosing a domain restructuring method

➤ Preparing to deploy your target environment

➤ Developing a rollback or recovery strategy

➤ Selecting the appropriate migration tools

➤ Identifying and documenting security principal details

➤ Determining how to migrate security principal details

Examining Your Existing Environment

Examining your current domain model will serve the following purposes:

➤ Allow you to choose the correct restructuring method for achieving your ideal Active Directory design goals

➤ Ensure that your existing network services continue to function and that resource access is maintained throughout the restructuring

➤ Identify obsolete or ineffective practices in your existing environment that you can eliminate in the new environment

When you examine your existing domain structure, do the following steps:

1. Document the existing domains, along with the projected need for maintaining the current structure. You might be able to eliminate multiple domains in favor of a single Active Directory domain.

2. Document all of the existing trust relationships so you can reestablish these after the restructure, if needed. This will ensure that user access is maintained to resources in domains that were originally trusted.

3. Document all applications and network services running on domain controllers. This is to ensure that they're compatible with Windows 2000 and to identify a backup plan for services that might not be available during the restructuring.

Choosing a Domain Restructuring Method

Depending on your migration plan, you might choose to restructure your domains immediately after upgrade, in place of an upgrade, or as a general domain redesign some time in the future. These options are described as follows:

➤ *Restructuring after the upgrade*—The most likely time for a domain restructuring is after an upgrade, as the second phase of migrating to Windows 2000. The upgrade has then already addressed the less complex migration situations, such as multiple domains in which the trust structure is essentially correct and in which there are no pending administrative issues.

When you choose to restructure after the upgrade, most likely your IT goals involve reworking the domain structure. Rework is principally used to reduce complexity. It is also used to bring administrators of resource domains into the Active Directory structure with delegated permissions instead of full administrative rights. You will also bring domains into a reworked structure to place resource domains into an OU with diminished authority or to limit resultant access to targeted groups.

➤ *Restructuring instead of an upgrade*—You might determine that your current domain structure cannot be salvaged (for example, if you need to redesign your existing directory infrastructure to take advantage of Active Directory), or that you cannot afford to jeopardize the stability of the current production environment during migration. In this case, the easiest migration path might be to design and build a pristine forest and then do a full reconfiguration. This is your ideal design for a Windows 2000 forest isolated from the current production environment. This allows your business to carry on normally during pilot project operations and allows the pilot project itself to eventually become the production environment.

After building the pilot project, you begin domain restructuring by migrating a small number of users, groups, and resources into the pilot domain. When this phase has been completed successfully, you can then switch the pilot project to a phased migration of resources into the new environment. The Windows 2000 pilot domain then becomes the production environment, and after a comfortable transition period, you can decommission the old domain and redeploy the remaining resources.

➤ *Restructuring after migration*—In this scenario, the source domain is migrated to 2000, forming a new forest. We would also create a new, pristine forest that is separate from the source. The necessary objects from the source forest are then restructured into the new forest. The largest advantage is if your business plans include mergers, acquisitions, or a complete business reorganization.

Preparing to Deploy Your Target Environment

This step is required only for an interforest restructure because you will be building a pristine forest to serve as the target environment when you migrate resources. When preparing to deploy your target environment, follow these steps:

1. Ensure that you have sufficient hardware available.

2. Ensure that there are no DNS namespace issues, like duplicate DNS names, between the source and target domains.

3. Ensure that sufficient OUs exist in the target environment so that you have to migrate accounts only once.

4. For target environments requiring multiple sites, verify that bandwidth and replication schedules will facilitate the redeployment of domain controllers, and place sufficient domain controllers in each site to provide fault tolerance.

5. Identify proposed changes to existing administrative roles and responsibilities, and communicate these changes to all affected parties. Use these proposed changes to define who is responsible for each area of the restructuring and how the new environment will be managed.

When you develop your test or pilot program, you should consider including the following steps, and then tailor your plan depending on the migration path and complexity of the migration project:

1. Develop an isolated test lab environment in which you can thoroughly test the configuration of a Windows 2000 server that you eventually plan to connect to your production network. The goal here is to ensure that the test environment will not have an adverse impact on the production network. This step includes creating a test domain that simulates the production LAN and WAN.

2. After you've validated your migration plan in a test lab, you can move into limited integration testing. During this phase, you move the test environment to a single LAN segment in your production environment to rule out any coexistence problems while both environments are operating on the same network. At this point, you do not want to introduce any new features or make configuration changes unless they are required for a peaceful coexistence between the two environments.

3. The next phase is extended integration testing, which includes scaling your deployment to multiple network locations within your enterprise network. The goal here is to completely integrate the Active Directory namespace into the DNS namespace; this integration allows you to address replication and authentication issues along with ensuring client access to resources.

4. Now you can continue deploying additional servers and domain controllers throughout your organization in a limited pilot test. This will include implementing any remaining required trust relationships, documenting areas such as application compatibility and user migration issues, and possibly deploying remote access to pilot users.

5. The final phase is extended pilot testing, in which you migrate large populations of users, resources, and computers, along with deploying any additional servers and solving application compatibility problems.

The success of your pilot program can make or break your migration plan, so you might consider enlisting technologically savvy users in the user migration phase. You can include IT support personnel in this process, but you should also include "average" end users as well because they will often experience the most difficult issues that need to be overcome before you migrate large groups of users to the new environment. To gain the most benefit from this step, make sure that these users are able and willing to participate, that they represent a cross-section of the installed hardware, and that they come from many departments. This will ensure that areas such as resource access and authentication are tested from a variety of locations.

Developing a Rollback or Recovery Strategy

Preparing a rollback strategy ensures that you can recover from any problems that might arise during the restructuring. The following are the minimum steps to include when you're creating a recovery plan:

1. Your first line of defense is a reliable backup of everything affected by your restructure. Back up all of your domain controllers, particularly your PDC, your member servers, and your pilot workstations prior to starting anything. You will need to verify that the backup was successful by performing a trial restore. Dead backups are worse than no backups at all.

2. Ensure that your source domains have at least two domain controllers so that you don't inadvertently orphan a domain during the migration.

3. Document applications and services running on domain controllers, and conduct a complete backup and restoration of these applications and services to ensure that your current disaster recovery plan works.

4. If you're migrating from an NT 4 source domain, one fully synchronized BDC should be kept offline until your new production environment is running smoothly. This will help ensure that if your restructure fails and takes the source domain with it, you can promote the reserved BDC to PDC, connect to the network, and continue operations of the old domain with minimal down time.

5. If you're migrating from a Windows 2000 source domain, perform a backup and test restoration of the Active Directory database in your Windows 2000 source domain.

Recovering a Windows NT 4 Source Domain

First remove all computers running Windows 2000 from the production environment. Then perform *one* of the following steps:

➤ Promote the offline BDC to the role of a PDC and connect it back to the network. This new PDC will replicate with any remaining NT 4 BDCs, thus returning the SAM database to its initial state.

➤ Restore the BDC from the backup media, promote it to the role of a PDC, and allow it to replicate with any remaining NT 4 BDCs.

Recovering a Windows 2000 Source Domain

Restore the original data from your backup media, and perform an authoritative restoration of the system state data.

Selecting the Appropriate Migration Tools

Microsoft has provided a number of tools for use in migrating to Windows 2000. The tools you use will be partially dictated by the restructuring method you choose. Each tool has various capabilities, administrative features, and security requirements that you should be aware of before choosing the set of tools you plan to use. You can use ClonePrincipal only for interforest restructuring, and you can use MoveTree only for intraforest restructuring. The Active Directory Migration Tool (ADMT) and Netdom can be used in both scenarios. Detailed descriptions of the tools will be provided in Chapter 8.

Identifying and Documenting Security Principal Details

In case you have to rebuild the security principal details, you should document them before the restructuring. Much of this work may have already been done as part of your organization's overall IT inventories, and there are additional tools in the Windows resource kits that can assist in documenting the rest. When you're documenting these details, do the following:

➤ Document the share, NTFS (New Technology File System), and Registry permissions on the source domain controllers. You can use the Showacls.exe, Subinacl.exe, and Perms.exe tools from the resource kits to document these in NT 4 or Windows 2000. You can also use a variety of Active Directory Service Interfaces (ADSI) scripts to collect this information in a Windows 2000 network.

➤ Document the membership of each source group that you plan to migrate. The NT 4 Resource Kit contains the Global.exe, Local.exe, Findgrp.exe, Showmbrs.exe, and Showgrps.exe tools to assist you in this task. Again, if the source domain is running Windows 2000, you can write ADSI scripts to gather this data.

➤ Identify global groups that you might be able to merge into a single group in the target domain, and use the Showmbrs.exe tool to identify empty groups that you can then delete prior to migration.

➤ Using the resource kit tool Usrstat.exe, identify when user accounts were last logged onto so you can delete unused or disabled accounts prior to migration.

Determining How to Migrate Security Principal Details

Migrating the details of your users, groups, and computer accounts has a direct impact on the SIDs and the nature of access tokens. Each access token granted to a user during a successful logon has a maximum number of entries that can exist before resource access issues occur. The limit in Windows NT 4 is 100 SIDs per access token; this limit has been raised to 1,023 SIDs in Windows 2000. Although these numbers may seem high, the possibility exists that a user, or a group, could be assigned more than this number, and this could result in a denial of resource access or even a failed logon. This will have a direct impact on the decisions you make in the area of migrating the **sIDHistory**.

 sIDHistory stores a user account's old security ID as an attribute of their new account. This old SID, as well as the new SID, can be used to access resources. The advantage is you don't have to change all of your resource ACLs as soon as you restructure.

Migrating the **sIDHistory** doubles the size of a user's access token, so you will want to identify any users in the source domain who belong to more than 500 groups; you can do this with the Showgrps.exe utility, which is part of the NT 4 and Windows 2000 resource kits. The implications and use of the **sIDHistory** attribute are discussed in more detail throughout this chapter.

 The global group membership is maintained during a cloning operation. You can migrate the users first and then the groups to which they belong, or you can migrate the groups first and then the users. Membership will be restored in either case.

When you create new administrative accounts in the target domain, they will not have a **sIDHistory** attribute, so any required special permissions or user rights will need to be assigned. For this reason, you will want to consider migrating source administrative accounts first and ensuring that they have all of the necessary rights in both the source and target domains. To retain the original permissions and user rights, you can add the source domain SIDs of well-known relative identifier (RID) accounts—including the Domain Admins, Domain Users, and Domain Guests—to the **sIDHistory** attribute of the corresponding accounts in the target domain.

 You can use either the Sidhist.vbs ClonePrincipal script or the Group Mapping And Merging Wizard in the ADMT to accomplish **sIDHistory** mappings to Domain Admins, Domain Users, and Domain Guests.

You can minimize the problem of large access tokens in several ways, including the following:

➤ Before migration, minimize the number of groups that a user belongs to in the source domain.

➤ Consider migrating some of your users or groups without retaining the **sIDHistory** attribute. This will require re-permissioning the associated discretionary access control lists (DACLs) in the target domain to allow resource access for migrated users.

➤ Clean up the **sIDHistory** of the migrated accounts before activating them.

Determining the Order for Restructuring within a Domain

Though you might prefer to restructure in any order that you choose, Microsoft has a recommended order in which objects should be migrated. This order is:

1. Restructure users and groups first in order to take immediate advantage of the improved features of Windows 2000.

2. Restructure Windows 2000 computer accounts shortly after migrating users so you can take advantage of the benefits of using group policies to administer and manage your network.

3. Restructure member servers after client computers because member servers are often more complicated to migrate. The experience you will gain from migrating users and clients first should prove valuable when you reach this phase.

4. With the exception of the PDC, move all other domain controllers last because BDCs will still be required to authorize access requests in the source domain for users located in other domains.

 Study the order of the following restructuring operations carefully. Commit the general steps outlined in Figures 7.8 and 7.9 to memory.

Figure 7.8 provides a block diagram of the recommended order for performing an interforest restructuring. Figure 7.9 provides a block diagram of the recommended order for performing an intraforest restructuring.

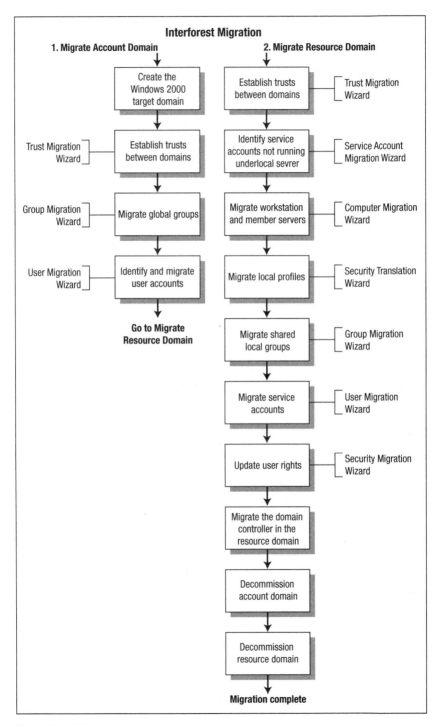

Figure 7.8 Interforest restructuring.

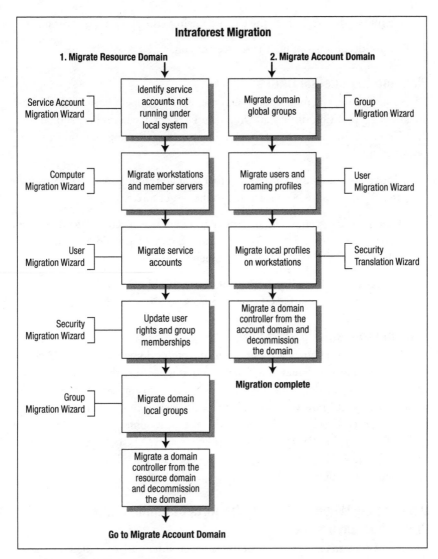

Figure 7.9   Intraforest restructuring.

Identifying Your Post-restructuring Tasks

After you've completed the restructuring, there will still be some administrative duties to perform to ensure that the new environment is operating and configured properly. The steps that should be included in this portion of the migration plan include the following:

➤ Plan for redefining DACLs (discretionary access control lists).

➤ Plan for cleaning up **sIDHistory**.

➤ Determine when to convert the target domain to the production environment.

➤ Plan for decommissioning the source domain.

Planning to Redefine DACLs

After a migration, you might notice that the security properties of a file or folder on an NTFS partition display an Unknown User entry where there should be a SID. To avoid this problem, you should include the following steps in your migration plan:

1. Move all of the computer accounts that contain resources as soon as possible after the users have been migrated to the target forest.

2. After all users, groups, and computer accounts have been migrated and the **sIDHistory** attribute is no longer required, remove the old SIDs from the DACLs, and perform any required repermissioning.

3. You can use the Security Translation Wizard in the ADMT to assist in the process of redefining DACLs on resources.

Planning to Clean Up sIDHistory

Removing the **sIDHistory** attribute from the target domain's resource DACLs raises some important issues. You'll want to first make sure that the appropriate DACLs have been redefined so users don't lose access to any resources. You'll also want to plan exactly how you will accomplish the task of cleaning up **sIDHistory**. Redefining each DACL individually could take quite some time, and there is no tool that can remove the **sIDHistory** attribute from a DACL, so you might consider using the ADSI application to write a script for querying and deleting the **sIDHistory** attribute on selected security principals.

Determining When to Convert the Target Domain to the Production Environment

The target domain is often the pilot or test environment that you built as a pristine forest, so determining when you can convert this target environment to your production environment will be extremely important. You will want to ensure that the Active Directory forest is fully operational before you do the conversion. You'll need to be aware of two key issues:

➤ Ensuring that migrated users, groups, and resources are all available for logon and access

➤ Ensuring that users have received their new passwords

Passwords are not maintained in an interforest migration. This requires either that you maintain two separate accounts for each user or that you disable the source accounts when you activate the target accounts.

Planning to Decommission the Source Domain

Your decommissioning plan will be implemented after you are satisfied that all resources have been migrated and are accessible and that users can use their new accounts to log on. A typical decommissioning plan will include the following steps:

1. Maintain the source domain as a recovery mechanism until you determine that all migration operations have been successfully completed. Perform spot checks to ensure that users can access resources in the new domain and that all network services are functioning properly.

2. Use the Netdom tool to remove all trusts between the source and target domains.

3. Upgrade any remaining domain controllers in the source domain to Windows 2000, or redeploy them in other roles in the target domain.

Choosing an Installation Strategy

There are various ways to minimize the IT-related requirements during your migration, and one of the best ways might be to plan for automating some of the new Windows 2000 installations. With this method, you can run the Windows 2000 Setup program with an answer file and perform the installation in an unattended fashion. To automate the Windows 2000 installation, you can use the Setup Manager Wizard, the **/syspart** switch with the Winnt32.exe command, the Sysprep utility, a bootable CD, or an automated deployment application like Microsoft Systems Management Server (SMS). SMS is beyond the scope of this book, but we will explore the other options in detail.

The Setup Manager Wizard

You can use the Setup Manager Wizard to create answer files, which can then be used in an unattended installation or upgrade to Windows 2000.

The /syspart Switch

The **/syspart** switch of the **Winnt32.exe** command can be used only for clean installations, but it does support dissimilar hardware. With **/syspart**, you first create a completely configured source machine; you then create a master image of that computer that can then be imaged onto another hard drive. The **/syspart** switch marks the target drive as active and as the boot device, so you may want to consider removing the imaged hard drive before restarting the computer.

The Sysprep Utility

The Sysprep utility is used for clean installations on computers that have identical hardware. Sysprep prepares the hard drive on the master source computer so that a third-party disk-imaging tool can transfer the image to other computers.

A Bootable CD

If your computer's BIOS supports booting from a CD-ROM (El Torito compliant), you can boot directly from the Windows 2000 installation CD.

 When you're performing disk duplication, check with your software vendor to make certain you are not violating the licensing agreement for installation of the software you want to duplicate.

Planning for a Smooth Transition to Windows 2000

You can perform many steps to ensure a smooth transition to Windows 2000. The following are the recommended steps for ensuring minimal interruption to your users, the network, and the core business functions of the organization:

1. Use a phased migration plan in which you incrementally migrate resources. This breaks your project down into "bite-size" chunks, which are easier to manage.

2. Keep your administrative and support teams fully informed, and provide advance training. This will maintain morale and ensure that the teams remain focused on the goals of the migration.

3. In order to minimize the impact on the business, schedule major migration activities around your business operations. This can include performing upgrades during off-peak hours or waiting for other projects to be completed so that deadlines are not affected.

In this chapter we discussed the specific aspects of a domain restructuring. If an organization conducts a thorough analysis of its existing domain environment and plans appropriately, it should not experience any issues that cannot be resolved during a migration from Windows NT 4 to Windows 2000. In the next chapter, we will look at specific steps for conducting your restructuring.

Practice Questions

Question 1

Why would you not want to convert all of your global groups to universal groups in an attempt to minimize the impact of migrating groups?

○ a. Global groups cannot be converted to universal groups; they can only be converted to domain local groups.

○ b. The use of universal groups raises important replication traffic issues within the forest.

○ c. Universal groups are available only in a domain that is running in mixed mode and therefore cannot be migrated to a target forest that is running in native mode.

○ d. Documenting universal group membership is not possible in a domain migration and therefore can lead to resource access issues in the target environment.

Answer b is correct. Universal group membership is stored on global catalog servers throughout the forest, and changes to universal group membership are replicated to every global catalog server throughout the forest. This leads to an increase in replication-related traffic whenever the membership of a universal group is changed.

Question 2

Which of the following Resource Kit utilities can help you with the process of documenting permissions and group membership information before you conduct a migration? [Check all correct answers]

❏ a. Local.exe

❏ b. Global.exe

❏ c. Subinacl.exe

❏ d. Perms.exe

Answers a, b, c, and d are correct. All of the tools listed can assist in the migration process. In addition, the following tools from the Resource Kit can also be useful when you're documenting permissions or group membership: Findgrp.exe, Showmbrs.exe, Showgrps.exe, and Showacls.exe.

Question 3

Which of the following migration tools support interforest restructuring?
[Check all correct answers]

❏ a. ADMT

❏ b. ClonePrincipal

❏ c. Netdom

❏ d. MoveTree

Answers a, b, and c are correct. ClonePrincipal can be used only for interforest restructuring, and MoveTree can be used only for intraforest restructuring. The Active Directory Migration Tool (ADMT) and Netdom can be used in both scenarios.

Question 4

What can be done to reduce the size of large access tokens? [Check all correct answers]

❏ a. Use ADSI to remove additional access tokens from the token attribute of the security principal.

❏ b. Migrate users without retaining **sIDHistory**.

❏ c. Consolidate group memberships of the migrated open set

❏ d. Minimize group membership in the source domain.

Answers b and d are correct. If you don't retain the **sIDHistory** attribute, you don't add those associated access tokens to the user account. If the user account is a member of only a limited number of groups, their list of access tokens will be minimized. Realize you will need to edit the DACLs on the target domain to accommodate resource access. Answer a is incorrect as there is no editable token attribute assigned to a security principal. Answer c is incorrect as group memberships are migrated as a closed set.

Question 5

What utilities can you use to migrate well-known RIDs, like Domain Admins, Domain Users, and Domain Guests? [Check all correct answers]

❑ a. sidhist.vbs

❑ b. RIDMerge

❑ c. ClonePrincipal

❑ d. ADMT

Answers a, c, and d are correct. Sidhist.vbs, ClonePrincipal, and the Group Mapping and Merging Wizard in the ADMT can map **sIDHistory** to well-known RIDs. RIDMerge is an application that has yet to be written.

Question 6

What is some selection criteria used to identify a good group to participate in a limited, pilot rollout of Windows 2000? [Check all correct answers]

❑ a. Selected users should come from a single department.

❑ b. Machines selected should come from a cross-section of installed hardware.

❑ c. Users should be selected regardless of desire to participate to get a good feel of the reaction to a migration.

❑ d. All users selected should possess some level of technical ability.

Answers b and d are correct. Machines should represent a good cross-section of installed hardware to help identify any issues with the upgrade. This helps you plan for equipment upgrades or replacement prior to the actual rollout. Answer d is correct because users should be somewhat technically savvy to help you by giving clear feedback. It is difficult to get a good idea if a problem is caused by the way a restructure was performed, or you just have a computer-challenged end user. Answer a is incorrect as users should come from several departments to ensure you have a representative cross-section of the population. Be aware of any disruptions in operations and ensure departmental willingness to participate. Answer c is misguided, as this is a limited rollout. Restructuring may cause some operator frustration and you may need to rely on the good graces of the end user to iron out all of the bugs. If you have a rollout comprised of disgruntled users to begin with, your chance of success is greatly impeded due to lack of participation and outright hostility.

Question 7

> Which operation(s) will retain the source security principal in the source domain? [Check all correct answers]
>
> ❑ a. Copying the user account to the new domain
>
> ❑ b. ClonePrincipal
>
> ❑ c. Moving the user account to the new domain
>
> ❑ d. MoveTree

Answers a and b are correct. Copying and cloning are the same operation that makes a destination account and leaves the source account intact. Answers c and d are incorrect as a move involves deletion of the source account.

Question 8

> Which domain migration scenario requires cloning user accounts to the target domain?
>
> ○ a. Interforest migration
>
> ○ b. Intraforest migration
>
> ○ c. Domain upgrade
>
> ○ d. Upgrade in place

Answer a is correct. Cloning is performed only in an interforest restructuring. Cloning copies the user accounts to the target domain while leaving the source domain account intact.

Question 9

> What is the default trust type that is created when you add a new Windows 2000 child domain to an existing Windows 2000 forest?
>
> ○ a. Shortcut trust
>
> ○ b. Transitive trust
>
> ○ c. Explicit trust
>
> ○ d. Nontransitive trust

Answer b is correct. When you add a new Windows 2000 child domain to an existing Windows 2000 forest, a two-way transitive trust is created automatically between the parent domain and the child domain. A two-way transitive trust is the default Windows 2000 trust relationship established between a parent and child domain or between two trees in the same forest.

Question 10

> What would you use to write a script to clean up the **sIDHistory** attribute of migrated accounts?
>
> ○ a. ADMT
>
> ○ b. ClonePrincipal
>
> ○ c. LDAP
>
> ○ d. ADSI

Answer d is correct. ADSI (Active Directory Service Interfaces) is a multiuse directory management application that can be used for a variety of Active Directory tasks, including cleaning up the **sIDHistory** of migrated accounts. ADSI enables administrators to automate common tasks, such as adding users and groups, managing printers, and setting permissions on network resources.

Need to Know More?

 Microsoft Corporation. *The Microsoft Windows 2000 Server Resource Kit*. Microsoft Press, Redmond, Washington, 2000. ISBN 1-57231-805-8. The encyclopedia of everything 2000 Server. The volume devoted entirely to deployment will be of particular interest to migration professionals. It has an outstanding poster of a fictitious migration and deployment that covers nearly every situation a true professional will face in the real world and the exam.

 Microsoft Corporation. Microsoft Official Curriculum course 2010 "Migrating from Microsoft Windows NT 4.0 to Microsoft Windows 2000". This is the official word on migration from Microsoft. It isn't completely exam-centric but does provide the Microsoft slant on the migration process.

 Microsoft Corporation. Microsoft's "Determining Domain Migration Strategies" document is a reprint from *The Microsoft Windows 2000 Server Resource Kit* Redmond, Washington: Microsoft Press, 2000, ISBN 1572318058. The section titled "Determining Your Migration Roadmap" gives outstanding guidance in identifying goals and procedures in the restructure process. This is located at: **www.microsoft.com/windows2000/library/resources/reskit/ samplechapters/dgbf/dgbf_upg_ovaw.asp.**

 Microsoft Corporation. Microsoft Windows 2000 Deployment Planning Guide. Microsoft white paper, 2000. Chapter 2, "Creating a Deployment Roadmap", contains excellent guidelines and various planning scenarios to help the reader understand the design methodology used in planning a Windows 2000 deployment. This is located at: **www.microsoft.com/windows2000/library/resources/reskit/ dpg/default.asp.**

 Microsoft Corporation. Microsoft Windows 2000 Domain Migration Cookbook. Microsoft white paper, 2000. Chapter 4, "Domain Restructure", and Chapter 5, "The Desired Structure and Migration Goals", are of particular interest when preparing for the design portion of the exam. This is located at: **www.microsoft.com/ WINDOWS2000/library/planning/activedirectory/cookbook.asp.**

Goth, Jen. Microsoft Interactive Training Tool online course, "How to Migrate Your Windows NT 4.0 Directory Services to Windows 2000 Active Directory". TNQ2000-3. The section that starts with "Restructure with Fallback" begins an excellent discussion about non-destructive methods of domain restructure and gives a nice discussion on using ADMT. The ADMT is a beta version, but the tips are valuable nonetheless. This is located at: **www.microsoft.com/TechNet/events/fall/ tnq20003/html/default.htm.**

 Microsoft Corporation. Microsoft Active Directory Service Interfaces (ADSI) application version 2.5 download can be found at: **www.microsoft.com/technet/winnt/winntas/adsi25.asp.**

 Microsoft Corporation. Microsoft System Preparation Tool (Sysprep) version 1.1 download can be found at: **www.microsoft.com/ windows2000/downloads/deployment/sysprep/default.asp.**

 Microsoft Corporation. Microsoft Windows 2000 Active Directory Migration Tool (ADMT) can be found at: **www.microsoft.com/ windows2000/downloads/deployment/admt/default.asp.**

8

Restructuring

. . . .

Terms you'll need to understand:

- ✓ Intraforest restructuring
- ✓ **sIDHistory**
- ✓ Closed sets
- ✓ Interforest restructuring
- ✓ ADMT (Active Directory Migration Tool)
- ✓ ClonePrincipal
- ✓ Netdom
- ✓ LDP
- ✓ MoveTree

Techniques you'll need to master:

- ✓ Using the proper Microsoft tools for restructuring Windows 2000 domains
- ✓ Selecting the order in which domains should be restructured or migrated
- ✓ Planning for the requirements and restrictions that must be met before performing an intraforest restructuring and an interforest restructuring
- ✓ Migrating users and groups
- ✓ Migrating local groups and computers
- ✓ Migrating domain controllers
- ✓ Using **sIDHistory**, deciding when to use it, when and how to remove it, and which migration tools maintain **sIDHistory** and which don't
- ✓ Determining the implications of moving or cloning security principals, including the effect on SIDs and resource access
- ✓ Troubleshooting common restructuring problems
- ✓ Choosing the appropriate restructuring tools based on the particular situation

The purpose of this chapter is to assist you in implementing either an intraforest domain restructuring or an interforest domain restructuring. Chapter 7 introduced some of the tools and concepts you'll need to master, and now it's time to take a look at the actual steps that you'll be required to perform based on the migration path that your organization chooses. Your choices will be affected by the migration plan, which is based on your organization's goals for the migration to Windows 2000.

Why Restructure

Windows 2000 Active Directory is more efficient than NT. You have greater scalability, administrative granularity, security, and stability. But in order to achieve the full benefit, you will have to change the way you do business.

An in-place upgrade is fairly straightforward, but it is a lot like repainting an old house: You may be able to change the look, but the previous structure, including its weaknesses, is still there. What we are talking about is the many issues that administrators had to deal with in overcoming with some of the limitations of NT. And in a straight migration, these limitations may be carried over.

With a restructure, it is like moving into a brand new home. You take your treasures, like users, member servers, and group memberships, and put them on shiny new shelves called organizational units and sites. A restructure lets you configure your domain to support your business goals without the baggage associated with an upgrade. The purest form is an interforest restructuring. That is where you create a new forest with a completely new structure. This requires more planning, but it does free you from the past. It offers some unique challenges, because you can't simply move from one domain to the other, but for many, the results are well worth it.

Sometimes you will have already built on to the old home. In other words, you have already moved into Windows 2000. You now want to tweak the configuration, maybe consolidate some domains. This is an intraforest restructure. You will find that this is inherently easier, but you lose some of the flexibility you normally enjoy with a completely new forest. Many choose to perform an intraforest restructuring to avoid excessive restructuring and reconfiguring. If you are mostly satisfied with your evolving enterprise, an intraforest restructure is more efficient.

Either of these restructuring scenarios (intraforest or interforest) can be carried out as part of a domain upgrade followed by a domain restructuring or as solely a restructuring of your existing domain model. Remember that in an interforest restructuring, you will copy (clone) security principals to the target domain. In an intraforest restructuring, you will be required to move security principals between the two domains. Computer accounts cannot be cloned, so these will always be moved from the source domain to the target domain, regardless of the migration scenario you choose. Both intraforest and interforest restructuring will require some advance preparation before you actually implement the cloning or moving operation. We'll cover each one separately so that when you face a scenario on the certification exam, you will be prepared to determine which path is the most appropriate based on the given circumstances. You will then be able to choose the appropriate tools to be used in the chosen migration path.

Intraforest Restructuring Scenarios

Intraforest restructuring is performed when accounts must be moved between domains in the same Windows 2000 forest. This restructuring method is most commonly used as the second phase of a two-phase migration in which an organization chooses to restructure after fully upgrading the existing Windows NT 4 domain model. You might also choose this migration strategy to perform the more complex Active Directory redesign required by a total corporate reorganization.

You Can Only Move, Not Clone

It is imperative that you understand that moving is the only migration operation possible in an intraforest restructuring scenario. Moving security principals between two Windows 2000 domains brings a fairly high degree of risk to the existing production environment because, in a move operation, the source account is deleted; this means that there is no built-in fallback mechanism. After an account is moved, you cannot easily recover the source account because it will no longer exist in the source domain.

Additional requirements and restrictions must be considered prior to the actual intraforest restructuring operation.

 Be sure to memorize the requirements for intraforest restructuring in the following sections.

Requirements for Intraforest Restructuring

Moving security principals is a security-sensitive operation. Therefore, you must prepare an appropriate environment before performing an intraforest restructuring. The requirements you must meet include the following:

➤ The target domain must be a Windows 2000 native-mode domain.

➤ The user performing the restructuring operation must have administrative privileges in both the source and target domains.

➤ Account auditing must be enabled in both the source and target domains. Audit Account Management must be enabled in the Default Domain Controllers group policy.

➤ Before you run the Active Directory Migration Tool (ADMT), you must disconnect any mapped network drives and similar connections between the source domain controller and the target domain controller on which the ADMT is running. Failure to do so may result in the failure of a migration operation due to a "credentials conflict" error.

➤ When you're migrating users and groups between domains in the same forest, the ADMT must communicate with the relative ID (RID) master in the target domain. To improve performance when you're migrating a large number of users or groups, you should install the ADMT on the RID master in the target domain. By default, this is the first domain controller installed in the domain. Use Active Directory Users And Computers or Ntdsutil.exe to locate the domain controller that holds the RID master role.

 If you want to migrate users and groups from a child domain to the forest root domain, the user account you log on with when you run the ADMT must have the permissions of the Enterprise Admins group, in addition to the security privileges normally needed to run the tool.

Restrictions for Intraforest Restructuring

In addition to the requirements just described, several restrictions also apply when you're performing an intraforest restructuring. These include the following:

➤ The source domain must be a Windows 2000 domain in the same forest as the target domain.

➤ Source objects must be users or security-enabled groups, computers, or organizational units (OUs). Security-enabled groups include global groups, Windows 2000 domain local groups, and Windows NT 4 shared local groups.

➤ Source objects cannot be built-in accounts (such as local Administrators, Users, and Power Users). Because built-in groups have well-known SIDs and RIDs, these groups cannot be moved. Built-in account security IDs (SIDs) are identical in every domain, so adding them to a **sIDHistory** attribute would violate the SID-uniqueness requirement of the forest. See the Microsoft Knowledge Base Article Q243330 for a list of well-known SIDs in Windows 2000.

➤ The SID of the source object must not already exist in the target domain, either as a primary account SID or in the **sIDHistory** attribute of an account.

➤ Administrative shares must exist on the computer where the ADMT is running and on any other computer on which the ADMT must install an agent.

You might recall that access to resources in Windows NT and 2000 is granted or denied on the basis of SIDs. Because SIDs are domain-specific, they must be changed as a result of migration. Although there are well-known SIDs that identify generic groups and users across all systems, the majority of security principals that you will be concerned with are identified in the context of a domain, and thus they cannot be moved between domains without their SIDs changing.

 In an intraforest restructuring, you can run the migration tools on either the source domain controller or the target domain controller. As you will see in the next section, interforest restructuring requires that you run the migration tools on the target domain controller.

Now that we have covered the prerequisites for an intraforest restructuring, it's time to discuss some of the details about moving security principals. In the next section, we'll cover the following: using closed sets to move users and global groups; using closed sets to move domain local groups; alternatives to moving with closed sets; moving computers and local accounts; and moving domain controllers.

Moving Security Principals

We have already discussed how intraforest migration operations require that security principals be moved from one Windows 2000 domain to another in the same forest. Moving a security principal creates a new, identical account in the target domain and removes the account from the source domain. Therefore, the move operation does not allow a return to the old account status if there are any problems with the migration. Moving a security principal between domains changes the security principal's SID.

To ensure that resource access permissions are maintained, the underlying APIs (application programming interfaces) used to move objects apply a constraint called a *closed set* on these types of operations. A closed set is a block of accounts that are moved at the same time. Both the MoveTree tool and the ADMT move security principals and provide the capability of retaining the source account SID in the **sIDHistory** attribute of the target account. This attribute allows continued access to resources in the source domain for the moved accounts. Cloning is not possible in intraforest migration because one SID would then be associated with two security principals, and this double association would lead to all sorts of authentication and resource access issues.

Using Closed Sets to Move Users and Global Groups

Using closed sets is required if you want to maintain the membership relationship between the users and groups you are moving, along with the permissions and access to resources that existed before the move. As an example, a closed set of users and groups is a set in which each global group that a user belongs to is moved with the user, and each global group's members are moved with the global group. To take this a step further, if the source domain is in native mode, global groups can contain other global groups; when this occurs, each nested global group's members, and all global groups to which its members belong, must be moved together, or the membership relationship will be broken. The key point here is that when a global group is moved, all of its members must also be moved.

Note: A global group can contain members from only its own domain.

Using Closed Sets to Move Local Groups

Closed sets are also used to move local groups. If an organization chooses to merge two or more domains, this will involve moving Windows 2000 domain local groups, and the domain controllers on which they reside, into the target domain. Windows 2000 domain local groups are valid in only the domain in which they were created; therefore, if a domain local group is moved independently of its members, any references to the group in the source domain's DACLs (discretionary access control lists) will be irresolvable. So to preserve group membership, and to retain access to resources, you must do the following:

➤ For each domain local group that is being moved, you must simultaneously move all domain controllers in the same domain with resource DACLs that refer to the group. Moving domain controllers means running DCPROMO to demote the machine down to a member server, joining the target domain, and then promoting the machine back to the ranks of a domain controller, if desired.

➤ For each domain controller that is being moved, you must simultaneously move all domain local groups that are referred to in DACLs on the domain controller's resources.

Alternatives to Moving with Closed Sets

The use of closed sets is particularly challenging because it adds administrative overhead. Using closed sets can require depopulating large groups in the source domain and then repopulating these groups in the target domain, and sometimes the smallest closed set possible is the entire domain itself. Three alternatives address the issues regarding using closed sets to move local groups:

➤ You can create parallel global groups in the target domain instead of moving them. Parallel global groups do not contain the **sIDHistory** attribute of the source group, so this raises additional requirements. You must redefine the new group membership and then modify all resources in the enterprise that contain DACLs referring to the original global group to include permissions for the parallel groups you created.

➤ You can leverage the new universal group type by changing the existing group type to a universal group. Universal groups have forest-wide scope, so they can be safely moved while retaining their membership and maintaining access to resources that are not migrated. After completing the restructuring, you can change the group type back to the original type.

 You want to be aware that, with this approach, the membership of universal groups is stored in the global catalog, and when universal group membership changes, the entire group membership is replicated throughout the forest. Therefore, this approach can result in a significant increase in forest-wide replication traffic.

➤ The third option is not so much a solution because it requires you to reconsider your migration strategy. Cloning security principals does not require the use of closed sets, but cloning works only when you're copying accounts between forests. Cloning would require that you perform the interforest restructuring directly from an existing Windows NT 4 domain or from a separate Windows 2000 forest.

Moving Computers and Local User and Group Accounts

Moving computer accounts between domains does not pose any additional issues because workstations and member servers have their own SAM (Security Accounts Manager) database, and they always take this database with them when they are moved. You can move computer accounts remotely by using the ADMT or the Netdom tool, or a user at the local computer can join the new domain manually.

Local user accounts and local group accounts are not affected during a move operation because they reside in the local SAM database. The resource DACLs will continue to provide the same access that existed before the move as long as the appropriate trust relationships are established between the source and target domains and any domains in which local group members reside.

Moving Domain Controllers

NT domain controllers cannot be moved between domains. Either you must upgrade Windows NT domain controllers to Windows 2000 and, in the process, join them to the target domain, or you must reinstall Windows NT. To move a Windows 2000 domain controller, you must first demote it to the role of a member server (using the Dcpromo.exe utility). You can then manually join the member server to the target domain, or use the ADMT or Netdom to move the computer account to the target domain. After the member server is joined to the target domain, you can promote the member server as an additional domain controller if your migration plan calls for this, or leave it as a member server. If security descriptors on the domain controller to be moved refer to any domain local groups, those groups must be moved before the server is moved. Moving domain controllers will be one of the final steps in an intraforest migration and will result in a decommissioning of the source domain.

Interforest Restructuring Scenarios

Interforest restructuring involves copying and moving accounts from a Windows NT 4 domain to a Windows 2000 domain, or from a Windows 2000 domain in one forest to a Windows 2000 domain in another forest. Interforest restructuring—which is also called *prune and graft* or *cut and paste*—is a more complex migration scenario that can be used to relocate security principals between two Windows 2000 forests. This can be a very effective migration scenario for use in corporate mergers or acquisitions. In this model, you will have two entirely separate yet parallel domains existing at the same time. This model will increase your overall hardware requirements and, at least temporarily, your administrative and support needs.

Copying Adds a Fallback Option

When you are restructuring a Windows NT 4 domain, you will be concerned with restructuring both account domains and resource domains. Restructuring account domains involves incrementally copying users, global groups, and shared local groups from the source domain to the parallel target domain. This migration path provides a built-in recovery strategy because the original accounts remain untouched during the migration process. You can also preserve the existing security, while migrating the **sIDHistory** attribute of the cloned accounts, until you have fully tested all of the newly cloned accounts' access to resources in the target domain. After all of the users and groups have been copied, the new environment has been tested, and the new accounts are in use, you can decommission the Windows NT 4 domain.

Restructuring resource domains allows you to "collapse" your existing Windows NT 4 resource domains into OUs in the destination Windows 2000 domain. This feature has the added benefit of reducing the number of domains, along with reducing the administrative overhead of managing multiple trust relationships. You can use a combination of moving and copying techniques in this scenario.

Note: At this time, you cannot combine forests because there is no way to merge the schemas of separate Active Directory forests. Microsoft has pledged to fix this in a future release, perhaps in a service pack or in the next-generation operating system.

Additional requirements must be met before you perform an interforest restructuring, and you need to be aware of several restrictions that may apply.

 Be sure to memorize the requirements for interforest restructures in the following section.

Requirements for Interforest Restructuring

Cloning security principals is a security-sensitive operation. Therefore, you must prepare an appropriate environment before performing an interforest restructuring. The requirements include the following:

➤ The target domain must be a Windows 2000 native-mode domain if the **sIDHistory** attribute will be migrated.

➤ You must create the TcpipClientSupport DWORD Registry value in the Registry key:

HKEY_LOCAL_MACHINE\System\CurrentControlSet\Control\Lsa\

This value must reside on the source domain controller to operate properly. AMDT will create this for you if needed. This step is only necessary when your source domain is a Windows NT 4 domain.

Note: You must reboot the domain controller after making this Registry change.

➤ The user performing the restructuring operation must be a member of the Enterprise Admins group in the target domain and must have administrative privileges in both the source and target domains.

➤ Auditing must be enabled in both the source and target domains. For a Windows NT 4 domain, you must audit the success and failure of any exercise of the Group Management right. For a Windows 2000 domain, Audit Account Management must be enabled on the Default Domain Controllers group policy.

➤ A local group named sourcedomainname$$$—for example, Yoohoo$$$—must be created in the source domain. The sourcedomainname is the NetBIOS name of the source domain. This group is used for auditing and must be empty.

➤ Before you run the ADMT, you must disconnect any mapped network drives and similar connections between the source domain controller and the target domain controller on which the ADMT is running. Failure to do so may result in the failure of a migration operation due to a "credentials conflict" error.

Restrictions for Interforest Restructuring

Several restrictions apply when you're performing an interforest restructuring. These include:

➤ The source domain controller must be the PDC (Windows NT 4) or the PDC Emulator of a Windows 2000 native-mode or mixed-mode domain.

➤ The source domain cannot be in the same forest as the target domain.

➤ The source object must be a user account or a security-enabled group.

➤ The SID of the source object must not already exist in the target forest, either as a primary account SID or in the **sIDHistory** attribute of an account.

➤ The migration tools must be run on the target domain controller. Physical access to the target computer is required unless Windows Terminal Services are used to run the tools remotely.

Now that we have covered the prerequisites for an interforest restructuring, it's time to discuss some of the details about cloning security principals. We'll cover the various aspects of cloning users, global groups, and universal groups; migrating computers and local group accounts; cloning local groups on domain controllers; and moving domain controllers.

Cloning Security Principals

A *clone* is an account in a native-mode Windows 2000 domain that contains properties that have been copied from a source account. The properties include user account properties and group memberships. Cloning (copying) security principals is the most common interforest migration operation. Although the clone has a different primary SID than the source account does, the **sIDHistory** attribute retains the original SID of the source account; this attribute allows access to network resources that were, or still are, available to the source account. For resource access to be retained, the proper trust relationships must exist from the resource domains to the clone's new account domain.

The advantage of cloning is that it does not disrupt the existing production environment in any way. When a cloned user account is properly configured, that user can log on to the new domain and can still fall back to the source account in the production environment if there are any problems. You can use the ADMT or the ClonePrincipal tool to clone security principals, and each source account maintains the original SID. A copy of the SID is also stored in the **sIDHistory** attribute of the cloned account. The ADMT gives you the additional ability to choose whether or not you want to migrate the SID.

Cloning is possible only between domains in different forests (interforest). Moving objects while updating the **sIDHistory** attribute is possible only between domains in the same Windows 2000 forest (intraforest).

Cloning Users

You can clone user accounts by using either the ADMT or ClonePrincipal. Each tool handles the process differently, so you'll need to be careful when choosing the appropriate tool. When you use ClonePrincipal, the source account is automatically disabled. When you use the ADMT, you can choose which account to disable, or you can elect to leave both accounts active, in which case both accounts can be used to log on to either the source or target domains. Not all of the source account properties are copied during cloning operations, but common properties—such as home directory, logon hours, and dial-in permissions—are copied.

Cloned users automatically become members of the Domain Users group in the target domain. In addition, global or universal group membership can be restored in the target domain as long as the groups to which a cloned user account belongs are also cloned to the target domain. The order in which the user and group migration is performed is not critical as long as both the users and the global or universal groups to which a cloned member belongs are both cloned to the target domain.

Cloning Global and Universal Groups

When you're cloning global or universal groups, the primary SID of the source group is retained in the **sIDHistory** attribute of the newly cloned group. The membership of the target group will also be restored to reflect that of the source group if member clone accounts exist. This is also true for nested groups when you're cloning from a Windows 2000 source domain. You can use ClonePrincipal or the ADMT to clone group accounts in an interforest restructuring.

You can also merge multiple source groups into a single target group; this merging allows you to combine multiple global groups from the source domain into one global group in the target domain. This allows you to collapse multiple Windows NT 4 account domains into the same Windows 2000 domain.

Migrating Computers and Local Group Accounts

Migrating computer accounts in an interforest scenario is functionally the same as moving computer accounts in an intraforest scenario. Computer accounts are never cloned; they are always moved to the target domain. You move computer accounts by using either the ADMT or Netdom, or you can manually join them to the target domain.

Local group accounts reside in the local SAM database. Local group accounts exist only on the computer where they are created, so their account properties are migrated when the computer on which they reside joins the target domain. This means that local groups are unaffected by migration, so their SIDs do not need to be changed. Permissions granted to local groups residing in resource DACLs on the moved computer will be maintained, and resource access will continue to function properly as long as the appropriate trust relationships exist in the target domain. If a local group contains members from trusted domains, trusts must be established between the target domain and any domains in which local group members reside.

Cloning Shared Local Groups on Domain Controllers

Shared local groups reside on Windows NT 4 PDCs and are shared between the PDC and all BDCs in the same domain. When you clone a shared local group, the **sIDHistory** attribute is retained, but the group itself is converted to a domain local group in the target domain. This occurs because the target domain is running in native mode. You can use ClonePrincipal or the ADMT to clone shared local groups, but the ADMT is the recommended method because it copies the local group and populates its membership automatically if the member accounts are migrated at the same time. You will still require the appropriate trust relationships to ensure continued access to resources in all affected domains.

 The Netdom and ADMT tools can help you identify and establish the appropriate trust relationships when you're cloning shared local groups.

Moving Domain Controllers

As it is with an intraforest restructuring, the task of moving domain controllers will be one of the final steps in an interforest restructuring. Domain controllers are never cloned; they must always be moved. To move an NT 4 domain controller, you can perform *one* of the following procedures:

➤ Upgrade the domain controller to Windows 2000 Server. When the Active Directory Installation Wizard runs, you can configure the computer to join the target domain.

➤ Reinstall the operating system as an NT 4 member server; then move or join it to the target domain in the same way as any other computer account. You can then leave it as a member server, or, if it is later upgraded to Windows 2000, you can promote it as an additional domain controller in the target domain.

> The only way to move a Windows 2000 domain controller is to first demote it to the role of a member server; then you manually join it to the target domain or use the ADMT or Netdom to move it like any other computer account.

Domain Restructuring Tools

Microsoft has provided several tools to help you with restructuring a domain. Various third-party tools are also available, but the certification exam will not address these, so even if you choose to use these third-party tools as part of your migration to Windows 2000, the certification exam will still expect you to know when and how to use the tools that are provided by Microsoft. Therefore, this section gives you the information you need to choose the right tools for conducting a successful migration, based on the scenario that is presented to you on the exam.

Migration Tools at 50,000 Feet

There are many Microsoft and third-party utilities available for migration. Lets start with the big picture. The tools and their capabilities that you will use for a domain restructuring include the following:

➤ *Active Directory Migration Tool (ADMT)*—The ADMT is a powerful tool that boasts a graphical user interface. ADMT is used for migrating security principals. It can be used in both an intraforest restructuring and an interforest restructuring.

➤ *ClonePrincipal*—ClonePrincipal consists of a set of Visual Basic scripts that clones users and groups to the target Windows 2000 environment. This tool can be used only in interforest migrations.

➤ *Netdom*—Netdom is a command-line utility that you use to query a domain for enumerating existing trust relationships. Netdom can also be used to create new trust relationships automatically and can add, move, and query computer accounts in a Windows domain. Netdom can be used in both an intraforest restructuring and an interforest restructuring.

➤ *LDP*—LDP is a graphical–user interface tool that uses LDAP (Lightweight Directory Access Protocol) to allow an administrator to display the attributes of objects in Active Directory. This tool allows you to verify that security principals have been migrated properly; you do this by displaying the **sIDHistory** attribute of a cloned security principal.

➤ *MoveTree*—MoveTree is a command-line utility that moves Active Directory security principal objects, such as users and groups, between domains in a single forest. MoveTree can be used only in an intraforest restructuring.

Now that you have had a brief introduction to some of the useful tools, let's delve deeper into some of the most popular, and testable, migration applications.

Active Directory Migration Tool

The ADMT is a wizard-based MMC (Microsoft Management Console) snap-in that is licensed from Mission Critical Software and that facilitates both intraforest and interforest migrations. You must download the ADMT from the Windows 2000 Web site because it is not shipped on the Windows 2000 CD-ROM. The ADMT should be installed only on Windows 2000 domain controllers in target domains. If you are using a terminal server as part of your migration, the ADMT can be run from any computer.

Make sure that the computer on which the ADMT is installed has the following:

➤ A Pentium II or later CPU.

➤ 10MB of RAM, plus 4K for each migrated user.

➤ 35MB of free hard drive space: 7MB for ADMT installation, and 25MB for data and log files.

The ADMT also dispatches an agent to each computer to perform operations that can only be performed locally. An agent runs as a service on the individual computer and can operate only on computers running the following operating systems:

➤ Windows NT 3.51 with Service Pack 5 (both Intel- and Alpha-based computers)

➤ Windows NT 4 with Service Pack 4 or later (both Intel- and Alpha-based computers)

➤ Windows 2000

Computers on which the ADMT agent will operate must meet the following requirements:

➤ The PC must have a hard-disk partition with at least 15MB of free disk space for the agent and agent log files.

➤ The ADMIN$ share, which points to the %systemroot%, must exist on computers running Windows 3.51 for the agent to install successfully.

➤ The ADMT user must be logged on with a user account that has Administrator or equivalent permissions on the target computer. Note that the built-in Administrators group normally contains the Domain Admins group from the computer's domain.

➤ Remote Registry access must be enabled.

➤ NetBIOS should be enabled.

➤ The NetBIOS Server service should be running.

➤ The target computer must be a valid member of a valid domain. Note that some computers might have been disconnected from the domain for some time and its password might have expired.

ADMT: The Swiss Army Knife of Migration

You use the ADMT to move users, groups, and computer accounts from one domain to another in an intraforest migration and to copy users and groups from one domain to another in an interforest migration. Because computer accounts can never be cloned, the ADMT is also used to move computer accounts from one domain to another in an interforest migration. The ADMT can be used to populate the **sIDHistory** attribute of migrated security principals so that access to resources in the source domain can be maintained until these resources are migrated to the target domain.

The ADMT is a comprehensive tool that allows you to analyze the migration both before and after the migration process. The ADMT also provides many additional capabilities, including reporting, fallback, and auditing features, in addition to allowing you to test migration scenarios before you perform the migration. With this tool, you can diagnose any possible problems before starting migrations to the Windows 2000 Server Active Directory. The ADMT also provides support for parallel domains, so you can maintain your existing Windows NT 4 domains while you deploy Windows 2000. A lesser-known capability of the ADMT is the ability to migrate Microsoft Exchange Server mailboxes.

Before performing the migration, you can test the process without actually migrating the accounts. You do this by selecting Test The Migration Settings And Migrate Later in all of the migration wizards.

Maintaining Access

Access to network resources (files, folders, printers, and shares) is protected by access control lists (ACLs) contained in security descriptors associated with each resource. The ADMT can change security descriptors that refer to a group or user account in a source domain so that they refer to another group or user account in a target domain.

For example, when you migrate a group or user account from domain X to domain Y, a new account is created in domain Y. This new account can have the same name as the original account in domain X, but this new account has a different SID. The ADMT changes the security descriptors for various resources to refer to the SID for the new account in domain Y. This process ensures that the new group or user account provides the same access to resources that the original group or user account provided. The process of changing the security descriptors is called *security translation,* which is performed by the Security Translation Wizard.

If the ADMT finds a source domain SID that it cannot resolve, such as a SID for an existing user account that does not have a matching user account in the target domain, the ADMT leaves the SID unchanged.

The security on resources does not need to be translated before the source account is deleted. However, to eliminate administrative confusion, you will most likely want to translate security before deleting the source account. After the source account is gone, the resource will no longer be able to resolve the SID to a name, and the security properties will show an "Unknown Account" name. The access will still work, but the system can't resolve the SID to a name. If you upgrade the resource domain to Windows 2000, Windows 2000 will be able to detect the **sIDHistory** attribute and then resolve the name properly. So, over time, you will want to manually clean up **sIDHistory** attributes and grant access to the new security principals.

ADMT Challenges

One sensitive area to be aware of is that Windows 2000 recognizes only the first 30 entries in Registry-key ACLs. If security translation is performed in Add mode, then more than 30 entries can exist at the end of the process. The large number of ACEs (access control entries) on certain Registry keys might result in users being locked out of the affected system because Windows 2000 stops examining the ACEs after the first 30 are compared.

To prevent this problem, if the Security Translation Wizard encounters an ACL with more than 15 ACEs while running in Add mode, the wizard will skip the Registry keys during the Registry security translation process. This will not occur if the security translation is run in Replace or Remove mode. An excess of ACEs will not occur if you have not manually changed any Registry-key ACEs on the affected systems.

ADMT and Exchange

The ADMT can also change the security descriptors for Exchange mailboxes, distribution lists, custom recipients, sites, organizations, and containers, as well as the primary Windows NT or Windows 2000 account for each mailbox, to reflect the SID for the new security principal in the target domain. This process ensures that the new security principal has the same access to resources and Exchange components as the original account.

To translate Exchange security, you must install Microsoft Exchange Administrator on a computer running the ADMT. If you want to translate Exchange security for Exchange mailboxes, distribution lists, custom recipients, organizations, sites, and containers, the account credentials you specify during the translation process must be a Permissions Admin in the Exchange site of the specified Exchange server.

Using ADMT

After you install the ADMT, you can access it through the Administrative Tools folder. The ADMT is often your primary tool for migrating security principals because of all of the functionality it offers. Additional information on the use of the ADMT is located within the ADMT help file. When you're performing a lengthy migration, always run the ADMT from the same domain controller. The ADMT stores information used during the migration process in a file on the computer on which the tool is run. If you must change domain controllers during the migration, you can move this information to the new domain controller by copying the protar.mdb file to the Active Directory Migration Tool folder on the new domain controller.

ADMT Wizards

The ADMT consists of a series of wizards, including the User Migration Wizard, the Computer Migration Wizard, the Security Translation Wizard, the Group Mapping And Merging Wizard, the Group Migration Wizard, the Service Account Migration Wizard, the Trust Migration Wizard, and the Reporting Wizard.

Before migrating groups, you can run the Group Mapping And Merging Wizard to map a group in the source domain to a new or existing group in the target domain. This mapping ensures that when the group's members are migrated from the source domain into the target domain, group memberships will reflect the mapping. You can also merge multiple groups into one group with this wizard.

Note: Contrary to its name, the Service Account Migration Wizard is not used to migrate service accounts; it is used only to identify the service accounts that must be migrated. You migrate service accounts with the User Migration Wizard. In addition, during the migration process, this wizard truncates service account names and user account names that are more than 20 characters long.

When you're running the Service Account Migration Wizard or the Computer Migration Wizard, you must be logged on to the source domain as an administrator or as a member of the Administrators group. When you're running the User Migration Wizard, the Group Migration Wizard, or the Security Migration Wizard, you must be logged on to the target domain as the administrator or as a member of the Administrators group.

Refer to Figure 8.1, which shows a fly-out window within the ADMT, displaying all of the wizards that can be used for migrating security principals and their properties.

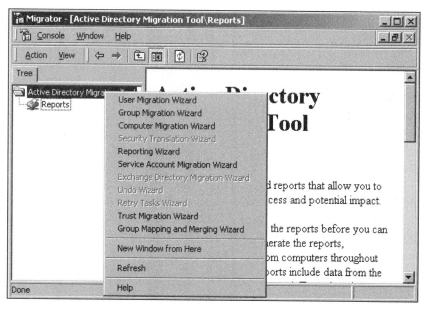

Figure 8.1   ADMT Wizards.

The ADMT's Reporting Wizard can provide you with the following detailed reports, which allow you to evaluate the migration process and the potential impact:

➤ *Migrated Users And Groups Report*—Summarizes the results of the user and group migration operations.

➤ *Migrated Computers Report*—Summarizes the results of the computer migration operations.

➤ *Expired Computers Report*—Lists the computer accounts with expired passwords.

➤ *Impact Analysis Report*—Lists the user accounts and groups that will be affected by computer migration operations.

➤ *Name Conflicts Report*—Lists the user accounts and groups that exist in both the source and target domains.

ClonePrincipal

ClonePrincipal consists of a suite of sample Microsoft Visual Basic scripts that copy users and groups from a source Windows NT 4 or Windows 2000 domain to the target Windows 2000 native-mode domain without affecting your production environment. Like the ADMT, ClonePrincipal populates the **sIDHistory** attribute of cloned accounts in order to retain the original access to resources in the source domain that existed before the migration.

The ClonePrincipal files can be found in the Support\Tools folder on the Windows 2000 Server CD. They include the following scripts:

➤ *sidhist.vbs*—Copies the SID of the source security principal to the **sIDHistory** attribute of an existing destination security principal.

➤ *clonepr.vbs*—Copies the properties of a source security principal, and copies the source SID to the **sIDHistory** attribute of the destination object. The destination security principal does not need to exist, but if it does, both the destination SAM name and the distinguished name must refer to the same object.

➤ *clonegg.vbs*—Clones all global groups in a domain, including well-known accounts such as Domain Guests, but excludes built-in accounts such as Backup Operators.

➤ *cloneggu.vbs*—Clones all global groups and users in a domain, including well-known accounts but excluding built-in accounts.

➤ *clonelg.vbs*—Clones all local groups in a domain, including well-known accounts but excluding built-in accounts.

You must memorize the names and functions of these ClonePrinicpal scripts. It isn't as nasty as it looks. Just remember what the letters mean: pr means property, gg means global group, ggu means global groups and users, and lg means local groups. They won't be so evil to give you a bogus file name with the letters pr tacked on.

When you install ClonePrincipal by using the Windows 2000 Support Tools setup procedure, the clonepr.dll file is automatically registered. If you install ClonePrincipal manually, however, you'll also have to register the clonepr.dll file manually by running the following command in the directory in which clonepr.dll resides: **regsvr32 clonepr.dll.**

For security reasons, Microsoft also recommends unregistering ClonePrincipal when it is not in use. You do this by entering the following command in the directory in which clonepr.dll resides: **regsvr32 /u clonepr.dll.**

Netdom

Netdom is a command-line tool that is one of the Windows 2000 Support Tools found in the Support\Tools folder on the Windows 2000 Server CD. Netdom can be used as part of an automated migration script to join a computer running Windows 2000 to a Windows NT 4 domain or a Windows 2000 domain while also specifying the OU (organizational unit) and generating a random computer password for the initial joining. Netdom also provides an option to move an existing computer account for a member workstation from one domain to another while maintaining the security descriptor on the computer account.

Netdom has many other useful features, including the ability to establish trust relationships between Windows NT 4 and Windows 2000 domains or shortcut trusts between two Windows 2000 domains. Netdom can also be used to verify and\or reset the secure channel for the following configurations:

➤ Member workstations and servers

➤ BDCs in a Windows NT 4 domain

➤ Specific Windows 2000 replicas

Netdom can also be used to manage trust relationships between domains. You can use Netdom to:

➤ View all trust relationships.

➤ Enumerate all direct and indirect trust relationships.

Netdom commands are case sensitive.

LDP

LDP has a Windows-Explorer-like graphical interface that allows you to perform various LDAP operations, including connecting, binding, searching, modifying, adding, and deleting objects in Active Directory or any other LDAP-compatible directory. This can be very useful when you want to view or delete the **sIDHistory** attribute assigned to a migrated object.

MoveTree

MoveTree is a command-line tool that can be used only in intraforest migrations to move Active Directory objects—such as users, groups, and OUs—between domains in a single Windows 2000 forest. MoveTree is also found in the Support\Tools folder on the Windows 2000 Server CD. MoveTree can add the source domain SID to the **sIDHistory** attribute of a migrated object, but this works only if the target domain is running in native mode. MoveTree can move global groups only as a closed set of groups in the source domain, so it has limited functionality in most migration scenarios. These types of operations primarily support domain consolidation or organizational restructuring operations.

Universal groups are moved intact during a MoveTree operation. However, because of group membership rules, only empty domain local groups and global groups can be moved. Computer objects are not moved during a MoveTree operation. Instead, use Netdom to move computer accounts between domains and to join computers to domains.

MoveTree allows for the creation of OUs, which is not possible with ADMT.

Overview of the Capabilities of the Migration Tools

MoveTree maintains a user's existing password; ClonePrincipal and the ADMT do not. ClonePrincipal sets the password to **NULL** on cloned user accounts. The ADMT can be used to generate a complex random password for migrated users accounts, or it can be used to set the password to the first 14 characters of the user account name.

When you're performing an interforest migration, the ADMT always sets the User Must Change Password option for migrated users. If the user account has the User Cannot Change Password option set, the target account won't be able to log on until one or both options have been changed.

MoveTree and the ADMT maintain the Active Directory object's GUID (globally unique identifier), but ClonePrincipal does not. MoveTree and ClonePrincipal are scriptable, but the ADMT is not. Refer to Table 8.1 for a detailed comparison of the features of each of the tools discussed in this section.

Table 8.1 Comparison of MoveTree, ClonePrincipal, ADMT, and Netdom.				
Feature	**MoveTree**	**ClonePrincipal**	**ADMT**	**Netdom**
Maintains existing passwords	Y	N	N	N/A
Generates complex passwords	N	N	Y	N/A
Moves NT 4 users, groups, and computers	N	N	Y	N/A
Populates the **sIDHistory** attribute of restructured objects	Y	Y	Y	N/A
Maintains the GUID of Active Directory objects	Y	N	Y	N/A
Can be scripted	Y	Y	N	Y
Moves local and global groups	N	N	Y	N/A
Moves universal groups	Y	N	Y	N/A
Moves computer accounts	N	N	Y	Y
Copies user accounts	N	Y	Y	N
Copies global group accounts	N	Y	Y	N
Copies Windows NT shared local groups (NT domain controllers)	N	Y	Y	N
Copies Windows 2000 domain local groups	N	Y	Y	N
Copies computer accounts	N	N	Y	Y
Moves built-in groups	N	N	N	N/A
Moves OUs	Y	N	N	N/A
Merges accounts	N	Y	Y	N/A

(continued)

Table 8.1 Comparison of MoveTree, ClonePrincipal, ADMT, and Netdom *(continued)*.				
Feature	MoveTree	ClonePrincipal	ADMT	Netdom
Sets primary group to Domain Users	N/A	Y	Y	N/A
Disables restructured accounts	N	N	Y	N/A
Migrates trusts	N	N	Y	Y
Disables source accounts	N	N	Y	N/A
Translates roaming profiles	Y	N	Y	N/A
Sets source account expiration	N/A	N	Y	N/A
Migrates service accounts	Y	Y	Y	N/A
Performs test migrations	Y	N	Y	N
Contains domain reporting capability	N	N	Y	N
Automatically identifies closed set for move operations	N	N/A	Y	N/A

 Memorize this table. It will be the subject of many of those "choose all that apply" questions we all know and love.

Windows 2000 Resource Kit Tools

The Windows 2000 Resource Kit contains more than 300 tools for administering a Windows NT 4 or Windows 2000 network. This section describes some of the tools that you might find useful when you're conducting a migration from Windows NT 4 to Windows 2000. This is not an exhaustive look at every tool in the Resource Kit; this is just an overview, which will provide you with enough information to pass this portion of the exam. You should not expect too many questions on the Resource Kit tools, so we'll limit this discussion to those tools that are most likely to be addressed on the exam. They are:

➤ *Global.exe*—Displays members of global groups on remote servers or domains.

➤ *Local.exe*—Displays members of local groups on remote servers or domains.

➤ *Findgrp.exe (Find Group)*—Finds all direct and indirect group memberships for a specified user in a domain. The Find Group tool can help you determine a particular user's access to Windows 2000 domain controllers in a domain by listing the groups in which the user is a member. The Find Group tool was created especially for use in a trusted domain model. Administrative access to either your domain or the user's domain is not required.

➤ *Usrstat.exe*—Displays the user name, full name, and last logon date and time for each user in a given domain.

➤ *Showmbrs.exe*—Shows the user names of members of a given group, even within a given network domain.

➤ *Showgrps.exe*—Shows the groups to which a user belongs, even within a given network domain. This is a command-line tool.

➤ *Showacls.exe (ShowACLs)*—Enumerates access rights for files, folders, and trees. It allows masking to enumerate only specific ACLs. The ShowACLs tool works on NTFS (New Technology File System) partitions only. The most useful feature of ShowACLs is the ability to show permissions for a particular user. ShowACLs does this by enumerating the local and global groups that the particular user belongs to and matching the user's SID, and the SIDs of the groups the user belongs to, to the SIDs in each ACE (access control entry).

➤ *Perms.exe*—Displays a user's access permissions for a specified file or set of files.

➤ *Gpolmig.exe*—Helps to migrate Windows NT 4 system policies to the Windows 2000 group policy object structure.

➤ *Subinacl.exe*—Allows an administrator to obtain security information on files, Registry keys, and services, and to transfer ownership from one user to another user, from a local or global group to another group, and from one domain to another domain.

➤ *Nlmon.exe (NLMonitor)*—Is used to list and test many aspects of trust relationships. NLMonitor uses the Computer Browser service to enumerate domain controllers; therefore, if browsing is not working correctly, NLMonitor might produce inconsistent results. Also, the computer on which NLMonitor is run and the computers providing the browsing services must share the same protocols that are used by the domain controllers to carry out their domain activity.

Additional Tools

A few other tools are worth mentioning in case you see them on the certification exam. These are ADSI Edit, the Active Directory Connector (ADC), Nltest.exe, and Lbridge.cmd.

ADSI Edit is a Microsoft Management Console (MMC) snap-in that is added to a Windows 2000 computer when you install the Windows 2000 Support Tools. ADSI Edit acts as a low-level editor for Active Directory. Using Active Directory Service Interfaces (ADSI), this tool provides a means to add, delete, and move objects within Active Directory. Using ADSI Edit, you can view, change, and delete the attributes of each object, including the **sIDHistory** attribute.

The ADC (Active Directory Connector) tool is located in the valueadd\msft\mgmt\ADC folder on the Windows 2000 Server CD. The ADC can be used to configure connection agreements between a Windows 2000 domain controller and an Exchange Server (running version 5.5). You can configure one-way connection agreements in either direction or configure a connection agreement in both directions, but the ADC is used primarily to extend the Windows 2000 Active Directory schema to include the Exchange Server attributes that are not included by default as Active Directory attributes. The ADC allows you to set a schedule for replication of the Exchange mailbox attributes in order to map them to Active Directory attributes.

Nltest.exe is a command-line tool that helps you perform network administrative tasks such as the following:

➤ Getting a list of PDCs

➤ Forcing a shutdown

➤ Querying and checking on the status of a trust relationship

➤ Testing trust relationships and the state of domain controller replication in a Windows domain

➤ Forcing a user-account database into sync on Windows NT 4 or earlier domain controllers (Windows 2000 domain controllers use a completely different mechanism for maintaining user accounts)

Nltest, which is one of the Windows 2000 Support Tools, can be used to test the trust relationship between a Windows computer that is a member of a domain and a domain controller where its computer account resides. Nltest can also verify the trust between the BDCs in a domain and their PDC. In domains where an explicit trust has been defined, Nltest can test the trust relationship between all domain controllers in the trusting domain and a domain controller in the trusted domain.

Domain controllers talk to each other using *secure channels*. These channels are used to authenticate Windows computer accounts. Secure channels are also used to authenticate user accounts when a remote user connects to a network resource and the user account exists in a trusted domain. This is called *pass-through authentication*, and it allows a Windows computer that has joined a domain to have access to the user account database in its domain and in any trusted domains.

For Windows 2000, Nltest no longer uses the Browser Service to enumerate domain controllers. Instead, you use the /dclist parameter with NlTest, which calls the DsGetDomainControllerInfo API to get the domain controller list from Active Directory.

Lbridge.cmd is a script that provides a bridge between the replication architectures of NT 4 and Windows 2000. You may see Lbridge referred to as "L-bridge", but the actual file is Lbridge.cmd. Either name applies to the Lbridge script. This sample script can be edited; it moves files from the Windows 2000 Sysvol folder to the Export directory used by the LAN Manager replication service on NT 4 servers. The benefit of this approach is that it keeps the two replication mechanisms physically separated from one another so that no legacy services are introduced onto the Windows 2000 domain controller. Lbridge.cmd is a sample batch file that you can adapt to your own needs. It can use either Xcopy or Robocopy as the file-copying application. Robocopy is the preferred method because it provides greater administrative control. Lbridge.cmd, Xcopy.exe, and Robocopy.exe are located in the Windows 2000 Resource Kit.

Practice Questions

Case Study

Mike Fos International

Mike Fos International is the leader in fashionable eyewear in the United States. Corporate headquarters are in Denver, Colorado; the research and development department is in Scottsdale, Arizona; manufacturing is in Edgerton, Wyoming; and marketing is in San Diego, California. These locations are all connected with a high-speed dedicated network.

Denver, Colorado

During their transition to a Windows 2000 environment, the local IT personnel set up the corporate headquarters domain **DenverFos**. This domain is Internal to the LAN and does not share the DNS namespace with their corporate Internet presence. Upon further examination, the CIO and the various directors want to completely centralize headquarters' operations into a central **MikeFos** domain. This is to be performed in a logical and cost-effective manner with minimal disruption to production operations. Fortunately, the IT department created a forest root named **ROOT** to hold the schema and domain naming FSMO servers. The only user accounts in this forest root are the default administrator and the disabled guest account.

Scottsdale, Arizona

The research and development domain, **ScottsRD**, joined the corporate network forest as a separate tree with **ROOT** as the common forest root. This was done to enhance security on local projects. The CIO wants to incorporate the R&D domain into the central **MikeFos** domain. The numerous projects in development require that the ACL of the files, shares, and other resources are unchanged. Barbara Jackson, the Java guru who spearheads the **COLOSSUS** project, has been given explicit permissions assigned to her user account throughout the enterprise, as well as trusting domains controlled by external companies. Re-creating her account and identifying and resetting ACEs would cost more than you make in a year and is not an option.

Edgerton, Wyoming

Someone in the manufacturing department in Edgerton, after reading a magazine article on how cool Windows 2000 is, rolled out Active Directory without centralized guidance. This domain, **Mikescowboys.mil**, was immediately populated with more than 3,000 user accounts, multiple global groups, and a security and share structure that can only be described as poorly designed, but thoroughly executed. To ensure a reliable restore option, all of the domain controllers were converted directly to Windows 2000 or were formatted as low-end internal Web servers. Backup tapes are something the facility is planning to roll out in Q1, 2006. The CIO has instructed Terry Sampson, the local administrator, that this rogue forest be brought into the central **MikeFos** domain while retaining usernames and group memberships. This set includes Terry's personal account and memberships. The CIO also believes that restructuring the security ACLs will be a good lesson on the perils of ignoring corporate policy. Because both local IT professionals are salaried, manpower costs are expected to remain the same, or slightly decrease, due to the flat Wyoming local job market.

San Diego, California

The marketing department in San Diego has yet to implement Active Directory and has been running off of a workgroup model to support access for its 15 employees to its three local Windows 2000 standalone servers. The user accounts will need to be created in the central **MikeFos** domain, but they should be disabled until all team members can attend a mandatory computer-security briefing.

Additional Services and Clients

All of Mike Fos International is running Exchange 5.5 and will not migrate to Exchange 2000 until late next year. The company is also running Microsoft SQL Server 7 to provide database tracking of order fulfillment and client tracking. There are currently no plans to upgrade the SQL server. All client machines are currently running Windows 2000.

Question 1

> What tool can you use to migrate system policies from the NT environment to the new Windows 2000 domain?
>
> O a. ADMT
>
> O b. Poledit.exe
>
> O c. Gpolmig.exe
>
> O d. Systogp.exe

Answer c is correct. Gpolmig is the utility that is used to convert NT policies to the group policy format of a Windows 2000 Domain. Answer a is incorrect because ADMT doesn't have a wizard for group policies. Answer b is incorrect because Poledit is used to create NT and Windows 9x system policies. Answer d is incorrect because Systogp doesn't exist.

Question 2

> Which of the following migration utilities will ensure that you don't lose the GUID of the source object? [Check all correct answers]
>
> ❑ a. ClonePrincipal
>
> ❑ b. MoveTree
>
> ❑ c. GUIDStore
>
> ❑ d. ADMT

Answers b and d are correct. MoveTree and the ADMT maintain the Active Directory object's GUID (globally unique identifier). Answer a is incorrect because ClonePrincipal does not maintain the GUID. Answer c is incorrect because GUIDStore does not exist.

Question 3

> Which ADMT Wizard will you use to migrate your Exchange and SQL user service accounts?
>
> ○ a. Security Translation Wizard
>
> ○ b. User Migration Wizard
>
> ○ c. Trust Migration Wizard
>
> ○ d. Service Account Migration Wizard

Answer b is correct. You migrate service accounts with the User Migration Wizard. Answers a and c are incorrect because the Security Translation Wizard and the Trust Migration Wizard do not migrate user accounts. Answer d is incorrect because the Service Account Migration Wizard is not used to migrate service accounts. It is used only to identify the service accounts that must be migrated. The Service Account Migration Wizard must be ran prior to running the User Migration Wizard or the service associations will not be properly identified.

Question 4

Which tools can you use to migrate the **ScottsRD** domain? [Check all correct answers]

❏ a. AMDT

❏ b. ClonePrincipal

❏ c. Netdom

❏ d. MoveTree

Answers a, c, and d are correct. Answer b is incorrect because ClonePrincipal can be used only in an interforest migration; because **ScottsRD** and **MikeFos.com** are in the same forest, ClonePrincipal cannot be used.

Question 5

Which objects can be moved without your having to reset the SID on the resource ACE? [Check all correct answers]

❏ a. Manufacturing group

❏ b. Scottsdale Engineering group

❏ c. **Barbara.Jackson** user account

❏ d. **Terry.Sampson** user account

Answers b and c are correct. Updating the **sIDHistory** attribute is possible only between domains in the same Windows 2000 forest. The **sIDHistory** attribute is what allows you to maintain the same access control entry, pointing to the same SID on the resource's access control list. The Scottsdale engineering group and the **Barbara.Jackson** user account reside in the ScottsRD domain and can be moved to the **Mikefos** domain, which is in the same forest.

The manufacturing group, and the **Terry.Sampson** user account are both from the **Mikescowboys.mil** domain, which is in a separate forest and you can't update a **sIDHistory** attribute between forests. This is an example of the level of extraction you will be required to perform during a live exam. Microsoft may throw you non-intuitive names. The exam may also hinge on the introductory information that identifies location roles and then expect you to extrapolate group memberships based on this shred of information. In a non-adaptive exam, always read the questions prior to reading the case study. Reading the questions will help you focus on just the required information and will assist in winnowing out the chaff from the kernels of worthwhile information in the multi-paragraphed case study.

If you find you are stuck, simply guess and move on. Any question you don't answer is marked wrong.

Question 6

Why can't the administrator in the **Mikescowboys.mil** domain migrate users to the **MikeFos** domain?

○ a. The Edgerton administrator has been trying to run the ADMT on the **Mikescowboys.mil** PDC Emulator. It needs to run on the domain naming master.

○ b. The user account that is being migrated doesn't have a duplicate SID in the **MikeFos** domain.

○ c. The ADMT cannot be executed via a terminal server connection to the target **MikeFos** domain controller.

○ d. The Edgerton administrator does not have physical access to a global catalog server in the **MikeFos** domain.

Answer d is correct. The ADMT must be executed on a domain controller in the target domain. A global catalog server in the **MikeFos** domain must be a domain controller and would perform a successful migration. Answer a is incorrect; you cannot run the application on the domain naming master because that is located in the **ROOT** domain and not the target **MikeFos** domain. Answer b is incorrect because an interforest restructuring requires that a migrated user account *cannot* have an existing SID or **sIDHistory** attribute in the target domain that matches the source SID. Answer c is incorrect because you can run the ADMT via a terminal server connection.

Question 7

Which of the following is required to restructure the **DenverFos** domain to the **MikeFos** domain? [Check all correct answers]

❑ a. **Mikefos** must be a native-mode domain.

❑ b. You must edit the TcpipClientSupport Registry key in the **MikeFos** domain.

❑ c. Audit Account Management must be enabled in the Default Domain Controllers group policy in both the **DenverFos** and **MikeFos** domains.

❑ d. All mapped drives between the **DenverFos** domain controller and the **MikeFos** domain controller must be disconnected.

Answers a, c, and d are correct. Answer b is incorrect because the Registry modification must occur in the source domain, not the destination domain.

Question 8

> What local group needs to be created, and where should it be located, for you to successfully migrate the Wyoming domain?
>
> ○ a. Mikescowboys.mil$$$ in the **Mikescowboys.mil** domain
>
> ○ b. Mikescowboys.mil$$$ in the **MikeFos** domain
>
> ○ c. MikeFos$$$ in the **Mikescowboys.mil** domain
>
> ○ d. MikeFos$$$ in the **MikeFos** domain

Answer a is correct. This group is created only in the source domain. The group is used for auditing and must be empty.

Question 9

> How can we move the domain controllers from the Denver, Scottsdale, and Edgerton, in that order, into the **MikeFos** domain? Put the steps below in the appropriate order. Use all of the entries.
>
> Run Dcpromo.exe on **grumpy.ScottsRD**
>
> Run Dcpromo on **con4.MikeFos**
>
> Rename **grumpy.ScottsRD** to **con3.ScottsRD**
>
> Run Dcpromo.exe on **main.DenverFos**
>
> Run Dcpromo.exe on **Wyatt.Mikescowboys.mil**
>
> Move **con4.Mikescowboys.mil** to the **MikeFos** domain
>
> Move **con3. ScottsRD** to the **MikeFos** domain
>
> Move **con2.Denverfos** to the **MikeFos** domain
>
> Run Dcpromo on **con3.MikeFos**
>
> Rename **Main.DenverFos** to **con2.DenverFos**
>
> Rename **Wyatt.Mikescowboys.mil** to con4.Mikescowboys.mil
>
> Run Dcpromo on **con2.MikeFos**

The correct answer is:

> Run Dcpromo.exe on **main.DenverFos**
>
> Rename **Main.DenverFos** to **con2.DenverFos**
>
> Move **con2.Denverfos** to the **MikeFos** domain
>
> Run Dcpromo on **con2.MikeFos**
>
> Run Dcpromo.exe on **grumpy.ScottsRD**
>
> Rename **grumpy.ScottsRD** to **con3.ScottsRD**
>
> Move **con3. ScottsRD** to the **MikeFos** domain
>
> Run Dcpromo on **con3.MikeFos**
>
> Run Dcpromo.exe on **Wyatt.Mikescowboys.mil**
>
> Rename **Wyatt.Mikescowboys.mil** to **con4.Mikescowboys.mil**
>
> Move **con4.Mikescowboys.mil** to the **MikeFos** domain
>
> Run Dcpromo on **con4.MikeFos**

The way you move a Windows 2000 domain controller is you run Dcpromo to drop it down to a member server, rename it, move it to the target domain and, if desired, promote it back to a domain controller. Remember that Windows 2000 Active Directory will not allow you to move, or rename, domain controllers so you have to drop them down to member servers.

Question 10

What must be done to ensure that local user accounts in the marketing servers will retain access to the local resources when the workgroup is transferred to the **MikeFos** domain?

- ○ a. The ADMT must be used to create a **sIDHistory** attribute for the local member-server user accounts.

- ○ b. The ClonePrincipal migration tool will ensure that the closed set of local groups and local accounts is retained. This will update the DACL on the resources automatically.

- ○ c. DACL entries must be re-created because there is no way to retain member-server local user account and group membership during a migration.

- ○ d. Nothing has to be done because local SAM databases are unaffected by an Active Directory migration.

Answer d is correct. The local user accounts and groups of member servers are not used, nor are they aware of Active Directory. The migration tools have no effect.

Question 11

What will be the biggest challenge in the enterprise restructuring of the Mike Fos International directory structure?

○ a. Edgerton's maze of permissions and group assignments

○ b. San Diego's addition to the **MikeFos** domain

○ c. Centralized administration with local delegation

○ d. Re-creating the forest root to support the new **MikeFos** domain structure

Answer a is correct. Edgerton's mixture of group assignments might make it difficult to reassign DACL access to the migrated resources. You might decide that a slash and burn policy of resource assignment is the most effective solution. Answer b is incorrect because migrating a workgroup to a domain is one of the easiest migrations to perform. Answer c is incorrect because the new structure really lends itself to centralized administration. When you consolidate all user accounts into a single domain and you have great connectivity, administrative delegation with centralized control is relatively simple. Answer d is incorrect because the forest root will remain unchanged. **MikeFos** will simply be added as a new tree in an existing forest.

Need to Know More?

 Microsoft Corporation. Microsoft Official Curriculum course 2010 "Designing a Microsoft Windows 2000 Migration Strategy". Module 5 "Restructuring Domains" is a wealth of information on tools and techniques for a successful restructure.

 Microsoft Corporation. *The Microsoft Windows 2000 Server Resource Kit*. Redmond, Washington: Microsoft Press, 2000. ISBN 1572318058. It has an outstanding poster of a fictious migration and deployment that covers nearly every situation a true professional will face in the real world and the exam.

 Microsoft Corporation. Microsoft Windows 2000 Support Tools Help Files. Microsoft has really done an outstanding job on the majority of its help files. The information on the ADMT will be of particular interest.

 Microsoft Corporation. Microsoft "Determining Domain Migration Strategies" document, which is a reprint from *The Microsoft Windows 2000 Server Resource Kit*. Redmond, Washington: Microsoft Press, 2000. ISBN 1572318058. The section titled "Domain Migration Tools" gives a wonderful overview of several of the tools you can use for your restructuring. This is located at: **www.microsoft.com/windows2000/ library/resources/reskit/samplechapters/dgbf/dgbf_upg_ovaw.asp**.

 Microsoft Corporation. Microsoft "Deployment Planning Guide" Web site. Chapter 10 "Determining Domain Migration Strategies" provides a road map for a medium to large migration. This is located at: **www.microsoft.com/windows2000/library/resources/reskit/dpg/ default.asp**.

 Microsoft Corporation. Microsoft Windows 2000 Domain Migration Cookbook. Microsoft white paper. 2000. Section 2, Migration Scenarios gives great examples of a migration process by walking you through a fictitious migration. This is located at **www.microsoft.com/ WINDOWS2000/library/planning/activedirectory/cookbook.asp**.

Microsoft Corporation. Chapter 3 of the Microsoft Exchange 2000 Server Upgrade Series "Deploying the Active Directory Connector". The section entitled "Creating an Interorganizational Connection Agreement" provides excellent insight into dealing with exchange deployments that are not part of the same Exchange organization—a typical problem in a reorganization. This is located at: **www.microsoft.com/TechNet/exchange/ guide/deploy/d_03_tt1.asp.**

 Goth, Jen. Microsoft Interactive Training Tool online course "How to Migrate Your Windows NT 4.0 Directory Services to Windows 2000 Active Directory". TNQ200-0-3. The discussion on **sIDHistory** and the demo of the Security Translation Wizard are excellent resources for combining domains in a single forest. This is located at: **www. microsoft.com/TechNet/events/fall/tnq20003/html/default.htm.**

 Microsoft Corporation. Microsoft Windows 2000 Active Directory Migration Tool download Web site at: **www.microsoft.com/ windows2000/downloads/deployment/admt/default.asp.**

 Microsoft Corporation. Microsoft Active Directory Service Interfaces (ADSI) application download can be found at: **www.microsoft.com/ technet/winnt/winntas/adsi25.asp.**

Post Migration and Restructuring

Terms you'll need to understand:

✓ Repadmin (Replication Administration) utility

✓ Replmon (Replication Monitor) utility

✓ Dsastat utility

✓ ADSI (Active Directory Service Interfaces)

✓ ADSI Edit

✓ DACL (discretionary access control list)

✓ Native mode

✓ Mixed mode

✓ Dcpromo (Active Directory Installation Wizard)

✓ DS Client (Directory Service Client)

Techniques you'll need to master:

✓ Using the Microsoft domain restructuring tools that are available for performing post-restructuring tasks in Windows 2000 domains

✓ Redefining resource DACLs

✓ Using the Backup program to back up source domains during and after the migration to provide a continuous history of the previous data and configuration

✓ Decommissioning source domains and redeploying the existing equipment

✓ Verifying the success of object migration

✓ Verifying the functionality of network services

✓ Removing the **sIDHistory** attribute of migrated objects

✓ Determining when to make the switch from mixed mode to native mode

This chapter discusses verifying that your domain migration has been successful. Regardless of whether you perform an upgrade, an intraforest domain restructuring, or an interforest domain restructuring, there are many tools and utilities you can use to check the status of the migration. Checking the status includes such tasks as verifying that your network services are configured properly and are functioning, checking log files for error messages, and backing up your source domain prior to decommissioning. You will also want to verify DNS resource records and determine how you will decommission and then redeploy the existing source domain equipment. You might have to redefine DACLs (discretionary access control lists) to avoid the Unknown User problem, which often occurs when the SIDs of the users and groups that have been migrated cannot be resolved. You might also have to clean up the **sIDHistory** attribute of migrated objects to minimize the size of access tokens. After your migration has been successfully completed, you will also need to determine when the target domain will be converted to production. The result of this will be the decommissioning of the source domain infrastructure so that you can redeploy the source domain hardware.

Verifying Network Services

Several critical network services should not only be maintained during a migration to Windows 2000 but must also be verified after the migration. This verification is needed to ensure that network clients are able to utilize all of the existing network services along with any new services that may have been deployed as part of the migration. The list of network services that should be verified will vary according to the services installed on your network, so this is not meant to be an exhaustive discussion of every possible network service that could exist in any organization. Instead, this section provides you with a high-level overview of some of the areas you need to consider when verifying that network services are functioning properly; you can then tailor this information to your production environment.

Perhaps the first place to start after you have upgraded your domain controllers is to verify the basic configuration of those domain controllers. The following are the minimum steps you should include in this process; they also apply to checking the configuration of network services and the configuration of the other computers on your network:

1. Verify the creation of DNS (Domain Name Service) resource records.

2. Verify domain controller promotion.

3. Verify domain controller functionality.

4. Verify the DHCP (Dynamic Host Configuration Protocol) Server service.

5. Verify the creation of WINS (Windows Internet Naming Service) resource records.

6. Check the Event Viewer.

7. Check services and applications (in the Services And Applications node in the Computer Management console tree).

8. Verify replication.

Verifying the Creation of DNS Resource Records

Besides A and PTR records that are registered by any Windows 2000 computer, additional records are registered by the domain controllers; the records vary according to their roles. Every time the Net Logon service starts (including restarting the domain controller), the service attempts to register some or all SRV resource records. The SRV resource records that are registered when you start the Net Logon service can be found in the Netlogon.dns file under the %systemroot%\System32\Config folder.

To reregister the domain controller SRV resource records, do the following: Open a command prompt; enter the **net stop netlogon** command; and then enter the **net start netlogon** command.

After you install Active Directory on a server running the Microsoft DNS (Domain Name Service), you can use the DNS Manager snap-in of the Microsoft Management Console (MMC) to verify that the appropriate zones and resource records are created for each DNS zone. Active Directory creates its SRV records in the following folders:

➤ _msdcs/dc/_sites/default-first-site-name/_tcp

➤ _msdcs/dc/_tcp

In these locations, an SRV record is displayed for the following services:

➤ _Kerberos

➤ _Lightweight Directory Access Protocol (LDAP)

If you use non-Microsoft DNS servers to support Active Directory, you can verify SRV locator resource records by viewing the netlogon.dns file, located in the %systemroot%\System32\Config folder. You can open and view this file by using a text editor. The first record displayed is the domain controller's LDAP (Lightweight Directory Access Protocol) SRV record, written in the format

```
_ldap._tcp.domainname
```

where *domainname* is the name of your domain.

You can also use the Nslookup utility to verify the creation of DNS resource records. To use this tool:

1. Open a command prompt.

2. Enter the following command: **nslookup set type=all**.

3. Enter the following command: **_ldap._tcp.dc._msdcs.***domainname* (where *domainname* is the name of your domain).

Nslookup returns one or more SRV resource, written in the format

```
hostname.domainname internet address = ipaddress
```

where *hostname* is the hostname of a domain controller, *domainname* is the domain to which the domain controller belongs, and *ipaddress* is the domain controller's IP address.

Another useful tool that can help you verify that your DNS server is operating properly is the Dnscmd.exe tool. Dnscmd.exe is a command-line tool that you can use to view the properties of DNS servers, zones, and resource records. Using the Dnscmd tool or the DNS Manager console, you can obtain information about the DNS server, including statistics about its performance. Dnscmd can also be used to manually modify DNS server properties, to create and delete zones and resource records, and to force a refresh of a DNS server's physical memory and DNS databases and data files.

Verifying Domain Controller Promotion

Several default files and folders are installed as part of the Active Directory installation process. These files and folders can be viewed in Windows Explorer, and they include ntds.dit, which is the Active Directory database file, located in the systemroot\NTDS folder. You can also verify that a computer is a domain controller by searching for the shared system volume. The shared system volume is a folder structure that exists on all Windows 2000 domain controllers. It stores scripts and some of the group policy objects for both the current domain and the enterprise. The default location for the shared system volume is %systemroot%\Sysvol.

The shared system volume must be located on a partition or volume formatted with the Windows 2000 version of the NT File System (NTFS 5).

Replication of the shared system volume occurs on the same schedule as replication of Active Directory. As a result, you might not notice file replication to or from the newly created system volume until two replication periods have elapsed (which typically takes 10 minutes). The first file replication period updates the configuration of other system volumes so that they are aware of the newly created system volume.

Another method for verifying domain controller promotion is to access the Network Identification tab of the System Properties dialog box for the computer that is the domain controller. This dialog box will state that the identification of the machine cannot be changed because this machine is a domain controller. Figure 9.1 shows an example of this tab.

 When you are confirming that this tab indicates the role of the computer on your network, you will also want to select the Advanced tab of the System Properties dialog box and confirm that the Application Response setting is correct; you do this by clicking on the Performance Options button in the Advanced tab and selecting the option for the role that server performs on the network.

Verifying Domain Controller Functionality

Additional tools exist for verifying that your domain controllers are functioning. The primary tool in this class is the Domain Controller Diagnostics tool (Dcdiag.exe). This utility analyzes the state of domain controllers in a forest or enterprise and

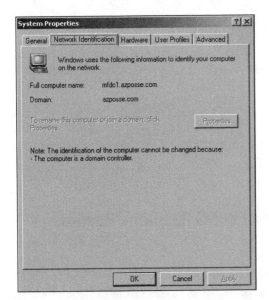

Figure 9.1   The Network Identification tab of the System Properties dialog box.

reports any problems. As an end-user reporting program, Dcdiag encapsulates detailed knowledge of how to identify abnormal behavior in the system.

Dcdiag consists of a framework for executing tests and a series of tests to verify different functional areas of the system. This framework selects which domain controllers are tested according to the user's scope directives, such as enterprise, site, or single server. Tests currently include: Connectivity, Replication, Topology Integrity, Check NC Head Security Descriptors, Check Net Logon Rights, Locator Get Domain Controller, Intersite Health, Check Roles, and Trust Verification. Dcdiag is the equivalent for domain controller functions of the Network Diagnostics tool (Netdiag.exe), another Windows 2000 Support Tool.

 Dcdiag /fix is designed to make safe repairs on your domain controller. It is a great tool, but it doesn't beat a good backup and recovery plan.

Netdiag is a command-line diagnostic tool that helps isolate networking and connectivity problems by performing a series of tests to determine the state of your network client (including whether it is functional). These tests, and the key network status information they provide, give network administrators and support personnel a more direct means of identifying and isolating network problems. Because this tool does not require you to specify any parameters or switches, you can focus on analyzing the output, rather than on training users how to use the tool.

Verifying the DHCP Server Service

To determine if the DHCP Server service is functioning properly, you can release and then renew your IP address by carrying out the following commands:

```
ipconfig /release
ipconfig /renew
```

If you still cannot connect the client to the domain controller (even though you have a good IP address), a Network Monitor sniffer trace of the connection attempt might be useful.

Verifying the Creation of WINS Resource Records

WINS is instrumental in maintaining down-level client's connectivity. Because the registration is dynamic, you will need to verify that records are being created. Windows 2000 also gives you the ability to create entries for queries in a text file if you want to run it more than once. To use the WINS Administration tool:

1. Load the WINS MMC from Start|Programs|Administrative Tools.

2. Select the WINS server you want to query.

3. Right-click on Active Registrations and select All Tasks.

4. Select Check Registered Names. And the Verify Name Records dialog box will appear.

5. Define your query in either the Look For Names Specified By or the In WINS Servers Specified By sections of the dialog box. You can use the asterisk, "*", wildcard characters to generate a broad query. This will give you the entire WINS database table.

 Another useful command is **NBTSTAT -c**. This command lists the contents of the local NetBIOS name table cache and displays the NetBIOS names and IP addresses that have been resolved for remote machines.

Verifying Replication

When you check network services, you'll also need to check various aspects of replication between the domain controllers on your network. For this task, you can use the Replication Administration tool and the Replication Monitor tool.

The Replication Administrator Utility

The Replication Administrator utility (Repadmin.exe), is a command-line tool used to diagnose replication problems between Windows 2000 domain controllers.

During normal operation, the Knowledge Consistency Checker (KCC) manages the replication topology for each naming context held on domain controllers. The Repadmin utility allows you to view the replication topology (sometimes referred to as RepsFrom and RepsTo) as seen from the perspective of each domain controller. In addition, you can use the Repadmin tool to manually create the replication topology, to force replication events between domain controllers, and to view both the replication metadata and the "up-to-dateness" vectors.

Note: During the normal course of operations, there is no need to manually create the replication topology. Incorrect use of the Repadmin tool may adversely affect the replication topology. The primary use of this tool is to monitor replication so that you can identify such problems as offline servers or unavailable LAN/WAN connections.

The **repadmin** command has the syntax

```
repadmin command arguments:[/u:[domain\]user /pw:{password|*}]
```

where *command* represents one of the supported commands, and *arguments* specifies the arguments applying to the command.

For a complete list of supported commands and their associated arguments, see the Windows 2000 Support Tools Help file. The arguments inside the brackets are as follows:

➤ /u:[domain\]user—Specifies an optional user (from an optional domain) as the administrator. If the username and password are not specified, Repadmin uses the credentials of the currently logged-on user.

➤ /pw:{password|*}—Specifies the password of the user specified by the /u: switch. If the username and password are not specified, Repadmin uses the credentials of the currently logged-on user.

The Replication Monitor Tool

Another tool that you might find useful when verifying replication is the Active Directory Replication Monitor (Replmon.exe). This is a Windows 2000 Support Tool that enables administrators to view the low-level status of Active Directory replication, to force synchronization between domain controllers, to view the topology in a graphical format, and to monitor the status and performance of domain controller replication through a graphical interface.

The Replmon utility works as a client of a COM object. You can use this tool to create your own applications or scripts, written in Visual Basic Scripting Edition (VBScript), to extract specific data out of Active Directory and act on it. The Replmon tool also includes functions that are wrapped APIs to make it easy to script replication between domain controllers with just a few lines of VBScript code.

 The file ladstools.doc, included with the Replmon tool, provides information on calling functions in the IADsTools ActiveX DLL from a script.

The Replmon tool must be installed on a computer running Windows 2000 Professional or Windows 2000 Server. The Replmon tool can be used to monitor domain controllers from different forests simultaneously.

When you're installing Replmon on localized builds of Windows 2000, the required Visual Basic controls might fail to register. This happens only if the Windows 2000 Support Tools are installed into a directory that contains extended characters. If this occurs, the workaround is to uninstall the Support Tools and then install them into the default folder (\Program Files\Support Tools).

The Dsastat Tool

A powerful diagnostic tool that can be used to compare and detect the differences between naming contexts on domain controllers is Dsastat. Dsastat can be used to compare two directory trees across replicas within the same domain or, in the case of a global catalog, across different domains. The Dsastat tool retrieves capacity statistics—such as megabytes per server, objects per server, and megabytes per object class—and compares attributes of replicated objects.

You specify the targeted domain controllers and additional operational parameters from the command line or from an initialization file. Dsastat determines whether domain controllers in a domain have a consistent and accurate image of their own domain. In the case of global catalogs, Dsastat checks to see if the global catalog has a consistent image with domain controllers in other domains. As a complement to the replication-monitoring tools Repadmin and Replmon, Dsastat can be used to ensure that domain controllers are synchronized with one another.

Backing Up Your Existing Source Domain

Both Windows NT 4 and Windows 2000 ship with built-in backup programs that can be used to back up the existing data and configuration information. These two backup programs are not the same program; therefore, the backup program you use will depend on whether you're backing up a Windows NT 4 source domain or a Windows 2000 source domain. For this discussion, we'll use the backup program that comes with Windows 2000. This backup utility helps you protect data from accidental loss if your system experiences hardware or storage media failure. For our purposes, the backup program will be used to create an historical record of our source domain; this record can then be used in the future for reference or for legal purposes.

You can use Backup to back up and restore data on either FAT (File Allocation Table) or NTFS (New Technology File System) volumes. However, if you have backed up data from an NTFS volume used in Windows 2000, it is recommended that you restore the data to an NTFS volume used in Windows 2000. If you don't, you could lose data as well as some file and folder features, such as permissions, disk quota information, mounted drive information, EFS (Encrypting File System) settings, and Remote Storage information. You can use Backup to:

➤ Archive selected files and folders on your hard disk.

➤ Restore the archived files and folders to your hard disk or any other disk you can access.

➤ Create an ERD (emergency repair disk), which helps you repair system files if they get corrupted or are accidentally erased.

➤ Make a copy of any Remote Storage data and any data stored in mounted drives.

➤ Make a copy of your computer's System State, which includes the Registry, the Active Directory database, and the Certificate Services database (if installed).

 It is the system state that holds Active Directory. Prior to a migration or restructure, make sure you have a good copy of the system state. You will use this backup in case your transformation fails.

➤ Schedule regular backups to keep your archived data up-to-date.

➤ Integrate with Windows 2000 Task Scheduler for automating backup jobs.

➤ Integrate with Remote Storage (storage management software in Windows 2000) for archiving data.

To open the Backup program, choose Start|Programs|Accessories|System Tools|Backup. This will open the Windows 2000 Backup And Recovery Tools dialog box, as shown in Figure 9.2.

The Backup utility supports five methods of backing up data on your computer or network. These include copy, daily, differential, incremental, and normal:

➤ A *copy backup* copies all selected files but does not mark each file as having been backed up (in other words, the archive attribute is not cleared). Copying is useful if you want to back up files between normal and incremental backups because copying does not affect these other backup operations.

➤ A *daily backup* copies all selected files that have been modified the day the daily backup is performed. The backed-up files are not marked as having been backed up (the archive attribute is not cleared).

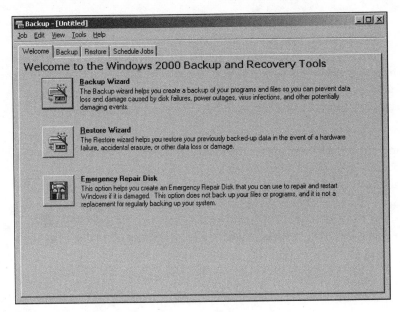

Figure 9.2   Windows 2000 Backup and Recovery Tools.

➤ A *differential backup* copies files created or changed since the last normal or incremental backup. It does not mark files as having been backed up (the archive attribute is not cleared). If you are performing a combination of normal and differential backups, restoring files and folders requires that you have the last normal backup as well as the last differential backup.

➤ An *incremental backup* backs up only those files that have been created or changed since the last normal or incremental backup. It marks files as having been backed up (the archive attribute is cleared). If you use a combination of normal and incremental backups, you will need to have the last normal backup set as well as all incremental backup sets in order to restore your data.

➤ A *normal backup* copies all selected files and marks each file as having been backed up (the archive attribute is cleared). With normal backups, you need only the most recent copy of the backup file or tape to restore all of the files. You usually perform a normal backup the first time you create a backup set.

An easy way to remember which type of copy affects markers is that if the name of the backup type has an "m" in it, it clears markers. Incremental and normal fit this description.

Figure 9.3 shows the Backup tab, which can be used to back up an entire hard drive or just selected files or folders on a hard drive. Figure 9.4 shows the Restore tab, which can be used to restore data that was backed up with the Backup program. Note that, as shown in Figure 9.2, you can also use the wizards supplied with the Backup program to assist you in creating or restoring a backup job, or you can use the Schedule Jobs tab to schedule a one-time or recurring backup job.

Backing up your data by using a combination of normal backups and incremental backups requires the least amount of storage space and is the quickest backup method. However, recovering files can be time-consuming and difficult because the backup set can be stored on several disks or tapes. Backing up your data by using a combination of normal backups and differential backups is more time-consuming, especially if your data changes frequently, but this combination makes it easier to restore the data because the backup set is usually stored on only a few disks or tapes.

Note: You must have Read access or be an administrator or a backup operator to back up files and folders.

When you're using Backup, you need to be aware of several issues. You can back up the System State data on only a local computer. You cannot back up the System State data on a remote computer. Backup files usually have the extension .bkf, although you can use any extension you like. Backup operators and administrators can back up and restore encrypted files and folders without decrypting the files or folders.

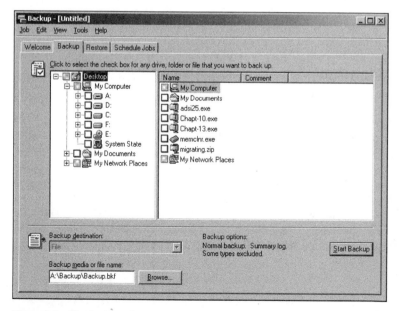

Figure 9.3 The Backup tab.

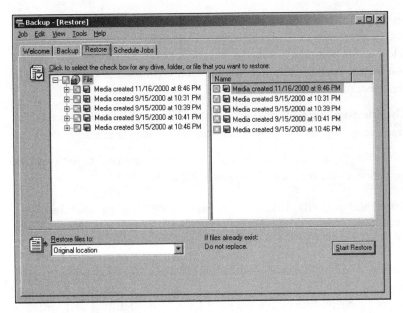

Figure 9.4 The Restore tab.

To capture Registry changes in your backup procedures, be sure to include the System State data in the backup set when you run Backup.

You must have certain permissions or user rights to back up files and folders. If you are an administrator or a backup operator in a local group, you can back up any file and folder on the local computer to which the local group applies. Likewise, if you are an administrator or backup operator on a domain controller, you can back up any file and folder (except the System State data as noted earlier) on any computer in the domain or back up any computer on a domain with which you have a two-way trust relationship. However, if you are not an administrator or a backup operator, and you want to back up files, then you must be the owner of the files and folders you want to back up, or you must have one or more of the following permissions for the files and folders you want to back up: Read, Read And Execute, Modify, or Full Control.

You can also perform backup operations at the command prompt or from a batch file by using the **ntbackup** command followed by various parameters. However, there are two important limitations to using batch files to back up your data:

➤ Using the **ntbackup** command, you can back up only entire folders. You cannot designate individual files for backup. However, you can designate a backup selection file (.bks file) from the command line; this file contains a list of files you want to back up. You must use the GUI version of the Backup utility to create backup selection files.

➤ The **ntbackup** command does not support the use of wildcard characters. For example, typing *.txt will not back up all files with a .txt extension.

The following is an example of using the **ntbackup** command to back up files and folders from the command line or by using a batch file:

```
ntbackup backup \\MikeFos\c$ /m normal /j "My Backup Job" /p
"Backup" /n "Command Line Backup Job 1" /d "Command Line Function-
ality Test" /v:yes /r:no /l:s /rs:no /hc:on
```

This example will perform a normal backup—named "My Backup Job"—of the remote share \\MikeFos\c$. This example will also pull a tape from the Backup media pool and name the tape "Command Line Backup Job 1." The description of the backup job will be named "Command Line Functionality Test." The backup will be verified after the backup job is complete; access will not be restricted to the owner/administrator; the logging level will be set to summary only; Remote Storage data will not be backed up; and hardware compression will be enabled.

Additional information on using the Backup program or the **ntbackup** command-line utility can be found in the Windows 2000 Help files and the Backup program Help files.

Verifying the Application of a Group Policy

The task of verifying that a specific group policy has been applied can be divided into verifying the application of a group policy to computers and verifying the application of a group policy to users. If you have upgraded from Windows NT 4 to Windows 2000, you will have a different level of default security applied to that computer than you would have for a clean installation of the Windows 2000 operating system on a previously blank hard drive. This statement applies to domain controllers, member servers, and Windows 2000 Professional clients.

Security Templates

To increase the security level of an upgraded computer, you will need to apply the appropriate security template based on the role that computer is performing in your network. Windows 2000 provides security templates, which are stored in the Systemroot\Security\Templates folder. Templates can be applied to local computer policy, imported to a group policy object, used for system security analysis, or assigned automatically with the Secedit command-line tool. These supplied templates can be customized using the Security Templates snap-in of the Microsoft Management Console (MMC), and they can be imported into the Security Settings extension of the Group Policy Editor snap-in.

When you use the security templates, you should be aware of the following issues:

➤ You cannot secure Windows 2000 systems that are installed on FAT file systems.

➤ These security templates are constructed with the assumption that they will be applied to Windows 2000 computers that use the default security settings for Windows 2000. In other words, these templates incrementally modify the default security settings if they are already installed on the computer. They do not install the default security settings and then perform the modifications.

➤ You should not apply these security templates to production systems without first testing to ensure that the right level of application functionality is maintained for your network and system architecture.

Security templates come in three flavors: those for professional, those for server, and those designed for domain controllers. The templates were designed to cover five common requirements for security.

Basic (basic*.inf)

The basic configuration templates are provided as a means to reverse the application of a different security configuration. The basic configurations apply the Windows 2000 default security settings to all security areas except those pertaining to user rights. These are not modified in the basic templates because application setup programs commonly modify user rights to enable successful use of the application. The basic configuration files are not intended to undo such modifications.

Compatible (compatws.inf)

The default Windows 2000 security configuration gives members of the local Users group strict security settings, while members of the local Power Users group have security settings that are compatible with Windows NT 4 user assignments. This default configuration enables certified Windows 2000 applications to run in the standard Windows environment for the Users group, while still allowing applications that are not certified for Windows 2000 to run successfully under the less secure Power Users configuration. However, if Windows 2000 users belong to the Power Users group in order to run applications not certified for Windows 2000, this compatible template might not be secure enough for some environments.

Some organizations might find it preferable to assign users, by default, as members of only the Users group and then reduce the security privileges for the Users group to the level where applications not certified for Windows 2000 run successfully. The Compatible template is designed for such organizations. By lowering the security levels on specific files, folders, and Registry keys that are commonly accessed by applications, the Compatible template allows most applications to run successfully under a User context. In addition, because it is assumed that the administrator applying the Compatible template does not want users to be Power Users, all members of the Power Users group are removed.

Secure (secure*.inf)

The Secure templates implement recommended security settings for all security areas except files, folders, and Registry keys. These are not modified because file system and Registry permissions are configured securely by default.

Highly Secure (hisec*.inf)

The Highly Secure templates define security settings for Windows 2000 network communications. The security areas are set to require maximum protection for network traffic and protocols used between computers running Windows 2000. As a result, computers configured with a Highly Secure template can communicate only with other Windows 2000 computers. They cannot communicate with computers running Windows 95, Windows 98, or Windows NT.

Importing a Security Template

You import a security template into a group policy object and this GPO is then assigned in the normal flow of policy inheritance. The security settings are applied when the system is started or as the group policy settings dictate. You can apply a security template directly to the local computer policy when a computer is not part of a domain. The system is immediately configured with the new template settings.

With the Security Templates MMC snap-in, Windows 2000 provides a centralized method of defining security. This snap-in is a single point of entry where the full range of system security can be viewed, adjusted, and applied to a local computer or imported into a group policy object. The Security Templates snap-in does not introduce new security parameters; it simply organizes all existing security attributes in one place to ease security administration. When used with the Security Configuration And Analysis MMC snap-in, security templates can also be used as a base configuration for performing security analysis. Figure 9.5 shows an MMC with both the Security Configuration And Analysis snap-in and the Security Templates snap-in added.

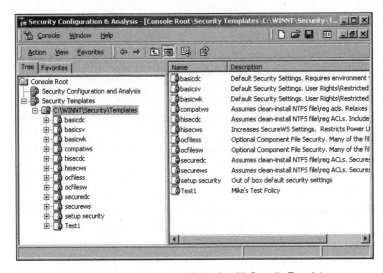

Figure 9.5   Security Configuration and Analysis with Security Templates.

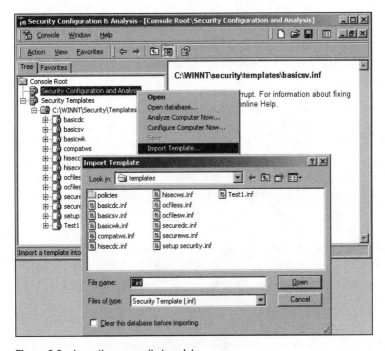

Figure 9.6   Importing a security template.

Figure 9.6 shows how you can use the Security Configuration And Analysis snap-in to import a template. After you import a template, you can analyze the impact that applying the template will have on the existing security configuration before you actually apply the template to that computer.

The Security Configuration And Analysis snap-in analyzes security by comparing the current state of system security against a security template that you have imported into a personal database. This template is the base configuration, and it contains your preferred or recommended security settings for that system.

The Security Configuration And Analysis snap-in queries the system's security settings for all security areas in the base configuration. Values found are compared to the base configuration. If the current system settings match the base configuration settings, they are assumed to be correct. If they don't match, the attributes in question are displayed as potential problems that need investigation.

You can create personal databases into which you can import templates for analysis. You can repeat the import process and load multiple templates. The database will merge the various templates to create one composite template, resolving conflicts in order of import; the last one imported takes precedence when there is contention. After the templates are imported into the selected database, you can analyze or configure the system.

The state of the operating system and applications on a computer is dynamic. For example, security levels might need to change temporarily to enable the immediate resolution of an administration or network issue; this change can often go unreversed. This means that a computer might no longer meet the requirements for enterprise security.

The Security Configuration And Analysis snap-in enables quick review of security analysis results; recommendations are presented alongside current system settings, and icons or remarks are used to highlight any areas where the current settings do not match the proposed level of security. The Security Configuration And Analysis snap-in also offers the ability to resolve any discrepancies revealed by analysis. Figure 9.7 shows some of the results of a security analysis.

Secedit

If you often need to analyze a large number of computers, as in a domain-based infrastructure, you can use the Secedit.exe command-line tool for batch analysis. However, analysis results still must be viewed in the Security Configuration And Analysis console.

Realize that Secedit can do the same things that Security Configuration And Analysis can do. The Secedit.exe command-line tool, when called from a batch file or automatic task scheduler, can be used to automatically create and apply templates and analyze system security. This tool can also be run dynamically from a command line. This tool is useful when you have multiple computers on which security must be analyzed or configured, and you need to perform these tasks off-hours. The Secedit tool supports several switches that can be used to analyze, configure, or provide reports on the various security templates that you might want to apply. These include the /**analyze**, /**configure**, /**export**, and /**validate** switches.

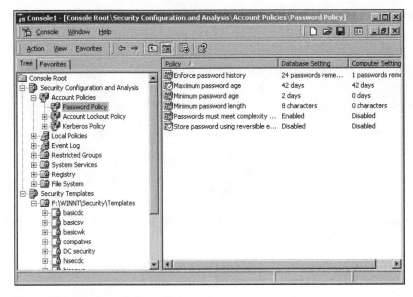

Figure 9.7   Security analysis results.

Secedit Switches

➤ **/analyze**—With the **secedit** command, it analyzes a system's security. This performs the same function as the Security Configuration And Analysis snap-in.

➤ **secedit /configure**—Configures system security by applying a stored template.

➤ **/areas area1 area2**—Specifies the security areas to be applied to the system. The default is All Areas. Each area should be separated by a space. The following areas can be used in this argument:

➤ **SECURITYPOLICY**—Local policy and domain policy for the system, including account policies, audit policies, and so on

➤ **GROUP_MGMT**—Restricted group settings for any groups specified in the security template

➤ **USER_RIGHTS**—User logon rights

➤ **REGKEYS**—Security on local Registry keys

➤ **FILESTORE**—Security on local file storage

➤ **SERVICES**—Security for all defined services

➤ **/export**—Exports a stored template from a security database to a security template file.

➤ **/validate**—Validates the syntax of a security template that you want to import into a database for analysis or application to a system.

Forcing a Policy Refresh

It is recommended that any time you apply a new group policy setting, you immediately force a manual refresh of the policy. You can do this at a command prompt or by choosing Start|Run and entering the following command:

```
secedit /refreshpolicy {machine_policy | user_policy}[/enforce]
```

The **secedit /refreshpolicy** command refreshes system security by reapplying the security settings to the group policy object. This command takes the following arguments:

➤ **machine_policy**—Refreshes security settings for the local computer.

➤ **user_policy**—Refreshes security settings for the local user account currently logged on to the computer.

➤ **/enforce**—Refreshes security settings even if the group policy object settings have not been changed.

Verifying Object Migration and Cleaning Up sIDHistory

One of your primary tools for verifying the successful migration of objects will be the Reporting feature of the Active Directory Migration Tool (ADMT). This tool provides detailed reports that allow you to evaluate the migration process and potential impact. You must generate the reports before you can view them. When you generate the reports, information is collected from computers throughout your organization. The reports include data from the time the reports were generated. To update the information in the reports, you must generate the reports again. You can generate the following reports:

➤ *Migrated Users And Groups Report*—Summarizes the results of the user and group migration operations.

➤ *Migrated Computers Report*—Summarizes the results of the computer migration operations.

➤ *Expired Computers Report*—Lists the computer accounts with expired passwords.

➤ *Impact Analysis Report*—Lists the user accounts and groups that will be affected by computer migration operations.

➤ *Name Conflicts Report*—Lists the user accounts and groups that exist in both the source and target domains.

To generate reports, choose Start|Programs|Administrative Tools|Active Directory Migration Tool. In the console tree, right-click on Active Directory Migration Tool, and then click on Reporting Wizard. Follow the instructions until you have finished generating the desired reports.

Most of the Resource Kit tools discussed in Chapter 8 can also be used after migration to provide feedback on the results of the migration. These tools include Global.exe, Local.exe, Perms.exe, Findgrp.exe, Showmbrs.exe, Showgrps.exe, and Showacls.exe. Refer to Chapter 8 for a discussion of the capabilities of each of these tools.

Most organizations will choose to retain the source domain's primary SID of the security principals in the **sIDHistory** attribute of accounts that have been migrated. This allows migrated users to retain access to resources in the source environment, but it also doubles the size of a user's access token, which can affect network access. The **sIDHistory** attribute is a temporary measure that will be required only as long as all of the source domain resources have not yet been migrated. After your users and groups have been fully migrated, you can clean up the **sIDHistory** value to minimize the size of access tokens.

Active Directory Service Interfaces

Your primary tool for deleting the **sIDHistory** value of your migrated objects will be the Active Directory Service Interfaces (ADSI). This tool abstracts the capabilities of directory services from different network providers in a distributed computing environment to present a single set of directory service interfaces for managing network resources. Administrators and developers can use ADSI to enumerate and manage the resources in a directory service, no matter which network environment contains the resource.

ADSI makes it easier to perform common administrative tasks, such as adding new users, managing printers, and locating resources throughout the distributed computing environment. ADSI also makes it easy for developers to "directory-enable" their applications. Administrators and developers deal with a single set of directory service interfaces regardless of which directory services are installed.

You can write ADSI client applications in many languages. For the majority of administrative tasks, ADSI defines interfaces and objects accessible from Automation-compliant languages—such as Microsoft Visual Basic, Microsoft Visual Basic Scripting Edition (VBScript), and Java—and from the more performance- and efficiency-conscious languages—such as C and C++. A good foundation in COM (Component Object Model) programming is useful to the ADSI programmer.

The ADSI runs on Windows 2000. However, client applications using ADSI can be written and run on Windows 95, Windows 98, Windows NT 4, and Windows 2000 systems. Client components for all of these operating systems are available on the MSDN Web site. In addition, developers will want the ADSI SDK (Software Development Kit), also available on the MSDN Web site.

ADSI 2.5 includes providers for several operating systems, including Windows NT 4, which means that it supports the Windows NT Server 4 directory. The Lightweight Directory Access Protocol (LDAP) provider works with any LDAP version 2 or version 3 directory, which means that it supports Novell NetWare Directory Services (NDS) and is NetWare-3-bindery-compatible (NWCOMPAT). This LDAP provider also works for the Windows 2000 Active Directory. ADSI integrates with many Microsoft products and technologies, including Active Directory, Microsoft Exchange 5.5, Microsoft Internet Information Server (IIS), and Microsoft Site Server.

Below is an example of an ADSI script (written in Visual Basic) that first gets a **fileshare** object on a server and reads its path property. Then the script gets a **fileservice** object on a server, uses it to enumerate the shares on the server, creates a new share (\\SERVER\newshare) for C:\, and deletes the share it just created. You can omit the **DOMAIN** in the code below, but you may see some performance degradation caused by additional browsing to find the **SERVER**.

Listing 9.1 ADSI sample script.

```
Sub foo ()

Dim comp As IADSComputer
Dim serv As IADsService
Dim fserv As IADsContainer
Dim share As IADsFileShare
Dim v As Variant

' Replace DOMAIN, SERVER & SHARE with the appropriate
' domain, server and share names

Set share = GetObject("WinNT://DOMAIN/SERVER/lanmanserver/Share")
v = share.Path ' Gets directory path on server
Set share = nothing

' Replace DOMAIN & SERVER with the appropriate domain and server
names

Set fserv = GetObject("WinNT://DOMAIN/SERVER/lanmanserver")

' Enumerate existing shares
```

```
For Each share in fserv
        v = share.class
        v = share.ADSPath
        v = share.HostComputer
        v = share.path
Next share

' Create share in fileservice container

Set shareNew = fserv.create("fileshare", "newshare")
shareNew.path = "C:\"

shareNew.SetInfo ' Commit new share

' Delete share

fserv.Delet "fileshare", "newshare"

' Fails since share is gone

ShareNew.GetInfo

End Sub
```

ADSI Edit

The Windows 2000 Support Tools include ADSI Edit, which is an MMC snap-in that acts as a low-level editor for Active Directory. ADSI Edit provides a means to add, delete, and move objects within the directory services. You can view, change, and delete the attributes of each object, including the **sIDHistory** attribute of migrated account objects.

ADSI Edit can also be useful for searching Active Directory. You can create a query and scope it to any level in the tree. You then create the query as a container; this provides continued browsing from the results and the results' children. Figure 9.8 shows an example of the ADSI Edit console.

When you're using ADSI Edit, you should be aware that Adsiedit.msc (the MMC snap-in for ADSI Edit) automatically attempts to load the current domain to which the user is logged on. If the computer is installed in a workgroup or otherwise not logged onto a domain, an error that displays the message "The specified domain does not exist" will occur repeatedly.

To avoid problems in this situation, open mmc.exe, add the ADSI Edit snap-in manually, make any connections that are appropriate for you with whatever credentials are necessary, and then save the console file. This procedure gives you

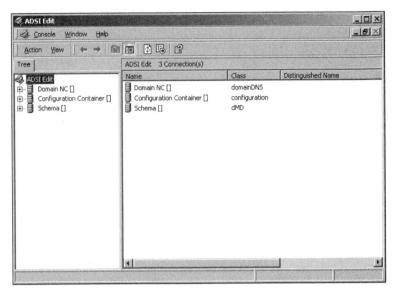

Figure 9.8   The ADSI Edit console.

your own default console that works with ADSI Edit. To make a connection, right-click on ADSI Edit in the Tree pane to open the Connection window shown in Figure 9.9. Then enter the connection information and select OK.

Redefining DACLS

Two Resource Kit tools can help you to identify existing permissions and redefine DACLs for individual users. These are Showacls.exe and Subinacl.exe.

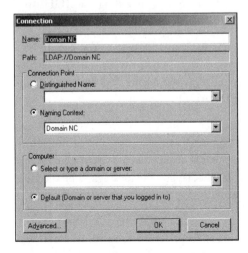

Figure 9.9   The ADSI Edit Connection window.

Showacls.exe is a command-line utility that works only on partitions or volumes formatted with NTFS. This utility shows you the rights for files, folders, and trees. Showacls.exe is great if you want to see an individual user's permissions for a resource. Showacls.exe enumerates the local and global groups that the user belongs to and matches the user's SID, and the SIDs of the groups that user belongs to, to the SIDs listed in each access control entry (ACE).

Subinacl.exe is a command-line utility that you can use as an administrator to obtain security information and to transfer the information from one user to another. The information can also be gathered for groups and be transferred from group to group and from domain to domain.

*Note: Kerberos authentication packages have a maximum size of 8KB for the access token within the package. The **sIDHistory** attributes may result in this limit being reached or exceeded.*

Converting to Native Mode

When your last NT BDC has been converted to 2000, you can convert your domain to native mode. Native mode is where the last shred of NT can finally be removed. You gain the true scalability of millions of objects and you get new types of objects to assist you in managing your new enterprise. This section is designed to give you a summary of the advantages and "gotchas" of a final conversion to native mode.

Native-mode conversion is done manually in the Active Directory Domain And Trusts snap-in. Before you click that convert button, there are several things to keep in mind:

➤ This is a one way process. The only way to convert back is to demote all domain controllers in the domain and start over.

➤ Native-mode conversion requires that all domain controllers in the domain are Windows 2000. Any NT BDCs still in circulation in your domain will prevent the conversion.

➤ Only Windows 2000 domain controllers can be added to the domain. If you try to sneak in an NT BDC, the request to join the domain will be denied.

➤ Native-mode conversion only affects the local domain. Your forest can be a combination of mixed and native-mode domains and still reap all of the advantages inherent in a forest structure.

➤ Down-level clients won't care what mode you are running in. The PDC Emulator takes a much smaller role in a native-mode environment, but it is still required to support legacy machines and keep the façade of NT alive for the Windows NT, Windows 95, and Windows 98 clients.

It is a good idea to be very aware of the requirements and effects of converting to native mode, particularly in the area of what has to occur to Windows BDCs in order to permit the conversion.

Native-Mode Group Changes

Day-to-day administrative functions are much easier when you apply the principals of group membership when assigning access and rights to users. Native-mode conversion enhances your flexibility and provides numerous options for a workable, yet scalable management structure.

The changes to the group structure starts with the addition of a new group scope called the universal group. This group can contain security principals from any domain in the forest and can be used to assign right and resource permissions in any domain in the forest.

Universal Groups: Flexibility with a Price

Universal group memberships are stored in all global catalogs throughout your domain. When you modify universal group membership, this change has to be replicated to every global catalog server in your organization. This is why Microsoft recommends that membership in universal groups should be limited placement in global groups. You would place the user and computer accounts into the appropriate global groups and then place the global group into the universal group. Users will inherit the rights and permissions assigned to the global and universal groups, but you don't replicate to the entire world every time you decide to make a change.

 You must be aware that universal groups only exist in native-mode domains and that they can cause replication problems when user accounts are directly placed in universal groups.

Group Nesting Expanded

Placing global groups into universal groups is just one example of the level of nesting you can gain with your conversion to native mode. You can also nest global groups into other global groups. This helps to shorten the number of access control entries (ACE) in the DACL. With the conversion, full nesting is now available. Global groups can be in universal, global, and domain local groups. Domain local groups can go into other domain local groups. In mixed-mode domains, only global groups could nest within domain local groups. This is, of course, in relation to security groups. Distribution groups are never under nesting limitations. Just make sure you document your levels of nesting and nest only when needed. Otherwise, it may get difficult to know who is assigned to which group and administration can easily get out of control.

Using Security and Distribution Groups

Distribution groups are new to Windows 2000. In a mixed-mode environment, once you create a group type, you are stuck. Many administrators have crafted group memberships only to find they created the wrong type. In a native-mode domain, you can freely convert from distribution to security and back. You can even convert global and domain local groups into universal. Universal, due to its potential wide spread use, cannot be "down-graded" to any other scope.

Local groups that are created on mixed-mode domain controllers can only be used to assign permissions to resources on Windows 2000 domain controllers and Windows NT BDCs. Once you are converted, domain local groups can be used to assign access to any resource in the entire domain.

The approved method of resource assignment is to place user accounts into global groups, global groups into universal groups, and universal groups into domain local groups, and you are to assign resource access to the domain local group. If you aren't going to use a universal group, you would simply place the global group into the domain local.

An easy way to remember the nesting order is (U)sers go into (G)lobal, global into domain (L)ocal, and (Y)es, you assign permissions. This adds up to UGLY. Universal groups make this really ugly by forcing the mnemonic device to transform into UGULY.

You can run your Windows 2000 domain in mixed mode indefinitely, but you won't be able to take advantage of all of the new functionality that switching to native mode gives you. Something to consider when you're pondering this decision is that Windows 2000 Active Directory provides excellent backward compatibility with your existing Windows NT-based environment. For example, you can continue to run Windows NT 4 member servers. You can even add new Windows NT 4 member servers to your environment after you've switched to native mode. In addition, the domain controllers you've upgraded will continue to support your existing Windows 95, Windows 98, and Windows NT 4 clients.

Decommissioning Source Domains and Redeploying Resources

The last step in the migration process is to decommission the source domains. When you decommission a domain, that domain ceases to exist. To decommission a Windows NT domain, after you have migrated all of the necessary accounts and resources and removed all trusts, you can simply turn off the last remaining domain controller in the domain. Then, you can either reinstall Windows NT 4 or install

Windows 2000 on that computer and join it to an existing domain. If you install Windows 2000, you can promote that computer to be a domain controller in another domain.

Note: The ADMT cannot change the domain affiliation of Windows NT PDCs and BDCs or Windows 2000 domain controllers. PDCs, BDCs, and Windows 2000 domain controllers must be migrated manually.

To decommission a Windows 2000 domain, use the Active Directory Installation Wizard (Dcpromo.exe) to demote the last domain controller to a standalone server. You can then join that computer to another domain or promote it to be a domain controller in another domain.

For more information about promoting a domain controller and the Active Directory Installation Wizard, see Windows 2000 Server Help. For more information about installing Windows NT, see the product documentation.

Final Tips for Advanced Administrators

Administrators who want to deploy Windows 2000 Professional in their environment still need to administer their network. The Windows 2000 Server CD-ROM includes an Administrative Tools setup file (located in the \I386\Adminpak.msi file), which will install the administrative tools on your Windows 2000 workstation.

You can also install the add-on Active Directory client software (Dsclient.exe) on workstations running Windows 95, Windows 98, or Windows NT. The Active Directory client is network client software for computers connecting to Active Directory networks. A computer configured with the Active Directory client can log onto the network by locating a domain controller. The client can then fully benefit from the features of Active Directory. The Active Directory client for Windows 95 and 98 is provided in a single upgrade pack in the \Clients\WIN9X folder on the Windows 2000 Server CD-ROM. The Directory Service (DS) Client software for NT 4 can be downloaded from the Microsoft Web site.

Because Windows 95, Windows 98, and Windows NT 4 clients lack many of the features provided by Windows 2000 Professional, you might want to install the Active Directory client to take advantage of the following Active Directory client features:

➤ *Site awareness*—Provides the capability to log onto a domain controller closest to the client.

➤ *Password changing*—Allows you to change the password on any Windows 2000 domain controller, rather than having to relegate all such requests to a Windows NT 4 PDC.

➤ *ADSI*—Provides scripting interfaces to Active Directory, which makes it easier for administrators to automate their work.

➤ *Access to Active Directory Windows Address Book property pages*—Decreases user management tasks by allowing the users to change the user-object properties (for example, a phone number or address) that they have the permission to change. User object pages are accessible by choosing Start|Search and selecting For People.

➤ *Client support for NTLMv2 authentication*—Provides improved encryption for user passwords.

One approach for deciding whether to install the DS Client software is to determine at what point you think you will install Windows 2000 Professional on your client computers. Use DS Client if the rollout will occur over an extended period of time. If your migration plan calls for a fast rollout, then do not install the DS Client software.

What the Active Directory Client Will Not Provide

If you got all of the bells and whistles, there would be no need to upgrade to Windows 2000. Some of the limitations of the Active Directory Client are:

➤ Kerberos is not supported. This lowers the level of security these clients can use.

➤ Group polices are not enabled. You are still stuck with system policies.

➤ IntelliMirror doesn't work. You must use some other method of automated software deployment, like System Management Server. Application assignment and publishing doesn't extend to non-Windows 2000 clients.

➤ Network level encryption isn't available. IPSec or L2TP aren't an option for down-level clients.

Add the above list to the stability, scalability, and hardware support that Windows 2000 Professional adds to the mix and you get a compelling set of reasons to make the leap. Until you retire the last legacy client, you aren't completely migrated.

Practice Questions

Case Study: Pillows and Such

Pillows and Such is an up-and-coming manufacturer of household decorating accessories. The company's main offices are located in Kutztown, PA, with satellite offices in San Diego, CA, Orlando, FL, and Mesa, AZ. The company used a single master domain model before the migration to Windows 2000. The master domain was **Pillowsandsuch**, and the company had three resource domains: **marketing**, **sales**, and **Southwest**.

Security

Robert Parker, Pillows' CIO, is concerned that the design for the newest trivets will be stolen by the company's chief competitor, Rugs and Things. To prevent the theft of corporate secrets, Robert mandates that EFS be installed on all laptops, and he wants himself to be the only recovery agent. This setup will require removing the default Administrator account from the list of recovery agents and will necessitate re-encrypting all files to replace the old recovery agent with Robert's account.

Domain Structure

In the initial migration to Windows 2000, the company did a straight upgrade to a parent/child tree structure. The forest root is **pillowsandsuch.com**. There are still two NT BDCs installed in the **pillowsandsuch.com** domain. These BDCs will need to be upgraded or removed. The child domains are **marketing.pillowsandsuch.com**, **sales.pillowsandsuch.com**, and **sw.pillowsandsuch.com**. The enterprise administrators have since done a domain reorganization, performing an intraforest migration of the marketing and sales domains to organizational units inside the forest root. Additional organizational units—namely, ITADMIN and Development—have been formed in the forest root. Amanda White and Thomas Clark are assigned members of the ITADMIN OU and are members of the Domain Admins group. All accounts in the ITADMIN OU should have all administrative tools installed.

Research Department

Brandon Pierce is assigned to the Development OU as a normal user account. He is primarily concerned with the advances in fluffy towels and needs the latest in CAD software installed. There is a mixture of Windows NT, 95, 98, and 2000 clients scattered throughout the sites. The research department has created a separate domain called **eus.pillowsandsuch.com**. All user accounts and resource machines have been migrated, and the process of removing the remaining domain controller has been started.

WAN Connectivity

The San Diego office is connected to the Kutztown office with a T1 Point-to-Point dedicated connection. This will be replaced at the end of next year by connections to a local ISP (Internet service provider) and then to a VPN (Virtual Private Network) to the remote offices. The company is using a Cisco PIX firewall and will need strong encryption that is compatible with Cisco products. The Orlando and Mesa offices are connected to each other using Routing and Remote Access Service (RRAS) and Network Address Translation (NAT). This solution will be replaced with a dial-on-demand router to connect directly to the Kutztown office via a local ISP and a VPN.

Name Resolution

Jakob Andersson is the Unix guru who controls the Unix DNS servers. Robert Parker, the CIO, has mandated that the initial domain records are to be manually created on the Unix DNS servers as a backup to the Windows 2000 Dynamic DNS that is to be installed on **DNS5.pillowsandsuch.com**. Jakob has ensured that the latest version of DNS is installed on his Unix machines and that they fully support SRV records.

Group Migration

During the migration, a **marketing.researchers** domain local group was created in the **pillowsandsuch.com** domain. This group was designed to access local resources on the various file servers.

Future Plans

Because **sw.pillowsandsuch.com** isn't quite ready to migrate, Charles Ballinger will perform on-site administration as a member of the Domain Admins group. The migration of **sw.pillowsandsuch.com** will occur in the next year.

Question 1

What is the name of the file you can use as a template to manually create the SRV records on the Unix DNS server?

○ a. Services.dns

○ b. Netlogon.dns

○ c. Resource.dns

○ d. DNSSRV.dns

Answer b is correct. The netlogon.dns file lists all SRV records that are registered when the Net Logon service is started. This file is located in the %systemroot%\System32\Config folder. The rest of the records listed (in answers a, c, and d) are names that aren't used in DNS.

Question 2

What should you do when you find that the shared system volumes haven't yet been replicated to the newly installed **dc3.pillowsandsuch.com** domain?

○ a. Wait 10 minutes.

○ b. Stop and then restart the Net Logon service.

○ c. Copy the winnt\system32 directory from **dc2.sw.pillows.com** to **dc3.ne.pillows.com**.

○ d. This is normal. The system volume isn't configured to replicate.

Answer a is correct because file replication will not be completed until two replication periods have elapsed on a newly installed system. The default replication period is five minutes. The first replication period updates the other domain controller's configuration, and the second period starts replication to the new domain controller. Answer b is incorrect because stopping and restarting the Net Logon service will force re-registration of the server's SRV record and no system volume replication. Answer c is incorrect because the settings contained in the system32 directory are specific to a particular machine. This form of copying will corrupt the destination system. Answer d is incorrect because the shared system volume is automatically configured for replication when Active Directory is installed.

Question 3

> Why am I unable to back up the System State of **bigguy.eus. pillowsandsuch.com** from my Windows 2000 Professional desktop before decommissioning the **eus.pillowsandsuch.com** domain?
>
> ○ a. You aren't a member of the Server Operators group.
>
> ○ b. Administrative Microsoft Management Consoles won't operate on Windows 2000 Professional machines.
>
> ○ c. You can't back up the System State data on remote computers.
>
> ○ d. You aren't a member of the Enterprise Admins group.

Answer c is correct because you can back up the System State data on a local computer only. Answer a is incorrect because you are a member of the Domain Admins group, which has sufficient permission to back up the System State. Answer b is incorrect because any MMC will run on any version of Windows 2000 if the user account controlling the MMC has sufficient authority to perform the desired action. Answer d is incorrect because backing up a domain controller doesn't require Enterprise Admins group membership.

Question 4

> What utility can you use to remove **sIDHistory** values from **pillowsandsuch.com** after the **marketing.pillowsandsuch.com** and **sales.pillowsandsuch.com** domains are converted?
>
> ○ a. Active Directory Users And Computers
>
> ○ b. Active Directory Service Interfaces
>
> ○ c. Active Directory Sites And Services
>
> ○ d. Regedit32

Answer b is correct. You use the Active Directory Service Interfaces (ADSI) to delete the **sIDHistory** value from migrated objects. None of the other tools listed have access to any form of **sIDHistory**.

Question 5

> Who can view the security log on **server5.pillowsandsuch.com**? [Check all correct answers]
>
> ❑ a. Amanda White
>
> ❑ b. Charles Ballinger
>
> ❑ c. Brandon Pierce
>
> ❑ d. Thomas Clark

Answers a and d are correct. Amanda White and Thomas Clark are domain administrators for **pillowsandsuch.com**. Domain administrators are automatically added to the local Administrators group on each member machine. Answer b is incorrect because Charles Ballinger is an administrator for **sw.pillowsandsuch.com**, and his permissions will not travel across domain boundaries. Answer c is incorrect because Brandon Pierce is a domain user with no special permissions. By default, only administrators can read the security log of any machine.

Question 6

> What are some of the reasons to install the Active Directory client on the non-Windows 2000 workstations that are members of the **pillowsandsuch.com** domain? [Check all correct answers]
>
> ❑ a. This forces Windows 95 and Windows 98 clients to communicate only with the PDC when user account passwords are changed.
>
> ❑ b. This permits users to update delegated Address Book property pages in Active Directory.
>
> ❑ c. This supports NTLMv4 authentication for enhanced security.
>
> ❑ d. This supports group policies assigned at the OU level for NT workstations.

Answer b is correct. Users are permitted to modify Address Book property pages by selecting Search|For People. Answer a is incorrect because communicating with the PDC to change passwords is the default behavior of Windows 95 and 98. The Active Directory client will permit these legacy machines to change their passwords on any domain controller. Answer c is incorrect because the version supported is NTLMv2. Answer d is incorrect because group policies are not supported at any level for NT workstations. NT still relies on system policies that are stored in the NETLOGON share of the validating domain controller. Remember, the ability to select multiple answers does not mean that multiple responses are correct.

Question 7

Which installation package should be installed on all desktops in the ITADMIN
OU computers to provide full administrative MMCs?

○ a. ADSI.msi

○ b. Adminpak.msi

○ c. MMC.msi

○ d. Setup.msi

Answer b is correct. Adminpak.msi gives the administrator all of the administration tools available to manage an Active Directory domain. The rest of the answers are bogus names.

Question 8

What command must you enter to force the member servers in the Development OU to download the latest group policy?

○ a. **secedit /refreshpolicy**

○ b. **replmon /replicate**

○ c. **secedit /replicate**

○ d. **replmon /refreshpolicy**

Answer a is correct. The Secedit command-line utility is used to refresh policy settings without waiting for the normal replication times. Answers b and d are incorrect because the Replmon utility is not used to replicate group policies. Answer c is incorrect because this is not the correct command switch.

Question 9

When **pillowsandsuch.com** is converted into native mode, Robert Parker will need access to the high-speed laser printer outside of his office. Place the following items in the recommended order to assign appropriate resource access. Not all items will be used.

Assign printer access to the Executives global group

Place Rparker user account into the HQ_Execs domain local group

Assign printer access to the Pillows_Executives universal group

Place the Executives global group into the Pillows_Executives universal group

Assign printer access to the HQ_Execs domain local group

Place Rparker user account into the Executives global group

Place the Executives Global Group into the HQ_Execs domain local group

Place the Rparker user account into the Pillows_Executives universal group

Place the Pillows_Executives universal group into the HQ_Execs domain local group

The correct answer is:

Place Rparker user account into the Executives global group

Place the Executives global group into the Pillows_Executives universal group

Place the Pillows_Executives universal group into the HQ_Execs domain local group

Assign printer access to the HQ_Execs domain local group

The correct method is to assign user accounts to global groups. You then assign global groups into universal groups. Universal groups are then assigned into domain local groups and domain local groups are assigned the appropriate permissions.

Question 10

> Marketing needs to move the **marketing.researchers** domain local group
> into a universal group. What must occur before this can be accomplished?
>
> ○ a. The Researchers group needs to have its members joined to a
>   different group that has the same SID.
>
> ○ b. Nothing. You cannot move domain local groups into universal
>   groups.
>
> ○ c. The **pillowsandsuch.com** domain will have to upgrade its last
>   domain controller and switch to native mode.
>
> ○ d. The enterprise administrators will need to clone the member
>   accounts of the Researchers group into a new universal group.

Answer c is correct. Before universal groups become available, the domain must
be in native mode. Answer a is incorrect because groups can never share the same
SID. Answer b is incorrect because you can move domain local and domain global groups into a universal group. Answer d is incorrect because you don't need to
clone accounts to convert a group.

Need to Know More?

 Microsoft Corporation. Microsoft Official Curriculum course 2010 "Designing a Microsoft Windows 2000 Migration Strategy". Module 8 "Planning to Deploy a Migration Strategy" provides insight into some of the complexities faced after the upgrade is completed.

 Microsoft Corporation. *The Microsoft Windows 2000 Server Resource Kit*. Redmond, Washington: Microsoft Press, 2000. ISBN 1572318058. The volume on deployment provides in-depth coverage for a post re-structure operation.

 Microsoft Corporation. Microsoft Windows 2000 Support Tools Help Files. Microsoft has really done an outstanding job on the majority of Help files. Remember it is context sensitive. Visit Help after the tool is installed.

 Microsoft Corporation. Microsoft "Determining Domain Migration Strategies" document, which is a reprint from *The Microsoft Windows 2000 Server Resource Kit*. Redmond, Washington, Microsoft Press, 2000. ISBN 1572318058. The section titled "Domain Migration Tools" gives a wonderful overview of several of the tools you can use for your restructuring. This is located at: **www.microsoft.com/windows2000/ library/resources/reskit/samplechapters/dgbf/dgbf_upg_ovaw.asp.**

 Microsoft Corporation. Microsoft "Deployment Planning Guide" Web site. Chapter 10 "Determining Domain Migration Strategies" provides a road map for a medium to large migration. This is located at: **www.microsoft.com/windows2000/library/resources/reskit/dpg/ default.asp.**

 Microsoft Corporation. Microsoft Windows 2000 Domain Migration Cookbook. Microsoft white paper. 2000. Section 2, Migration Scenarios gives great examples of a migration process by walking you through a fictitious migration. This is located at: **www.microsoft.com/ WINDOWS2000/library/planning/activedirectory/cookbook.asp.**

 The Microsoft "Step-by-Step Guide to Using the Security Configuration Tool Set". This gives you the literal step-by-step procedures for analyzing and configuring Windows 2000 security. This can be found at: **www.microsoft.com/TechNet/win2000/seconfig.asp.**

Jen Goth. Microsoft Interactive Training Tool online course "How to Migrate Your Windows NT 4.0 Directory Services to Windows 2000 Active Directory".TNQ2000-3. The discussion on **sIDHistory** and the demo of the Security Translation Wizard is an excellent resource for combining domains in a single forest. This is located at: **www.microsoft. com/TechNet/events/fall/tnq20003/html/default.htm**.

 Microsoft Windows 2000 Active Directory Migration Tool download Web site is located at: **www.microsoft.com/windows2000/downloads/ deployment/admt/default.asp**.

 Microsoft Windows Active Directory Client download Web site is located at: **www.microsoft.com/windows2000/news/bulletins/adextension.asp**.

Troubleshooting

Terms you'll need to understand:

- ✓ Active Directory Migration Tool (ADMT)
- ✓ ClonePrincipal
- ✓ Upgrade
- ✓ Access rights
- ✓ Migration
- ✓ SID and **sIDHistory** attribute
- ✓ System policy and group policy
- ✓ Trusts, one-way trusts, nontransitive trusts, and Kerberos trusts
- ✓ Service account
- ✓ Rolling back

Techniques you'll need to master:

- ✓ Choosing the proper migration tool for a successful migration
- ✓ Using the correct configuration steps for each migration tool
- ✓ Ensuring that the proper hardware is used for the migration and upgrade
- ✓ Troubleshooting incorrect shares, resources, and NTFS permissions after migration
- ✓ Resolving network service issues with DHCP, DNS, and WINS after migration
- ✓ Solving problems related to the Remote Access Service (RAS) after migration
- ✓ Troubleshooting issues related to application compatibility and service accounts
- ✓ Properly planning for a rollback of either an upgrade or a migration failure

Although Microsoft has done a fair job of creating a suite of toolszfor migrating your Windows NT 4 enterprise to Windows 2000, there are still going to be problems that you'll need to address during the process. One thing to keep in mind is that the Microsoft tools that are available for migration need to be handled with great care and given extreme attention to detail. If any configuration is missed or incorrect, the migration will fail. Another important issue related to the migration is the proper configuration of account-related services. Again, if one configuration is incorrect, the migration could fail.

Other important aspects of the migration that must be properly controlled include user resource access, network services, and application management. Many of these issues will not fail the migration; they will just cause hours of frustration, as you attempt to troubleshoot why a user cannot access a particular resource.

The final issue that this chapter will tackle is disaster recovery. If the migration or upgrade is not going as planned, it may be best to go back to the beginning. If this is the case, you will need to have this strategy mapped out beforehand. The exam will require you to know details related to all of these issues, so let the troubleshooting begin.

Applicable Tools

As earlier chapters have already discussed, Microsoft provides a handful of migration tools that you will need to use for the migration of the existing network to the Windows 2000 network. These tools are:

➤ Active Directory Migration Tool (ADMT)

➤ ClonePrincipal

➤ Netdom

➤ MoveTree

Refer to Table 8.1 in Chapter 8 for the fine details about each tool. You will need to make an educated decision on which tool will work for your migration. After you have selected the right tool for the job, you also need to make sure that the tool is being used properly and the configurations are set correctly. Each tool has a unique set of guidelines that *must* be met. If you don't have all of the required configurations established, the migration is bound to fail. As the following sections describe in detail, each tool requires a unique set of parameters to function properly.

Note: To get more detailed information about each tool, the required configurations, and why each configuration is necessary, see Chapter 8.

ADMT Requirements

If the ADMT tool is just not functioning properly, you might need to take a step back and make sure that all of the configurations are correct. As the exam will emphasize, it's important to have all of the configurations completed before the tool is initiated. The following is a list of configurations that are required (or highly suggested) to successfully use ADMT for migrations:

1. The ADMT tool should be installed and run from the Windows 2000 domain controller that has the PDC Emulator Flexible Single Master Operations (FSMO) role.

2. The target domain must be Windows 2000 running in native mode. Figure 10.1 illustrates the error that you will receive if you have failed to perform this task.

3. The source domain can be one of the following types of domains:

   ➤ Windows NT 4 with Service Pack 4 or later

   ➤ Windows 2000 mixed mode

   ➤ Windows 2000 native mode

4. The source domain needs to be configured to trust the target domain.

Note: This is required for the ADMT to migrate the users, groups, and computers to the target domain.

5. The Domain Administrators global group from the source domain needs to be added to the Administrators local group in the target domain.

6. The Domain Administrators global group from the target domain needs to be added to the Administrators local group in the source domain. Figure 10.2 illustrates the error generated when this configuration is incorrect.

7. In the source domain, create a new local group called SourceDomain$$$. This group should be empty, and the name should be identical to the source domain. For example, if the source domain name is ECNT, then the group name needs to be ECNT$$$. The ADMT will create this group if it is not present, as illustrated in Figure 10.3.

Figure 10.1   Error indicating that the target domain is not in native mode.

Figure 10.2   Error indicating that you do not have administrative rights on the source domain.

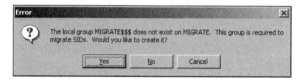

Figure 10.3   Error indicating that the SourceDomain$$$ group is not created.

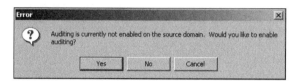

Figure 10.4   Error indicating that auditing is not turned on properly.

8. Both Success auditing and Failure auditing need to be enabled on the source domain for User and Group Management. Figure 10.4 shows the error message that is generated when auditing is not enabled. Notice that the ADMT can turn this on automatically.

9. Both Success auditing and Failure auditing need to be enabled on the target domain for Audit Account Management. Figure 10.4 will be similar for the target domain, and this auditing can also be turned on automatically through the ADMT.

Note: This configuration needs to be done within the Default Domain Controllers policy.

10. The PDC (for the source domain) needs to have a Registry value added. The path, value, value type, and data value in the Registry are:

```
PATH:
HKEY_LOCAL_MACHINE\System\CurrentControlSet\Control\LSA
VALUE:      TcpipClientSupport
VALUE TYPE:    REG_DWORD
DATA:      0X1
```

Error
TcpipClientSupport registry key is not set on the source domain. Would you like to add this registry key?
Yes
No
Cancel

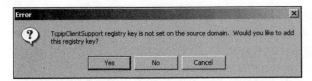

Figure 10.5 Error indicating that the TcpipClientSupport Registry key needs to be configured.

This value will be created automatically by the ADMT if it is not present when needed (Figure 10.5 shows this error message). The correct configuration will require a reboot of the PDC. If the value is not created when the ADMT is run, you will receive an error message in the log, and the remainder of the migration will fail, as shown in Figure 10.6.

11. The administrative shares need to be active on the domain controller in the target domain that is running the ADMT. Additionally, any computers that have a migration agent dispatched against them need to have the administrative shares active. This agent helps resolve security related issues and gather information for analysis.

12. The user account that will perform the migration from the ADMT needs to have the following rights:

    - Domain Administrator rights for the target domain
    - Administrator rights in the source domain
    - Administrator rights on each computer that will be migrated
    - Administrator rights on each computer that will have the security translated

    An excellent account to perform the migration would be the <*SourceDomain*>\Administrator. This account will typically log on to the target domain controller to perform the migration with the ADMT. If this account

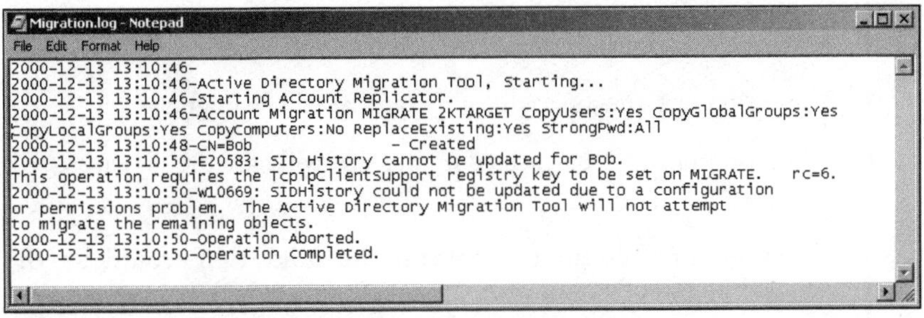

Migration.log - Notepad
File Edit Format Help
2000-12-13 13:10:46-
2000-12-13 13:10:46-Active Directory Migration Tool, Starting...
2000-12-13 13:10:46-Starting Account Replicator.
2000-12-13 13:10:46-Account Migration MIGRATE 2KTARGET CopyUsers:Yes CopyGlobalGroups:Yes
CopyLocalGroups:Yes CopyComputers:No ReplaceExisting:Yes StrongPwd:All
2000-12-13 13:10:48-CN=Bob - Created
2000-12-13 13:10:50-E20583: SID History cannot be updated for Bob.
This operation requires the TcpipClientSupport registry key to be set on MIGRATE. rc=6.
2000-12-13 13:10:50-W10669: SIDHistory could not be updated due to a configuration
or permissions problem. The Active Directory Migration Tool will not attempt
to migrate the remaining objects.
2000-12-13 13:10:50-Operation Aborted.
2000-12-13 13:10:50-Operation completed.

Figure 10.6 Migration log indicating that the TcpipClientSupport Registry key was not properly configured.

is selected, be certain that the <*SourceDomain*>\Domain Administrators group is still configured to be a member of each computer's local Administrators group. This will be a requirement for the computer to be migrated to the target domain.

The ADMT creates a log file (the migration log file), which can be found in the Logs folder under the ADMT folder. The location of the ADMT folder will vary depending on where you installed the application.

ClonePrincipal Requirements

This tool requires precise detail not only with the configurations of the source and target domains, but also with the syntax of the commands that you create. This tool consists of multiple scripts that will perform many of the same duties as the ADMT but without a friendly GUI interface. Refer to Chapter 8 for the list of required steps for a standard interforest and intraforest migration. Below is a list of additional measures that you will need to consider for the ClonePrincipal tool if the migration is having any problems:

➤ The source domain needs to have the scripts applied to the PDC.

➤ The source domain can be one of the following types of domains:

  ➤ Windows NT 4 with Service Pack 4 or later

  ➤ Windows 2000 mixed mode

  ➤ Windows 2000 native mode

➤ The source domain cannot be in the same forest as the target domain.

➤ The source domain needs to be configured to trust the target domain.

➤ The user account that will perform the migration with the ClonePrincipal tool needs to have the following rights:

  ➤ Domain Administrator rights for the target domain.

  ➤ Administrator rights in the source domain.

  ➤ Administrator rights on each computer that will be migrated.

  ➤ Administrator rights on each computer that will have the security translated.

    ➤ An excellent account to perform the migration would be the <*SourceDomain*>\Administrator. This account will typically log on to the target domain controller to perform the migration with ClonePrincipal.

If this account is selected, be certain that the *<SourceDomain>*\Domain Administrators group is still configured to be a member of each computer's local Administrators group. This will be a requirement for the computer to be migrated to the target domain.

As you can see, both ClonePrincipal and the ADMT have the same base steps, with minor alterations for configuring the domains. The key difference between the two tools with regard to overall capabilities is that ClonePrincipal supports customization of specific migration steps. Therefore, if you are failing to get a portion of the migration to perform as you wish with the ADMT, take a good look at the scripts that come with ClonePrincipal to see if they provide more detailed control of the migration.

 Because the ADMT and ClonePrincipal tools use different methods to determine whether objects have been moved, it is best to use either one or the other tool. A mixture of the two tools for the same migration would most certainly produce an unpredictable result.

Netdom

The Netdom tool is a command-line tool that is designed to verify and establish trust relationships between domains. No specific configurations need to be established for this tool before it can be used. Therefore, if there is an issue with the tool during use, it is most likely either a physical network issue or an issue with name resolution. In either case, the problem does not lie in the tool, but lies in the network itself. For more information about the core functions of Netdom, refer to Chapter 8.

 The Netdom tool has a built-in capability to check Kerberos trust relationships between Windows 2000 domains.

MoveTree

The MoveTree utility was designed to move directory objects from one Windows 2000 domain to another Windows 2000 domain. This command-line tool is not as powerful as the ADMT or ClonePrincipal, but MoveTree can be used to move OUs, groups, users, and computer accounts between domains in the same forest. Refer to Chapter 8 for more information about MoveTree. Other limitations that will help you troubleshoot potential problems include:

1. The target domain must be running Windows 2000 in native mode.

2. The source domain can be one of the following types of domains:

   ➤ Windows 2000 mixed mode

   ➤ Windows 2000 native mode

3. The source domain must be in the same forest as the target domain.

4. Global groups need to be empty for the migration between domains.

Note: The best way to perform this step is to remove all users from the global group, move the global group to the target domain, and then repopulate the global group with the correct users.

5. All objects must be moved in a closed set.

Note: A closed set would include global groups for user migration. When you're migrating computers, local or domain local groups could be shared across multiple computers, but that would break the rule for a closed set.

Failed Upgrades

A failed upgrade is certainly not what anyone is looking for when it comes to moving from Windows NT 4 to Windows 2000. However, there are many aspects of the upgrade that could go astray. A single problem could render the enterprise lifeless. There is good news, though. Any one of these problems can be avoided if there is proper care and preparation for the upgrade. There are three distinct areas that could fail during an upgrade: hardware failures; access rights associated with upgrading; and domain name resolution issues. These three areas will be the focus of the exam and should also be the focus of your planning and preparation for the upgrade.

Hardware Failures

It might seem rather strange to think about the hardware failing during the upgrade of such an important aspect of your network, but remember that we are dealing with Microsoft products that are notorious for hardware incompatibility. True to form, there will be hardware that runs perfectly fine in Windows NT but does not run in Windows 2000. For this issue, you will need to test the hardware with Windows 2000 before you perform the upgrade. Here are the two tests that you should perform to achieve a confidence level in the 90 percent range:

1. Install a fresh copy of Windows 2000 as a domain controller on a computer with the same hardware that you will be upgrading to Windows 2000.

2. Upgrade a Windows NT PDC to Windows 2000 on a computer with the same hardware that you will be upgrading.

Testing the PDC Upgrade

One excellent way to test a PDC upgrade is to follow these steps:

1. Install a Windows NT BDC in the same domain as the PDC that needs to be upgraded.

2. Take the PDC offline.

3. Promote the BDC to a PDC, and make sure the network functions properly.

4. Perform the upgrade of the offline PDC on an isolated network. Then ensure that all hardware, software, users, groups, and configurations function properly.

5. When the test is complete, reinstall the offline PDC as a BDC.

6. Promote the BDC to a PDC, and you are back to where you started.

 When upgrading an NT domain, the PDC must be SP4 or later. The BDCs can be at a lower Service Pack, unless they will be upgraded later, in which case they too need to be SP4.

These steps will take care of two items for you. First, they will ensure that the hardware will work with the default Windows 2000 drivers. Of course, if there are any drivers not included with the OS, you can install your third-party drivers. This will prove that these third-party drivers are compatible with Windows 2000 as well. Second, these steps will give you an idea of whether or not the upgrade process will work successfully with regard to hardware and the drivers.

Note: When you're upgrading from one operating system to another, the hardware drivers may or may not be upgraded automatically. There is really no way to determine this without performing the upgrade.

As you can see, there is virtually no way to control whether or not the hardware will work with Windows 2000 after an upgrade. With this in mind, you'll need to take more precautions than just testing the upgrade process. You'll need to have a contingency plan in place before you even perform the upgrade test. Here are some items to include into your contingency plan:

➤ Consider how users will gain access to resources if a problem occurs. Either have the resources mirrored on another portion of the network, or have another server ready to go in case the resources become unavailable.

➤ Hardware components can go bad, so be certain to have spare parts readily available. You probably have the more common parts in stock, but the more expensive and unique parts should be accessible, too.

➤ A tape backup is the only true way to have your information archived. If you have not performed a mock disaster recovery, now would be a good time to perform that process. A tape backup is only as good as the ability to restore the information.

➤ Try to anticipate all possible problems that might occur. Document a solution to each failure point. If you have a plan for all anticipated problems, the recovery process will go much more smoothly.

Last, but certainly not least, know the requirements for using Windows 2000 Server and Advanced Server as a domain controller. Both of these operating systems have the same minimums according to Microsoft:

➤ *Processor*—133MHz or higher Pentium-compatible CPU

➤ *Memory*—256MB RAM (128MB minimum supported)

➤ *Hard disk*—2GB

Note: Although this hardware will allow the installation of Windows 2000, most environments will quickly find out that more hardware is required to effectively run Windows 2000.

Of course, if you only want to run a clock server, these minimums would suffice. However, for your hardware to perform as a domain controller in the enterprise, you will need to beef it up. The following minimums are what I have found to be a good starting place for minimum hardware, your mileage may vary. If you have any network services or applications, or a large number of users per domain controller, these numbers should be increased accordingly:

➤ Processor—Pentium II 300MHz or greater

➤ Memory—256MB RAM as a minimum

➤ Hard disk—5GB

Whether you are upgrading or installing fresh, the critical Windows 2000 domain controller files and folders (SYSVOL, NTDS.dit, and the NTDS log) need to reside on NTFS volumes.

Remember that you can install the Active Directory database on a different physical hard drive than the operating system. This will not only give you better performance, but also allow you to limit the size of the operating system's drive.

Access Rights Required

The rights needed to upgrade a Windows NT PDC will be less stringent than the rights required to migrate users, groups, and computers by using a tool such as the ADMT or ClonePrincipal. The reason for this is the simplicity of the network domain structure with only a Windows NT domain. There are, however, two scenarios that you must consider when making the upgrade from NT to 2000. The first scenario is that of upgrading the PDC to become the first Windows 2000 domain controller, in the first Windows 2000 domain, tree, and forest. The other scenario is that of upgrading the PDC to become the first Windows 2000 domain controller in a new domain, but located in an existing Windows 2000 tree or forest.

If you consider the first scenario, you will need to have fewer rights than if you consider the second scenario. For the first scenario, you will only need to be aware of the rights that you require in the Windows NT domain. The Windows 2000 domain does not even exist yet. The rights that you will need for the Windows NT domain will be Administrator privileges. If you don't have the appropriate rights, then using the automatic upgrade process (accomplished by placing the Windows 2000 Server CD in the computer and having the CD autoplaying) or running the Dcpromo.exe utility from the PDC will give you an error indicating that you need to be an administrator to perform the function.

For the second scenario, you will need the appropriate rights not only in the Windows NT domain but also in the Windows 2000 enterprise. Of course, you would not want to just allow anyone to add a domain to the Windows 2000 Active Directory structure. Therefore, to add another domain to the existing tree and forest, you will need to have the Enterprise Administrators privileges within the Windows 2000 Active Directory.

Domain Name Problems

When you upgrade your Windows NT domain to Windows 2000, you'll have to name your new Windows 2000 domain. This name, as you have experienced, must be a DNS (Domain Name Service) domain name. An example of such a name would be **examcram.com**. A couple of issues could make your domain name fail. As you work through the exam, be cognizant of these issues and how they might manifest themselves in an upgrade scenario. The issues are as follows:

➤ The DNS server that will house the Windows 2000 namespace must support SRV records. The DNS should also support dynamic updates for ease of administration of the DNS entries.

 Other important benefits of a Windows 2000 DNS server are the support of incremental zone transfers and the ability to make the DNS Active Directory integrated. Be sure to notice any exam question that is focusing on issues related to these benefits.

➤ The new DNS structure must fit into the existing DNS namespace, or else a new DNS namespace should be created. For example, the existing DNS namespace might be based on business units (**marketing.ec.com** and **sales.ec.com**), and the new Windows 2000 DNS namespace might be based on geography (**east.ec.com** and **west.ec.com**).

➤ The DNS structure might create a security hole between the internal network and the Internet. Be careful when you're selecting the name of the internal DNS namespace compared to the Internet namespace. Unless there is a security team in place, it might be best to keep the two namespaces separate (**ec.com** for the Internet and **ec.local** for the internal network).

➤ An upgrade of an NT domain must be placed into an existing Windows 2000 forest to gain the benefits of Kerberos trusts, common global catalogs, and common schema. Domain names within the same forest must be unique.

➤ If the new upgraded Windows 2000 domain is not the forest root domain, the PDC must be able to communicate with the parent domain (if the PDC is a child in an existing tree) or with the forest root domain (if the PDC is the root of another tree).

➤ For a new domain to enter into an existing forest, the first domain controller in that forest must communicate with the domain naming master. This is one of the FSMO (Flexible Single Master Operations) servers that controls the names within the forest.

If the domain migration seems to have succeeded, but the new domain is not responding to other domains in the Windows 2000 forest, there could have been an error with the domain name during the upgrade process. The Nltest.exe tool is designed to help you determine and test the domain status of servers and domain controllers. If the Nltest.exe tool is used with the **parentdomain** switch, it will specify the parent domain of the server in question. If there is a problem with the new upgraded domain communicating with the parent domain (or apparent parent domain), the result will be an error message indicating that the parent domain could not be located.

Account Issues

As you migrate users, groups, and computers from the Windows NT environment to the Windows 2000 environment, certain issues will surround these accounts. In Windows 2000, unlike Windows NT, the issue of duplicate computer SIDs will play a major role. The reason for this is that a computer is a security principal within Active Directory. Therefore, you need to worry about duplicating SIDs of computers along with users and groups when you migrate from Windows NT to 2000.

Duplicate SIDs are not the only things that you need to be concerned with when it comes to account issues. You also need to be aware of how logon scripts are migrated and replicated. Finally, system policies and group policies can play havoc on your newly migrated Windows 2000 environment. The exam will certainly test you on all of these possible pitfall areas, so this chapter will provide the details for you.

Duplicate Accounts That Have Different SIDs

As users, groups, and computers are migrated from the Windows NT domain to the Windows 2000 domain, there's bound to be some form of duplication of accounts. There can be many reasons for this duplication. This section will describe the possible reasons for duplication and specify the best solution for each case. We will also discuss why the **sIDHistory** account plays an important role in the migration of users to the target domain.

Reasons for Duplicate Accounts

Figure 10.7 illustrates the scenario of duplicate accounts. As you can see from the graphic, it will be difficult to migrate an account from the source domain to the target domain with an existing account already there. This situation could be caused by several things.

First, someone might create an account in Active Directory with the same name as an account in the source domain. This could be by design or by accident.

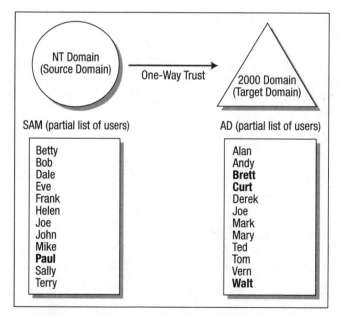

Figure 10.7 Duplicate accounts in source and target domains.

Because a large migration could take place over a period of time, an account might be required in both domains for administration or testing.

Second, there might have been an earlier migration of the user account. This is typical when the migration process takes a long time due to the size of the enterprise being migrated to Windows 2000. For example, the global group might be migrated in the early stages of the migration process. Then, while both the source domain and the target domain are using the global group for authentication, new users are added to the source domain global group. In this scenario, the global group would need to be cloned again to reflect changes made during the migration process.

Third, multiple source domains might be migrated to a single target domain. In this scenario, the initial source domain could create an account that has the same name in another source domain. When the second source domain is migrated, you will choose how to deal with the existing account that was migrated from the initial source domain.

Controlling Duplicate Accounts

The best bet for controlling duplicate accounts is to use the ADMT wizards. The wizards will walk you through each step and allow you to determine how to control duplicate users, groups, or computers. Figure 10.8 illustrates the possible options for conflict resolution for the migration of users. (The options for groups and computers include the exact same options for name conflict resolution.)

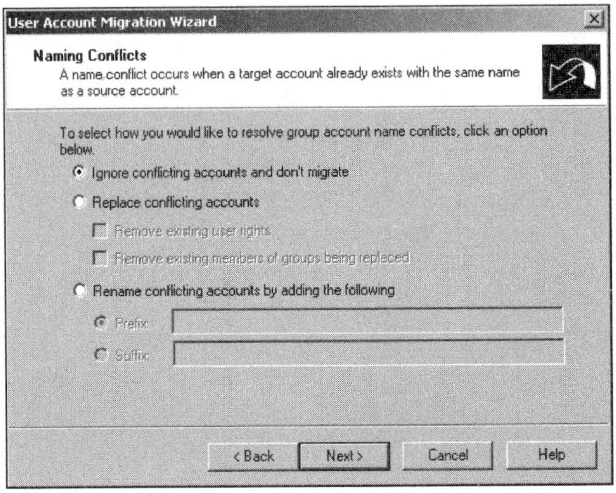

Figure 10.8 The Naming Conflicts page of the ADMT's User Account Migration Wizard.

As you can see in Figure 10.8, there are options that will take care of almost any detail. As you decide which option will best suit you, be certain that you are fully aware of what your result will be. Following are descriptions of each option and the resulting configuration for the migrated user:

➤ *Ignore Conflicting Accounts And Don't Migrate*—This option leaves the target domain account unchanged. This is the obvious choice if the account that you're migrating is truly a duplicate or if you're just not certain of the outcome.

➤ *Replace Conflicting Accounts*—This option changes the properties of the existing account in the target domain to reflect the properties of the duplicate account in the source domain. This option only updates the properties and does not change the SID of either account.

➤ *Remove Existing User Rights*—This option updates the target account's user rights, ensuring that the updated account does not have more access rights than the source account configuration. This option goes along with the Replace Conflicting Accounts option.

Note: If you select this configuration, the target account will have only the user rights that are common to both the source and the target duplicate accounts. This might cause results that you don't want. If the goal is to have only the source user rights, do not select this option. Simply select the Update User Rights box in the User Options Wizard.

➤ *Remove Existing Members Of Groups Being Replaced*—This option configures the members of the migrated groups in the target domain to ensure that they are the same as the members of the corresponding groups in the source domain. This option goes along with the Replace Conflicting Accounts option.

➤ *Rename Conflicting Accounts By Adding The Following*—This option takes a passive approach and adds the user but with a prefix or suffix added to the name of the migrated account. This ensures that the new account in the target domain is unique. The SID and the name are different.

Tackling Duplicate Accounts

Now that both the problems and the configurations have been discussed, which option should you use to get the results that you want after the migration? This will be rather straightforward when you begin to play with the problems and possible configurations to solve your issues.

Consider the first possible configuration to handle duplicate accounts: Ignore Conflicting Accounts And Don't Migrate. This solution will work well for those organizations with many user accounts that need to be migrated. Consider an organization that has 20,000 users in the source domain. It would be a great idea to break up the migration into multiple phases in order to handle the possible problems of authentication, resource access, user rights, and normal operations. After the users in the initial phases have been migrated, however, it may become difficult to distinguish between the migrated users and those users who have yet to be migrated. Therefore, for the next couple of phases, the ADMT could be configured to simply ignore conflicting accounts, and this would eliminate the confusion as to which option should be selected.

Be certain that you keep track of which users were created manually and which users were migrated from another domain. The **sIDHistory** attribute will need to be updated and bound to the target account, even if it is a duplicate account.

The second configuration is to Replace Conflicting Accounts. This by far will be the most used configuration for migrations. The reason is that the **sIDHistory** attribute will need to be added to any duplicate accounts, and the user rights and group memberships will also need to be modified to account for the source domain settings. All of the reasons for duplicate accounts could fit into this category and require that you replace conflicting accounts.

Note: When an existing target account is replaced, the SID is not changed. The original SID remains the same, regardless of how the account was initally created. However, if the account needs to be updated for the sIDHistory or user rights, this is the only configuration in the ADMT that will allow for this duplicate account control.

The third option, Rename Conflicting Accounts By Adding The Following, will be used only when the plan calls for user accounts to have a prefix or suffix. Some organizations will use this option to quickly determine the location of the user within Active Directory. This solution might not be used that often because of the change that the user will incur. The user will now be forced to use a different username—one that has a prefix or suffix attached to the logon account. If thousands of users have been migrated, it will take awhile for all these users to remember to use their new usernames.

The sIDHistory Attribute

By far, one of the most important facets of the migration process is the inclusion of the **sIDHistory** attribute. As you will recall, the **sIDHistory** attribute allows a migrated account to be known in the new target domain as well as in the old source domain. The goal here is to allow the new account access to the source and resource domain files, folders, and printers.

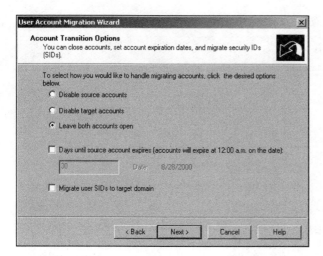

Figure 10.9   sIDHistory configuration through the ADMT's User Account Migration Wizard.

As you migrate the users, groups, and computers, no matter which migration tool you're using, you must specify that you want the **sIDHistory** attribute. Figure 10.9 illustrates the ADMT interface for configuring the **sIDHistory** attribute for a user.

When an issue arises that forces you to verify that the **sIDHistory** attribute is migrating successfully, you might have to query the Active Directory account to verify that the **sIDHistory** attribute is being configured. The tool to perform this task is the LDP tool (located on the Server CD in the /Support folder). This tool allows you to query any object within Active Directory to find the current attributes and their values. Figure 10.10 shows the result of querying the user Bob. Note that the **sIDHistory** attribute is properly assigned for this account.

A final note about **sIDHistory** is that there can be only a single instance of a **sIDHistory** in the entire forest. If there is a duplicate SID for a user, group, or computer, you will typically receive the **rc=8539** error. If you run the **net helpmsg 8539** command, it will verify the meaning of the error message.

Logon Script Failures

The concept of a logon script is familiar. First, the client logs onto the domain and is authenticated by a domain controller. The user has a configuration that states that he is to receive a logon script (usually a batch file, but sometimes a script). If the logon script is available on the domain controller that authenticates the user, that user gets configured with the information that is in the logon script.

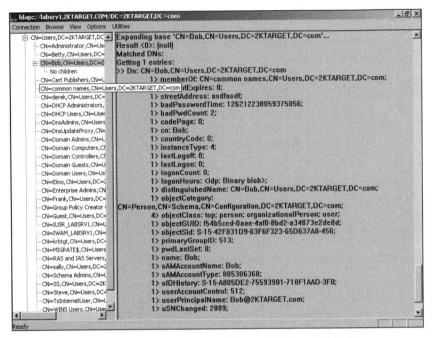

Figure 10.10 Results of using the LDP tool to verify the **sIDHistory** attribute for a user.

This final phase of the logon script process is the key to the proper functioning of the logon script. There can be many reasons for the logon script not being correctly configured on all domain controllers. The exam will require that you know why the logon script has failed and how to fix the problem. You'll need to be aware of two environments: native-mode domains and mixed-mode domains. (Of course, an NT-only domain has problems with logon scripts, but this is a Windows 2000 exam.)

Native Mode

First, we'll tackle the easier of the two scenarios. Remember that a native-mode domain simply means that there are no more down-level domain controllers in the domain. Therefore, you will not need to concern yourself with any Windows NT issues if the exam's case study states that the environment is a native-mode domain.

However, you will need to concern yourself with any problems that can occur if the user is not receiving the logon script that you have configured. The two main issues related to the failure of logon scripts after a migration are the misconfiguration of the user account and the failed replication of the NETLOGON share, which is located in the SYSVOL on the domain controllers.

The first situation is quite simple. The administrator failed to configure the user account. Therefore, the administrator can simply go to the user (or group of migrated users) and ensure that the logon script is configured properly.

The second situation can be as simple as a missing logon script or as complex as a misconfigured site topology. The NETLOGON share uses the Knowledge Consistency Checker, site links, and replication schedule that are built for the replication of the Active Directory database. However, these two replications are separate. With the native-mode configuration, the replication will occur automatically unless you have tweaked the site links or the replication schedule. If these have been tweaked, then ensure that the replication can occur because it's possible to set up a site topology that never replicates.

Mixed Mode

A mixed-mode domain can get a little sticky with regard to logon scripts. The first two reasons for a failed logon script can be taken from the previous section. If the user account is incorrectly configured or replication of the SYSVOL share among the Windows 2000 domain controllers is not functioning, the logon scripts won't work.

However, with a mixed-mode domain, there is another very important situation that you need to be concerned about. The Directory Replication Service in Windows NT (also referred to as the LAN Manager Replication Service or LMRepl) does not communicate with the File Replication Service in Windows 2000. The key to solving this problem is getting the two domain controllers to exchange this important data. There are two options for this. The first solution is to use the Lbridge.cmd file that copies the NETLOGON portion of the SYSVOL share from a Windows 2000 domain controller to the Windows NT domain controller that's functioning as the export server within the NT BDCs. The other solution is to create this simple batch file yourself to do the same thing. In either case, the only way to get the two domain controllers to replicate the NETLOGON share is to manually copy the files from one platform to the other. This manual process could be formatted in the new Windows 2000 scheduler as well, making the process occur periodically.

Still one more issue has not been solved. This involves the upgrading of the PDC to the first Windows 2000 domain controller. If the PDC is the export server for the Directory Replication Service among the Windows NT domain controllers, then the replication between the NT domain controllers will halt. The solution to this problem is to ensure that the PDC is not the export server before the upgrade. Configure one of the BDCs as the NT export server by using Server Manager, and then upgrade the PDC. Then use the Lbridge.cmd file to copy the files from the Windows 2000 domain controller to the configured export BDC.

System Policy and Group Policy Problems

You might think that a group policy is an extension of Windows NT system policies, but it isn't. Although a group policy can include some of the functionality that was available in system policies, many more configurations are available with group policies. As you make the migration from NT to 2000, you will certainly need to know how to recover from any problems related to your existing system policies and how they interact with group policies. This section will describe the key aspects of this interaction as well as how system policy problems could affect your migration attempts.

Policy Interaction

During the migration process, you'll need to have both system policies and group policies. Even after the final migration step is complete, you'll probably still need system policies in the organization because of the existence of legacy Windows computers—namely, Windows NT 4, Windows 95, Windows 98, and Windows ME. These operating systems cannot compile group policies and will still need to have the system policies be controlled by the administrators.

There are special cases that you will need to consider when you have both system policies and group policies. For example, you might have a user who is a member of the Windows 2000 domain (being authenticated from Active Directory), but the user's computer is part of an NT domain or is a Windows 95/98/ME system. In a case like this, the user would be able to obtain some of the group policies and the system policies, but the computer would be able to compile only system policies. If you considered the many possible combinations, you would end up with the matrix that is displayed in Table 10.1. This table shows which policies apply, depending on where the user and computer accounts are located. (In this table, "SP" stands for "system policy," and "GPO" stands for "group policy object.")

As you can see, the interaction of system policies and group policies becomes pretty messy, depending on the location of the user and the computer within the domain structures. As you take the exam, be certain to pay close attention to the locations of the user and the computer; these will basically give away the answer to the question.

A note of caution: If you have system policies on the NT domain controllers and the 2000 domain controllers, the results might be very mysterious because of how the clients implement system policies. Although this is not specifically on the exam, do plenty of testing to determine what your result will be well before you introduce the migration into the mix.

Table 10.1	System policy and group policy application.				
Computer Membership	User Membership	Computer SP	Computer GPO	User SP	User GPO
NT domain (NT or 2000 client)	NT domain	•		•	
NT domain (NT client)	2000 domain	•		•	
NT domain (2000 client)	2000 domain	•		•	•
2000 domain (NT client)	NT domain	•		•	
2000 domain (2000 client)	NT domain		•	•	
2000 domain (NT client)	2000 domain	•		•	
2000 domain (2000 client)	2000 domain		•		•
N/A (95/98/ME client)	2000 domain	•		•	

System-Policy Specifics

The migration of system policies can be a smooth transition or a rough transition; it just depends on the time and detail that you spend with them in the planning phase. This section will review the specifics about system policies with regard to a migration and a Windows 2000 production environment.

One item on the agenda that must be discussed is how system policies actually update a computer. A system policy is nothing more than a Registry change. When the computer starts or the user logs on, the Registry is changed based on the configurations that were made within the ntconfig.pol file (config.pol for 95/98/ME computers). This Registry change is a permanent change and can be removed only manually or by another system policy. All computers (2000/NT/95/98/ME) can be affected by this permanent change (or *tattoo*) in the Registry. If a system policy has permanently affected a computer, then an upgrade to the OS or a change in how the computer receives the policies (see Table 10.2) could adversely affect the desired outcome.

Note: Windows 2000 group policies do not tattoo the Registry. They actually update two secure Registry locations, which are flushed when the computer is rebooted or the user logs off.

If the system policy has tattooed the Registry, and the computer has been upgraded from a Windows NT to Windows 2000 client, there are a couple of ways to remedy the problem. Of course, this will affect only those Windows 2000 clients that do not compile system policies. First, you could manually go into the Registry and change the value back to the original configuration. If multiple computers are affected, this could take too much time. Another option is to alter the Windows 2000 Group Policy Administrative Templates. Similar to the system policies, the Administrative Templates can be customized to change any Registry setting.

Note: These group policy customizations will tattoo the Registry.

The final option for changing the Registry for a system that has been tattooed is to reinstall the Windows 2000 client. This is somewhat drastic, but it is a solution. If you have to reinstall after the upgrade from NT to Windows 2000 due to this Registry issue, it would have been a much better solution to just reinstall in the first place. This is the preferred method of going from NT to 2000 clients.

Conversion of System Policies

There is not an option to migrate system policies directly to group policies. However, there is a way to utilize a system policy's information and configuration in a group policy. The method for this is to convert the system policies using the Gpolmig.exe tool. This tool allows you to migrate settings from your system policies to the group policy object (GPO) structure.

Miscellaneous Tools and Troubles with Policies

Other tools are also available:

➤ *Gpresult.exe*—This tool gives you insight into the system information about the group policies applied to the current user and computer. This information includes a detailed list of the group policy settings that are being applied.

➤ *Gpotool.exe*—This tool allows you to create and delete group policies from the command line. The tool also helps you check the replication status of group policies as well as of the Sysvol folder.

➤ *Netdiag.exe*—This tool helps you with more global network-related issues as well as with verifying DNS connectivity. Both of these issues could cause policies to fail.

➤ *Replmon.exe*—This tool is an excellent method of verifying the replication of the Active Directory.

Access Issues

After an upgrade or migration to a completely new environment, there are bound to be issues with users and servers gaining access to resources. The access issues can be related to security issues, such as client connectivity or authentication. Many access issues will be related to the new NTFS structure and the **SIDHistory**. There are bound to be problems with trusts between domains, since Windows 2000 handles trusts so different than the NT OS did.

Client Connectivity

For Windows 2000 Active Directory to function properly, the client needs to communicate with and connect to different aspects of the environment. The reason for this is that Windows 2000 Active Directory relies on more than broadcasts and WINS (Windows Internet Naming Service) to function properly, and those are what much of the legacy Windows NT domain relied upon. Now with advancements with DNS and DHCP (Dynamic Host Configuration Protocol), clients need to communicate with and connect successfully to more network services and locations than before.

One of the first issues that is typically brought up about Windows 2000 Active Directory is the need for WINS. WINS is still an integral part of the Microsoft world and is needed most of the time (see the section on name resolution for details). However, it's possible to configure the Windows 2000 standard protocol, TCP/IP, with no NetBIOS support. The reasons to get rid of NetBIOS are good ones, but you must consider how the client will now communicate with the rest of the network before you tackle such a task. The key thing to remember is that DNS can now resolve network services to IP addresses for Windows 2000 clients. Therefore, if you decide to eliminate NetBIOS from your Windows 2000 clients, you must be sure that the DNS is configured properly and you must have some form of backup DNS server for fault tolerance.

DNS is critical when NetBIOS is eliminated on the network in addition to finding network resources. For your Windows 2000 clients, DNS is going to replace WINS for your clients' connection to network resources. A good example of this reliance upon DNS includes the configurations that Active Directory can force upon clients via *group policies*. Because the client relies on DNS for the network service location, group policies will fail if the client is not properly configured with the appropriate DNS server.

Another item to consider with regard to DNS and clients is the new interaction that a client must have when communicating with the network services. This query is now done through DNS, not WINS or a broadcast. The client must be able to communicate with the DNS Server. Although this sounds easy enough, consider another factor that might prohibit this communication: the HOSTS file. If the HOSTS file is configued on a client to use an old domain controller for authentication, the client will never use DNS to use a legitimate domain controller. In this case the client will not be able to authenticate, or perform many other imoprtant functions in the domain.

A final issue related to client connectivity involves user profiles. When a user is migrated from NT to 2000, a new SID is generated for the new 2000 account. The unfortunate thing is that a profile is resolved by checking the primary SID on the user's token or ticket. Because the primary SID is checked, the **sIDHistory** attribute will not help with this situation. The only thing that can be done to fix this problem is to use a tool to reapply the ACL (access control list) to the local profile. The ADMT provides this option, as shown in Figure 10.11. This option will translate the SID that is used for the profile.

Shares and Shortcuts

After migration, users might experience strange behavior with referential objects, such as shortcuts or shares. Typically, shortcuts are located on the desktop and point to local executables or programs. Shares are mapped through logon scripts, published in Active Directory, or browsed to via the new Network Neighborhood that is buried in the My Network Places icon. Sometimes these shortcuts and shares are not available or do not function properly after migration.

When you're dealing with a migration of users, computers, and the associated applications that need to come along for the ride, you are bound to wind up with a shortcut that is pointing to an unknown folder or application. Keep in mind that upgrades and migrations do not take care of the fine details; that is left up to you. When you run up against such an issue, though, you now will have some ammo to battle the task. When shortcuts are not migrating properly, simply use the Chklnks.exe tool to find the incorrect links and give you the opportunity to remove the links.

Access to shares might be more complex due to the new, migrated and most likely complex environment of Windows 2000 and NT domains. If you cannot access a share, but you can see the share published in Active Directory, be certain that you have the right permissions for the file. The right permissions might be obtained in a couple of ways, depending on the originating problem. Here are some tips:

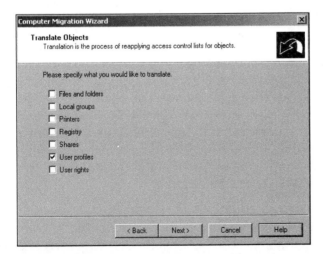

Figure 10.11 The Translate Objects page of the ADMT's Computer Migration Wizard.

➤ Ensure that the **sIDHistory** attribute correctly migrated with the user accounts.

➤ Ensure that the correct trust relationships are established for your new account to gain access to the resource in the resource domain.

➤ Check the ACL (both share and NTFS permissions) on the shared folder to see if your account (or **sIDHistory**) has the proper permissions.

If you can't even see the share, but you know that it was there yesterday, you will need to investigate Active Directory to see if you have the proper permissions through the OU or share that is located in the structure. You can hide shares and entire portions of the Active Directory structure by setting permissions on the objects contained within the Directory database. This can be a very powerful way of controlling access, but it can also be frustrating if the results cause problems with users or administrators not gaining access to shared resources.

NTFS Security

If you have decommissioned the source domain before migrating the resource domains, you will most likely see the "Unknown Account" in the ACLs and groups of the resource domain. However, the user will still gain access. This is due to the inability of the NT 3.51, NT 4, or mixed-mode 2000 domain to successfully translate the SID to the user account without the source domain still available. If you implemented **sIDHistory**, the user will still be able to access the accounts. To fix this, run the Security Translation Wizard, as shown in Figure 10.12, to replace the source account SID with the new target account SID for all affected resources. However, this problem should not occur if you decommission the source domains all at once as a final step in the migration process.

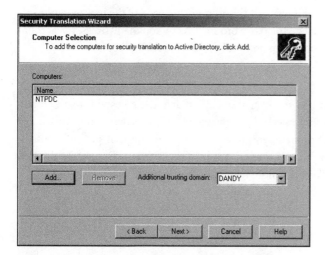

Figure 10.12   The Security Translation Wizard in the ADMT.

In this particular Wizard, notice that you have the option of specifying additional trusting domains for the translation of security on computers in these domains, too. To gain access to these trusting domains, you will need to have administrative rights to this source domain.

Authentication

Although the authentication of users will work properly for most successful migrations, there are a couple of sticking points that you need to be aware of. One is for an interforest migration, and the other is related to an intraforest migration. A final issue is related to communicating with your users, which usually needs some attention in most organizations.

As a reminder, an interforest migration occurs when accounts from a domain in one forest are migrated to another domain in another forest. For most organizations, this will be the typical method of migration. The catch is that after an interforest migration, the user accounts are set so that users must change their passwords at the next logon. A problem can occur if the target domain already has the user accounts set so that users cannot change passwords. The users won't be able to log on if this is the case, so an administrator will have to change one or both of these settings to give the users access.

An intraforest migration occurs between two domains in the same forest. This will be a popular task after many organizations realize the power that Windows 2000 provides—after the first failed migration to 2000. A key item to remember with an intraforest migration is that the passwords are maintained. If the password policy from the source domain is not complex enough for the target domain, the users will not be able to log on with their original passwords. The system will prompt users to change their passwords. However, if the users are unaware of the new requirements and they attempt to change the password incorrectly too many times, the account lockout will certainly lock them out until you enable their account.

Trusts

Remember to review the trust relationships that must be established before a migration can function properly. If you have migrated accounts from the source domain to the target domain, you have obviously set up that part of the trust relationship correctly. You might still run into some snags, though. As the first part of the chapter indicates, more trusts need to be established so that users can gain access to all resources in the enterprise. A scenario and a graphic will help clear up this issue.

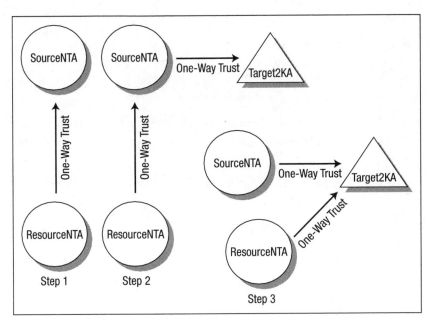

Figure 10.13   Trust migration scenario.

Scenario for Trusts

Figure 10.13 includes three domains. There is a source domain, SourceNTA, with users that will be migrated to Windows 2000, Target2KA. There is also a resource domain, ResourceNTA, which has resources that users in SourceNTA have access to in Step 1. To complete the migration, you must establish a trust between SourceNTA and Target2KA, in Step 2. After the migration of the users, the users are in the Target2KA domain, and another trust must be established between the ResourceNTA and Target2KA.

Here are some things to keep in mind to help you troubleshoot trust issues:

➤ Windows 2000 domains in the same forest use two-way, transitive Kerberos trusts.

➤ Windows 2000 domains not in the same forest use one-way, nontransitive Kerberos trusts.

➤ Windows NT domains to any other domains use one-way, nontransitive trusts.

Network Services

Windows 2000 relies heavily on the network services compared to the NT world. With this in mind, there will undoubtedly be issues that need resolution as you migrate from one version to the other. The critical network services that will cause the most problems include DHCP, DNS, WINS, and RRAS. This section will walk through the most common problems and how to troubleshoot them.

DHCP

One of the most changed services from NT to 2000 is the DHCP service. The service has become a centerpiece for the network with the requirement of TCP/IP as the protocol and Dynamic DNS. Many things can go wrong with DHCP, but the following is a list of issues and the solutions to those issues:

➤ *Problem*—A client could have received a duplicate IP address and cannot gain access to network resources. The initial IP address could have been dynamically allocated or statically assigned.

Solution—Configure the DHCP service for IP address conflict detection, as shown in Figure 10.14.

➤ *Problem*—The DHCP scope is not activated and is therefore not available to clients. Usually this will be noticed when a client receives an IP address from the 169.254.0.0 to 16 range.

Solution—The DHCP scope simply needs to be activated in the DHCP administrative tool.

➤ *Problem*—The DHCP server has not been authorized, and clients are not obtaining an IP address from the correct range. Usually this will be noticed when a client receives an IP address from the 169.254.0.0 to 16 range.

Solution—Authorize the DHCP server from the DHCP administrative tool.

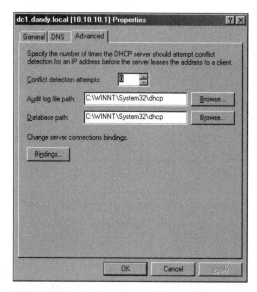

Figure 10.14 Configuring the DHCP service for IP address conflict detection.

➤ *Problem*—The DHCP server is not updating DNS for Windows 2000 or down-level clients.

Solution—Upgrade or install a Windows 2000 DHCP server to support this function.

Name Resolution Issues

Name resolution is still an important issue on a Windows 2000 network, just as it was on the premigrated Windows NT network. The main goal is to have a solid, efficient, and hands-free name resolution environment. Sounds too good to be true, but that is exactly what Windows 2000 offers. The two name resolution services, DNS and WINS, can have some trouble after migration, but will probably work just fine on your network. If they don't, see if the following information helps you solve your problem.

DNS

DNS is an essential part of a Windows 2000 network that has Active Directory installed. The first domain controller for the 2000 domain must communicate with a DNS server. The DNS server that it communicates with must meet the Active Directory requirements. If you continue to have trouble with the upgrade of the PDC due to a DNS issue, do one of the following:

➤ Install DNS on the server that is being upgraded. This will install the Dynamic DNS service, which meets all of the Active Directory requirements.

➤ When prompted for a DNS server for the new Windows 2000 domain, you can point to another DNS server that supports the Active Directory requirements. This server does not have to be a Windows DNS server, but make sure that you select the correct DNS version if you go to another platform (see Chapter 4 for details).

After you get your initial upgrade complete and the Windows 2000 domain is running, you can still get snagged on a couple of issues related to DNS. The advanced features of a Windows 2000 DNS make it a very solid solution for a 2000 network. As you attempt to solve problems that are related to DNS and domain name resolution, be sure to consider these additional DNS features that just might solve your problems:

➤ DNS can be configured as Active-Directory-integrated. This will make the DNS database fault-tolerant by adding the DNS database to the Active Directory database. When a single Active-Directory-integrated DNS server fails, the other Active-Directory-integrated DNS servers are still running and are all considered to be primary because they can all update the DNS database.

➤ After DNS has been made Active-Directory-integrated, the DNS server can also be configured to accept only secure dynamic updates. This will protect the DNS server from any rogue updates that do not accept secure dynamic updates. All Microsoft products that support dynamic updates can communicate with the DNS server in this secure manner.

➤ The forward lookup zone is automatically created and updated by default. If you need to resolve names from the IP address, you will need to configure the reverse lookup zone, too. Services such as SQL, IIS (Internet Information Server), and Exchange could benefit from this zone to help with decrypting the log files that are created by these services.

 Remember that you will need to have correct versions of BIND for certain functionality. BIND 4.9.7 is the lowest version that will support AD and BIND 8.1.2 is the lowest version to suport Dynamic updates.

WINS

There are debates for a Windows 2000 network with regard to the WINS service: Is it required, or can I just use DNS? There really is no debate because the guidelines for requiring WINS are clear-cut. If you are experiencing problems with your migrated or upgraded Windows 2000 network, they might be due to a missing WINS. Remember that WINS will resolve an IP address to the NetBIOS name. If you have one of the following situations, you will need to continue to run WINS on the network:

➤ You have clients that are running Windows for Workgroups, Windows 9x, or Windows NT 4. These would also include servers running Windows NT 4.

➤ There are applications that require NetBIOS and therefore NetBIOS name resolution in order to function on the network.

➤ You have multiple forests (this would also include NT domains) that are trusted or trusting domains outside of the forest. The legacy trusts (one-way, nontransitive) use LAN Manager to establish the trusts and therefore require NetBIOS.

Remote Access Permissions Failures

The issue with RAS (Remote Access Service) in an upgrade or migration scenario is quite simple, but can seem to be complex. However, even though the issue is simple, it's essential that you take care of it before problems arise for the remote access users. The problem is related to the fact that Windows NT 4 RAS uses the LocalSystem account to run the service. This LocalSystem account uses NULL credentials (no username or password) to log on to the system and run the service. When this account with NULL credentials attempts to authenticate against Active Directory, the authentication fails. Following are some solutions to this problem; as you go down the list, the solutions become less attractive, due to security concerns:

➤ Upgrade your Windows NT 4 RAS servers to Windows 2000.

➤ Add the Everyone group to the Pre-Windows 2000 Compatible Access local group.

➤ During the installation of the domain controllers, select the option to loosen Active Directory security. This will grant Everyone permissions to read any property on any user object.

 If you are concerned about weakening security, you should upgrade Windows NT 4 RAS servers prior to upgrading your PDC.

Application Failures

During the migration of your NT domain to a Windows 2000 domain, you will need to migrate and reconfigure applications on the servers. Many of these applications will be affected by different problems during this process. The next two sections will cover the two main problems that will affect these applications. The first problem is related to the service accounts that drive these applications, and the other is the incompatibility of these applications with Windows 2000.

Failures Due to Service Accounts

Many third-party applications require an account to run the service that drives the applications. Examples of applications that require this include Exchange, SQL, anti-virus programs, and backup programs. The accounts that are running these services need to be documented, migrated, and configured properly on each server that is running the associated service. If these steps are not performed, the service will almost certainly fail, leaving the application lifeless. To ensure that each and every step along the way is taken care of correctly for a smooth migration, follow these steps:

1. Run the ADMT Service Account Migration Wizard, as shown in Figure 10.15. This wizard allows you to retrieve a list of service accounts and to place the list in a log. The log is named DCTLog.txt, and it's stored in the Temp directory on the system drive of the computer that was tested.

2. The next step is to migrate the users, including the service accounts, from the source domain to the target domain. In Step 1, a special flag is placed in the ADMT database for the service accounts that need to be updated. The

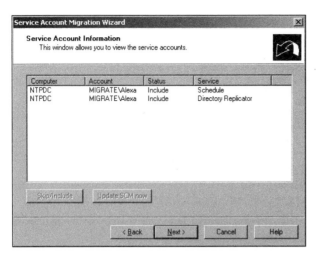

Figure 10.15   The Service Account Migration Wizard.

ADMT will make the proper changes in the service account configurations on the member servers.

3. If the service account was also a member of any group that provided special rights, you'll need to run the Security Translation Wizard to update the rights for the service accounts.

If the service is still not functioning just right, it might be due to the rights not being translated properly. If you ran the Security Translation Wizard with failed results, you might need to go into Active Directory and give the user account specific rights to function as a service. You can do this by modifying the group policy for the organizational unit that contains the server running the application.

Note: Always remember to change the password for service accounts, for the specific service, when the password for this account changes at the domain level. This requires that each instance of the service be modified at each server.

Sometimes the service account will fail and the previous steps will just not fix the situation. If you have performed all of the steps listed, but the service account still won't function properly, there is another option. This option is to use the LocalSystem account and to configure this account to Allow Service To Interact With Desktop, as shown in Figure 10.16. This modification will only affect the local computer, and will not suffice for multiple server interaction.

Incompatibility

This is quite a large topic, but you need to be aware of specific issues for your network migration and for the exam. The main areas that you need to be focused

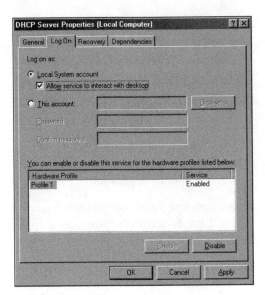

Figure 10.16   LocalSystem account configuration to control applications on the desktop.

on are the new application requirements from Microsoft and the testing regimen that you need to perform on all applications as you migrate from NT to 2000.

First, the Windows 2000 Application Specification was developed by Microsoft to force vendors to adhere to the Windows 2000 API and to regression-test the applications before they were released and signed with the Microsoft seal. There are two specifications: one for desktop applications and one for distributed applications. Both sets of applications go through intense testing to prove that they are compatible with the basic and advanced features of Windows 2000.

If you find that an application is not compatible with Windows 2000, you might not have much ammo with which to combat the problem. You should call the vendor and investigate the Microsoft Web site to see if the application might be compatible. If the vendor or Microsoft indicates that the application is compatible, you might be running another application or device that is making it incompatible. This is a lot of work and can cause the stress level to rise dramatically. One way to help with the stress level is to test before you implement. Following is a set of guidelines for testing applications before you migrate:

1. Run the Winnt32.exe program with the **checkupgradeonly** switch. This will check the compatibility of the current system and configurations before you upgrade the system.

2. Upgrade the computer that is running the application, and then test the most-used features for any errors or failures.

a. If the testing in Step 2 fails, then try to uninstall the application before the upgrade; then reinstall the application after the upgrade and perform the same tests.

b. If Step 2a does not work, then install a fresh copy of Windows 2000, install the application, and perform the tests. If this does not work either, you might have an application that is not compatible with Windows 2000.

3. Test your applications with all of the other applications that will be running on the computer. Applications often conflict with other applications or devices, causing strange behavior with one or more applications.

4. Test data access and printing. Permissions and network access can often cause applications to fail. The more testing that is done with this aspect of the application, the fewer calls you will get from users after the migration or upgrade.

5. Test the application on a computer that has all of the group policies applied that will be applied in the production environment. An application will often require special permissions or access that can be removed by a group policy.

6. Use the testing tools that are provided in the Windows 2000 Resource Kit. A couple of tools that are extremely useful for testing applications include the following:

➤ Dependency Walker—This tool recursively scans dependent modules that are required by an application. This tool detects files that are missing or invalid, mismatched files, and modules installed on mismatched computers.

➤ APIMON—This tool monitors running applications for all API calls. It tracks them and returns any errors or dependencies that could cause a problem.

Implementing a Rollback for Disaster Recovery

A rollback plan is certainly needed before you tackle the migration or upgrade of the existing environment to Windows 2000. However, the rolling back of the environment is different depending on whether you upgrade the PDC or migrate users from NT to 2000 through the ADMT. This section will look at both scenarios and give the best ways to recover from a failed migration.

Rolling Back an Upgrade

When you do an upgrade, you take the NT PDC and upgrade it to the first Windows 2000 domain controller in a Windows 2000 domain. Because you have now taken the critical domain controller from your NT environment and converted this system to a totally different OS, changes might have occurred that you do not want. This might happen because of the replication of the new Windows 2000 domain controller back down to the legacy NT BDCs. To recover from this problem of an undesirable Windows 2000 upgrade, you would have needed to take precautions *before* the upgrade. Here are those precautions:

1. Select a BDC from the source domain that will be sufficient to function as the PDC.

2. Synchronize this BDC with the PDC before you promote the PDC.

Note: Do not make any changes or alterations to the PDC database after this step.

3. Take the BDC offline, and then move forward with the migration of the PDC.

This procedure will create a snapshot of the NT domain before the upgrade is attempted. If the upgrade fails or you want to roll back to the NT configuration before the upgrade, you can bring the BDC back online. After it is back online, you will simply promote it to a PDC, and it will replicate the database to the BDCs, changing any configurations that might have occurred while the BDCs were getting changes from the Windows 2000 domain controller.

Rolling Back a Migration

If the NT domain has been fully or partially migrated to 2000, there are ways to get the NT domain fully functional again (if you have not destroyed the original accounts during the migration). Depending on the steps that have occurred and the configurations that were made during the migration, the following steps will help you return to the previous NT environment if the migration fails or if the 2000 environment is no longer desired:

1. Disable all of the user accounts in the Windows 2000 Active Directory domains.

2. If user accounts were disabled in the source domain during the migration, then enable them again.

3. If the computer accounts were migrated to the Windows 2000 domain, you'll need to manually change them back to the Windows NT domain.

4. If you ran the Security Translation Wizard, you'll need to undo all changes and restore the original configurations. These include rights and ACLs.

Note: This will be a very complex and nearly impossible task. This task should be one of the last items in the migration process, so if the rollback is needed, the ACLs might not have changed yet.

5. If trusts were deleted from resource domains, you'll need to establish them again.

6. Verify that profiles, system policies, and logon scripts are working properly and that the replication of the NETLOGON share is functioning.

7. Replicate any changes that were made to target global groups and domain local groups on the equivalent source global and local groups.

Practice Questions

Question 1

You are running the Active Directory Migration Tool, and you receive an error message indicating that you do not have the correct Registry configuration. The error message states that the ADMT will automatically update the Registry for you. You select this option and continue with the migration. The remaining configurations were completed before the ADMT was started.

You decide to migrate a pilot group of users for this first attempt. You select the option to update the **sIDHistory** attribute for the users. After the migration tool finishes running, you notice that it did not complete the migration of all of the users and it attempted to migrate only one user. What could be the reason for this failure?

○ a. You do not have the correct administrative rights to transfer the SIDs from the source domain.

○ b. The trust between the source and target domains is going in the wrong direction.

○ c. The source domain controller needs to be rebooted due to the configurations you have selected.

○ d. The target domain controller needs to be rebooted due to the configurations you have selected.

Answer c is correct. When the ADMT configures the Registry setting for the TcpipClientSupport key, the source domain controller must be rebooted for the change to take place. Answers a and b are incorrect because the ADMT would have failed before this point if the correct administrative privileges and trusts were not configured properly. Answer d is incorrect because the target domain does not need to have the Registry changed for this setting; only the source domain controller does.

Question 2

> You are attempting to upgrade the Windows NT PDC from the **dandy** domain to become the first domain controller in the Windows 2000 child domain **sales.examcram.local**. At this stage of the Windows 2000 network, you want to keep things simple. You are going to use the existing DNS, DHCP, and WINS servers until the network has proved itself to be stable.
>
> During the upgrade, you specify the DNS server and the new domain name, **sales.examcram.local**, but the upgrade continues to fail at this point. You test the DNS server, and it is still running and accessible. What could be causing this upgrade to fail?
>
> ○ a. The PDC is unable to contact the DHCP server during the upgrade.
>
> ○ b. The PDC Emulator master from the parent domain cannot be contacted for initial replication.
>
> ○ c. The domain naming master cannot be contacted.
>
> ○ d. The domain name **sales.examcram.local** is not a valid domain name due to the domain extension **local**.

Answer c is correct. When a new domain is entering the forest, the domain naming master must be contacted to ensure that the domain name is unique and valid. Answers a and b are incorrect because these services do not need to be contacted during the upgrade process of a PDC to Windows 2000. Answer d is incorrect because the domain name is valid in all DNS servers, not just Microsoft DNS servers.

Question 3

Your network has just been migrated from a Windows NT domain to a Windows 2000 mixed-mode domain. You currently have four BDCs and only one Windows 2000 domain controller. You implement system policies on all Windows NT and Windows 9x clients in the enterprise. The current replication configuration is shown in the exhibit below.

After you change the system policy through the System Policy Editor on one of the BDCs, you notice that the change is occurring on some of the clients, but not all of them. The implementation of the policies is random and sporadic. What is causing this problem?

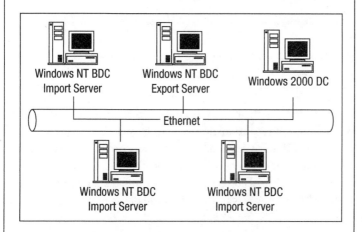

○ a. The system policies need to be modified on the Windows 2000 domain controller.

○ b. Changes first need to be made in the Group Policy Administrative Template section.

○ c. The Windows 2000 domain controller needs to be made an import server.

○ d. The Lbridge.cmd application needs to be run.

Answer d is correct. Windows 2000 and NT do not replicate system policies and the NETLOGON share the same way. The Lbridge application will copy the NETLOGON portion of the SYSVOL share from the Windows 2000 domain controller to the BDC export server. Then the BDC export server will replicate the information to the import BDC servers. Answer a is incorrect because system policies can be changed on the BDCs even in a mixed-mode domain. Answer b is incorrect because group policies do not affect NT or 9x computers. Answer c is incorrect because Windows 2000 domain controllers cannot be configured as import servers.

Question 4

The user migration of the source domain, **ecnt** , has gone very smoothly so far. The resulting Windows 2000 domain, **ec2k.local**, now has two Windows 2000 domain controllers and four Windows NT domain controllers.

After the migration, users complain that they cannot gain access to the resource domain **resnt**. What is the likely cause of this problem?

- ○ a. The domain needs to be migrated to Windows 2000 before the users can access these resources.

- ○ b. A trust must be established so that the **resnt** domain trusts the **ec2k.local** domain.

- ○ c. A trust must be established so that the **resnt** domain trusts the **ecnt** domain.

- ○ d. A trust must be established so that the **ec2k.local** domain trusts the **resnt** domain.

Answer b is correct. Because the users were migrated from the **ecnt** domain to the **ec2k.local** domain, the **resnt** domain needs to have a new trust established such that it trusts the **ec2k.local** domain. Answer a is incorrect because users in a Windows 2000 domain can access resources in any other NT or 2000 domain, as long as the trusts are established correctly. Answers c and d are incorrect because these trusts will not allow the users in the **ec2k.local** domain to access resources in the **resnt** domain.

Question 5

You have just migrated your NT domain to a Windows 2000 domain. This migration included the users, groups, and computers. All clients are using Windows 2000 Professional. All services—including DNS, DHCP, and WINS—have been converted to Windows 2000 as well. Multiple group policy configurations control the users' desktops, security settings, software installations, and Internet Explorer settings.

The developers need to configure the custom firewall application to log FQDNs instead of just IP addresses because it is hard to track down users that are DHCP clients. What will the administrators need to do with this new migrated environment?

○ a.   Create a reverse lookup zone for the Windows 2000 domain in DNS.

○ b.   Create a custom group policy that will have users enter the hostname into DNS when they register.

○ c.   Use the Security Translation Wizard to help resolve the names to the IP addresses.

○ d.   Configure DNS to use WINS for this name resolution.

Answer a is correct. The custom application can be directed to DNS if the DNS has a reverse lookup zone. This zone will perform a reverse lookup to give a name to an IP address. Answer b is incorrect because these clients will already update DNS with their hostnames, without a group policy. Answer c is incorrect because this tool is used for translating user rights and permissions. Answer d is incorrect because the addition of WINS will not help in this case; the DNS needs to have a reverse lookup zone.

Question 6

> You are migrating users, groups, and computers from your NT domain, named **sourcent**, to the Windows 2000 domain, named **target2k**. You have successfully migrated all of the user and group accounts. You have also migrated all of the user computers to the new domain. You are now ready to migrate the servers to the new domain.
>
> After you migrate one of the application servers from the NT domain to the Windows 2000 domain, the application does not function properly. Other application servers have not had any problems. What are possible problems with this server and application? [Check all correct answers]
>
> ❏ a. The service account password is not synchronized with the Windows 2000 Active Directory.
>
> ❏ b. The Security Translation Wizard was not run.
>
> ❏ c. The Service Account Migration Wizard wasn't run after the users were migrated.
>
> ❏ d. The **sIDHistory** attribute was not updated properly.

Answers a and b are correct. If the password is not synchronized with the Active Directory database, the service account will fail. The Security Translation Wizard updates user rights, groups, and permissions. If this service account needed certain rights, the wizard would have established them correctly. Answer c is incorrect because this wizard needs to be run before the users are migrated. Answer d is incorrect because **sIDHistory** is not a factor in this case.

Question 7

> The ACME company has migrated its 6,000-seat NT domain to a Windows
> 2000 domain. After the migration, the IT department finds a major problem
> with the structure and plan of the Windows 2000 domain. They now need to
> roll back to a Windows NT domain. They realize that this is not possible
> because of one of the steps performed during the migration process. Which
> two actions would eliminate the option to use a rollback process? [Check all
> correct answers]
>
> ❑ a. The Windows 2000 domain was changed to native mode.
>
> ❑ b. There are no BDCs in the NT domain.
>
> ❑ c. The NT accounts were deleted after the migration.
>
> ❑ d. A BDC was not taken offline before the migration took place.

Answers c and d are correct. If there are no more accounts in the NT domain, the
domain is empty and there is nothing to roll back to. If a BDC were taken offline,
it would still have the user accounts, and this computer could rebuild the NT
domain. Answer a is incorrect because a migration requires that the Windows
2000 domain be in native mode before the migration can begin. Answer b is
incorrect because a PDC is all that is required to roll back to a Windows NT
domain.

Need to Know More?

 ADMT help file—Search the ADMT help file after you have installed the ADMT. The help file provides details for configuring, implementing, and troubleshooting.

 Microsoft Technet CD—Search the TechNet CD (or its online version through **www.microsoft.com**) and the *Windows 2000 Server Resource Kit* CD, using the keywords "migration," "cookbook," "upgrade," and "troubleshoot."

 Windows 2000 Resource Kits: Web Resources—Search the following Web site: **http://windows.microsoft.com/windows2000/reskit/webresources**. This link describes information about the Windows 2000 Application Specification and process.

Sample Test

Case Study 1

Braincore, Inc., is a group of medical doctors who specialize in treating head injuries and brain-related illnesses. The doctors have offices around the world, and are known for their cutting-edge approach to medical practice and for their Web presence, **www.braincore.com**. The main office for the Braincore group is located in Paris, France. The company also has branch medical offices in New York, NY; Los Angeles, CA; Tokyo, Japan; Sydney, Australia; and Bonn, Germany.

The Task at Hand

Reconfigure the existing locations so they are all part of a Windows 2000 Active Directory structure.

Existing Network Configuration

Braincore currently functions on a multiple-domain infrastructure in Windows NT 4. Each office is a unique domain. The current domain model and trust relationships can be seen in Figure 11.1.

Each office has at least two BDCs in addition to the PDC. Administrators in each office maintain their NT domains. The network service servers are all configured on Windows NT 4 servers. Figure 11.2 shows the locations of the different network service servers.

The existing clients are all running Windows 98 and Windows NT 4 Workstation. Figure 11.3 shows the current WAN configuration. Note that there are no connections between the branch offices.

Each branch office has dial-up capability to access the Internet. The main office in Paris has a fractional T1 line for access to the Internet. The Paris office

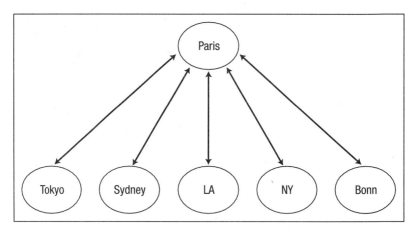

Figure 11.1 The current domain model.

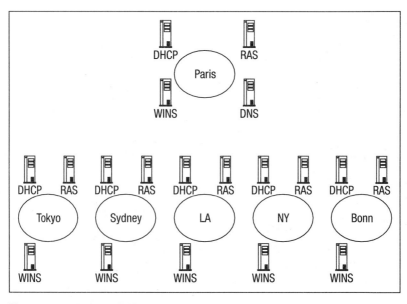

Figure 11.2 Windows NT network services topology.

currently uses an ISP for its Web hosting services. When the doctors travel, they can use dial-up access on the RAS server in their location to gain access to their files. Each office has implemented NT system policies. The offices that use dial-up currently use the highest form of security that Windows NT offers for authentication and data encryption.

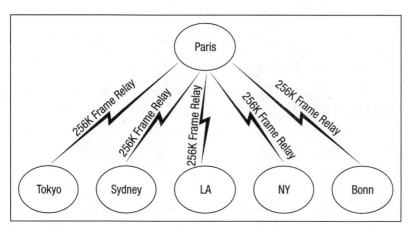

Figure 11.3 Braincore WAN connections.

Proposed Network Configuration

One goal, after the move to Windows 2000, is to have a single domain. The domain name desired is some form of the company name, Braincore. Another goal is to locate the network service servers in the proper location to optimize the network traffic. There are capable administrators in each office to support the servers. All client computers will run Windows 2000 Professional.

The best security possible is needed for communications between WAN links. The only changes that will be considered for WAN connectivity will be those that reduce the cost of the existing WAN topology.

The Paris office would like to bring the Web hosting into the office to make sure that the information is secure and to cut down on the cost of the hosting at the ISP.

The doctors would like to use a VPN (Virtual Private Network) connection instead of a dial-up connection while traveling. This change is to reduce the long-distance costs that are currently very high.

The existing NT system policies must be migrated to Windows 2000. Because these policies are configured on a per-NT-domain level, the administrators at each office will need to control their own policies in the Windows 2000 environment.

Task Obligations

It will be extremely important to ensure that security is a top priority for access to the Active Directory database. This security will also include any DNS communications, which will contain resource record mappings.

Network administrators will remain in each branch location to administer the users, groups, and computers in that branch. The Active Directory database should be configured so that this structure is upheld.

Question 1.1

After the migration is complete, how will a user in Bonn locate a domain controller?

- ○ a. By broadcasting
- ○ b. By querying DNS
- ○ c. By querying WINS
- ○ d. By querying Active Directory

Question 1.2

It has been decided to use the ADMT to migrate users to the new Windows 2000 structure. Which steps would you need to do before starting the migration? [Check all correct answers]

- ❏ a. Create a native-mode Windows 2000 domain.
- ❏ b. Create a mixed-mode Windows 2000 domain.
- ❏ c. Create trusts such that the Windows 2000 domain trusts all of the NT domains.
- ❏ d. Create trusts such that the Windows NT domains trust the Windows 2000 domain.

Question 1.3

What will be the best Active Directory structure based on the criteria in the case study? [Check all correct answers]

- ❏ a. A single domain
- ❏ b. Six domains
- ❏ c. One tree
- ❏ d. Six trees
- ❏ e. One forest
- ❏ f. Six forests
- ❏ g. One organizational unit
- ❏ h. Six organizational units

Question 1.4

What tool will be used to implement the proposed policy?

○ a. Gpotool

○ b. Gpolmig

○ c. Grpcpy

○ d. Nltest

Question 1.5

Based on the case study's stipulations for DNS, what would be the best solution for the DNS configuration?

Answer by creating the proper DNS configuration under each location. (Use only items that apply; you may use items more than once.)

List of possible locations:

Paris

Los Angeles

New York

Tokyo

Sydney

Bonn

List of possible DNS configurations:

Primary DNS zone

Secondary DNS zone

Active Directory Integrated zone

Caching-only DNS server

Dynamic updates

Secure dynamic updates

Question 1.6

The network administrator is trying to determine which tool would be best for the job. Which tools could successfully complete the task of migration as indicated in the case study? [Check all correct answers]

- ❑ a. ADMT
- ❑ b. Netdom
- ❑ c. MoveTree
- ❑ d. ClonePrincipal

Question 1.7

During the implementation of the Windows 2000 domain, the Active Directory domain was given the name **braincore.com**. What might cause problems with this naming convention, as indicated in the case study?

- ○ a. Adding additional trees to the forest with a different root name than **braincore.com**
- ○ b. Bringing the Web services into the company and using the same DNS server as the Active Directory
- ○ c. Having syntax problems with the Windows 98 clients
- ○ d. Having NetBIOS name registration issues with WINS

Question 1.8

You have decided to perform an upgrade from the NT domains to the Windows 2000 structure. Arrange the following steps in the recommended order for the process of upgrading to Windows 2000. (Use only steps that apply.)

Upgrade the Paris PDC.

Upgrade the Paris BDC.

Upgrade the branch PDCs.

Upgrade the branch BDCs.

Use the ADMT.

Create trusts with the Netdom tool.

Use the MoveTree tool.

Question 1.9

After you upgrade the PDC to Windows 2000 in the Paris location, the remote users are complaining that they cannot gain access to the RAS server. What should you do?

○ a. Install a RADIUS server.

○ b. Configure at least one RAS policy.

○ c. Upgrade the RAS server to Windows 2000 RRAS.

○ d. Configure at least one group policy.

Case Study 2

Certcore International is a company that produces a full array of training services for the automotive industry. Certcore is based in Detroit, MI. There are branch offices in Seattle, Dallas, Miami, and Newark. The company has become the number-one training service for most of the American car manufacturers.

The Task at Hand

Upgrade the existing environment to Windows 2000 in stages.

Current LAN/WAN Configuration

The Certcore group has a master domain model with the resource domains at the branch offices. All client computers are running Windows 98.

The Detroit office has a PDC and four BDCs for the **CERTCORE** domain. The PDC is configured as the export server, and all other BDCs are import servers. There are approximately 4,000 users and computers in the domain. All client computers obtain an IP address from the DHCP server.

The branch offices all have a single PDC with one BDC. The resources in these domains include a proprietary application that is used for training purposes; these resources also include file and print servers. Each branch office has a DHCP server, and all clients are configured as DHCP-enabled clients.

Proposed LAN/WAN Configuration

The ultimate goal is to have the entire enterprise running Windows 2000. For now, the goal is to have the master domain running Windows 2000 with Active Directory. The next phase will have the branch offices upgrade their domains to Windows 2000 domains or have the resources migrated into the existing Windows 2000 domain. The final phase of the upgrade will have the Windows 98 computers migrated to Windows 2000 Professional.

The Detroit office will have as many Windows 2000 domain controllers as possible. Administrators still need to investigate which Windows NT servers can run Windows 2000.

The branch offices will need to have at least one domain controller during the second phase of the migration plan.

Question 2.1

It has been decided to have the branch offices migrate into the master domain. The master domain has the PDC and one BDC upgraded so far. At what point can the Windows 2000 domain be moved to native mode?

○ a. After the Detroit BDCs have been upgraded

○ b. After the branch office PDCs have been upgraded

○ c. After the branch office BDCs have been upgraded

○ d. Never, because there are legacy clients

Question 2.2

You are consulting for the Certcore company, and it wants a list of steps to follow to use universal security groups at the end of phase one. Arrange the following steps in the recommended order for the process of upgrading to Windows 2000, based on the case study and the requirements of the upgrade result.

Upgrade the BDCs.

Upgrade the PDC.

Check the server hardware for compatibility.

Synchronize the BDCs with the PDC.

Change the domain to native mode.

Take a BDC offline.

Question 2.3

The PDC in the Detroit domain has been successfully upgraded to Windows 2000. During the week of testing in this new environment, the logon scripts are functioning sporadically. What could be the reason?

○ a. The PDC Emulator has not been started.

○ b. The global catalog is not configured for the new server.

○ c. The logon scripts are not being replicated.

○ d. The domain needs to be in native mode.

Question 2.4

The network administrator would like to use group policies to control some security on all computers that are in the Sales department. How would this process be optimized?

○ a. There should be a domain for each department in the company. The GPO should be applied to the Sales domain.

○ b. There should be a tree for each department in the company. The GPO should be applied to the Sales tree.

○ c. There should be a site created for each department in the company. The GPO should be applied to the Sales site.

○ d. There should be an organizational unit for each department in the company. The GPO should be applied to the Sales OU.

Question 2.5

The network administrator has decided to upgrade the resource domains as child domains of the Detroit Windows 2000 domain. What will be required for this domain to be successfully upgraded? [Check all correct answers]

❑ a. The RID master must be online.

❑ b. The domain naming master must be online.

❑ c. There must be a DNS server capable of secure dynamic updates.

❑ d. There must be a DNS server capable of supporting SRV records.

Question 2.6

> After you upgrade the Detroit DHCP server to Windows 2000, the DHCP-enabled clients are not receiving any IP address configurations. What should you do?
>
> ○ a. Authorize the DHCP server.
>
> ○ b. Reinstall the DHCP server.
>
> ○ c. Run the Jetpack tool against the DHCP database.
>
> ○ d. Configure the RRAS server as the DHCP Relay Agent.

Question 2.7

> A new application is going to be beta-tested in the Seattle office. The new application requires the use of Active Directory and uses name resolution through DNS lookups. What steps will need to occur for the application to function properly in the Seattle office? Arrange the following steps in the recommended order for the application to function properly. (Not all steps need to be used.)
>
> Install a DNS server.
>
> Configure the DHCP server to update DNS for clients that don't support dynamic updates.
>
> Upgrade the BDC to Windows 2000.
>
> Upgrade the PDC to Windows 2000.
>
> Upgrade the WINS server to Windows 2000.
>
> Upgrade the DHCP server to Windows 2000.
>
> Configure the DHCP server scope option for the DNS server.

Case Study 3

Cactusflats, Inc., is a company that ships automobiles all across the United States and overseas. The company has two offices: one in Los Angeles and one in Atlanta. The company wants to expand to cover more regions and absorb more regional moving business.

Both locations have a call center available 24 hours a day, seven days a week, to handle any problems for the truck drivers and individual car drivers. There are a total of 500 employees, including the truck drivers, car drivers, and sales staff.

The Task at Hand

The final goal will be to have a single Windows 2000 domain that can dynamically incorporate the expansion of adding other companies to the domain when they are purchased. ADMT will be used to migrate the existing NT domains to Windows 2000.

Existing LAN/WAN Configuration

There are two Windows NT domains: one in Los Angeles and one in Atlanta. There is a two-way trust between the two domains. LA domain is named **LA-CF**, and the Atlanta domain is named **ATL-CF**.

The network topology consists of a PDC and two BDCs in each domain. There are also file and print servers, a proxy server, an Exchange 5.5 server, WINS and DHCP servers, a backup server, and RAS servers in each domain. All servers are running Windows NT 4 with SP4. All Internet traffic must travel through the proxy server and firewall to gain access into or out of the office.

Each location has a team of network administrators who handle the support of all servers and users' desktop clients. PCAnywhere is installed on many of the servers so the administrators can perform remote administration when they are at home or on the road.

The current security on the network is very lax. The password policy is the default configuration for both domains. The network administrators have done a superb job of using the global and local groups properly and efficiently.

Proposed LAN/WAN Configuration

The goal is to have a single Windows 2000 domain named **cactusflats.com**. A structure should be created so that the existing administrators can manage their own users and computers but not the other locations' users or computers. Built-in flexibility is needed to have the newly acquired companies join the domain. The existing network administrators will need to administer these new users and computers when they are configured in the domain.

The network should be optimized to reduce the traffic on the 128K Frame Relay connection that exists between the two locations. Future locations will have a 128K Frame Relay connection installed. The connection will be to only one of the first two main offices, whichever one is closest to the new facility.

Task Obligations

A more complex password policy must be in place for the new domain.

Only two administrative groups will control the entire domain structure.

The RAS servers need to have the best security possible for the Windows 98 laptop users who use them while on the road.

Question 3.1

What must be done to start the initial migration?

○ a. The PDC in LA must be upgraded.

○ b. The PDC in Atlanta must be upgraded.

○ c. The Windows 2000 domain must be created.

○ d. A BDC in LA should be taken offline after being synchronized with the PDC.

○ e. A BDC in Atlanta should be taken offline after being synchronized with the PDC.

Question 3.2

What will be the most efficient steps for performing a pilot migration? Arrange the following steps in the correct order. (Not all steps are required.)

In the **cactusflats.com** domain, create a group called **pilot**.

Monitor the users in the **cactusflats.com** domain.

In the **LA-CF** domain, create a group called **pilot**.

Run the ADMT Group Migration Wizard.

Copy a small number of user accounts from the **LA-CF** domain to the **pilot** group.

Run the ADMT User Migration Wizard.

Create a small number of user accounts in the **cactusflats.com** domain.

Copy the users in the **cactusflats.com** domain to the **pilot** group.

Question 3.3

After you migrate all of the users from the **ATL-CF** domain to the **cactusflats.com** domain, the tape backup server fails to back up properly. What should you do?

○ a. Migrate the users again.

○ b. Add the service account for the backup server to the Backup Operators group.

○ c. Configure a group policy that gives the service account the Backup and Restore rights.

○ d. Configure the backup application to point to the new service account.

Question 4

Your company has completed its Active Directory design, which includes creating a universal group that contains several global groups. You complete your domain upgrade successfully and attempt to carry out your plan, but you find that universal groups are unavailable. What should you do?

- ○ a. Use the **NET GROUP** command to manually create a universal group.

- ○ b. Upgrade all your Windows 9x clients to Windows 2000 Professional.

- ○ c. Open Active Directory Domains And Trusts and switch to native mode.

- ○ d. Add your user account to the Enterprise Administrators group.

Question 5

You have three Windows 2000 domains: **sales.corp.com**, **marketing.corp.com**, and **research.corp.com**. You upgraded only your PDCs to Windows 2000. You plan to upgrade your remaining BDCs later. Now you want to restructure all objects into **sales.corp.com**. You use MoveTree to move your global groups to **sales.corp.com**. The operation fails.

What should you do? [Choose two]

- ❏ a. Change the domain to native mode.

- ❏ b. Populate the global groups.

- ❏ c. Upgrade the BDCs.

- ❏ d. Use ClonePrincipal.

Question 6

> Your network consists of a master domain. The domains are **ACCT1** and **RES1**. **RES1** trusts **ACCT1**. A backup application, BACKSERV, resides on a Windows NT 4 member server in the **RES1** domain. This application backs up your entire network. You plan to upgrade your network to a single Windows 2000 domain. You upgrade the PDC and BDC from **ACCT1**. You then migrate the member server over to the new Windows 2000 domain. The backup operator later reports that the BACKSERV application is no longer making backups of the **RES1** domain. What should you do to resolve this problem?
>
> ○ a. Migrate the member server into the new domain again by using the Active Directory Migration Tool.
>
> ○ b. Delete the account for the application in the new domain.
>
> ○ c. Create an explicit trust from the new domain to **RES1**.
>
> ○ d. Create an explicit trust from **RES1** to the new domain.

Question 7

> You have a network with three domains—**CORP**, **SALES**, and **MARKETING**—configured as a multiple-master domain. You want to upgrade to Windows 2000. Your envisioned network design will have all three domains with a similar DNS suffix, and all three domains will have control over their password policies. What should you do?
>
> ○ a. Set up two root domains with one having a child domain.
>
> ○ b. Set up one domain with three organizational units.
>
> ○ c. Set up three root domains and no child domains.
>
> ○ d. Set up one root domain with two child domains.

Question 8

You are concerned about security of passwords as you migrate user accounts. What can you do to ensure that password security is maintained throughout the migration? [Check all correct answers]

- ❑ a. Choose Complex Passwords in the User Migration Wizard.

- ❑ b. Require users to change their passwords before the migration.

- ❑ c. Require users to change their passwords after the migration.

- ❑ d. Choose Same As User Name in the User Migration Wizard.

Question 9

You are the administrator of a mixed-mode domain. You want to upgrade to native mode. You have directory replication configured on different servers as shown below:

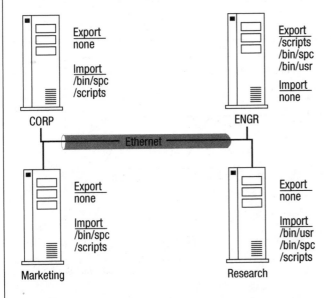

You want to ensure that the servers hosting export directories are available during the upgrade. What is the order of the upgrade? Arrange the following servers in the correct order:

CORP

ENGR

RESEARCH

MARKETING

Question 10

You currently administer a Windows NT network. You plan to migrate to Windows 2000. You create a pristine Windows 2000 forest. You want to establish trusts to the forest to maintain resource access, and you want to clone source global groups into the target domain and decommission the source domain. What could you do? [Check all correct answers]

❏ a. Use Netdom to establish any trusts that do not already exist.

❏ b. Use ClonePrincipal to clone the source users into the target domain.

❏ c. Use ADMT to clone users into the target domain.

❏ d. Use Adsutil with the **/test** switch to verify established trusts and with the **/accesswrite** switch to implement trusts that do not already exist.

❏ e. Use MoveTree to clone users from the source domain into the target domain.

Question 11

You need to simplify your network design, which currently is configured as shown below:

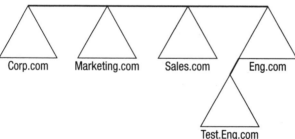

(continued)

Question 11 *(continued)*

Your envisioned network design is configured as shown below:

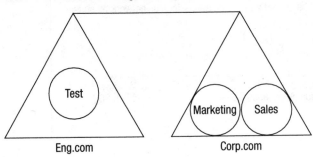

Eng.com   Corp.com

Arrange the tasks below in order to achieve your envisioned network design. (Not all answers are required.)

Collapse the **Sales.com** domain by demoting all domain controllers to member servers.

Join the member servers previously in **Sales.com** to **Corp.com**.

Collapse the **Marketing.com** domain by demoting all domain controllers to member servers.

Join the member servers previously in **Marketing.com** to **Corp.com**.

Collapse the **Eng.com** domain by demoting all domain controllers to member servers.

Join the member servers previously in **Eng.com** to **Corp.com**.

Collapse the **Test.eng.com** domain by demoting all domain controllers to member servers.

Join the member servers previously in **Test.eng.com** to **Eng.com**.

Join the member servers previously in **Test.eng.com** to **Corp.com**.

Question 12

You are the administrator of a mixed-mode domain. You want to upgrade to native mode. You have configured the servers in your network as shown below:

Name: Engr
OS: Windows NT 3.5
Function: Application Server

Engr

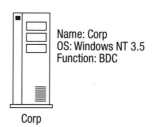

Name: Corp
OS: Windows NT 3.5
Function: BDC

Corp

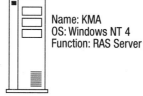

Name: KMA
OS: Windows NT 4
Function: RAS Server

RAS Server

What should you do to ensure that the upgrade to native mode is successful? [Check all correct answers]

❏ a. Upgrade the RAS server to Windows 2000, and then use Dcpromo to promote the server to a domain controller.

❏ b. Upgrade ENGR to Windows 2000.

❏ c. Upgrade CORP to Windows NT 4, and then upgrade to Windows 2000.

❏ d. Upgrade ENGR to Windows NT.

Question 13

Your network's configuration is shown in Figure 11.8. Your envisioned structure consists of a single security boundary with resources being administered within the security boundary.

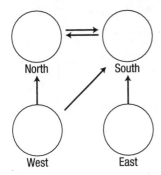

Which step or steps should you take to construct your envisioned design? [Check all correct answers]

❑ a. Upgrade the **EAST** domain as the root in a new forest, and collapse the **SOUTH** domain into an OU in the **EAST** domain.

❑ b. Upgrade the **SOUTH** domain as the root in a new forest, and upgrade the **WEST** domain and make it a child of the **SOUTH** domain.

❑ c. Upgrade the **NORTH** domain as the root in a new forest, and collapse the **SOUTH** domain into an OU in the **NORTH** domain.

❑ d. Upgrade the **SOUTH** domain as the root in a new forest, and collapse the **WEST** domain into an OU in the **SOUTH** domain.

❑ e. Collapse the **EAST** domain into an OU in the **SOUTH** domain.

❑ f. Collapse the **EAST** domain into an OU in the **NORTH** domain.

❑ g. Collapse the **NORTH** domain into an OU in the **SOUTH** domain.

Question 14

You have a Windows 2000 domain named **hawthorn.com**, which you are migrating to another Windows 2000 domain, named **santafe.com**. You plan to use the ADMT to migrate the following groups to **santafe.com** in the following order:

*hawthorn.com/ExchangeAdministrators

*hawthorn.com/Staff

*hawthorn.com/Helpdesk

*hawthorn.com/SecureDev

You are concerned about a failed migration. Which group migration will you be able to undo using ADMT?

○ a. **hawthorn.com/ExchangeAdministrators**

○ b. **hawthorn.com/Staff**

○ c. **hawthorn.com/Helpdesk**

○ d. **hawthorn.com/SecureDev**

Question 15

You want to use Ntbackup.exe to back up the Active Directory of your enterprise, as shown below. On which machine or machines must you execute the application? [Check all correct answers]

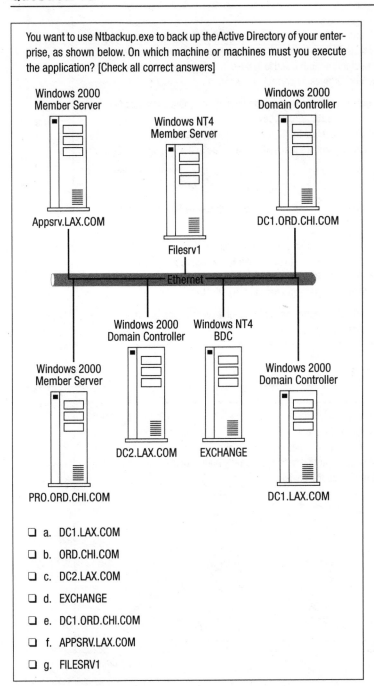

Windows 2000
Member Server

Appsrv.LAX.COM

Windows NT4
Member Server

Filesrv1

Windows 2000
Domain Controller

DC1.ORD.CHI.COM

Ethernet

Windows 2000
Domain Controller

DC2.LAX.COM

Windows NT4
BDC

EXCHANGE

Windows 2000
Member Server

PRO.ORD.CHI.COM

Windows 2000
Domain Controller

DC1.LAX.COM

❏ a. DC1.LAX.COM

❏ b. ORD.CHI.COM

❏ c. DC2.LAX.COM

❏ d. EXCHANGE

❏ e. DC1.ORD.CHI.COM

❏ f. APPSRV.LAX.COM

❏ g. FILESRV1

Question 16

You are planning the pristine Windows 2000 environment. You want your DNS servers to support secure dynamic updates. You want to ensure that all client computers are authorized to make only secure dynamic updates. What should you do? [Check all correct answers]

- ❏ a. Configure the client computer for secure dynamic updates by adding **UpdateSecurityLevel** to HKEY_LocalMachine\System\CurrentControlSet\Services\ Tcpip\Parameters and setting the value to 256.

- ❏ b. In the DNS console, select Zone. In the Allow Dynamic Updates dialog box, select Only Secure Updates.

- ❏ c. In the DNS console, select Zone. In the Allow Dynamic Updates dialog box, select Yes.

- ❏ d. Configure the client computer for secure dynamic updates by adding **DisableReplaceAddressInConflicts** to HKEY_LocalMachine\System\CurrentControlSet\Services\ Tcpip\Parameters and setting the value to 1.

- ❏ e. In the DNS console, select Zone. Change the Zone Type to Standard Primary.

Question 17

You have a network with three domains—**CORP**, **SALES**, and **MARKET-ING**—configured as a multiple-master domain. You want to upgrade to Windows 2000. Your envisioned network design is to have the same domain name suffix, yet maintain separate security boundaries. Choose the design that best describes the envisioned network.

○ a.

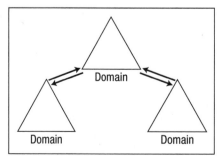

(continued)

Question 17 *(continued)*

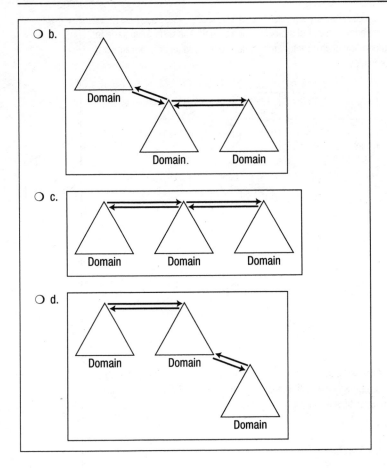

Question 18

You are the administrator of a mixed-mode domain. You want to upgrade to native mode. You have directory replication configured on different servers, as shown below:

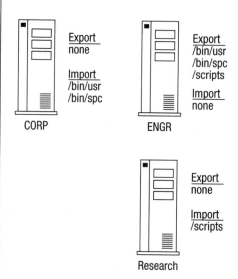

CORP	Export none Import /bin/usr /bin/spc
ENGR	Export /bin/usr /bin/spc /scripts Import none
Research	Export none Import /scripts

You want to ensure that the servers hosting export directories are available during the upgrade. What is the order of the upgrade? Arrange the tasks below in order to achieve your goal.

Upgrade CORP.

Upgrade ENGR.

Upgrade RESEARCH.

Question 19

You are the CIO of your company. The network is configured as shown below:

sales.com   marketing.com   research.com

Your network team wants to migrate the entire environment to a single Windows 2000 domain. The new environment will be configured as shown below, and the domain will be called **corp.com**.

corp.com

The user accounts, group accounts, and computer accounts from **sales.com**, **marketing.com**, and **research.com** need to be migrated. The team also wants to simplify administration by consolidating domains. What type of migration should the team employ?

- ○ a. An in-place upgrade only
- ○ b. An in-place upgrade and then a restructuring
- ○ c. A domain restructuring only
- ○ d. A domain restructuring and then an upgrade

Question 20

During the planning stages of your migration to Windows 2000, you have decided to manually configure DNS to support Active Directory. You decide to use the Configure DNS Server Wizard to configure DNS on a member server. This server will not be the root DNS server. How should you configure DNS to ensure a successful configuration?

○ a. Configure the member server's network connections to point to another DNS server in the network. Run the DNS Server Wizard. After it is run, create a forward lookup zone that is authoritative for the locator records that Netlogon will add. Enable dynamic updates on that zone. Add a delegation to the new forward lookup zone in its parent zone.

○ b. Configure the member server's network connections to point to the domain controller. Run the DNS Server Wizard. Add a delegation to the new forward lookup zone in its parent zone.

○ c. Run Dcpromo on the member server. After it is run, create a forward lookup zone that is authoritative for the locator records that Netlogon will add. Add a delegation to the new forward lookup zone in its parent zone.

○ d. Run Dcpromo on the member server. Configure the server's network connections to point to another DNS server in the network. Enable dynamic updates on that zone. Add a delegation to the new forward lookup zone in its parent zone.

Question 21

You have an organizational unit in the **examcram.com** domain. The objects within the OU require a DNS suffix that is different from the Active Directory domain name. The modified domain name suffix you want to use is **coriolis.com**. You want to enable the modified domain name to be registered in both the DNS hostname attribute and the Service Principal Name attribute in Active Directory. What should you do?

○ a. Modify the DACL for **examcram.com** in Active Directory Users And Computers.

○ b. Create a GPO that will assign the **coriolis.com** domain suffix to all computers in the OU.

○ c. Add the modified name to the search order in DNS.

○ d. Add the primary DNS suffix **coriolis.com** to the HOSTS file on all computers.

Question 22

You have a DNS server named Server1 running Windows 2000. You want to configure Server1 so that it will not be the root DNS server or the domain controller. There is already an existing DNS infrastructure in place. After you install DNS, you want to configure DNS to support Active Directory. Arrange the following steps in the correct order:

○ a. Configure Server1's network connections to point to one or more DNS servers in the network.

○ b. In the DNS console, select Zone. In the Allow Dynamic Updates dialog box, select Yes.

○ c. From the parent zone of Server1, add a delegation for this zone.

○ d. Add a forward lookup zone that is authoritative for the resource records registered by Netlogon.

Answer Key

For asterisked items, please see textual representation of answer on the appropriate page of this chapter.

1.1 b	2.5 b, d	11. *
1.2 a, d	2.6 a	12. a, c, d
1.3 a, c, e, h	2.7 *	13. d, e, g
1.4 b	3.1 c	14. d
1.5 *	3.2 *	15. a, c, e
1.6 a, d	3.3 d	16. a, b
1.7 b	4. c	17. a
1.8 *	5. a, c	18. *
1.9 c	6. d	19. c
2.1 a	7. d	20. a
2.2 *	8. a, c	21. b
2.3 c	9. *	22. *
2.4 d	10. a, b, c	

Question 1.1

Answer b is correct. Because the final migration topology will include only Windows 2000 servers and clients, DNS will be used as the method for finding the domain controller for authentication. Answer a is incorrect because broadcasting is the old method of finding the domain controller; the new DNS method is more efficient and reduces network traffic. Answer c is incorrect because WINS is the Windows NT method of finding the domain controller. Answer d is incorrect because Active Directory is what you are trying to find on the domain controller. If you could just query Active Directory, then DNS would not be required.

Question 1.2

Answers a and d are correct. To migrate users, groups, and computers from an NT domain to a Windows 2000 domain, you must establish a trust such that the Windows NT domain trusts the Windows 2000 domain. The Windows 2000 domain must also be configured as a native-mode domain. Answer b is incorrect because the Windows 2000 domain must be in native mode for the Active Directory Migration Tool to work. Answer c is incorrect because the trust must go from the source domain to the target domain for the ADMT to work.

Question 1.3

Answers a, c, e, and h are correct. According to the case study, there is a proposed solution for a single domain. With a single domain, there is inherently a single tree and forest. However, there should be six organizational units to accommodate the desired administration model. Answer b is incorrect because the case proposes a single domain. Answers d and f are incorrect because a single domain will require only a single tree and forest. Answer g is incorrect because the proper administrative model will require six OUs, one for each location.

Question 1.4

Answer b is correct. The Gpolmig tool is designed to migrate system policy settings into a group policy. Answer a is incorrect because this tool is designed to manipulate GPOs, and it has nothing to do with the migration of the Windows NT system policies to Windows 2000. Answer c is incorrect because this tool is designed to copy user names from one group to another group in an NT enterprise. Answer d is incorrect because the Nltest tool is designed to administer the domain trusts, services, and other domain-controller-related issues.

Question 1.5

The correct answer is:

Paris
> Active Directory Integrated zone
> Secure dynamic updates

Los Angeles
> Active Directory Integrated zone
> Secure dynamic updates

New York
> Active Directory Integrated zone
> Secure dynamic updates

Tokyo
> Active Directory Integrated zone
> Secure dynamic updates

Sydney
> Active Directory Integrated zone
> Secure dynamic updates

Bonn
> Active Directory Integrated zone
> Secure dynamic updates

The zones need to be Active Directory Integrated to allow for the secure dynamic updates. The secure dynamic updates need to be configured to ensure the most secure transfer of the DNS information. Each location needs to have a DNS server to reduce the name resolution traffic across the WAN.

Question 1.6

Answers a and d are correct. ADMT and ClonePrincipal can both migrate users from a Windows NT domain to a Windows 2000 domain. Answer b is incorrect because the Netdom tool is used to verify and establish trusts between domains and to migrate computers only. Answer c is incorrect because the MoveTree tool is used to move directory objects between Windows 2000 domains.

Question 1.7

Answer b is correct. If the internal Active Directory domain name and the Internet domain name have the same name, security and DNS problems can arise. It is recommended to have the internal Active Directory name and the Internet name be different. An example would be **braincore.local** and **braincore.com**. Answer a is incorrect because additional tree names can have different root names. This is actually what makes the definition of a tree in the same forest. Answer c is incorrect because the Windows 98 clients will be able to understand the syntax **braincore.com**. Answer d is incorrect because domain names are not related to WINS; only NetBIOS names are.

Question 1.8

The following steps and order are correct:

> Upgrade the Paris PDC.
>
> Upgrade the branch PDCs.
>
> Upgrade the Paris BDC.
>
> Upgrade the branch BDCs.
>
> Use the MoveTree tool.

For the recommended approach, it will be best to upgrade the PDCs from each domain first to ensure that the upgrade is successful. Paris is made unique because it is the main office and has the most impact on the upgrade. Then the BDCs should be upgraded. (You can upgrade either the Paris BDC or the branch BDCs, in any order.) After the upgrade of all domains, you will need to restructure. The MoveTree tool will work very well to move the users, groups, and computers from the upgraded domains to the single domain that is required in the case study. The ADMT and Netdom tools will not be required because they are migration tools, not upgrade tools.

Question 1.9

Answer c is correct. The Windows NT RAS server is having trouble authenticating against the new Windows 2000 domain controller. The solution is to upgrade the RAS server to Windows 2000 so it can use Kerberos for authentication. Answer a is incorrect because a RADIUS server would not help with the failed authentication from the NT RAS server to Active Directory. Answer b is incorrect because there is a single RAS policy configured by default. Also, RAS policies cannot be configured on Windows NT RAS servers. Answer d is incorrect because group policies would not affect the authentication of the RAS user in this manner. The company should have upgraded the RAS server prior to the PDC to avoid the problem described in the question.

Question 2.1

Answer a is correct. Because the branch offices are going to be migrated into the existing Windows 2000 domain, the domain can be moved to native mode as soon as the BDCs in Detroit have been upgraded to Windows 2000. Answer b is incorrect because the branch office PDCs can't be upgraded to the existing Windows 2000 domain in Detroit. Answer c is incorrect because BDCs can't be upgraded to the existing Windows 2000 domain in Detroit. Answer d is incorrect because the existence of legacy clients has no bearing on whether or not the domain is mixed or native mode.

Question 2.2

The following order is correct:

Check the server hardware for compatibility.

Synchronize the BDCs with the PDC.

Take a BDC offline.

Upgrade the PDC.

Upgrade the BDCs.

Change the domain to native mode.

There is no certainty that any of the hardware on the Windows NT domain controllers can support Windows 2000. Therefore, a hardware check should be done first. After you check the hardware, you need to develop some form of backup plan, which includes synchronizing the domain controllers and taking a BDC offline in case the upgrade fails. After the upgrade of the PDC is successful, the BCDs can then be upgraded. After the upgrades are complete, the domain needs to be moved to native mode to support the universal security groups.

Question 2.3

Answer c is correct. Because the export server was promoted to the Windows 2000 domain controller, the logon scripts will work sporadically. One of the BDCs should be configured as the export server for the Windows NT domain controllers, and the Lbridge tool should be used to replicate from Windows 2000 to NT. Answer a is incorrect because the PDC Emulator is automatically configured and started on the first Windows 2000 domain controller. Answer b is incorrect because the global catalog service is automatically configured and started on the first Windows 2000 domain controller. Answer d is incorrect because the domain logon scripts will function whether the domain is in native mode or mixed mode.

Question 2.4

Answer d is correct. The implementation of OUs is usually the most effective method to organize users and computers, especially for the administration of GPOs. Answers a, b, and c are incorrect because these methods of designing the Active Directory structure are not as effective or efficient as using organizational units to represent departments in an organization.

Question 2.5

Answers b and d are correct. The domain naming master must be available when the PDC is upgraded from each resource domain. This master will ensure that the name is valid and not existing already. The DNS server must support SRV records for the new domain to be installed. Answer a is incorrect because the RID master is domain-specific, not forest-wide. Therefore, the new domain would generate its own RID master. Answer c is incorrect because the DNS server does not have to support secure dynamic updates to function as the DNS server for a Windows 2000 domain.

Question 2.6

Answer a is correct. Windows 2000 DHCP servers need to be authorized with Active Directory before they can allocate IP addresses to clients. Answer b is incorrect because this is a drastic measure for a simple fix. Also, the newly installed DHCP server would need to be authorized after installation. Answer c is incorrect because the Jetpack tool will help eliminate any errors in the database as well as compress the database, but Jetpack won't make the database start allocating IP addresses. Answer d is incorrect because the Relay Agent is required only for DHCP servers that are on different network segments from the clients.

Question 2.7

The following steps and order are correct:

Upgrade the PDC to Windows 2000.

Install a DNS server.

Upgrade the DHCP server to Windows 2000.

Configure the DHCP server to update DNS for clients that don't support dynamic updates.

Configure the DHCP server scope option for the DNS server.

For this process to work correctly, you'll need Active Directory, DNS, and a Windows 2000 DHCP server. The DHCP server needs to be configured to update DNS for the down-level Windows 98 computers. The DHCP server will also need to have the DNS server scope option configured to ensure that the Windows 98 clients receive the IP address of the DNS server when they receive the other IP configurations.

Question 3.1

Answer c is correct. A Windows 2000 domain must be installed first. Answer b is incorrect because this is a migration, not an upgrade. The PDC will not be upgraded, and there is no reason to take a BDC offline because the PDC will not be altered.

Question 3.2

You need a small group of user accounts for the pilot migration. You also need a group to migrate from the Windows NT domain to the Windows 2000 domain. Therefore, first create the group, and then place a small number of users into the group. This needs to be done in the NT domain. (This could be LA-CF or ATL-CF.) Then run the ADMT Group Migration Wizard to migrate the users and group to Windows 2000. After the migration, monitor the users and group interaction with the new configuration for any errors.

Question 3.3

Answer d is correct. When the service account user was migrated, the SID changed, as did the location of the user. The backup application needs to be reconfigured to point to the new account in Windows 2000. Answer a is incorrect because migrating the users again will not solve the problem and could cause serious problems with other aspects of the migration. Answer b is incorrect because the users will already be in this group after the migration because they were in the group in Windows NT. Answer c is incorrect because the service account will have the Backup and Restore rights due to the membership in the Backup Operators group.

Question 4

Answer c is correct. Universal groups exist only in domains that are in native mode. Answer a is incorrect because the **NET GROUP** command will not create a universal group. Answer b is incorrect because upgrading down-level clients has no impact on the creation of universal groups. Answer d is incorrect because even though Enterprise Administrators have sufficient permissions to create universal groups, universal groups require a native-mode domain.

Question 5

Answers a and c are correct. MoveTree requires the target domain to be in native mode; for a domain to be in native mode, there can be no down-level domain controllers in the domain. Answer b is incorrect because MoveTree requires that global groups be unpopulated. Answer d is incorrect because using ClonePrincipal will not move a group, but will copy it.

Question 6

Answer d is correct. When the member server was migrated to the new Windows 2000 domain, the existing trust became invalid. A completely new explicit trust from **RES1** to the new domain is necessary for the application to function properly. Answer a is incorrect because the Active Directory Migration Tool will not create the necessary trust between the two domains. Answer b is incorrect because it will not solve the problem, but will create a new one: no backup application would exist. Answer c is incorrect because the trust is in the wrong place.

Question 7

Answer d is correct. One of the requirements is that there be a contiguous namespace throughout the domain. There also must be unique password policies, and this requires unique domains. Answers a, b, and c are incorrect because they do not have a contiguous namespace or they will not allow for unique password policies.

Question 8

Answers a and c are correct. Complex passwords include uppercase and lowercase letters plus numbers. If a user changes his password after the migration, no one but that user will know what it is. This will maintain the best security. Answer b is incorrect because the password will be changed during the migration to either a complex password or the default. Answer d is incorrect because this option is not secure; it is too easy to guess.

Question 9

The following order is correct:

> CORP
>
> RESEARCH
>
> MARKETING
>
> ENGR

Because the ENGR server is hosting the Export directory, this server needs to be the last one upgraded. The others can be upgraded in any order.

Question 10

Answers a, b, and c are correct. ADMT and ClonePrincipal can be used for an interforest migration. MoveTree can be used only for intraforest migrations. Netdom is a command-line tool that can be used to establish trusts. Answer d is incorrect because the Adsutil tool is not used to implement trusts. Answer e is incorrect because MoveTree is used only for intraforest migrations.

Question 11

The following steps and order are correct:

Collapse the **Sales.com** domain by demoting all domain controllers to member servers.

Join the member servers previously in **Sales.com** to **Corp.com**.

Collapse the **Test.eng.com** domain by demoting all domain controllers to member servers.

Join the member servers previously in **Test.eng.com** to **Eng.com**.

Collapse the **Marketing.com** domain by demoting all domain controllers to member servers.

Join the member servers previously in **Marketing.com** to **Corp.com**.

This process requires that you decommission the existing domains by demoting the domain controllers in those domains. Then the servers need to be joined to the new domains to continue their roles as file and print servers, or they can be promoted to domain controllers in the new domain. (There are multiple variations of this answer, but the collapsing of the domains is required before the servers are joined to the new domain.)

Question 12

Answers a, c, and d are correct. All of these servers should be upgraded to Windows 2000. Watch out for the OS levels here because some upgrades require two steps. Answer b is incorrect because you must first upgrade to Windows NT 4 before you can upgrade to Windows 2000.

Question 13

Answers d, e, and g are correct. To accomplish the design, which is a single Windows 2000 domain with three OUs, you upgrade one domain and collapse the rest into OUs. Answer a is incorrect because **EAST** trusts **SOUTH**. Answer b is incorrect because your goal is a single Windows 2000 domain. Answer c is incorrect because there are no other answers concerning the collapse of **WEST** into **NORTH**. Answer f is incorrect because it goes with answer c, and there is no answer concerning the collapse of **WEST** into **NORTH**.

Question 14

Answer d is correct. The ADMT will allow you to undo only the most recently performed user, group, or computer migration. Answers a, b, and c are incorrect because they cannot be undone through the ADMT.

Question 15

Answers a, c, and e are correct. Ntbackup.exe must be run on all domain controllers to back up the Active Directory. Ntbackup.exe is not run on non-domain controllers to back up the Active Directory. Answers b, d, f, and g are incorrect because they cannot back up the Active Directory information due to their role as servers, not domain controllers.

Question 16

Answers a and b are correct. By adding the Registry key and setting the value to 256, you will ensure that clients will *only* make secure dynamic updates. You can also perform this from the DNS console. Answer c is incorrect because it will allow the client to choose between secure and nonsecure updates. Answer d is incorrect because it will have no effect on whether the client makes secure updates or not. Answer e is incorrect because it has nothing to do with secure updates.

Question 17

Answer a is correct. It is the only design where the namespace is contiguous throughout. Answers b, c, and d are incorrect because the namespace is not contiguous.

Question 18

The following order is correct:

>Upgrade CORP.

>Upgrade RESEARCH.

>Upgrade ENGR.

The server acting as the export server should be the last server migrated to ensure that the directories are available during the upgrade. The CORP and RESEARCH migration order doesn't matter.

Question 19

Answer c is correct because the company needs to redo its Active Directory design. Answers a, b, and d are incorrect because there is already a Windows 2000 environment, so there is no need for an upgrade.

Question 20

Answer a is correct because you must configure the server to point to another DNS server because it is not the root. Answer b is incorrect because the network connections need to point to another DNS server, not just to a domain controller. Answer c is incorrect because running Dcpromo will not configure the server's DNS configuration. Answer d is incorrect because running Dcpromo will not configure the server's DNS configuration.

Question 21

Answer b is correct. When a group policy exists, the suffix set in the group policy supersedes the local primary DNS suffix, which by default is the same as the Active Directory domain name. Answer a is incorrect because although you can modify the DACL, if you do so, any computer in the domain can register itself under a different name, and you want a specific name. Answer c is incorrect because just adding the modified name will not change the suffix on your clients. Answer d is incorrect because modifying the HOSTS file on all computers will not change the suffix on which it exists.

Question 22

The following order is correct:

a. Configure Server1's network connections to point to one or more DNS servers in the network.

d. Add a forward lookup zone that is authoritative for the resource records registered by Netlogon.

b. In the DNS console, select Zone. In the Allow Dynamic Updates dialog box, select Yes.

c. From the parent zone of Server1, add a delegation for this zone.

Because the DNS server is not on a domain controller, there are critical steps that need to be performed. The previous list contains the steps for this process.

Glossary

Account domain

A specific Windows NT 4 domain created specifically to hold user and group accounts. Traditionally, account domains are created to overcome limitations of the Windows NT 4 SAM database within a single domain.

Active Directory

The directory management structure for Windows 2000. Active Directory provides greater scalability, ease of use, and flexibility than does the Windows NT domain structure.

Active Directory Integrated zone

A DNS zone that has been integrated into Active Directory to take advantage of increased security and Active Directory replication.

Active Directory Migration Tool (ADMT)

Useful for assisting with domain restructuring, the ADMT is a Microsoft Management Console snap-in that contains several wizards that assist with the migration of users, computers, and other network objects.

Active Directory Service Interfaces (ADSI)

A Microsoft interface that allows the integration of several directory services into a single administrative interface. Directory services that can be integrated include NetWare Bindery, x.500, Notes, and NDS.

Administrative template

Similar to Windows NT system policies, administrative templates are used to restrict access to applications, desktop settings, and network and system configuration options.

Assigned software

A software distribution option, included with group policies, whereby an application can be automatically installed or available on a machine or for a user.

Auditing

Accessible within the Event Viewer, auditing is a means of monitoring network and system-related events such as accessing specific resources, logging in, and logging out.

Backup domain controller (BDC)

The backup domain controller is one of potentially many computers designated as having the capability to handle user authentication and security access if the primary domain controller (PDC) fails or becomes unavailable.

Berkeley Internet Name Domain (BIND)

The engine behind DNS, BIND contains specific guidelines and protocols regarding how DNS resolves and registers data. Active Directory requires SRV record and Dynamic Update features that are supported in BIND version 8.1.2 and above.

Clonegg.vbs

A ClonePrincipal script that clones global groups in a domain.

Cloneggu.vbs

A ClonePrincipal script that clones global groups and users in a domain.

Clonelg.vbs

A ClonePrincipal script that clones local groups but not built-in local groups.

Clonepr.vbs

A ClonePrincipal script that clones security principal properties and copies the SID of the security principal into the **sIDHistory** attribute of the target security principal object.

Cloneprincipal.exe

A restructuring tool that is used to clone user and group accounts from Windows NT or Windows 2000

domains into a separate Windows 2000 domain located in a different forest.

Closed set

Commonly referred to as a constraint on moving objects with the **sIDHistory** attribute. A closed set is a single entity that consists of component parts. This can get complicated when a component part can be a member of more than one entity. For example, a family might consist of a mother, a father, and two children. The mother also has her parents and siblings, who also constitute another family. The two families together would be a closed set.

Complete trust domain model

A multiple domain network model in which each domain trusts all other domains. All domains are responsible for administering their respective resources.

Dcdiag.exe

The Domain Controller Diagnostics tool. Dcdiag analyzes the state of domain controllers in a forest or enterprise and reports any problems to assist in troubleshooting.

Dcpromo.exe

Also known as the Active Directory Installation Wizard, Dcpromo installs Active Directory on any server, thus making that server into a domain controller.

Delegated DNS subdomain

Created specifically so that Windows 2000 can function within a legacy DNS system, a delegated DNS subdomain is a new DNS domain that exists within another DNS domain. An example of a DNS domain is **widgetsrus.com**. Examples of delegated DNS subdomains are **denver.widgetsrus.com** and **detroit.widgetsrus.com**.

DHCP scope

A portion of the DHCP database dealing with an administrator-defined range of TCP/IP addresses available for lease.

Directory service

A network process that targets all network resources and allows those resources to be accessed by users and by applications.

Discretionary access control list (DACL)

Located in the header of every object in Active Directory, the DACL contains SIDs and permission levels for each SID of the object to which the DACL is attached.

DNS zone

Fundamental to the DNS hierarchical structure, DNS zones are lists of resolved network resources and computers. A DNS forward lookup zone must exist for every DNS server. Reverse lookup zones are also highly recommended. Each forward lookup zone can contain multiple DNS domains and subdomains.

Domain

See *single domain model.*

Domain local group

A group used to assign access to resources located within a single domain.

Domain Name Service (DNS)

DNS is a name resolution service that resolves fully qualified domain names into TCP/IP addresses.

Domain naming master

One of several FSMO operations, a domain naming master is a Windows 2000 server process that tracks and maintains domain names throughout a forest.

Domain restructuring

The process of migrating from Windows NT to Windows 2000 by completely changing the network infrastructure, hardware, operating system, and resources.

Domain upgrade

The process of migrating from Windows NT to Windows 2000 by upgrading existing network hardware and resources.

Dsastat.exe

A command-line utility that can be used to monitor replication status within a domain and across domains.

Dynamic Host Configuration Protocol (DHCP)

A protocol (and service) designed to assign TCP/IP configuration information dynamically to requesting clients. DHCP is valuable in that it eliminates the need to statically assign and manage IP addresses on client computers.

Dynamic DNS (DDNS)

Active-Directory-integrated DNS in which the DNS database is dynamically updated by authenticated hosts.

Dynamic Host Configuration Protocol (DHCP)

A protocol (and service) designed to assign TCP/IP configuration information dynamically to requesting clients. DHCP is valuable because it eliminates the need to statically assign and manage IP addresses on client computers.

Event Viewer

A built-in Windows NT and Windows 2000 utility that monitors system events and specialized network events. The Windows NT Event Viewer tracks system, security, and application events. The Windows 2000 Event Viewer tracks application, security, system, directory service, DNS server, and File Replication Service events.

Explicit trust

Any one-way trust that is manually created for purposes such as inter-forest resource access, or shortcut trusts.

External trust

A trust between a Windows 2000 domain and a Windows NT domain.

Flexible Single Master Operations (FSMO) Servers

Within a network, specific servers that are designated owners of specific processes that should not be performed concurrently in multiple instances. Some process types include time synchronization, PDC Emulation, and domain naming.

Folder redirection

A Windows 2000 feature that allows a folder or a set of folders to be redirected to another location on the network. Traditionally, folder redirection is used to replicate otherwise static data, such as a user's documents, into the roaming profile data in such a manner that this data also becomes available when a user logs into multiple computers.

Forest

A set of Active Directory trees that use trusts to access resources and data among themselves. All trees within a forest share the same global catalog and schema.

Forward lookup zone

A type of DNS zone that contains fully qualified domain names and their IP addresses.

File Replication Service (FRS)

File Replication Service is the Windows 2000 equivalent to Windows NT's LMRepl. FRS automatically replicates any data contained within the SYSVOL share of any domain controller to all other Windows 2000 domain controllers.

Global catalog

An index of commonly used object attributes for every Active Directory object in every domain belonging in a forest.

Global group

A group used to assign resource access to resources located within a domain.

Gpolmig.exe
A utility that migrates Windows NT system policies into Windows 2000 group policies.

Gpotool.exe
A utility used to administer group policies and group policy replication from the command line.

Gpresult.exe
A utility that displays the group policies that are being applied to the current system and user.

Group policy
The Windows 2000 equivalent of Windows NT system and group policies. A Windows 2000 group policy is an Active-Directory-integrated feature that allows you to place system and user restrictions on user and computer objects within Active Directory.

Group Policy container (GPC)
An Active Directory object that is assigned to every object capable of sustaining group policies. The Group Policy container holds group policy objects.

Group policy inheritance blocking
A group policy attribute that allows group policy inheritance to *not* apply to the specific group policy.

Group policy link (GPL)
A process whereby group policies residing in a source OU container can be linked for usage to any other OU container within an Active Directory forest.

Group policy loopback
The process of enabling a more restricted group policy to override any lesser restrictions associated with a user's given group policy. Loopbacks are ideal for high-security environments such as kiosks and ATMs.

Group policy object (GPO)
An Active Directory object containing information specific to a group policy. All GPOs are stored in the GPC (Group Policy container).

Group policy template (GPT)
A group policy storage facility located in the SYSVOL share.

Host
Any network resource that communicates via TCP/IP.

Intersite replication
Replication that occurs across multiple sites.

Intrasite replication
Replication that occurs within a single site.

Ipconfig.exe
A Windows 2000, Windows NT, and Windows 98 utility that displays and manipulates IP configuration information. Ipconfig can be used to test the functionality of a DHCP server.

Jetpack.exe
A DHCP and WINS utility that is used to compress and optimize the DNS and WINS databases.

Kerberos

A method of authentication—originally developed by MIT (Massachusetts Institute of Technology)—that assigns a unique key identifier to each user who logs into a network.

LAN Manager Replication Service (LMRepl)

The file replication process supported by Windows NT. LMRepl has been replaced by FRS (File Replication Service) in Windows 2000.

Lightweight Directory Access Protocol (LDAP)

An open network protocol that allows access to information located in a directory information tree, such as Active Directory.

Local groups

User groups available within Windows 2000 to assign resource access to the local Windows 2000 system. Local groups cannot be accessed or used outside of the Windows 2000 computer to which they belong.

Master domain model

A domain model consisting of a single domain, containing user and computer accounts, and one or more child domains, containing resources. User login authentication for all domains occurs on the account or master domain via the appropriate group memberships and trusts established between the resource domains and the master domain.

Microsoft Management Console (MMC)

An open-source administration tool that is used to administer Active Directory and other Windows 2000 services.

Mixed mode

A domain structure that contains both Windows NT and Windows 2000 domain controllers.

MoveTree

A Windows 2000 utility, available in the Resource Kit, that allows Active Directory objects to be moved from one Windows 2000 domain to another Windows 2000 domain in the same forest.

Multiple-master domain model

Similar to a master domain model, a multiple-master domain model is a set of domains containing more than one master domain. Multimaster domain configurations are usually created to handle larger enterprises where the size of the SAM database and its limitations become factors in network and directory services design. Resource domains trust their master domains but not other resource domains.

Native mode

A domain structure that contains only Windows 2000 domain controllers. Windows 2000 universal and domain local groups are enabled, and group nesting is made available, when a domain is changed to native mode.

Nbtstat.exe

A NetBIOS utility designed to determine what current NetBIOS name resolution is occurring on the system.

Netdiag.exe

A utility that assists in troubleshooting network and DNS connectivity issues by determining the status of the current network client.

Netdom.exe

Similar to ClonePrincipal, Netdom moves computer accounts and re-creates trusts from a Windows NT or Windows 2000 domain into a Windows 2000 target domain.

NETLOGON share

The standard Windows NT share that contains logon scripts and replication directories.

Netstat.exe

A utility that displays current TCP/IP connections.

Network Address Translation (NAT)

A standardized method of making secure Internet connections.

Nontransitive trust

A single one-way trust. Windows NT trusts are all nontransitive trusts. Nontransitive trusts are not dynamic and are restricted to the two domains involved. All of the following are nontransitive trusts: Windows 2000 domain/Windows NT domain; Windows 2000 domain in forest 1/ Windows 2000 domain in forest 2; Windows 2000 domain/Kerberos v5 realm.

NTBackup

A data backup utility provided with Windows NT and Windows 2000.

Ntdsutil.exe

A command-line utility commonly used to change operations masters on Windows 2000 servers.

NTLM (NT LAN Manager)

An authentication process whereby the authenticating server challenges the requesting host, receives a response, and authenticates the user without transmitting passwords across a network.

Organizational unit (OU)

The fundamental Active Directory container that allows logical segregation and administration of users, groups, computers, and other resources within a domain.

Primary domain controller (PDC)

A Windows NT domain controller that has been specifically designated as the single source for user login and authentication. The PDC also maintains security changes that are reflected in the SAM (Security Accounts Manager) database for the entire domain.

Primary zone

A DNS zone that contains a read/write copy of the zone file.

Published software

A software distribution option, included with group policies, whereby an application can be listed for optional network installation from within the Control Panel (choose Add/Remove Programs).

Repadmin.exe

A Windows 2000 utility that can be used to check the replication status of a given server with the parent domain.

Replication

The process of copying and maintaining duplicates of a particular set of data. Replication also includes synchronization in such a manner that changes made in one instance of a data set are synchronized appropriately with all other instances of the same data set.

Replication bridge

A single point of replication between two systems. A replication bridge is ideal for reducing replication bandwidth by isolating replication through a single source and for reducing replication redundancy across several systems on the network.

Replication partner

Specific Windows 2000 servers that are automatically designated by Windows 2000 as replication partners to a given server. Replication partners are assigned based on the most efficient replication paths available in order to thoroughly and completely replicate data across the enterprise.

Replmon.exe

The Windows 2000 Replication Monitor. A utility that enables administrators to monitor Active Directory replication status, force domain controller synchronization, and view topology, status, and performance.

Resource domain

Similar to an account domain, a resource domain contains computers, peripherals, and other network resources. A resource domain traditionally exists only in environments where the number of resource and user accounts exceeds the limitations of the Windows NT SAM database.

Resource record

The fundamental building block of DNS. All DNS objects are defined in terms of resource records. A, RR, SOA, and CNAME are all resource record types within DNS.

Restore

The process of replacing current data with older, stored data.

Reverse lookup zone

Similar to a forward lookup zone, a reverse lookup zone also contains fully qualified domain names (FQDNs) and their respective IP addresses. A reverse lookup zone is used to provide a FQDN when queried with an IP address.

Roaming user profile

A user account's desktop and personalized settings that are available upon login to any computer within a given domain.

Operations master

Any domain controller that is acting as a FSMO server.

Routing and Remote Access Service (RRAS)

The Windows 2000 equivalent of RAS (Remote Access Service) with several improved features, including increased security via NAT (Network Address Translation) and built-in VPN support.

Schema
The structure of the Active Directory database.

Schema master
A mechanism that defines and controls the types of objects that are available in the Active Directory structure. The schema master maintains the Active Directory data integrity by maintaining lists of object template attributes, similar to the way a database defines required fields and input masks.

Secedit.exe
A command-line utility that analyzes system security and creates system templates.

Secondary zone
A DNS zone that contains a read-only copy of the DNS database.

Security Accounts Manager (SAM) database
The central data store for security and resource information for Windows NT. The SAM database is accessed before resource access is allowed.

Security identifier (SID)
A unique identifier that is assigned to every object within Active Directory. The SID is used to refer to a specific object when security checks are performed against the Windows 2000 Active Directory database.

Security principals
Any Active Directory object that contains a SID (security identifier). Security principals include user objects and group objects.

Service account
A hidden logon account that is designed to start server services without requiring a live user login.

Services for Macintosh
Microsoft-provided network service support for Macintosh connectivity. Also one of the Windows NT components that is upgraded from Windows NT to Windows 2000.

Share
A specific folder or directory that has been flagged as available for access by other network resources.

Shortcut trust
A specialized explicit trust that is manually created to reduce or eliminate time-consuming associative layers from a multitrust authentication process.

sIDHistory
An Active Directory feature that allows a security principal to contain historical information about prior SIDs that were attached to an object throughout its existence.

Sidhist.vbs
A ClonePrincipal script that copies the SID of the source security principal into the **sIDHistory** attribute of the target security principal.

Single domain model
A network model in which all user accounts, groups, and resources are located within the same administrative location.

Single-master domain model
A network model in which all user accounts and global groups are located within a single domain, with resource domains and trusts being established to handle local groups and domain-specific resources.

Site
An Active Directory object that is usually defined as a specific TCP/IP subnet.

Site link
An Active Directory object that is dynamically created between at least two sites that is based upon least-cost routing and scheduled directory replication. Site links are necessary for intersite replication to occur. Site links can also be manually created, however, several considerations should be taken into account prior to doing so.

Source domain
The original, or starting, domain in a restructuring process. Generally considered a Windows NT domain, but a source domain can also be a Windows 2000 domain.

System policies
An administrative tool for enforcing specific system-based criteria within a single computer or on a network. Primarily used within Windows NT and Windows 9x networks, system policies have been largely replaced by Windows 2000 group policies. System policies, however, are permanent registry changes whereas Windows 2000 group policies are temporary.

SYSVOL share
A standard Windows 2000 share that contains login scripts and that is replicated automatically by Windows 2000.

Target domain
A destination, or final, domain in a restructuring process. The target domain is usually created and then subsequently populated with the source domain's security principal objects.

Task Scheduler
A utility, built into Windows NT and Windows 2000, that is used to automate specific tasks, such as tape backup and system maintenance.

Transitive trust
A two-way trust that is dynamically and automatically created by Windows 2000 to link two Windows 2000 domains. Transitive trusts exist between all domains in a Windows 2000 forest and do not cross forest boundaries.

Tree
A set of several Windows 2000 domains linked by transitive trusts. All domains within a given tree share the same global catalog, schema, and contiguous namespace.

Universal group

Available only within native mode domains, universal groups are used to assign resource access in any domain and can contain user accounts and global groups from any domain.

Universal Naming Convention (UNC)

A networking standard by which resources and servers are addressed. The UNC standard consists of the server name followed by the share name in the following format: \\server\share.

Windows Internet Naming Service (WINS)

A Windows NT/2000 service that handles NetBIOS name resolution.

Index